Birds' Nests: Business and Ethnicity in Southeast Asia

BIRDS' NESTS
Business and Ethnicity in Southeast Asia

An Anthropological Study of Business

KASEM JANDAM

The translation and publication of this book were funded by The Thailand Science Research and Innovation (TSRI).

Birds' Nests: Business and Ethnicity in Southeast Asia
Kasem Jandam

Thailand Science Research and Innovation (TSRI)
14th Floor, SM Tower,
979/17-21 Phaholyothin Road, Samsan Nai, Phyathai, Bangkok 10400
Tel: 0 2278 8200
Fax: 0 2298 0476
E-mail: webmaster@tsri.or.th
Website: www.tsri.or.th

Birds' Nests: Business and Ethnicity in Southeast Asia
Original Thai text © TSRI, 2017
English text © TSRI, 2021
All rights reserved

ISBN: 978-616-215-167-5

No part of this publication may be reproduced, stored in a retrieval system, or transmitted, in any form or by any means, electronic, mechanical, photocopying, recording or otherwise, without the prior permission in writing of the Thailand Science Research and Innovation (TSRI).

First edition published in 2021 by
Silkworm Books
430/58 Soi Ratchaphruek, M. 7, T. Mae Hia, A. Mueang Chiang Mai,
Thailand 50100
info@silkwormbooks.com
http://www.silkwormbooks.com.

Typeset in Minion Pro 11 pt. by Silk Type

Printed and bound in the United States by Lightning Source

Contents

Message from the Director of the Thailand Research Fund vi
Acknowledgement viii

Introduction 1
1. Communities and Bird's-Nest Resources in Vietnam 7
2. Ethnic Groups and Bird's-Nest Resources in Indonesia 55
3. Ethnic Groups and Bird's-Nest Resources in Malaysia 107
4. Culture and Edible Birds' Nests in the Philippines 174
5. Ethnic Groups and Bird's-Nest Resources in Thailand 235
6. Birds' Nests and Ethnic Groups in Hong Kong 314

Endnotes 347
References 370
Index 384

Message from the Director of the Thailand Research Fund

The Thailand Research Fund (TRF)* was established in response to the 1992 Research Endowment Act. Its primary duty is to support science, technology, humanity, and social science for economic and social development and higher education.

The knowledge of the bird's nest and bird's-nest business is a particular issue. The bird's-nest business is enormous in the global business system and is a closed business that is not easy to access data sources, including being associated with various groups of people of multi-ethnicity. Thailand is one of the vital bird's nest production sites in the world but still lacks research data to make policy recommendations in all dimensions.

In 2009, the Thailand Research Fund (TRF) with the National Policy and International Relations Division (Division 1) provided the research fund to the "Ethnicity relates to the resource-backed bird's nest in Southeast Asia" project, which Mr. Kasem Jandam, an independent researcher, was its leader. He researched significant producers of bird's nests, such as Vietnam, the Philippines, Indonesia, Malaysia, Thailand, and Hong Kong, the center of the world bird's-nest market.

---

* In 2019, TRF and other government funding agencies for higher education were merged, for efficiency, into The Thailand Science Research and Innovation (TSRI), established by the National Higher Education, Science, Research, and Innovation Policy Council. The organization is a government entity holding the status of a juristic person. Its objective is to enhance, support, and drive the national research and innovation systems.

Message from the Director of the Thailand Research Fund

The research findings presented in this volume range widely and cover, for example, the characteristics of belief in the bird's nests of each group, the moral requirements that the community has about bird's nests, and the life of people in bird's-nest regions throughout Southeast Asia. As the author points out, that the bird's nest is an 'intermediary' that contributes to ethnic relations, reflecting ethnic characteristics and power of access to social resources and capital. The study compares the history of bird's-nest use in various countries and wisdom in the bird's-nest business world. It examines bird's nest consumption beliefs, grade classification, food hierarchy classification of bird's nest products, and the essential equipment and innovations used in the bird's-nest business. The researcher also covers gender privilege to access and allocate bird's-nest resources, the legal system related to the benefit and property of the public, private, community, and non-exclusive economic nesting resources. The impact of bird's-nest business on ecology and environment. The bird's-nest business and the relationship of ethnic groups within the state, across the state, and the influence of Hong Kong's bird's nest market on the bird's-nest business in Thailand and Southeast Asia.

TRF is delighted to support the research and the publication, in Thai and English, to disseminate knowledge on this subject. This book, *Birds' Nests: Business and Ethnicity in Southeast Asia*, An Anthropological Study of Business results from the risk and perseverance works in the field. Mr. Jandam paid attention to every detail; his dedication of more than seven years will not only open the knowledge and deepen the dimensions of the bird's nest. The TRF hopes that the data resulting from this research project will be applied to policy areas in the bird's-nest trade, both natural and farm-settings: the legal system, and in the bird's-nest trade, development of bird's-nest resources in various dimensions according to the needs of consumers and the market, locally and internationally.

Professor Dr. Suthiphan Jitphimonmat
Director of the Thailand Research Fund

Acknowledgement

Birds' Nests: Business and Ethnicity in Southeast Asia, An Anthropological Study of Business is a product from the Transnational Research Project: "Ethnicity and Birds' Nest Resources in Southeast Asia." For the accomplishment of the book, I would like to express my gratitude to the following people.

Prof. Dr. Piyawat Boon-long, Dr. Chayan Vaddhanabhuti, Dr. Patrick Jory, Assoc. Prof. Dr. Pattamawadee Potchnukul, Prof. Dr. Issara Santisart, director of National Policies and International Relations Division, the Thailand Research Fund, Suwit Maprasong, and Ruengrong Rungrasmi.

For the Vietnam chapter: the first friend in Ho Chi Minh City – Luat, the three interpreters – Nguyen Thi Kim Chi, Tran Thi Hai Thuy, Vo Chi Mai Huong; the interviewees – Nguyen Tan Trung (Mai Vang Restuarant owner), Nguyen Duc Vinh, Nguyen Van Dung, Nguyen Thi Lai, Nguyen Nhuu Tri, Dieb, Nguyen Tien Duong, and the female owner of a steamed duck shop in Nguyen Sau Ngao, Nha Trang.

For the Indonesia chapter: Dr. Kamaruzzaman Bustamam-Ahmad; the bird's-nest collectors of Lampuuk – Mulia, Mahya, Muzakir, and Baeit, Rizal-Syahrizal Djam'an, Dr. Abdul Rani Usman, H. Fainal, an owner of a birds' building in Sigli; Zafril, bird's-nest merchant and owner of a birdhouse in Bireuen, Aceh; owner of the birdhouse at the Suzuki motorcycle dealer in Bakri Samalanga, E. Nugroho and Harry Kusumo Nugroho, bird's-nest researchers and business people in Semarang, Central

Java; Aman Sitanggang, Indonesian employee of oil company; Thai academics, Dr. Onanong Thippimol, Dr. Davisak Puaksom, Razak Panaemalae, Somjai Somkid, Rasamee Mahmudey, Thatri Nimitsomsakul.

For the Malaysia chapter: Earl of Cranbrook, Nuar Bin Haji Jaya, Siri Bin Neng Buah Penan ethnic of the Niah bird's-nest cave; Sunni Mahli, Niah National Park officer; Haidar Bin Ali, Head of the Niah Miri Sarawak National Park Office; Michael Bueng, an Iban ethnic bird's-nest merchant in Rumah Panjang Kampung Chong, Batu Niah; Johnson Chew, a Chinese ethnic bird's-nest merchant; Tan Boon Siong, researcher, and owner of Longevity Wellness Industries Sdn Bhd, Johor; Tan Yoke Tian, owner of the bird's-nest building and Swiftlet Eco Park business in Manjung-Perak; Chen Vunwo, owner of birds' building and Jonker Bird House restaurant in Melaka, Jia Lijuan, Dr. Kwancheewan Buadaeng, Tabuang Jandam.

For the Philippines chapter: Fidel E. Mondragon Jr., vice-chairman of Saragpunta Federation Brgy. Dobcauon I.; Roy Abella and Aldrin G. Caballero, Tagbanua ethnic bird's-nest collectors on Coron Island, Busuanga, Violeta Francisco, and Medardo Pe – Filipino ethnic bird's-nest buyer in Coron Town Busuanga: Uncle Bird-De Guia Merlindo Aguilar, Uncle June – Perfecto B. Dabuit Jr., Tagbanua ethnic owner of the bird's-nest cave in Black Island, his wife and his son Rey D. Dabuit; Mark Anthony S. Bianco (Ton-Ton); Bong, owner of Salatan boat; Garcia Dennis, former Filipino ethnic bird's-nest collector on Cadlao island of El Nido; Merlindo de Guia (Boy), Saragpunta boat driver; Jhovert Guadian, Dr. Thirawut Senakham, and Jirawat Saengtong.

For the Thailand chapter: Kamolsak Lertphaiboon, president of the Association of Bird's Nest Entrepreneurs in Thailand, Kitti Kittipinyo, a birds' building business owner; Thai bird's-nest concessioners; bird's-nest collectors; and bird's-nest bandit.

For the Hong Kong chapter: Vieng-Vachira Buason and Nui-Piyanart Thamawattana helped to coordinate the field works; interpreters – Queeny Nui and Kamkaew Maneerot; Chan Shun Wan, researcher, and lecturer, Helen-Tam Hoi Lun, coordinator at Hong Kong Polytechnic University; Dr. Ng Kar Man Alexander, TCM doctor, Lo Moon Fai, the owner of a Chinese medicine store in Ma On Shan new territories; Frank Pak, Stella Blade, Allen Pang, of Home of Swallows Limited at Siu Lek Yuen, Shatin, N.T.; Tim, the owner of a fruit shop on Wing Lok St., for kindly explained the Hong Kong measurement system.

Prof. Dr. Anan Ganjanapan, Prof. Dr. Craig J. Reynolds, Rapeeporn Sitti, Patthamakon Khatithammanit, Kanokrat Sivaraksa, Rawipat Suato, Dr. Aranya Siriphon, Dr. Amporn Marddent, Dr. Supakorn Pattanavivat, Chanida Puranapan, Roengwut Mitsuriya, Din-Dan Book Publisher, Thanasak Phosrikhun, and many whose names are not mentioned.

For the English edition of this book, thank you very much for the unwavering support from Assoc. Prof. Dr. Phakpoom Tippakoon, Prapapon Kaorop of the Thailand Science Research and Innovation (TSRI); Trasvin Jittidecharak and Silkworm Books team.

Special thanks to Patjira Jandam, who has been supportive of my research and life.

Kasem Jandam
January 2021

Bird's-nest collector at Viking Cave at Phi Phi Ley Island, in front of a hoof made of long bamboo beams used as a ladder to climb along the cave wall. On the left-hand holds a long bamboo handle, in the end, there is a holder to hold the candle holder for lighting. And a three-pronged iron device used to stab shovel the nest, on the cliff wall. He carries a flashlight around his neck and a waist bag for a nest. Photograph by Vinai Dithajohn, 2001.

Inside the Viking Cave, Phi Phi Ley Island, Andaman Sea, Krabi Province, Thailand. Inside the cave, there are paintings of elephants and various ships such as European or Arabian sailboats, junk boats, sailing ships, turbines, steamboats, etc. These paintings could be by sailors or pirates while resting during the monsoons seasons to unload cargo or repair boats. There is a rock that resembles a dragon's head, worshiped by the bird's-nest collectors. Photograph by Vinai Dithajohn, 2001.

Bird's-nest collector at Viking Cave, riding on a hamper, moving along a rope vertically and parallel to the cave hall. Photograph by Vinai Dithajohn, 2001.

At the mouth of Viking Cave, bird's-nest collectors start working in the early morning. Photograph by Vinai Dithajohn, 2001.

Introduction

Edible-nest swiftlets are birds belonging to the order of *Apodiformes*, in the swift family, *Apodidae*, and *Collocaliini* tribe. The birds build nests using their own saliva, and in some parts of the world people consume the nests as food or medicine, hence the 'edible-nest' moniker.

The 26 species of this swiftlet dwell in limestone caves and abandoned buildings. Their habitats are scattered across a wide range of locations: Mascarene Islands in the western Indian Ocean, the eastern area of the Himalayas mountains, southern Asia, southeastern Asia, New Guinea and northern Australia in Queensland, including the southwestern Pacific Islands in the area of India, Sri Lanka, Nepal, Sikkim, Bhutan, Thailand, Myanmar, Malaysia, Indonesia, Cambodia, the Philippines, China, Timor, the Fijian Islands, Papua New Guinea, and Australia.

In Southeast Asia, home to a highly diverse number of cultures; one of the most recognized natural resources is the swiftlet's nest, and as a result this region is renowned for birds' nests and the and bird's-nest trade. These birds' nests are so highly valued they've been labelled 'White Gold' and 'Caviar of the East.'

The culture of bird's-nest consumption can be traced mainly to ethnic Chinese, with the earliest recorded mention appearing over a thousand years ago during the Tang Dynasty (618–907 A.D.), when chronicles stated the nests served as food and medicine.

Bird's-nest consumption nowadays is a substantial industry oriented towards health and beauty. The raising and breeding of the swiftlets has moved from natural cliffs and stone formation to any house-like structure that can be built to lure wild swiftlets to build nests in them. The first instance of such construction is believed to have occurred in Sedaya, Java, approximately 200 years ago. This modern farming later became widespread throughout southeast Asia after the economic crisis of 1997.

In 2014, in Southeast Asia alone, construction of artificial swiftlet houses was estimated at 400,000 and worth hundred thousands of billions baht. In each country in southeast Asia, nests are collected in different seasons. Harvesting birds' nests from inside houses or buildings, for all countries, depends on the number of birds, but generally, the birds' nests are collected about once a month.

Many in Southeast Asia believe the swiftlet to be a powerful, sacred creature that bless or curse any life it encounters. Because collection of the birds' nests is a risky profession, many spiritual rituals have developed over the ages and are performed both before and after collection. In many cases, there are also restrictions on behavior in the caves, and the language spoken around the bird's-nest habitats may also differ from that of everyday life.

Highly valued as an anti-aging serum that raises libido, boosts immunity, promotes brain function, and improves overall body health, swiftlet nest consumption used to be reserved for nobility and the rich. The Chinese believe that the birds' nests are a magical potion, one of the five most prestigious Chinese delicacies, along with abalone, fish maw, ginseng and shark fins.

Nowadays, with globalized capitalism and the society of consumerism, eating birds' nests remains a status symbol, and the cultural-spiritual myth is somewhat supported by scientific evidence. However, each society has its own way of checking, resisting, and arguing with both the myths and scientific proofs.

In Southeast Asia of the past, when kings and sultans occupied the center of power, they granted ownership rights to ethnic groups who discovered nest-bearing caves, while collecting taxes on the material. Until the postcolonial period or the latter half of 20th century (1945–68), the rights and laws related to the region's swiftlet nests changed along with transformations towards a modern state system.

Ownership rights and legal systems are now more diverse, involving: personal ownership rights for individuals and family; co-ownership rights; and concessions granted by government to private business. Such rights and laws vary from one country to another, but what they share in common is that the owner of a swiftlet-house or any artificial bird's-nest resources, regardless of ethnicity, can lawfully will their rights to their children or family members via inheritance.

An exception is Hong Kong, where, despite being a global center for the bird's-nest market, there are no laws or taxes related to the bird's-nest trade. Here the birds' nests are simply considered a food product, and most nests are imported by individuals carrying them into the country. Hong Kong Cantonese control the trade, which is part of a larger Chinese business network.

No one really knows the real overall worth of the bird's-nest trade, but there are estimates for different countries. Important bird's-nest producers in Southeast Asia include Myanmar, Vietnam, Indonesia, Malaysia, the Philippines and Thailand. In 2014, the production of raw bird's-nest for these countries was estimated to be a minimum of 2,817,000 kilograms, worth more than THB 120 billion per year. Regardless of the source in Southeast Asia, it is China, Hong Kong, Taiwan and Chinese communities around the world that serve as the primary markets for the birds' nests.

Hong Kong used to represent the world's biggest bird's-nest market and biggest per-capita consumption. In 1990, an estimated 60 percent of nest consumers were Hong Kong Chinese. Until 2009, raw birds' nests in Hong Kong's market were estimated at around 1,000 tons a year, and the annual trade in Hong Kong was worth at least 10 billion Hong Kong Dollars. That volume continued until China found fake red bird's-nests imported from Malaysia in July 2011, which led to a prohibition on bird's-nest imports from Malaysia and other countries. This was a turning point for both the edible bird's-nest tade, and the 'red' bird's-nest consumer culture in China.

After China's prohibition of bird's-nest imports in July 2011, the trade among Southeast Asian ethnic became subject to China trade restrictions. China enforced regulations for the inspection and potential detention of persons entering or exiting the country with birds' nests beginning in November 2012. Today China prohibits the importation of all edible birds' nests, other than the canned product.

In the future, the edible bird's-nest business will continue to grow, especially in China. The bird's-nest trade will expand investments in China, as the Chinese bird's-nest market is estimated to be worth many billions of dollars. Marketing technologies, E-Commerce and E-Business related to the bird's-nest trade are developing at the same time.

From consumption based on Chinese culture and belief, to the large-scale production and processing of raw birds' nests for distribution worldwide, the swiftlet nest business is one of the largest businesses in today's global economy.

The bird's-nest trade supports a unique relationship between ethnic groups. As the product's popularity in Asia has grown, so has the fighting over resources and the competition between trading rivals.

The global trade is also inextricably involved with the swiftlet's ecosystem, speciation and other environmental variables. The widespread existence of bird's-nest resources, both in natural and artificial settings, also deals with bird's-nest management and benefit allocation among ethnic groups, related to ethnic belief and ritual systems around benefiting from the birds' nests. These relate to swiftlet myths, collecting, consuming the bird's-nest, food and medicine nutrition and the creation of tales, myths, stories, literature, songs and so on. It also includes applied knowledge in inventing tools employed for collecting the birds' nests, preparing ready-to-eat birds' nests, and other related products. Business systems and management vary accordingly, to explain the nature and relative sizes of the business, the methods for import and export of the raw and ready-to-eat bird's-nests, branding and marketing from what is essentially a family-based industry.

The fact that the bird's-nest market in Hong Kong is significant to both local markets and international Southeast Asian markets and ethnic groups, leads to common interests as well as domestic and international conflicts. This also affects the bird's-nest trade both within Hong Kong, and for other ethnic groups in Southeast Asia.

Finally the social and political systems involved with both natural and artificial swiftlet house is involved both in regulation of the trade and in swiftlet conservation. Business and resource management models vary in a way consistent with the unique characteristics of different Southeast Asian ethnic groups.

1
Communities and Bird's-Nest Resources in Vietnam

INTRODUCTION

The Socialist Republic of Vietnam is approximately 331,690 square kilometers. The country is diverse with mountainous terrain, highlands, lakes and thousands of islands scattered along the coastline, with a length of 3,440 kilometers from the Gulf of Tonkin to the Gulf of Thailand.

The country's population is approximately 98.7 million (2020 est.). The 54 ethnic groups in Vietnam divided into Kinh (Viet) 85.7%, Tay 1.9%, Thai 1.8%, Muong 1.5%, Khmer 1.5%, Mong 1.2%, Nung 1.1%, Hoa 1%, other 4.3% (2009 est.).[1] 70 percent of hill tribes are Mahayana Buddhist, the rest are Roman Catholic or Protestant Christians, Muslims Hoa Hao, and Cao Dai,[2] and animists. This country is rich in natural resources both energy and mineral resources. It has important raw materials for investment including adequate soil and water resources, for agriculture.[3]

The country is home to more than 1,000 bird species of bird, with the swiftlet ranked as one of the most essential national resources.

1. HISTORY OF THE INDIGENOUS PEOPLE AND BIRDS' NESTS

1.1 Swiftlets in Nature

The oldest Vietnamese writings on swiftlets and their nests come from Ly Thoi Tran (Li Shizhen, 1518–1593) in 1578. He wrote that birds' nests had been consumed for at least 400 years. In the past, the Vietnamese people harvested the nests conservatively, with strict regulations. Given the numerous swiftlet caves along the rocky coastline of Vietnam and their enormous production potential, it would not be surprising that the practice of eating nests started in the kingdom of Vietnam.

Much of the knowledge of birds' nests and their origins comes from longstanding trade with southern China.[4] Local nest-collectors in Cu Lao Cham Island in Hoi An, Quang Nam Province, tell stories of Le Ong To, as the first and most important local person gathering nests.[5] Likewise, a former fisherman of the Thu Bon River in Hoi An, said that around 70–80 years ago, a Vietnamese man named Jad was the pioneer in collecting the nests. He was the one only who knew the collection techniques and prices. After he died, others entered the business. The locals see him as the father or pioneer of the nest business.[6]

One formal perception says that the Nguoi Cham had learned about the swiftlet birds' nests collecting before then. In the late 1500s, the Dai Viet, or Vietnamese Ethnics moved in Hoi An, and in the 17th century in the reign of the Nguyen Dynasty who loved eating the nests, the Dai Viet in Thanh Chau village started collecting nests as a profession.[7] The nests collectors would use bamboo ladders to climb up and pick nests at Cu Lao Cham. At that time, they had to pay taxes in two provinces: Binh Dinh and Khanh Hoa.

Another story at Cu Lao Cham is that Tran Cong Tien, and his wife got lost at sea. They finally beached on a deserted island without food, and ended up eating some kind of unknown birds' nests to survive. After eating the nests, they felt strong. After they returned home, they arranged a team to collect the nests on the island. The locals also believe that the first groups of nest-collectors (*dau tien*) in Hoi An started business in 1806, during the reign of the Emperor Gia Long (r.1802–1820). The leading instructor was Ho Van Hoa; a person who was later appointed by the emperor to be *Quan linh tam tinh yen ho*, to supervise the collecting of nests in three provinces.[8]

Harvesting nests in Binh Dinh has been going for a long time according to the book, *Dai Nam Nhat Thong Chi* (Official geographical record of Vietnam's Nguyen Dynasty), and there is also a tax on the practice on the island. Each collector must pay 10 kg. of nests as tax to the government each year.[9]

Nest collection has been passed down continually for over 400 years, creating a history, culture, and belief system that perseveres to the present day. There's evidence in storytelling, buildings, locations and rituals. For example the shrine (*mieu tho*) built by ancestors who were nest-collectors or *ong to nghe yen*.[10] passing down the swiftlet nest culture in Dao Tan Hiep – Cu Lao Cham, Hoi An, Quang Nam Province. There is an annual ceremony to express gratitude to the Hoi An pioneers[11]

Likewise, in other areas there are birds' nests cultural events (*nen van hoa yen sao*) on 10th day of the 3rd month of the Vietnamese calendar every year. This is the ceremony to give thanks and ask for the blessing of a safe and prosperous harvest. This event is held at the Ho Van Hoa shrine, in Thon Bai Huong and Cu Lao Cham of Quang Nam Province.

Chapter 1

On the swiftlet island in Nha Trang, Khanh Hoa Province, the ceremony is held on June 2 to pay respect to Le Thi Huyen Tram and Le Van Quang, who lived during the reign of Emperor Quang Trung (r. 1788–92) and fought and died in a war protecting the nests.

Le Thi Huyen Tram in particular was considered to be a pioneer in harvest, and the first woman to become a chief of the birds'-nests islands or *Ba Chua dao Yen*. Her shrine is on Noi Island. The collecting ceremony (Le hoi yen sao) is held after the first collection each year. While on Noi Island, there's the Ho Yen shrine, built to memorialize Ho Van Hoa, the male pioneer in birds'-nest harvesting in Binh Dinh and Khanh Hoa, during the reign of Emperor Gia Long. At the time, the collectors had to pay an annual tax of 80 kg. to the state. Ho Van Hoa is also considered the first person who contributed to the harvesting concession in Khanh Hoa.[12]

However, a formal record of the nest harvesting business, carved in marble in front of the Noi Island shrine in Lich Su Nghe Yen Sao, Khanh Hoa, says:

> In 1328, during the Tran Dynasty, Le Van Dat, the emperor's assistant sailed in the emperor's ship to Hon Tre and founded the Bich Dam community on the Khanh Hoa Island, beginning the harvest there.

In 1769, Le Van Quang's assistant, the head of Bich Dam village, who was in charge of the island, and his daughter, Le Thi Huyen Tram, controlled the business and had the most power in collecting and selling the nests to other countries.

Before unifying modern Vietnam, Gia Long Emperor, then King Nguyen Anh, fought with Le Thi Huyen Tram in Binh Khang Sea battle. Le Thi Huyen Tram won the first battle. However, in a later battle, Le Thi Huyen Tram and her father Le Van Quang, and all their nest-collectors were killed on May 10, 1793. Le Thi Huyen Tram has become a legend and respected figure for the locals. She was called Dao Chu Thanh Mau, goddess of the birds' nests islands. Thus her shrine was built.

In 1831, Minh Mang, the 12th emperor, heard of these swiftlet islands and sent an envoy to resume the nest business. Since then, the business has continued to develop.

In 1858, there was a war against a group of the birds'-nest island protectors led by Bao Nghia Kien Nghiep Hoi, whose name has changed twice to Bao Quoc Doan, and finally, Binh Tay Cuu Quoc Hoi.

In 1873, the new group were nest supervisors and collectors, trading nests for guns provided to soldiers in the South and Central regions to fight with the French. After that, the Khanh Hoa birds' nests have become legendary throughout the country, since they helped them eventually free the country from the French.

From 1930–70, France and Saigon permitted Chinese investors to invest in harvesting nests here, which reduced the number of birds and nests. Vietnamese bird's-nest collectors at Vinh Nguyen and Vinh Truong had long experience in harvesting nests so knew how to preserve the bird population.

In 1971, Vietnamese people pressured the government to cancel the birds' nests collection concession for Chinese capitalists. That year, the Vietnamese government in Saigon allowed the Vietnamese in Vinh Nguyen to look after and collect the nests, though the state imposed taxes. Nonetheless, a group of collectors in Vinh Nguyen tried their best despite many difficulties to run the business.

In 1987, Nha Trang the local government business group, Xi Nghiep Quoc Doanh Yen sao Nha Trang, was founded and followed by the Yen sao Khanh Hoa Company, which was established in 1990.

The company had a good management in harvesting the nests and caring for the swiftlets. The harvest increased in volume compared to 1970, ultimately increasing eightfold, and the income from exports was 10 times higher. The business was well received by the government. The collectors of Yen sao Khanh Hoa were proud to take part in the care of Vietnam's natural resources.

These people, both dead and still alive earned the respect of the company. The staff who had co-invested and founded the company donated to building the main shrines of the nest island to show appreciation. Nest-collectors have shared feeling of love bound to the business and its 650 year heritage.[13]

1.2 Development of the Swiftlet House Farming Business

It is not clear when swiftlets first started nesting in houses and other buildings in Vietnam. However, according to the Cong ty (company) Yen sao Khanh Hoa, in the 1980s in Nha Trang, Khanh Hoa Province, swiftlet nests were found in a movie theater. At the time it was built in 2000, around 200 swiftlets nested in the Thanh Binh – Ninh Thuan movie theater, in Ninh Thuan Province.

In 1993, there were about 20 swiftlets nesting in a house on Le Thanh Phuong road, in Nha Trang City, Khanh Hoa Province. In 1996, the construction of nesting houses began, and about 100 swiflets moved in to the building on Thong Nhat road, Nha Trang City, where the birds are still nesting and growing in numbers.[14]

One important factor that encouraged Vietnamese people to start swiftlet house farming was due to soaring nest prices, which were around USD 600 per kilogram in 1978,[15] but now command USD 5,000 per kilogram.[16]

The Vietnamese began studying house farming in Indonesia in the 90s,[17] as well as techniques from Malaysia, Singapore, Thailand, Cambodia and Hong Kong.[18]

Swiftlets have nested in houses in Da Nang, Quang Ngai and Ho Chi Minh as well. During the early period in Vietnam, people who had swiftlets nesting in their houses would keep it a secret. They thought of it as having a platinum ingot (*mo vang trang*) in the house.[19]

The Yen sao Khanh Hoa Company experimented with 50 house farms and all were successful. The company published the methods of establishing swiftlet house farms for several provinces: Khanh Hoa, Da Nang, Binh Dinh, Phu Yen, Binh Duong, Binh Thuan, Ninh Thuan, Tien Giang, Ho Chi Minh and Vung Tau.

The house farms that initially produced nests were Phu Yen, Khanh Hoa, Binh Duong and Kien Giang. It is estimated that there are now at least 200 nest-farm buildings throughout 24 provinces.[20] At the same time, the Yen sao Khanh Hoa company conducted field research under a project named, "The Industrial process in hatching and raising swiftlets in houses during an expansion period." (*Quy trinh congnghe, ky thuat ap no nhan tao va nuoi chim yen hang qua tung giai doanphat trien*). It was a successful breeding program, increased nest value and developed the business in general, winning the first prize in the 2nd Provincial Creative Technology Competition (2006–2007).[21]

From the research project, the company first used Swiftlet eggs from natural sources after collecting the first birds' nests. Egg types are divided by temperature and humidity control, and then placed in an incubator to be artificially hatched. After hatching, the birds are placed in a baby bird nursery; where they are cared for and kept in a training machine, where they learn to fly. The resulting swiftlets are released into artificial bird farms or *ngoi nha yen*. The project has increased the number of the baby Swiftlets, both in farms and natural caves.[22]

According to a study of swiftlet propagation in 2003, the Yen sao Khanh Hoa project has had the best success breeding swiftlets from Hon Ngoai Island to Hon Rom Island. In 2006, two of the swiftlet bird's caves were found: hang Gom and hang Sao Cao in Nha Trang City. Swiftlets propagating in natural caves has continued and reached the islands in Van Ninh District.[23]

The swiftlets raised in the hatchery were able to live with the naturally born swiftlets. Until 2007, this industrial process allowed the company to increase the number of swiftlet caves to 21. In Nha Trang City, there are 83 swiftlet caves. The harvesting of birds' nests has increased as a result of the industrialized process, growing the swiftlet populations of Vietnam.[24]

At present, the government focuses on swiftlet conservation, and researchers are also studying the raising of swiftlets in house farms. In addition to the Binh Dinh birds' nests collecting company, wealthy people in Quy Nhon have also built nest farms.[25]

Before 1976, there were six swiftlet bird islands in Khanh Hoa Province. But at present, the Yen sao Khanh Hoa Company owns the rights to 12 of the Swiftet islands (*dao yen*), with 40 caves (*hang*). In 1961, the total nest yield was 350 kilograms. In 2009, it was around 2,500 kilograms. There are estimates that the Yen sao Khanh Hoa Company produces about five times more than all of Thailand.[26] The amount of birds' nests harvested in the central region (*mien Trung*) of Vietnam is around 2,500 kilograms per year.[27] Each year, the artificial nest farms produce two kilograms on average per house. The nest harvest in the whole country is around 3,000 kilograms.[28]

However, even though Vietnam generally has good management and cares for the nest resources to maintain or increase the swiftlet population, some provinces are not well managed. The management needs to be improved to ensure the swiftlet population will grow in the next 5–10 years.[29] Meanwhile, a businessman in the ready-to-eat bird's-nest industry, as well as nest farms, has noted that as in Indonesia, breeding swiftlets is challenging.

The nursery process is difficult, especially feeding the fledgling birds until they can fly. Moreover, even though research showed that raising new-born birds can be managed, it is very difficult to ensure the birds from the hatchery remain in the nest farms or caves where humans place them.[30]

2. THE NATURE OF SWIFTLETS: FREE BIRDS OF THE SPRING

Swiftlets, which the Vietnamese commonly call *chim yen* or *chim yen Hang* also have other names, such as *hai yen*: sea swiftlet, *chim bien*: seabirds, *chim en bien*: sea-backed birds, *Viet yen* or *chim yen dat Viet*: Swiftlets of Vietnam, *Nam yen* or *chim yen mien Nam*: Birds of the South, *Ho Yen* or *chim yen xu Ho*: Bird of the Ho, *at dieu*: named for the bird's flying route, *huyen dieu*: named for its color, *Chi dieu, du ba*, *thien nu oa*. Other names less commonly used are, *yen oa, yen thai, quan yen, kim ty yen, – du ha uu dieu*: birds that fly above water.[31]

Their scientific name is *Collocalia fuciphaga germaini oustalet*. In 1996, Vietnam had approximately 750,000 Swiftlets,[32] most of them nesting in island caves and various buildings spread in the coastal areas of the central region and southern region. In 2010, Khanh Hoa alone has about 500,000.[33] In the Hang Ca caves, Phuong Mai Island, Quy Nhon city, Binh Dinh Province, there are about 100,000.[34]

2.1 Natural Characteristics

Swiftlets prefer to build their nests in high places in caves and tall buildings. The birds are small at about 115–125 mm long. Males and females weigh about 15–20 grams. Their bellies are gray with a black upper body[35] and a long, dark gray tail divided into two lobes.[36] It can cling to rocky cliffs and likes to eat insects such as ants and mosquitoes. This small bird heads out for food early in the morning at about 5 AM and settles back into the nest at about 8 PM[37] and can fly as much as 200[38]–500 kilometers per day.[39] They travel in pairs and lay two eggs at a time, three times per year from January to September.[40]

They begin building nests in December.[41] After the father and mother birds select a nesting place, they start building the nest using their saliva, which dries out when exposed to air. Around April, their salivary glands will grow and produce more saliva. The first nest takes four months (120 days) to build and then they start building a new nest. The birds can remember the precise location their nest, even if it is harvested, but the bird will nest there again. Some may build three or four nests, but they are smaller than the first and have a lower value.[42]

The eggs weigh 0.6–1 grams. Once hatched, the father bird and mother bird will feed the fledgling three times a day[43] and take care of them for up to six months.[44]

In Vietnam, edible swiftlets nests can be divided into two types. White nest swiftlets (*C. fuciphaga germani*), also known as chim yen hang. *Yen to trang* or *chim yen co to an*[45] is subdivided into two types: *yen bien di mau long* and *yen bien di to*[46] (swiftlet *Collocalia Esculenta*), a swiftlet nesting with saliva mixed with other materials.[47] They're known as Grass Birds, and are raised in the nest farms to help attract the other type (*C. fuciphaga germani*) from the caves[48] to come and nest there.

The Black-nest Swiftlet called *yen do den*,[49] whose scientific name is *Aerodramus maximus*, its nest contains a significant percentage of feathers with the saliva. The Vietnamese call these nests *Yen Sao* or *To chim yen*. In Vietnam, each of these nests have an average weight of 12–20 grams,[50] while the feathers will weigh about 7–15 grams,[51] so require 100–120 nests per kilogram. In Hoi An, there are 60 birds' nests per kilogram.

2.2 Swiftlets Habitat in 63 Provinces

Currently, the habitat of the birds in both natural and nest farms In Vietnam covers more than 24 provinces: Quang Ninh, Thanh Hoa, Quang Binh, Da Nang, Quang Nam, Quang Ngai, Binh Dinh, Phu Yen, Khanh Hoa, Ninh Thuan, Binh Thuan, Binh Phuoc, Binh Duong, Dong Nai, Vung Tau, Ho Chi Minh, Tien Giang, Vinh Long, Tra Vinh, Soc Trang, An Giang, Kien Giang, Bac Lieu and Ca Mau.

The nesting place of the swiftlets in natural sources covers around 50 islands scattered in the mentioned provinces. In Quang Ninh Province, they are Ha Long Island, Thanh Hoa Island, and Me Island. In Quang Binh Province: La Island and Vung Chua Island. In Quang Nam, Hoi An Town, Cu Lao Cham Islands. In the Cua Dai Sea, they are Lao Island, Tai Island, Dai Island, Mo Island, Kho Me Island, Tan Hiep Island, and especially in Kho Con Island, there are caves with the most birds' nests such Kho Cave, Tai Cave, To Vo Cave, Ca Cave, Tran Cave.[52]

In Quang Ngai, Sa Huynh Mountain, Sa Huynh Island, and Cu Lao Re Island. In Binh Dinh Province, Phuong Mai Island, Ca Cave, and in a village in Nhon Hai Island, Nhon Ly, Nhon Chau. Quy Nhon Town[53] has several caves, such as Rung Cao Cave, Doi Cave, Ba Nghe Cave, Can Cave, Hep Cave. The most habituating swiftlets cave is the Ca Cave,[54] Yen Island, Ong Can, and Phuoc Mai. In Khanh Hoa Province, Ninh Hoa, Van Ninh, Hon Rom, and Hai Dang Districts,[55] they are Ngoai Island, Noi Island, Ho Island, Cha La Island, Dun Island, Mun Island, Ngoc Island, Xa Cu Island, Co Ong Island, Doi Moi Island, O Ga Island, Trao Do Island,[56] Doi Island, Tre Island, Nhan Island. In the Thuan Hai Sea, Thu Islands, Bong Lau Island, and Con Son Island. In Kien Giang Province, Phu Quoc Island, Nhan Island, Rai Island, Tho Chu Island, Nam Du Island, and An Thai Island.

The well-known ones are in Kho Cave, Thuong Island, Ca Cave, Thien Island, Tay Cave, Tay Island, Vo Vo Cave, Ca Island, Mui Yen Mountain in Phuoc Mai Island, Yen Du Isle in the Cham Islands, Yen Xa and Lang En Villages in Hoi An; Phan Rang City in Ninh Thuan Province,[57] and Con Island in Vung Tau.[58]

2.3 Birds' Nests Collecting Season (*Mua khai thac*)

In Vietnam, there are two or three sanctioned times a year to collect birds' nests in various natural areas. The first period is from March to April, with a second gathering in August. In the past, the nests were collected after the fledglings were hatched around April (*thang tu*). After that, the birds build a new nest, and the second collection

(*thang bay*) is over a one to two month period. The second nests are smaller, about half of the size of the first, and the quality is not as good.

To conserve the swiftlets, nest-collectors will harvest them during the day after the fledglings birds have flown. Some areas will have third collection (*thang bay*), but the nests will be very small and contain a lot of feathers. There are also fewer to harvest and they can be red in color. There is no third nest collection anymore.[59]

From field data, a nest collector from Cu Lao Cham, Hoi An in Quang Nam Province says that each year the birds' nests are collected twice in the 3rd and 7th month. The harvest lasts for four to five days.[60]

In the province of Nha Trang, Khanh Hoa, the swiftlets begin nesting in December (*thang 12 hang nam*). The harvest here is twice a year. The first from March[61] to May, and the second in August.[62]

Information on Binh Dinh Province shows that the birds spend about 70 days nesting in the Vietnamese New Year period (*tet*) until the 3rd month, according to the lunar calendar. After the birds have completed their nests, the collectors harvest the first round of nests without letting the birds lay their eggs. The birds will build a second nest around the end of the 4th month (*thang tu*). Fourty-five days after, the mother bird will lay eggs and after the fledglings birds (*chim con*) can fly, and the *nguoi tho khai thac Yen sao* or nest collector will collect them. After harvesting, the birds will cling to the cave wall. At present, the conservation of the species means the period has been increased between the first and second harvests, so the birds numbers increase.

In Binh Dinh, the third collection is in the middle of the sixth month (*thang sau*), after the birds will build a third nest to replace the second harvested one. Construction takes approximately 45–50 days; and these are the last ones the collectors harvest in a given year.[63] Also in Binh Dinh, the first nest collection (*dau mua*) is in February and March (*thang 2, 3*); the second is (*thu hai*) after the fledglings bird flies from the nest to find food. The third harvest (*Vu ba*), is small.[64]

3. BELIEFS AND RITUALS RELATED TO SWIFLETS

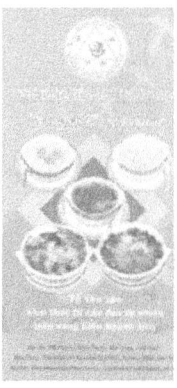

3.1 Beliefs and Rituals

Beliefs Related to Swiftlets

Since the Swiftlets have been a part of Vietnamese life for nearly a thousand years, many of beliefs have taken shape. The Swiftlets are birds of the Spring, and sign of integrity and loyalty (*chung thuy*) with their lifelong partners. Since when they are out, the birds normally do not stop along the way but go straight to their nests, they're regarded as the birds of pure heart.[65] In relation to royalty, Emperor Minh Mang who favored edible birds' nests, had a statue of swiftlet lovers in his Dai noi Hue palace.[66]

In Hang Trong Hon Ngoai Cave in Khanh Hoa, there is a rock carving with the following inscription:

> Swiftlets build their nests to raise their offspring, and gracefully contribute to the people and the country.

Poems are written about them, as one sample below:

> Swiftlets build their nests, where they do not reside.
> Bees create honey, which they do not taste.

Bach Van, a poet of Nha Trang wrote a poem titled, "Ngoai Island" below:

> A long time ago, this island was filled with swiftlets,
> Where boats, alongside waves of the ocean, often visited.
> Traveling through mazes of the sea,
> To the lands of mysterious caves on the island,
> The sounds of the birds in the sky blended harmoniously with waves the of the sea,
> White nests filled the caves like stars in the night sky,
> Enriching with prosperity, abounded with the precious white gold of the island[67]

In modern society, the Vietnamese value swiftlet nests as "white gold" (*vang trang*) and believe that they are birds of faithfulness, since despite the distance they fly, they always return to their nests. This inspired Van Le's movie, *Yen va nguoi*, or *Swiftlets and Man* (1999). The movie tells a story of the loving characteristics of the birds, as well as raise awareness of preserving the swiflet species.[68]

Beliefs and Rituals Related to Swiftlets' Nests

Swiftlets are unique and valuable than other birds. The Vietnamese nest-collectors and those related to the birds were reproduced and inherited as a ritual around the birds and collected their nests.

Climbing high cliffs in the dark caves, climbers risk their lives. In addition, humans can never fully access the world of the swiftlets. These experiences that take place beyond human control, contributed to the beliefs, and the relationship between humans and the supernatural. Humans can neither control nor own nature, so the true owners are supernatural beings.[69] The night before a harvest, a ceremony to pay homage to the sacred, Le Ong To, is held on the island to receive a blessing to collect nests for medicine, food and as a specialty for the privileged.

The collecting of swiftlet nests is dangerous work, so the collector must be a smart, diligent and courageous person. However, some of the men who fell from the cliffs were buried in the caves, to remind others of how dangerous their mission is. Unless a collector is very careful and patient, he won't make it out alive.[70] The nest-collectors or *cong nhan*, need to be experienced, and physically and mentally prepared before climbing 40 meter high scaffolding built from bamboo (*tre*)[71] and tied with rattan (*may*).

Collectors in Hoi An, Quy Nhon, Binh Dinh or Nha Trang have practiced their profession for 600–700 years, and so developed beliefs about the swiftlets.

In Cu Lao Cham, Hoi An or Phi Pho and Dai Jian in the past, in Quang Nam Province, the night before harvesting, they would perform a ritual to pay respects to sacred Le Ong To,[72] the pioneer of the bird's-nest collectors on the island.[73] By the 10th day of the 3rd month of the Vietnamese calendar, the collectors must come to Cu Lao Cham to pay homage at a ceremony to worship lu cung To nghe Yen; a two-day sacrifice ceremony for safety in collecting the nests. There are also fun activities such as singing, dancing, games, and tours from Hoi An to Cu Lao Cham.

In Nha Trang, there is a ceremony to worship the spirits on Ngoai Island, expressing both praise for and fear of the supernatural beings. Offerings are presented to negotiate benefits with spirits, similar to ceremonial day of the king's death in the past. Here, it is to pay respect to Le Thi Huyen Tram, a woman who owned the island around 350 years ago. The collectors and anyone else involved with the birds'-nests island must know its history and respect the island's spirits.[74] All of the nest-collectors must attend to ensure their missions are productive.

At the same time, the nest-collectors, or *nguoi gat yen* or *sao chia* in Vietnamese, must be patient, clever and strong men. Normally, the guards (*doi bao ve*) live alone on the island, and enjoy the company of the collectors only in the havesting season.

Chapter 1

The collectors must be careful and be able to keep secrets (*song rat muc can trong*). They must not drink alcohol (*khong bao gio*), or smoke (*han che hut thuoc, hut thuoc*), and must maintain strong health. On the mission, they will not say anything bad or inauspicious (*do su ton nghiem o tren dao*) to show respect for sacred things, where the shrines of the collectors' ancestors are located.

The collection of birds' nests in Vietnam is gender specific, and women are prohibited from entering the caves[75] or collecting the nests because it is dangerous.[76] However, in the nest business establishments in stores, companies or manufacturing plants of ready-to-eat bird's-nest products, most of the sales staff are women.

Belief and Truth in Nest Collection

Vietnamese people have collected birds' nests for consumption since the 10th century, and the swiftlet nest has been featured as one of eight most delicious and best cuisines (Bat Tran) – the caviar of the East.[77] It is a special food of the rich and kings. In the past, kings would eat birds' nests every day, instead of rice. At the royal audience or the court parties, serving birds' nests is the gesture to honor the guests. The Emperor Qin Shi of China and the Emperor Minh Mang of Vietnam believed that eating nests contributed to eternal life.[78]

Bird's-nest soup, which has a texture is similar to glue, mixed with flour or sugar, is one of the world's most expensive foods. It's believed to have help erectile dysfunction (*tang cuong tinh duc*), and to increase immunity and concentration.[79]

Ancient Vietnamese books outline beliefs about swiftlet nests and consumption. An example is *Tra pho tap van*, which asserted that swiftlets use fish to make their nests. Another book, *Lanh Nam tap ky* (Southern Sky Miscellaneous Records), said that they eat seaweed but do not digest it, and regurgitate it to build their nests.

The book *Viet luc* or The Six Vietnamese believes that they eat algae as a food; while the book, *Tuyen Nam tap chi* (Tuyen Nam Journal) said that the consumption of birds' nests started during the Minh Dynasty. It said that the birds eat oysters as food and can't digest the hard but valuable part, so they spit it out as saliva.

Swiftlet nests are also used to make medicines and can be used in many ways. All the ancient tomes state that the nests can stimulate sexual desire, and many Chinese people use it for this purpose. One ancient book on swiftlet nests concluded that it nourishes the body, brain, and helps seriously ill people to recover from near death.

The Chinese book translated in Vietnamese, *Ban thao cuong muc thapdi* (Supplemented Itemized Pharmacopoeia) (1765) said that the swiftlets nests taste sweet, and can be medicine, food and helping to dissolve phlegm, cure cough, asthma, and fever. The book, *Huong to but and Hoan dubut ky* (Huong to, Writings and World-wide Travel Accounts) mentions red birds' nests (*to chim do*) and blood birds' nests (*yen huyet sao*) and that the bird's blood is mixed in the birds' nests, which is a very valuable food and can be used in traditional medicine. For example, *Truyen thi lao trai hoan* is made of five-blood nests as well as traditional medicine called, *tu ha xa*.

At the same time, the Vietnamese ethnic community has referred to knowledge from Hong Kong restaurants advertisement that swiftlet nests can cure tuberculosis, HIV positive, lung disease and various sicknesses.

In Vietnam, the Swiftlet nest is used to make medicine in a pot: using about 6–12 grams in a cloth bag, boiled in hot water. After letting it cool, it can be eaten daily.

In addition, Vietnamese people believe that the nest has medicinal properties, in particular, *Yen nhuc thao*, which is a wet and waste element in Birds' nests. The book, *Trung Viet*, mentioned Chinese herbalist named Ly Thoi Tran (Li Shizhen) using the swiftlet nests to make medicine (*Trien kim phuong*) to prevent *dai duong* or diabetes. In addition, the birds' nests have *Yen phan*, urine and feces, that is made into tablets and taken daily. The toxins in the body will be driven out by the urine (*Sao yen noi tu*).

Dead swiftlets found in the nests can also be used as a fever remedy and cough; plucking, cleaning, cooking with the birds' nests and formed into tablets to take as medicine.

The most important use of the nest is to make food. The first step is to clean them, removing small hairs and soaking for 1–2 hours, so only the bird saliva is left. Nests can be cleaned by boiling with *dau phung* or bean oil. When all the hairs have been removed and the remainder used as food, mostly are boiled nest soup, chicken soup, or beef. It is also cooked with birds, *bi cau tan Yen sao*, by boiling the birds until cooked and then seasoning. A dessert is made with 750 ml of water, 2 nests and rock sugar (*duong phen*). To eat with lotus seeds (*hot sen*), 1 nest of with 30 lotus seeds, half of sugar, half the amount of lotus seeds boiled with 7–8 times the amount of water than the lotus seed. While the red birds' nests (*huyet, mau*) is believed to contain bird blood, which are believed were made made when the birds were very tired, is the most valuable. It is believed that eating will improve mood, especially for those who are very stressed.[80]

Initially, it was believed that birds' nests are not a food, but a remedy, though the reason is unclear.[81] At present, in the medical community, research has shown that nests are high in protein at 42.8–54.9 percent, glucose, vitamins B, C, E.[82] with low fat, about 0.0–0.13 percent. There is a large amount of useful amino acids with acidic acid (acid sialic) 8 percent with 16 vitamins, and the DNA in the birds' nests has useful qualities. Consuming regularly will help the brain[83] and body, promoting beautiful skin and immunity. Nests are very useful to pregnant women, small children who are not very smart, and old people when eating birds' nests will see improved health and a more youthful appearance.[84] The nests beautify facial skin, improve sleep, aid in recovering quickly form illnesses for children and the elderly. It's recommended to drink hot nest soup before going to bed. One hundred grams of birds' nests should be divided into 20 portions and eaten[85] daily.

3.2 Equipment and Tools in Collecting Birds' Nests and its Industry

In the process of collecting nests, Vietnamese collectors have employed local wisdom to create methods and devise equipment in. The collectors dress simply, and important tools are prongs, torch, cloth bag, bamboo (*caytre*). Bamboo poles are lashed together along the cave faces as scaffolding. For safety, the bamboo is replaced every year.[86]

In the book, *Binh Dinh, Danh Thang* wrote that the collection of birds' nests is dangerous work passed down from generation to generation. The collectors must be experienced, climb and walk on the bamboo structure to collect the nests. They must be gentle and not damage the nests or their value will drop. When the weather is dry, the nests will be brittle, so they sprinkle them with water to soften them before collecting.[87]

After North and South Vietnam merged to form the Socialist Republic of Vietnam in 1976, the country was faced with a social and economic crisis that later led to the announcement of a reform policy (*Doi Moi*) or official "Renovation" in 1986. It was believed that without a free market economy, socialism in Vietnam would collapse. This resulted in the "Market Economy, One Political Party" economic policy, and multi-directional foreign policies.[88]

This transformed Vietnam's traditional birds' nest from local consumption into small enterprises, factories, and industrial plants that produce nest products using modern technologies. In a village in Nha Trang, Khanh Hoa Province, a famous birds' nests products brand Sanest produces ready-to-drink nest in bottles and cans in 29 provinces across the country. The Vietnamese have developed new flavors, and designed and advertised nest products for modern day consumption. Popularity has grown, along with more private brands of companies in other provinces i.e. Doi quan ly & khai thac Yen sao Hoi An, and Binh Dinh company.

3.3 Culture, Traditions and Wisdom in Birds'-Nests Business of Ethnic Groups

Tradition and culture related to swiftlet nests formed over 400 years ago and continues in areas where the nests are found, i.e Dao Tan Hiep – Cu Lao Cham Island, where a swiftlet cultural fair is held to express gratitude to the Nest-Collecting pioneers in Hoi An, and has become a tourist attraction in Quang Nam Province. Both Vietnamese and foreigners travel specially to the island to enjoy the celebration.

The birds' nests collection rituals originate from a belief in supernatural powers, or animism, arising from fear and appeasement. Like fertility rites the rituals eliminate fear.[89] The ceremony is held on the 10th of the 3rd month on the Vietnamese calendar at nest collector ancestral shrines in Hon Lao Island, Thon Nai Huong and Cu Lao Cham. This is to pay respect to the ancestors and ask for protection from the spirits during the harvest. Professional collectors, or nguoi lam nghe khai thac yen, prepare the ceremony prior to harvest season.[90]

Such ritual has two purposes: 1) To show appreciation of those who came before, and 2) To ask for property for the two-day harvest. There are also contests and folk games, showing off the unique identity of Cu Lao Cham that can be found only in Hoi An.[91] The traditional ceremony is called, *Ong to nghe yen*. It is intended to worship spirits, and to enjoy fun community activities.[92] A similar ceremony is held at the *Ho Van Hoa* shrine in his remembrance, on 7th of the 3rd month of every year.[93]

As for Nha Trang, Khanh Hoa, there is a ceremony in to commemorate Le Van Dat, one of the first nest-collectors in the area. The legend was that he had died in a war protecting the island 700 years ago. This ceremony is therefore to show gratitude for his sacrifice, and hope that his spirit will bless the harvest.[94]

The harvest ritual (*Le hoi yen sao*) here, is held on the 10th day of the Vietnamese calendar's 5th month, honoring the pioneer collector of the first nests, who was a woman, Tran Le Thi Huyen Tram, called *Ba Chua deo Yen* or the chief of the birds'-nest island. The ritual is held after the year's first harvest. On one of the nest islands, is the Hoh Yen shrine built for Ho Van Hoa, the man who collected the first nests at Binh Dinh during the King Ya Long Period.[95]

4. RIGHTS AND LEGAL SYSTEMS IN VIETNAM

Vietnam was under the jurisdiction of China for 1,000 years, from about 140–86 B.C. to the year 938 before independence was restored.[96] Under the yoke of the Chinese government the Vietnamese were cruelly persecuted. As a result, the Collective Consciousness of Ethno-History has been filled with bitterness reflected the form of

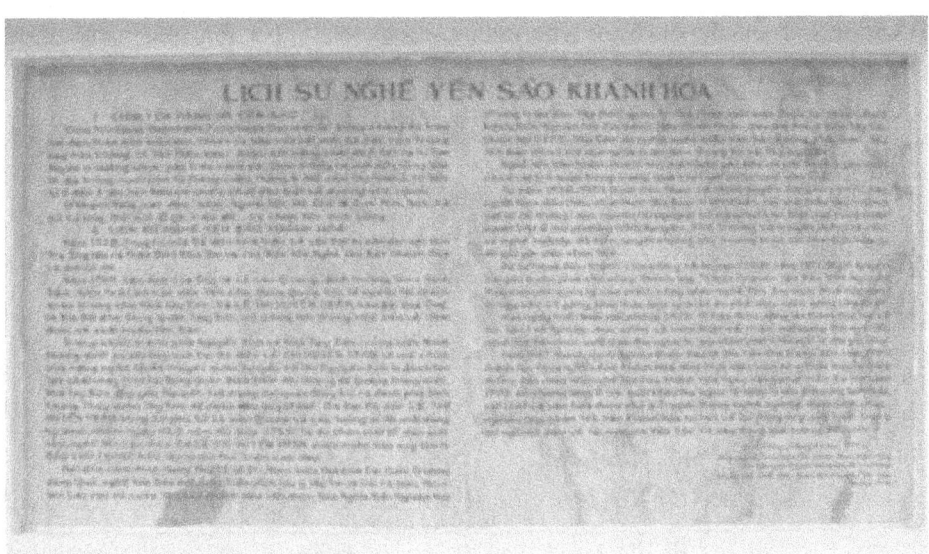

writing, such as a poem that declared victory, "Binh Ngo Dai Cao" by Nguyen Trai (A.D. 1380–1442), the military expert who mobilized people, together with Le Loi, Emperor of Le Dynasty (1428–1789), which was written after the Ming army of China departed in 1428. One section goes,

> "... Keep the peace for the people. That is the essence of humanity and justice. Eliminate violence, that is the first goal of our soldiers. Dai Viet, our country is a land with a long culture. The rivers and mountains have their own way of life and tradition different from the North [meaning China]. The Trieu, Dinh, Ly, Tran dynasties established the sovereignty of independence. We came up to stand prominently, the same as the Chinese Han, Tang, Sung, Yuan dynasties. We experienced both the day of greatness and the day of defeat, and we never lacked heroes ..."[97]

The 3rd chapter of a history textbook for 4th graders speaks of oppression:

> "... They forced us to enter the forest, hunting elephants, rhinos, good birds, fragrant wood, and dive in the deep sea finding pearls, catch beautiful fish; bringing them the

seashore. They are the Hans who came to live with us, but forced us to follow Han tradition and learn the Han alphabet..." [Hans = Chinese]

Or this:

"... Our country was occupied by the North, ruling us for more than a thousand years. At that time, even though we were heavily exploited, we did not become slaves. We never stopped resisting, until glorified winning of the Battle of Bach Dang. We brought independence back..."[98]

Vietnam however remained under the influence of China until the French colonized the country in the years 1858–1945. The structure was influenced by the Chinese hierarchies of power relations, that is the fundamental value system. The value that emphasizes human dignity expressed in the form of rules, that is, customs or law or power in the right to participate in various social, cultural activities of the society.

This includes the right to resources,[99] and Chinese feudalism. At the same time through nationalism as a political project created by political conditions; it separates the "them" and "us" in the country. This caused ethnic groups to leave behind their identities,[100] in the new history that the modern state created as part of the nationalism process. This is a state tool to create attributes for those who live within the national borders by ethnic classification, which is a kind of technology of powers that helps the state to know, its people.

By creating ethnic border lines, various ethnic groups' differences become more distinctive, and separated. Even though the dividing lines were created by the state and not related to how members of ethnic groups define themselves, it affected the formation of a new ethnic consciousness. Ethnic groups use it to differentiate between one another.[101]

The use of swiftlet nesting resources from natural sources in the past, left traces of access rights to nest resources in Hoi An, Quang Nam. On Cu Lao Cham Island of birds' nests, the Cham ethnic group (*nguoi Cham*) had traditionally collected the nest before others.

Until the end of the 15th century, the ethnic group of Dai Viet or Vietnamese ethnics came. And in the 17th century, ethnic Vietnamese people living in Thanh Chau village had the right to gather birds' nests. This indicates that since the 17th century, Vietnamese ethnic people have assumed the rights to such lands. The Cham ethnic group who originally collected the nests were pushed out. However, due to the arrangement of social power relations in Vietnam that follows the feudal system, access rights and use of swiftlet nesting resources proceeded according to the order of social stratification or power relations.

In the past, the person who granted the authority to access, manage and use nest resources was decided in accordance with social power relations systems in the feudal system; in which the king was the center of power. In addition to the aforementioned Cham ethnic group who had the right to harvest the birds' nests resources, Vietnamese ethnic people were granted the right by the king to collect nests. They paid a tax to the state or the king.

Other groups, such as Dai Viet or Vietnamese people in Thanh Chau village had the right to collect nest as well as pay tax to the state. In Emperor Gia Long reign, Ho Van Hoa was bestowed a title *Quan linh tam tinh ye ho*, acting as a master, supervising the harvest in three provinces: Quang Nam, Binh Dinh and Khanh Hoa. A group of Vietnamese ethnics in Binh Dinh also said the nest-collectors must pay tax to the state in the form of nests.

In 1793 before Emperor Minh Mang let the new ethnic group, the Bao Nghia Kien Nghiep Hoi to collect nests in the island. These Vietnamese groups, who collected the nests during French colonization—before the Chinese came in 1930–70, pressured the government in Saigon to withdraw the rights from Chinese investors. They requested that the Vietnamese from Vinh Nguyen district be allowed to supervise and collect the nests in 1971.

According to local collectors concerning the rights systems of nest resources in Cu Lao Cham, none mentions hereditary rights within families. As these are related to the Vietnamese society as hierarchal social relations, within which only one person or institute holds the rights. Its "linear system of management" and "linear concept of rights" takes the form of 'exclusive rights' because it prevents others from participating.[102] However, other field information says that knowledge of nest collection is passed on within families of the same bloodline.

This was so until modern times, after Vietnam integrated the country into the Socialist Republic of Vietnam in 1976, ruled with Democratic Centralism. Through more recent economic reforms or *Doi Moi* since 1986, the Vietnamese government shifted the economy into a more liberal capitalist system, allowing the private sector freedom in small scale operations, as well as increasing foreign trade.

The government announced the 4th constitution in 1992 which, according to Article 15, states that the economic system is supported by various elements. Article 16 states the needs of the people both material and psychological. Article 20 states that the industrial sector can have freedom in voluntary administration based on democracy and mutual benefits. Articles 21–23, ensure that individual and private capitalists can manage production and trade as needed with the state's support, the economic development of households, production and trade equally in accordance with the law. Article 23 says the government will not seize private businesses. Article 50 provides that political rights, civil rights, economic, social and cultural rights are respected. It is also part of civil rights that all have the right to religion. In Article 112, the government protects the rights and legitimate interests of the people and creates conditions that allows people to exercise their rights and perform their duties[103] and allows provinces to have organizations independent from the central government resource management of the swiftlet nest resources in Nha Trang, Khanh Hoa.

The ethnic groups with access to power and management, especially the nest-collectors are still the Vietnamese ethnic groups from Vinh Nguyen district, later called themselves, *Hop tac xa Yen sao Vinh Nguyen*, took control of the trade. The local government here founded the bird's-nest business group, Xi Nghiep Quoc Doanh Yen sao Nha Trang in 1987 and became Cong ty Yen sao Khanh Hoa in 1990.

This is the largest corporation in Vietnam that has continuously run their business to the present day (2011).

The result of the hiearchical social order that lasted such a long time, and the ruling central government has eliminated the traditions of the bird's-nest collection. The government holds the rights to the resource, which used to be passed within the local community. In case of house nest farms, after the declaration of 1992 constitution, all citizens have the right to run their business freely. This resulted in people running birds'-nests businesses in house farms, companies, and retail stores selling both raw and ready-to-eat birds' nests.

Though there were only 50 swiftlet houses in 2007, this increased to more than 200 by 2011, both as domestic and international businesses. It is tax-free[104] and can be inherited legally.

There is no law controlling the swiftlet houses, only the conservation of the natural habitats. The 47/2008 law, enacted on August 1, 2008, covers conservation in different categories.[105] It bars outsiders from entering the bird's-nest islands and prevents the collectors from selling the nests to business contacts. The collectors must be honest, especially the supervisors, in case of theft and bribery. If caught, they must be fired from the job.

The nest-collectors work for the government and receive relatively high pay. They receive welfare, insurance and retirement benefits.[106] It is considered a dream job. Only those who have connections will get the jobs on the island.[107]

One source insisted that in Nha Trang, a mafia-type person has the monopoly to Hong Kong auction access. However, even though the Vietnamese ethnic groups who have access to the nest resources and have the most power, within one ethnic group there are unequal levels. Since management power is with the central government, the rights and power are related so closely that it has destroyed the traditional inherited rights of the descendants. In contrast, the owner of a swiftlet-house building can lawfully pass the rights to their children.

Chapter 1

5. BUSINESS AND MANAGEMENT SYSTEM OF THE BIRD'S-NEST BUSINESS IN VIETNAM

5.1 Bird's-Nest Business from Ancient Times – Conservative Society

The traditional collection of birds' nests uses centuries old local technology. The most important one is the bamboo scaffolding used for climbing the cave face. The nests are consumed as medicine and as food within Vietnam's ethnic groups. It has been this way for hundreds of years and it either spread into China, or it originated in China and spread to Vietnam. Either way, the nests are part of the cultural identity in Vietnam. The nests can be made into various special products, but Vietnamese scholars who study birds' nests and the cultural aspects of their consumption refer to the journal *Tuyen Nam tap chi*, which says that eating swiftlet nests has been practiced since the China Ming Dynasty[108] (A.D. 1368–1644), which deeply reflects the acceptance of Chinese culture in Vietnam.

It appears that the Cham ethnic group used to collect nests before the 15th century. They are the dominant ethnic group who established the business and its history, establishing it as an ethnic space and excluding others geographically.

In the year 1328 nobleman Le Van Dat, founded a community—Bich Dam village—and ran a business collecting nests there. In 1769, Le Van Quang, the chief teacher of Bich Dam and Le Thi Huyen Tram, his daughter, controlled the business, including selling them to foreign countries. Other evidence is found in the writings of herbalist Ly Thoi Tran (1578), saying that nests were traded as food and used to make *Thien kim phuong*, a medicine to treat diabetes.

External evidence on Vietnam's nest business appears in the memoirs of the French ambassador, Simon de la Loubère, who traveled to Ayutthaya, Siam (Thailand) after 1686, and recorded that in Ayutthaya, nests were traded freely. The nests came from Tonkin.[109]

Vietnamese ethnic groups have established a mythology on the subject. It emphasizes the value and special quality of the birds' nests. It refers to Chinese Emperor Qin Shi, and Vietnamese Emperor Minh Mang (1820–1841) who believed the nests would give them eternal life. The myth was retold repetitively, in various forms, in many generations beyond these groups,[110] which became the base of the nest business system in Vietnam.

This accords with written evidence in Khanh Hoa; The Emperors would grant people whom they favored the bird's nest business. For example, in 1806, Emperor Gia Long appointed Ho Van Hoa to supervise harvesting in three provinces. In 1831, Emperor Minh Mang granted only a few people to run the bird's-nest islands in Khanh Hoa Province. In return of the favor, according to the Official Geographical Record of Vietnam's Nguyen Dynasty, each year the particular amount of the collected birds' nests belonged to the government, as tax. The rest could be trade, both domestically and internationally. The practice continued until the French colonization changed it to a free trade system.

In 1858, during the war between France and Vietnam, the Vietnamese ethnic group known as *Binh Tay Cuu Quoc Hoi* became the protector of the nest island until 1873. Later on, the French and Vietnam government in Saigon granted permission for the Chinese to run the business spanning 1930–70, which was resisted and eventually stopped by the Vietnamese. In 1971, the Vietnamese from Vinh Nguyen were the main caregivers and nest-collectors. Their name was changed to Hop tac xa Yen sao Vinh Nguyen in 1975. However, they were the main nest-collectors, who have traded with foreign markets ever since.

Chapter 1

In the past, birds' nests were divided into different categories. According to the book *Trung Quoc*, they were categorized by color: black, white, and red. The red nest (*yen huyet sao*), or blood nest is the most expensive and valuable, and mainly used to make medicine.

In Hoi An, they are catergorized into 3 levels:
1. The first is *quan Yen sao*, or a white big and thick bird's nest.
2. The second is *thien tu Yen sao*, or blue nest, not as thick as the first level.
3. The third is *dia tu Yen sao*, a yellow or black nest, thinner and smaller than the other two. There are some yellow materials mixed in the nest.

There are also *bai tu Yen sao* (*yen bai*), or an incomplete nest, and *mao yen*, a bird's nest that has been recently completed.[111] All of them are sold as raw birds' nests. In 1976, after the country became the Socialist Republic of Vietnam, the government took control of the nest business. The declaration of the 4th constitution in 1992 granted authority to each province with nest resources to run its own business, keeping 14 percent of the income within the province, with the rest going to the central government.[112]

5.2 Business of Birds' Nests in Food Sovereignty Time: Modern Society

After 1992, the socialist government Vietnam adjusted the social system to keep up with changes to compete in global trade. The management of the nest business changed accordingly. In addition to each province that is the source of birds' nests running its own bird's-nest business after 1996, a private business invested in nest-farm buildings and set up a company.

In 1978 the bird's-nest price reached USD 500–600 per kilogram, a sevenfold increase compared with 30 years earlier. In 2004, the price was USD 3,000–3,500 per kilogram. From 1978 to 1991, rose 20 times and more recently, it increased by a further tenfold.

In the early 21st century, the bird's-nest prices rose to USD 5,000 per kilogram. The Vietnamese birds' nests are valued at five times higher than the Thai birds' nests in the Hong Kong market; 22 times higher than Malaysian's, and 74 times higher than Indonesia's prices.[113]

In Nha Trang, Khanh Hoa Province, one of the important bird's-nest resources in Vietnam, the local government established a company called, Cong ty Yen sao Khanh Hoa in 1993. The one-stop service company covers the whole range of nests resources, storage, and a production plant.

Size of Vietnam Bird's-Nest Business

Even though birds' nests from natural sources are available in many provinces, the top one in quantity, quality and reputation is the one in Binh Dinh. Nest collection is about 800 kilograms per year in Binh Dinh, and in Da Nang Province, about 700 kilograms per year. In Cu Lao Cham, Yen sao Hoi An, it is up to 1–1.5 tons per year. The price here is higher than in Binh Dinh and Khanh Hoa.

Some years ago, it exported nests to Taiwan and Singapore at a price of USD 3,000–4,000 per kilogram, and the income from selling the birds' nests was 20 percent of Hoi An's total taxable income. Another important nest source is Nha Trang, Khanh Hoa.

In 1961, 370 kilograms of the birds' nests were collected here, by 1970, it was eight times that amount, and the export product worth was 10 times more. At the same time, the province of Khanh Hoa advertised that its birds' nests were the most expensive in the world and five times the quantity of Thailand's.

Each year, Cong ty Yen sao Khanh Hoa collects nests for the government of Vietnam, totaling around THB 80 million per year. In 2002, the company can handled 2,145 kilograms, in 2007, collecting 2,356 kilograms with a value of THB 102 million, in 2008, 2,445 kilograms and in 2009, 2,500 kilograms.

Cong ty Yen sao Khanh Hoa is a nest collection company that produces Sanest bird's-nest beverage, in addition to selling bird's-nest products in various sub-stores in hotels, airports or direct sales services and on the Internet. It has showrooms selling nest products in 29 provinces. There are 18 government stores, and 19 private, locating in the major cities in all regions. Most of the stores are in the south.

In the major cities, Ho Chi Minh City, Nha Trang, Da Nang and Hanoi where there are approximately 200 swiftlet houses, producing 400 kilograms per year. However, Vietnamese businessmen estimate production at around 1,500 kilograms per year.[114]

When combining from the country's natural sources and swiftet houses, the total is approximately 7,000–8,000 kilograms per year. Excluding the ready-to-drink nest products, the average price is USD 1,666 per kilogram. Vietnam sells raw nests worth about THB 350–400 million per year. Vietnam has companies that buy and sell raw nests, produce ready-to-drink birds' nests and construct swiftet houses. Companies belonging to local governments are Cong ty Yen sao Khanh Hoa, Doi quan ly & khai thac Yen sao Hoi An, Cong ty Yen sao Binh Dinh, and to private companies such as Hoang Yen, Yen Viet, Cong Ty Co Phan Yen sao Viet Nam.

Table 1.1: Bird's-nest production in three provinces

	Provinces					
	Khanh Hoa (1)		Da Nang (1)		Binh Dinh (2)	
Year	Island (3)	Output (kg.)	Island (3)	Output (kg.)	Island (3)	Output (kg.)
1980	6	940	3	186	3	210
1981	6	1008	3	167	3	-
1982	6	1205	3	156	3	-
1983	6	1213	3	212	3	-
1984	6	ca. 1300	3	159	3	-
1985	7	ca. 1300	3	220	3	393
1986	7	ca. 1500	3	381	5	486
1987	7	ca. 1500	3	433	5	486
1988	7	ca. 1450	3	461	5	502
1989	7	ca. 1450	4	539	5	478
1990	7	ca. 1300	4	644	5	568
1991	12	2100	4	638	5	-
1992	12	1450	4	-	8	-
1993	12	2321	4	-	8	-
1994	12	1330	4	-	8	-
1995	12	2136	4	648	8	754
1996	12	2275	4	668	8	715[115]

Table 1.2: Amount of bird's-nest production in Nha Trang, Khanh Hoa[116]

Year	Kilogram
1953	60
1961	370
1991	2,150
2002	2,145
2007	2,356
2008	2,445
2009	2,500

Chapter 1

Type and Price of Nests in the Vietnamese Market

In the Vietnamese bird's-nest business market, there are different types of birds' nests:

(A) Nests categorized by nesting area and color are divided into 5 types:

1. *To Yen Hoang / Trong Dong* or *Yen Hoang* or Wild / cave nests

    There are 2 types of nests in caves obtained from Edible-nest Swiftlets (Fuciphaga) and Black-nest Swiftlets (Maxima). For the Cave Swiftlet (*yen hang*), the color of the nests is an important factor in pricing.

2. *To Ye Trong Nha* or House Nest is a swiftlet nest that can be obtained from swiftlet houses, called white bird's-nests (*bach yen*).

3. *Huyet Yen* or Red Nest is blood red (*mau do* or *Hong Yen*), a rare type popular with the biggest spenders, representing less than 10 percent of the international nest market.

4. *Hong Yen* or Gold Nest as well as red nests are expensive and rare. Hong Yen is orange colored. The color tone is from orange to yellow, and the closer to orange, the higher the price.

5. *Bach Yen* or White Nest is the most prominent type in the market, which is about 75 percent of the total sold in the world market.

(B) Swiftlet's nests divided according to the quality and color of the nests are:

1. *yen huyet*
2. *yen thien*
3. *yen quang*
4. *yen bai*
5. *yen dia*
6. *yen vun*

The average price is USD 3,000 per kilogram

(C) **Swiftlet's nest is divided into 5 grades:**

1. *Yen sao to nho* is a pure swiftlet nest that is 100 percent bird saliva, weighing 6–7 grams. The price is USD 1,666–1,904.
2. *To yen bai* birds' nests with a weight of 3–5 grams per nest, priced at USD 1,190–1428 per kilogram.
3. *To yen vun* or broken birds' nests, 3–5 grams, USD 476–714 per kilogram.
4. *To yen dia* or *yen dia* is a nest that has a little saliva and lot of grass, feathers or other materials, USD 380–476 per kilogram.
5. After sorting the nests into grades, and sorting out the best quality ones, a fifth grade is grade is *to yen mau hong* or Pink, with a price of USD 1,904–2,380 per kilogram.

(D) **10 types of birds' nests categorized from location of the nest, color, and cleaning process:**

No.	Name	Quality	Price (THB)
1	House-birds' nests (cleaned)	X	8,000
2	Island birds' nests (cleaned)	X	14,000
3	House birds' nests (not cleaned) (no. 1)	8 nest/100 g., 12.5 g./nest	10,000
4	House birds' nests (not cleaned) (no.2)	10 nest/100 g., 10 g./nest	9,000
5	House birds' nests (not cleaned) (no. 3)	12 nest/100 g.	8,000 (bit)
6	House birds' nests (not cleaned) (no. 4)	15 nest/100 g.	8,000
7	House birds' nests (not cleaned) (no. 5)	17 nest/100 g.	7,000
8	Island birds' nests (not cleaned) (no. 1)	12 nest/100 g.	16,000
9	Island birds' nests (not cleaned) (no. 2)	15 nest/100 g.	13,000
10	Red birds' nests (not cleaned)		30,000[117]

Source: www.yensao.vn bang gia (thong nhat tren toan quoc)
Note: The birds' nests prices calculated from VND 500 to THB 1

Incentive and Welfare System for Bird's-Nest Collectors

The welfare and compensation and way of life for nest workers, including collectors, guards on the bird's-nest island, factory workers, management, etc. are not easy to discover. Bird's-nest businesses keep their information strictly confidential. However, some people were willing to share information on aspects of the world of Vietnamese bird's nest businesses.

Here is Hoi An, Quang Nam!

Nguyen Duc Vinh, a 35 year-old man with one daughter, is a furniture technician, and a former bird's-nest collector in Cu Lao Cham, Hoi An, Quang Nam Province. He met us in the evening in a European style restaurant, and told us his story:

"… In 1990, around 18 years ago, after finishing high school, I was looking for work, and applying as a worker on bird's-nest island in Cu Lao Cham, knowing nothing about swiftlets.

When I first started working at the island, there were about 30–40 workers on 3 months shifts. The work included guarding the island and collecting the birds'-nests. There was a chief of the birds' nests called, Doi truong. The island was well protected from thieves. The nests were harvested twice a year, in the 3rd and 7th month, 4–5 times daily. Each worker collecting 2–3 kilograms per day.

The government managed this operation, and the chief or manager of the company was the wealthiest. Collectors retire at 60. Workers at bird's-nest islands received a monthly salary of 85,000 Dong. The collectors had to stay 2–3 months on the island before returning home. The money I earned went to my mother, and family.

Daily life on the island meant getting up at 6 o'clock in the morning and taking care of things, and patroling the island. During the harvest times, we'd collect the birds' nests. The company provided food and we cooked for ourselves, mostly fish. The company also provided accommodation. There were strict laws forbidding theft. At night, there would be a boat patrolling around the island. And once a year, everyone on the island helped each other to construct new bamboo scaffolding used for collecting the birds' nests …"[118]

Nguyen Van Hung, is a former fisherman who used to catch fish near the bird's nest islands. He's now an owner of a tourist boat in the Thu Bon River. He used to collect birds' nests when they were not worth nearly as much as now. He has seen the islands and the way of life of people who worked there.

> "... Bird nest-collectors received a monthly salary of THB 10,000. Police officers would accompany us to the island during harvest time. They'd inspect every collector before leaving. There were 50 people on the island, and 10 people per week would rotate, working on Cu Lao Cham Island.
>
> They'd wait until the birds finished building their nests, and then travel to the island. Police officers were on guard the whole time. The company inspected and separated birds' nests into various types. Everyone who sorts the birds' nests must change clothes before working. We were under police supervision at all times. We changed to our normal clothes again after work. This was to prevent theft. But the collectors wouldn't steal, because they already made good money. If they stole, they'd be arrested. The birds'-nests collectors are not ordinary people, they're connected or related to powerful people in the province. They make really good money of around THB 10,000 per month throughout the year. They receive this salary even when not working. The collectors are government employees. People, outside the province would like to become birds'-nests collectors too, but it's impossible. It's very difficult ..."[119]

Here, Binh Dinh!

On the Internet, there are websites that share stories about the bird's-nest islands:

> "... At Binh Dinh, there are 40 nest-collectors for 16 caves. There are many rules to keep the island under control. No outsiders are allowed to visit the island. As well, people working there are not allowed to speak about the island to anyone outside. If any birds' nests are stolen, the police investigate on the island. In the past, the island wasn't well supervised nests disappeared. The person in charg of collecting birds' nests, had to pay for the missing birds' nests, and was fired. This was according to legal requirements. Any income from selling birds' nests must be paid as a tax to the provincial government

first, and the rest goes to the collectors. The government must deposit the tax money in a government bank in each province..."

Here, Nha Trang, Khanh Hoa!

Nguyen Nhuu Tri, a 43-year-old tour guide of the Yen sao Khanh Hoa Company, who was leading tourists on the bird's-nest island, told us.

"... On the islands, there are only guards, and outsiders are not allowed to enter. They are responsible for protecting the islands from theft. There are about 20 people working there. Only two groups of people are allowed to enter the islands – guards and collectors. They can enter the caves during harvest time. At other times, they remain at home. The collectors are 25–60 years old. They do not need to have high education, and you can be a successor if your father was a collector. The birds' nests are collected in cloth bags.

On the island, there is a chief supervisor from the company called *dao truong*. There's an accountant to check how many birds' nests are collected. The collectors must sign off on the number collected. The collectors cannot eat any birds' nests. Every island has surveillance cameras..."[120]

Nguyen Tien Duong, a young taxi driver in the city of Nha Trang, told his story in the early afternoon while driving for a group of researchers after visiting one of the Sanest bird's-nest shops in Nha Trang...

"... bird's-nest business is a closed shop in Vietnam; foreigners are not allowed to join the business. You have to pay 10,000 Dong up front to the company before you can work for them. All employees are Vietnamese and can work until they retire at 60 years old.

Even people in Nha Trang have a hard time getting in the company. Only those with connections, or who have fathers working there have the opportunity. People do want to work there, but it is difficult. I'd also like to work for a birds'-nest company, but it's impossible..."[121]

Another taxi driver is an insider in Nha Trang, yet an outsider of the bird's-nest business. He refused to tell us his name while telling us about the bird's-nest business in Vietnam. As he was driving us to one manufacturer that produces ready-to-drink bird's-nest products around 12 km outside the city, he said:

> "… People who collect birds' nests, or work for the bird's-nest company get paid really well. However, people who work on the island get better pay than the ones in the office; with a fixed rate salary set by the government. A guard on the island gets paid around 4,000,000–8,000,000 Dong; and a collector, 2,005,000 Dong. Supervisors in the company have a better life than most people in Vietnam. Opportunities to work in these companies are hard to come by. You must be knowledgeable, and smart. If you work on the island, or in the factory, it's not as difficult because you don't need much education. The companies are all government owned.
>
> No foreigners are allowed on the island; I've only been to small caves. I'd love to work in the birds' nests company, but it's impossible. In a factory, there are many departments. Everyone finishes work at 5 PM …"[122]

A 40 year old woman, owner of steamed duck shop called, Kim Kook. Her shop is in front of the Sanest factory, of the Yen sao Khanh Hoa Company, in Nguyen Sau Ngao, outside Nha Trang city. She said:

> "… This factory has been open for almost three years now. They start work at 7.30 AM, with an hour break, then finish at 5 PM. There are about 200 workers; mostly males – all young. They must have a bachelor's degree. A cleaner in the factory must finish high school, and gets paid 2,000,000 Dong; it is 3,000,000 Dong for a factory worker, and 2,800,000 Dong for a security guard. You must have a degree to apply for this job; they'll consider your application and let you know. There's no other test. Here they work in three shifts, eight hours per shift. There is OT work at the factory at night as well – like today, some will work until 9 PM. During the working hours, the factory provides them with free food."[123]

Yen sao Khanh Hoa is a very big company that produces bird's-nest beverages, and other products under the brand Sanest. In addition to the company's showrooms around the country, they also have an online sales channel offering various of products; it is to distinguish the status of a customer, whether middle or high-class. The website tells about both the birds' nests and its business.

> "... the company staff on bird's-nest islands are not allowed to contact anyone on the shore – zero chance to talk to outsiders. They are isolated. There are two boats, large and small, that deliver everything they need like food, and water. They have accommodation with TV, telephone, and a radio to communicate between the islands and the patrols. The caregiver can use the telephone to contact only family members. The company has built accommodation for people in the island with a kitchen and bathrooms. The company also provides life insurance; the quality of a birds'-nest collector's lot has improved. It's unlike the past, when there was no welfare ..."[124]

Meanwhile, the government has allowed the company, which is government owned to do more product research i.e sweets, more variety of bird's-nest beverage, raw birds' nests. tours.[125]

Export Market

Vietnam's important nest markets are both domestic and international. Vietnamese consumers favor both raw, and ready-to-drink bird's-nest products; however, 90 percent are exported to Hong Kong, Taiwan, China and Singapore.

Nest-Trade Relationships with the Birds' Nests as a Link for Ethnic Relations

Nest-Trade Relationships with Swiftlet's Nest as a Link for Ethnic Group

Swiftlets' nests have unique characteristics in food hierarchy: they are a natural food, medicinal drug, healthy food, food industry, food as a gift, and symbolic food for the wealthy. Similarly, the swiftlets producing edible nests, have a fluidity within the social property systems: State, Private, and 'communal property' regimes. At the same time, they are considered *Res nullius* regimes or open access regimes.[126] The swiftlets are generally state property, which are conserved and protected by law as with any other state properties. They become private property when the birds build nests in a private house; they're also communual property since they grow in community area.

They are open access property, under the condition that the bird chooses to build its nest in a house or building, beyond human influence. In the Vietnamese business, the resource is a mediator for relationships of people in the state, and ethnic groups. The Vietnamese ethnic group is the 'dominant ethnicity'; they have monopoly power to manage access and use of swiftlet nests in natural sources. Futhermore, they have the authority to control and manage the people involved, whether they are researchers, bird's-nest collectors, guards, or workers in the state-owned industries.

At the same time, within the Vietnamese ethnic group alone, there is another layer of power relationship in accessing and using the overlapping birds' nests resources. The relationship both 'includes' some at the center of power, and 'excludes' others.

The 'inclusive' relationships are for example, when children can succeed their fathers as collectors, or those who have connections and have a better chance to work in the birds' nests company. The birds' nest people reinforce their unity as seen in the inscription in the history on Noi Island that all collectors on the island have inherited the shared tradition of collecting nests for more than 650 years. Another example is when bird's-nest auctions by the state are monopolized by Vietnamese companies for export to international markets.

On the other hand, even within the same ethnic groups, not everyone has access to or allows bird's-nest resources. The excuse is that the federal government forbade the disclosure of information. A third party or any outsider is banned from entering the island or cave. People on the island cannot contact or provide information on the birds' nests with outside parties and can only talk with their families.

Once the birds' nests are collected, the company will not allow outsides to see anything, with laws prohibiting theft, and patrol boats are used to prevent any unauthorized person from entering the island. Tourists can only go on a company boat to see smaller caves specified by the company.

At the same time, the smaller ethnic groups, who are blocked from the power to access and use resources, have fought back with criticism, gossip, or even stealing the birds' nests when the opportunity arises, and hence the police presence and patrol boats.

Nest-Trade Relationships Across Ethnic Groups

Vietnamese private companies compete at auction for birds' nests from the local government company, then export to markets in Hong Kong, Taiwan, China and Singapore. Some of these companies, such as Hoang Yen and Yen Viet also import nests from Thailand, Malaysia and Indonesia.

The local and international business contacts have developed a deep mutual trust. The birds' nests for import or export must be consistent in volume to meet market needs.

A manager of the Home of Swiftlet company, the top company that sells raw and ready-to-drink bird's-nest beverages in Hong Kong, says that the Vietnamese birds' nests have the highest quality and fetch the highest prices in Hong Kong. However, the volume is less than from Malaysia or Indonesia.[127]

Nonetheless, although the consumption in Vietnam is high; ethnic Chinese are the most powerful in determining global market prices. Hong Kong also has a significant influence on pricing in the Vietnamese market. Yen sao Khanh Hoa Company, which is a government-owned company with bird's-nest resources and a ready-to-drink industry, Sanest has no problem obtaining raw materials for their factory, importing raw birds' nests from Thailand, Malaysia and Indonesia.

Though the birds' nests produced in the country are sufficient for domestic consumption, there is greater financial potential in exporting, so 90 percent of birds' nests produced in the country are exported, and this contributes to the Birds'-Nests Business company monopoly in winning the auctions from the state company. However, even though global society has changed quickly, bird's-nest collection is still carried out using bamboo scaffolding, as in the hunter and gatherer society, disregarding the modern view of food production.

6. BIRDS' NESTS IN POLITICS AND SOCIETY

The Republic of Vietnam is governed with Democratic Centralism, with the economy controlled by a centralized bureaucracy. The management power is vertical with the Communist party at the center of power. The state controls the economy, banking, state enterprises and foreign trade.

After experiencing economic development failures following unification, with slow growth and inflation as high as 774.7 percent in 1986, the party decided to reform the country to survive, and prevent socialism and the Communist Party from collapsing.

Vietnam opened up and reformed its economy by integrating the centralized economy with the market economy or the "Socialist Market Economic system" – a more flexible socialist ideology. The state administration system was reformed with an open foreign policy. The Foreign Policy of multilateralism and diversification focused on diplomatic and multi-party operations, participating in international organizations at a global and regional level.

Vietnam became a member of ASEAN in July 1995, and AFTA, ASEM (ASEAN Regional Forum), and APEC at the end of 1998. They attended summits such as the South Summit in Havana, in 2000 and the 10th UN Conference on Trade and Development, as well as the World Trade Organization (WTO) in January 2007. This was to accelerate the country to industrialization and modernization by 2010 and lay out the foundation for the country to be fully industrialized by 2020.

Vietnamese politics is currently more liberal, though still adhering to a single political party system, namely the Communist Party of Vietnam as in socialism and as a political system, only not strict.[128]

However, there has not been much improvement in the politics of bird's-nest resources, despite the new international policies. Reflections from the local Vietnamese reveal inequality in access and use of bird's-nest resources. The inclusion of some people and the exclusion of others from the center of power remains and can be seen in job opportunities such as bird's-nest collectors, factory workers, and monopolizing state concession. Some companies keep information about bird's-nest resource confidential, and many relevant laws maintain their old structure. An exception is the private business owners' swiftlet houses or bird's-nest companies, who have freedom to operate their businesses. However, these business owners are a wealthy minority.

When considering the birds' nests in the dimension of politics and social practices of everyday life, this is a movement of everyday life struggle and symbolic politics. People in society who are inferior, whether a birds' nests collector, a fisherman who knows the benefits of birds' nests resources, boat driver, bird's-nest businessman, taxi driver, restaurant owner or even Vietnamese bird's-nest thieves, have expressed in the form of everyday life resistance in many forms: gossip, intransigence, silent protests and stealing.

In one dimension, it's because those who are excluded from access to bird's-nest resources do not wish to protest openly; but rather use a method called, the 'weapons of the weak' to avoid being suppressed, arrested, or lose help from the authorities.[129] Such characteristics are the thoughts of the underprivileged people to criticize the state power system.[130] It is an instrument to express criticism of domination. The nature of such countermeasures is a way to challenge state power in Vietnam's bird's-nest business, where there is an inequality of power. However, according to field data, there is no evidence of murder due to "The War of the Bird's-Nest Resources" in the Vietnamese ethnic community.

7. ENVIRONMENTAL AND ECOLOGICAL FACTORS

Vietnam has a variety of climates and terrain, with abundant natural resources including tropical forests, coal, manganese, wild animals, oil and marine resources. There are more than 12,000 plant species, of which 2,300 are used to produce human and animal food, medicine, and other purposes, and there are over 1,000 species of birds.[131] However, the forest has been quickly destroyed, as well as wild animals. The cause of the problem is management that lacks balance between human needs and natural resources due to rapid development.[132] After the government began to develop a plan based on capitalism, starting with a community system, and returning the land to the citizens, and opening a free market, the resulting development has seen Vietnam grow swiftly.

Previously, Vietnam still had no specific environmental laws but later, the government began to discuss laws to prevent deforestation and preserve rare wildlife. However, law enforcement is still weak. The country has adopted laws through economic mechanisms to collect taxes and fees such as the use of natural resources tax laws in 1991.

Though the government has accelerated the development of environmental education, people's environmental awareness is still low. Public cooperation and the work of NGOs doesn't play a large role.

Being a Socialist country, Vietnam may have both advantages and disadvantages in political management or policy formulation, but law enforcement is not strict, and the legal system emanates from the center, causing weakness in local governments. Bribery, lack of law enforcement and lack of awareness of the importance of environmental protection slow the progress of government policies. There is also inadequate cooperation from the people. Vietnam has just started developing the country amid the current trend of environmental awareness around the world, and it can learn from other countries by boosting economic growth while simultaneously building in environmental protections.

Swiftlet resources in the natural environment are related to the birds and their habitats, the case of the birds' nests islands in Nha Trang Province, which had been heavily degraded, only 60 kilograms of nests produced in 1953. However, the production has increased, by 2009, more than 2,500 kilograms of birds' nests were collected. It demonstrates that caring for the environment and ecological systems helps economic progress.

At present, Vietnam has a good level of swiftlet resource management. In some provinces, there is still much to improve, but they have been alerted to do so.

Vietnam is still primarily an agricultural country, with vast rice fields that are a food source for swiftlets. Bird's-nest harvesting has been cut from three times a year to two. The collecting time has extended, waiting for fledgling birds to leave before harvesting. Thus, bird's-nest production in natural resources has increased.

For this reason, CITES has accepted the Yen sao Khanh Hoa as a state company that may collect a large amount of birds' nests. It has been praised as the best company in Southeast Asia in caring for the swiftlet population.

In the case of birds' nests outside of natural resources, there are around 200 swiftlet houses scattered from the central to the southern region in 24 provinces. The density of these buildings is still low. In addition, birdhouses are often spread outside the community. Vietnamese people have respect for their neighbors, so they do not play the bird attraction sounds too loudly. Therefore, there's little noise pollution from the swiftlet houses, nor any impact on community health.

APPENDIX

Vietnamese Ethnics with Birds' Nest Resource

Swiftlet Characteristics in Vietnam.

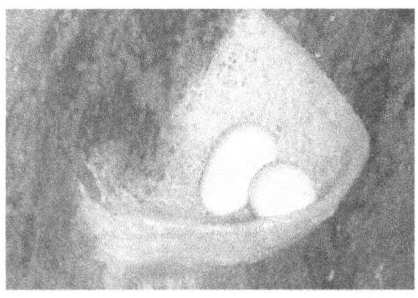

Swiftlet birds' nests and eggs in Vietnam.

The hut for guarding birds' nests on Noi Island, Nha Trang, Khanh Hoa.

The birds'-nests cave and the hut for guarding birds' nests on Noi Island.

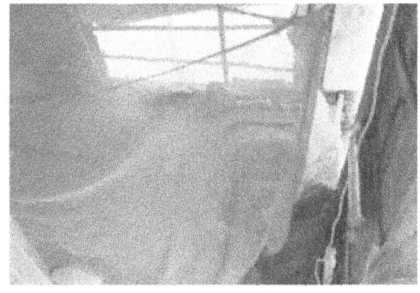

Inside the hut for guarding bird's-nest island on Noi Island, Nha Trang.

A gun inside the hut on the bird's-nest island on Noi Island.

Chapter 1

A shrine and the sacred pioneer spirits of birds'-nests collection in Noi Island, Nha Trang.

Bird's-nest collectors on Cu Lao Cham Island are building a scaffold for climbing to collect birds' nests.

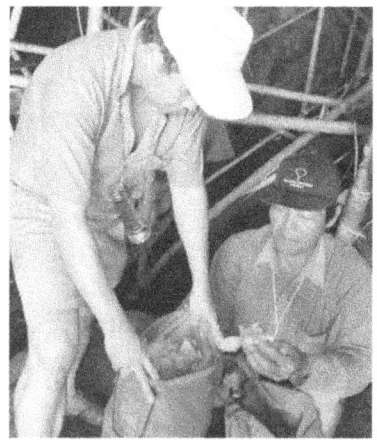

Bird's-nest collectors on Cu Lao Cham Island are gathering birds' nests from the birds'-nests cave in bags.

A supervisor of the bird's-nest collectors on Cu Lao Cham Isand worshiping sacred spirits before entering to collect birds' nests in a cave.

Bird's-nest collectors in Nha Trang are collecting birds' nests in a cave.

The headquater of Yen sao Khanh Hoa Company, the producer of bird's-nest products brand Sanest in Nha Trang.

Communities and Bird's-Nest Resources in Vietnam

The ready-to-eat birds' nests factory of the Yen sao Khanh Hoa Company in Nha Trang suburb, Khanh Hoa.

Vietnamese female workers of Yen sao Khanh Hoa Company are cleaning birds' nest inside the facotry, in Nha Trang.

A Sanest birds' nests advertisement, common sights in Khanh Hoa and Vietnam.

The canned SANEST ready-to-drink bird's-nest products.

Sanest bird's-nest products are available at the Cam Ranh International Airport.

Chapter 1

Sanest birds' nests product stores can be found in Nha Trang, Khanh Hoa and all over Vietnam.

Sanest birds' nests products salesperson on Noi Island in Nha Trang.

A Vietnamese child from a well-to-do family enjoys drinking Sanest ready-to-drink birds' nests.

2

Ethnic Groups and Bird's-Nest Resources in Indonesia

INTRODUCTION

The Republic of Indonesia gained dependence from the Netherlands in 1949. It is the world's largest archipelagic state and the third most populous democracy. It is the world's largest Muslim-majority nation, 83% of the total population of 267 million (2020 est.). It is the world's largest producer of swiftlet birds' nests.[1]

Indonesia has a large variety of ethnic groups and cultures, as well as vast quantities of biological and natural resources, such as natural gas, forests, and minerals (charcoal, lead, copper, nickel, bromide, gold, silver, and iron). Of its 1,500 bird species, the swiftlet bird is the most significant. It has influenced Indonesia's history, economy, culture, politics, environmental awareness, and ethnic group awareness.

1. INDIGENOUS PEOPLE'S USE OF BIRDS' NESTS

1.1 Swiftlets in Nature

It is unknown when and where in Indonesia people first began to harvest birds' nests, but there is support for the belief that Dutch merchants, first arriving on Java in 1596, greatly influenced the increased production and sale of the nests. Partnering with

Nest-collectors in Middle Java sorting the nests and putting them into bags.

indigenous people, the Dutch founded the United East India Company in the capital city of Jakarta (then known as Batavia).

The birds' nests brought wealth and power. Evidence shows that by 1637, the birds' nests were already being used as a valuable symbol of honor, when the embassy in Palembang sent birds' nests as tribute to the Dutch governor-general in Batavia.[2] According to historical records, birds' nests began being sold in 1625,[3] with the oldest records dating from the 17th century.[4]

Since the indigenous people who first sold birds' nests were in Middle Java, near the city of Gombong Selatan, they began to call the birds' nests Karang Bolong, as recorded in 1720.[5] Then in 1840, the Dutch colonial government obtained sole rights from the feudal lord in the area to harvest the nests.

The Dutch colonial government later leased out the swiftlets' caves to a private company. The caves provided nests from two species of the edible-nest swiftlet – the Germain's swiftlet and the black-nest swiftlet. These two species are native to

Tjiampea in Java. Normally, indigenous people disregard the Black-nest Swiftlet because their nests are not so valuable.[6]

During the 17th century, the birds' nests increased in value, and China began selling them throughout Southeast Asia, then known as Nanyang. Even though the indigenous people controlled the bird's nest supply, the Chinese merchants controlled the international trade because they owned the boats.[7]

Since the birds' nests became an important product in the 18th century, the United East India Company mandated that all sales of all Java birds' nests go through Batavia. During 1740–1750, those selling to Chinese merchants had to pay taxes on all sales. At the beginning of the 19th century, the Dutch controlled all merchandise being transported throughout Indonesia's seas. In 1860, Singapore became the center for imported birds' nests from the Dutch East Indies. Singapore re-exported the birds' nests to China, but during WWII (1942–45), the Japanese shut down international trade in the region.[8] This greatly impacted the industry.

East Kalimantan is a rich source for the bird's nest industry. The Dayak ethnic group of the area have harvested the birds' nests and sold them to Chinese merchants for many decades.[9]

In the basins of the Rian River at Desa Langap, the Kenyah ethnic group hold the sole rights to the area's swiftlet caves. Ownership of these caves has been passed down for 13 generations, with each generation harvesting the birds' nests for 25 years. Counting back from today, that means the first generation began in 1675.[10]

The modern industry in East Kalimantan began in 1940, when many communities began harvesting the birds' nests in Telang Teba and Sungai Peta. Some of the families pass down ownership of the caves to each new generation. In 1942–45, following the Japanese invasion, the industry in that area shut down, but resumed in 1960. Records show that the birds' nests have been an important commodity for the local groups since the late 1700s because there are records of them trading birds' nests with Chinese merchants for expensive porcelain.[11]

At the beginning of 1980, the influence of the world market sharply increased the value of birds' nests in Long Apari, which is also in East Kalimantan. Then in 1987, the nests were in even higher demand, equal to the demand for *gaharu* (eaglewood). By 1990, the price for the birds' nests had increased to 500,000 rupees per kilogram. The rate of harvesting had also increased to 4–5 tons per year.

Due to this high demand, the Aoheng (Penihing) ethnic group found itself fighting against incoming ethnic groups in their region of Long Apari[12] because the local government auctioned off the cave rights to the highest bidders. This led to armed gangs fighting each other as well as an uprising against the local government to fight for sole ownership of the East Kalimantan caves.[13]

At the same time, the Acehnese ethnic group in Aceh revealed that their province was an untapped source of bird's nests. In the past, whoever first discovered a swiftlet cave became its owner. Once this information went public (during the fourth generation of Acehnese ownership), the local government seized control of the caves. Now the caves are considered government property, so require government permission to harvest. A direct result of that was the decrease in the harvest. The tsunami of 2004 also greatly reduced the output in Aceh Province. However, in 2011, efforts were begun to establish a community cooperative that seeks to improve the management of the caves, in the hopes of making the industry more fair for all concerned. The primary strategy is to have the collectors pay management costs to the community cooperative in the Kampung Sub-District.

Before the 2004 tsunami, the Acehnese had to bid for the caves and pay money the local government, but once harvesting was severely reduced by forest fires and the tsunami (from 1,200 kg. to 20 kg. per year), the government abandoned the auction system and conceded management to the local people.[14]

The collectors in Aceh Province tell of their history with the birds' nests. In the past, local people would go into the forests for agriculture and to gather forest resources. They discovered the swiftlet caves, but were unaware of their value. They ate the birds' nests but were oblivious to the international market for them.

Once they learned of their value in 1970, however, they began to collect the birds' nests from the Guha Rayeak on the Guha Siblah Mountain in Kampung Meunasah, Lampuuk, Lhoknga District, Aceh Provinces. This continued for 3–4 generations, until annual government auctions began. Participants had to be Acehnese, though the money could come from outsiders.

From 1976–2005, the Indonesian government engaged in civil war with the Acehnese. During this time, government forces made the Guha Rayeak one of their bases, and they fired guns and torched the birds' nests to force the swiftlets to leave.

Though the Acehnese had loved to eat birds' nests, very few were able to afford them, so the practice fell out of style. Over time it has become popular again, especially at parties and as an ingredient in soups mixed with coconut oil, pineapple, other fruits.[15]

For almost 30 years, GAM (Gerakan Aceh Merdeka-Free Aceh Movement) of the Acehnese ethnic group wanted to be free from Indonesia. The Acehnese supported this group by selling cattle, rice and eggs. The birds' nests became an important product to make money to buy weapons for GAM,[16] through the birds' nests network in the Andaman Sea of Thailand.[17] The birds' nests became a natural resource to fund arms purchases and support the group until 2005. Under a peace agreement concluded during that year at Helsinki, the Acehnese received special autonomy, and the birds' nests were no longer used to fund war.

1.2 Swiftlets in Swiftlet Farming Business

There have been building development projects in Java for over 500 years,[18] But swiftlet house farming in Indonesia, which is the model for modern swiftlet farming instead of harvesting from the caves,[19] accidentally started in north Java almost 200 years ago when someone found swiftlets building nests in an empty building and adapted the building for swiftlet farming.[20] Some people believed that swiftlet farming first started in East Java in 1880. It became very popular.[21]

Some people said it came from a house owner in Sedaya or Sedayu of Gresik, on the Java Island of Tohir Sukarama.[22] The house owner left the house to do Haj ceremony for many months and closed off some rooms. When he came back, he discovered that swiftlets had made their nests in one of the rooms; so after that, he tried to improve the environment of the other rooms to encourage swiftlet nest-building. This was the prototype of the swiftlet house farming technique, although it was kept secret in the beginning.[23]

There are three periods of swiftlets house farming in Indonesia:

1. The original swiftlet house farming (1850–1950)

The original swiftlet house farm would allow the swiftlets make their nests in the house naturally without altering any environmental factors in the house. It depended on luck. During this period, there was scant success. The house owners collected the nests once or twice a year.

During this period, people possessed little knowledge of how to house farm swiflets. Most of the locations looked like normal houses and were located along the coast. The swiftlets would make their nests on the ceilings or the house pillars, and it was considered bad luck if they entered then left the house. However, concerning the swiftlet species *C. esculenta*, people would intentionally force them out of the houses, as the nests weren't valuable and the birds created cleaning problems.

2. Semi-primitive swiftlet house farming (1950–90)

There were a lot more swiftlet houses in the cities and countryside during this time. People started building concrete houses, which are very suitable for swiftlets. The house owners would move out if the swiftlets started to come. This time period saw slow improvement in the industry through trial and error, as they observed the swiftlets' behaviors. Successful strategies were kept secret, even from other family members, and mythical and magical reasons were still prevalent in explaining how certain results were achieved. One major breakthrough was the observation that the presence of the swiftlet *C. esculenta* could encourage the arrival of the swiftlet *C. fuciphaga*, which was the desired species.

3. Intensive swiftlet house farming (1990–2011)

During the modern swiftlet house farming period, experts of swiftlet farming and swiftlet enthusiasts shared their knowledge and experience. The first international seminar on farming the birds' nests was on January 7, 1989 at the Sky Garden Hotel, Semarang. It was led by E. Nugroho. There were 423 attendees. From this seminar, the Indonesian Swiftlet Lover's Association was established, and during that same year, there was another seminar on November 3 at the Metro Hotel, Semarang. They also published the swiftlet house farming booklet and set up a workshop for interested people.

In the 1990s, swiftlet farming developed very quickly, especially in Java, and spread throughout Sumatra, Bali, Kalimantan, Sangihe, and Sulawesi. The Indonesian Swiftlet-Lovers' Association handed out a swiftlet house farming booklet and provided information centers and training once a month in Semarang.

This movement influenced people to share their secrets and experience, which was a dramatic shift from the original thinking. This resulted in more development and increased farming knowledge, especially in the small cities. There are now 60–150 swiftlet houses in Cilamaya, Cirebon, Pemanukan, Haurgeulis, Pekalongan, Tegal, Rembang, Purwodadi, Brora, Tuban, Pasuruan, Garut, Wonosobo, Salatiga, and Magetan. Farmers design the buildings and employ proper equipment in order to create an environment suitable for the swiftlets. They also manage the timing of the harvest in order to avoid negatively affecting the swiftlets' hatching periods, contributing to the preservation of the swiftlet populations. The bird's nest farmers take more responsibility for the swiftlets than ever before.[24]

At the beginning of 1990, there were a lot of wealthy Chinese businessmen who invested in the industry. By the mid-1990s, the price for nests of good quality increased from USD 400 to 3,000 per kilogram.[25] In 1992, a lot of people were excited by the industry and started building more swiftlet houses, so that by 1995, there swiftlet houses throughout Indonesia.[26] It has become common to see swiftlet house farming in cities, and most of the building-owners are Chinese.[27] This has increased the swiftlet populations and the production of the nests increases up to 25 percent each year.[28] In 1993, a census of the species *C. fuciphaga* found that there were 35,159,736 birds, and 75 percent of them were house farmed, while only 25 percent were found in natural caves.[29]

However, since the government hadn't granted permission to construct entire buildings for swiftlet house farming, most farmers used the upstairs areas of their personal buildings and shops for farming. Thus, it is hard to know exactly how many buildings there are. In 2011, there were approximately 250,000 swiftlet house farms, with only around 70 percent of those having specialized swiftlet residence and nest constructions.[30]

Even though it is difficult to tell how many birds' nests from Indonesia are sold in the central Hong Kong market (due to sellers shipping their products on privately-owned planes), it is estimated to be around 80 percent of the entire global market. That is about 2,000 tons per year.[31]

There are nest-collectors from many ethnic groups in Indonesia, including the natural cave and house farming methods, such as Javanese, Dayak or Acehnese; however, Hong Kong and China are the biggest markets in the world, so the birds' nests primarily go through channels that use Chinese language to do business with Chinese exporters.[32]

2. THE NATURE OF SWIFTLETS

2.1 The Blessing Swiftlet from Allah

The ethnic groups in Indonesia call the swiftlet *Burung Walet* in the Bahasa Indonesia anguage, and the bird's nests are called *Sarang Burung Walet*. The scientific name for the swiftlet is Genus Collocalia.[33] Altogether, there are 14 species of swiftlets,[34] but only four species build edible nests.[35] In Indonesia, there are three species of edible-nest swiftlets. The first is *Walet Sarang Putih,* which has the scientific name *A. fuciphagus*. It produces the white bird's nest, which is considered to be the best quality. The second species is *A. germanicus* or *A. vestitus*. This species produces yellowish-brown nests, which is the second highest-quality nest. The last species is *Walet Sarang Hitam* (*A. maximus*), which produces black nests. 80 percent–90 percent of these nests are composed of the swiftlets' feathers.[36] In Kalimantan region,

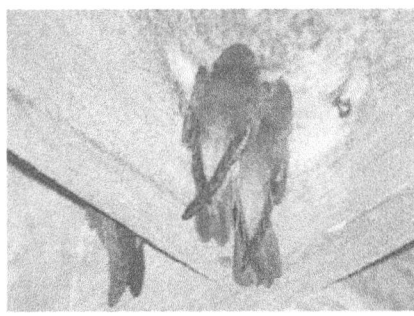
Swiftlets living in a house farm in Semarang city, middle Java, Indonesia.

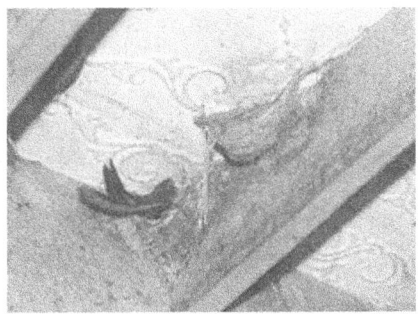
Seriti swiftlets in a house farm in Semarang city.

birds' nests are separated into five categories: *sarang putih*-white nest, *sarang hitam*-black nest, *sarang lumut*-mossy nest, *sarang gundul*-bald nest, and *sarang merah*-pink nest.[37]

Natural Characteristics

There are four types of important swiftlet farming, including for edible-nest swiftlets and non-edible-nest swiftlets.

1. **Walet Sarang Putih** (*A. fuciphagus*) is about 12 cm long and weighs an average of 8 grams, which makes it a medium-sized bird. The feathers are blackish-brown, and paler on the upper part. Its rump is light gray or light brown, it has a brown iris, and the bill and feet are black. It lives in coastal regions 500 meters above sea level and dwells in limestone mountains. Its diet consists of flying insects. These birds use echo-location to locate their nests in dark caves with only 0.2 Lux intensity light. Most importantly, they produce white bird's nest from their saliva. Both female and male birds work to build a nest within 30–45 days. During the rainy season (April to September), they can complete the nests in 30 days because there are plenty of insects. Otherwise, completion can take up to 80 days. During the breeding season, the swiftlets breed at night for 4–8 days after finishing the nests and then lay 2 eggs in each nest. The second egg will hatch three days after the first one. Each egg (both male and female) weighs around 1.2 grams.

The *Walet Sarang Putih*'s incubation period for the first egg is 23 +/- 3 days, and for the second one, it is 21–25 days. After 2 weeks, the baby bird will hang at the nest's edge and be fed by its parents until maturity at around 43 days (+/- 6 days). The nest is used again during the next breeding season if left unharvested. However, if the nest is collected, the birds will build a new nest. The *Walet Sarang Putih* in house farming prefers a cave-like room with 0–2 Lux light intensity, at 28 degrees celsius, and with 85 percent–95 percent humidity.[38]

2. ***Walet Sarang Goa*** (*A. germanicus* or *vestitus*) is the same size as the Walet Sarang Putih (*A. fuciphagus*) at 12 cm. long, making it a medium-sized bird. Its feathers are blackish-brown. Visually, it is difficult to tell the difference between this species and the *Walet Sarang Putih*. However, this species produces a yellow-brown bird nest with some feathers added. The nests are shaped like a bowl, but deeper, and the Walet Sarang Goa lays two eggs each time.[39]

3. ***Walet Sarang Hitam*** (*A. maximus lowi*) is about 12 cm long, making it a medium-sized bird. The feathers are blackish-brown and paler on the upper section. It also has feathers on its legs. Its iris is dark brown and its bill and tail are black. Its appearance is very similar to that of the edible-nest swiftlet. It lives in coastal regions and dwells in limestone mountains. Its diet consists of flying insects. It produces the black bird nest, 80 percent of which consists of feathers. These nests are a lot cheaper than the white ones because more time and labor is needed to clean them.[40]

4. ***Seriti*** (*C. esculenta*) is 10 cm. long, making it a medium-sized bird. It makes its nest out of hay. It lives in the same area as other swiftlets, but it needs more light than other species because it cannot use echo-location to find its nest in the dark. The *Seriti* is very useful in luring other swiftlet species to nest in swiftlet farming houses. Farmers use it to hatch other swiftlet species' eggs, and the *Seriti*'s eggs can be sold. Overall, farmers use the *Seriti* species to increase swiftlet breeding of all species.

Acehnese nest-collectors at the Guha Rayeak of Guha Siblah Mountain in Kampung Meunasah, Lampuuk, Lhoknga District, say that there are 2 types of swiftlets in those regions—the *Sarang Puteh* or white nest swiftlet and the *Sarang Hitam* or black nest swiftlet.[41]

Swiftlet Habitats

There are 25 out of 33 provinces in Indonesia that serve as a swiftlets' habitat, including natural caves and swiftlet-houses sites. These include: Aceh, Sumatera Utara, Sumatera Barat, Sumatera Selatan, Riau, Bengkulu, Jambi, Lampung, Bangka Belitung, Java Barat, Java Tengah, Java Timur, Yogyakarta, Bali, Kalimantan Tengah, Kalimantan Timur, Kalimantan Barat, Kalimantan Selatan, Maluku, Madura, Sulawesi Utara, Sulawesi Tengah, Sulawesi Barat, Sulawesi Selatan, and Sulawesi Tenggara.[42]

Birds' Nests Collecting Season

Harvesting occurs 2–4 times a year in the natural caves of Indonesia. Harvesting time also depends on the area. For example, the East Kalimantan's first harvest takes place from January to April to achieve themaximum yield of the best quality. The second harvesting period occurs in August. The Kampung Meunasah, Lampuuk, Lhoknga District, Aceh Provinces. harvest four times a year except when there was a civil war between the Acehnese and Indonesian government in 1980.[43]

During that time, the harvest, from 200–300 kilograms per year for the white bird's-nests, and 800 kilograms per year for the black bird's-nests, decreased to 20 kilograms a year. It was because no one was available to look after the swiftlet caves.

The same problem occurred after the tsunami on December 26, 2004 and the ensuing forest fires. After that, the government canceled the auction and let local people manage the harvesting themselves. This decision led to an increase in the quantity of nests harvested in Indonesia. In 2011, the swiftlet caves in the Kampung Meunasah, Lampuuk, using community cooperatives to manage the harvesting process, produced enough nests to harvest twice a year in February and June.[44]

As for swiftlet house farming, harvesting depends on the number of nests but typically occurs once a month.

3. BELIEFS AND RITUALS RELATED TO SWIFTLETS

The bird's-nest collectors monument in Kebumen, the south part of middle Java.

3.1 Beliefs and Rituals

Beliefs Related to Swiftlets

The people who live in Rongkop and Karang Bolong, in the south part of middle Java, believe in the Indonesian goddess Nyi Roro Kidul, the patron goddess of birds' nests gatherers. She is the queen of the southern sea in Javanese and Sundanese mythology. The gatherers perform a ritual to Nyi Roro Kidul before harvesting the nests, so that she will bless them. This ritual is performed at the Gua Karang Bolong in the 9th month of the Javanese calendar. The gatherers ask the goddess for a bountiful harvest.[45]

At the same time, some of the swiftlet-house owners in Java believe in particular spirits that have magic powers and lead the swiftlets to the farming houses. They bring offerings, such as food, flowers, and incense, to these spirits.[46]

Additionally, some of the swiftlet-house owners who have suffered the departure of swiftlets from their building will hire diviners to perform black magic rituals to bring the swiftlets back. These farmers also believe that whoever has swiftlets come and stay in their house will receive blessings from their gods or God.[47]

The Acehnese ethnic group in Aceh Province believe in the swiftlet legend of the Gua Mirapati or Pigeon Cave, which has a lot of swiftlets. To get there from Kampong Mumnasa, Lumpuuk, one has to walk for two days. The journey is very dangerous, due to wild animals, such as tigers, elephants, and snakes. Not many people risk the journey. The Acehnese believe that if a bird's-nest collector is to reach this cave, they must be a good person, holy, and have powers. A person like that will be able to reach the cave and harvest as many birds' nests as they want, but can only do so once. The legend of this cave mentions a particular fisherman who made it to the cave.[48]

The Acehnese ethnic group believes that after constructing a swiftlet house, they must invite the Ulama to perform an Islamic ritual for Allah to bless the building so the swiftlets will come and build their nests.[49] They believe they have to wait for Allah to provide the swiftlets, and this provision and blessing from Allah will only be given to good and faithful people.[50]

In Kebumen, in the south part of middle Java, where the Gua Karang Bolong is located, the local people give special value on the swiftlets. Besides using the swiftlets as a symbol of the city, they have also built a monument to bird's-nest collectors in the middle of the town.

Beliefs and Rituals Related to Nest-Collecting

The swiftlet became more valuable and important than other birds through the ritual of the bird's-nest collectors and some ethnic groups in Indonesia, due to the danger of harvesting birds' nests from natural caves. From the past until now, the relationship between humans and the uncontrollable forces of nature have inspired the rituals of these ethnic groups in their attempts to receive favor and blessings from angels or guardian spirits before the harvest season, as well as protection for the collectors who harvest the bird's nests for medicine, food and special gifts to the high people of the community.

On the seacoast in the south of Java, there is a traditional *wayang kulit* performance which is held before the harvesting season and used as a ritual to ask the guardian spirits for safety and a bountiful harvest. During the ritual, animal sacrifices (goats, cows, and buffalos) are performed, and the ritual finishes with a big celebration.[51]

Another harvesting ritual is performed in the ninth month of the Java calendar near Gua Karang Bolong, Karang Bolong village, Gombong Sub-District, Kebumen, in the southern part of middle Java.

The people who live in Karang Bolong village believe that swiftlets are assets of their goddess Nyi Roro Kidul. They will do rituals to Nyi Roro Kidul for the safety of bird nest-collectors (*upacara keselamatan*) by making offering such as *Kain lurik hijau gadung, udang wulung*, scarfs, mattresses and white pillows. The head collector leads this ritual. At the same time at the front beach at Gua Karang Bolong Cave is a *wayang kulit* performance with gamelan orchestra and tari tayub dance which is the local art performance dance of Java.

The wayang kulit performance started with Dalang who leads the show and prays for the permission from Nyi Roro Kidul, the queen of the south sea along with Joko Suryo, Suryawati, Den Bagus Cemeti, Kiai Bekel and Kiai Surti. These are held for the safety and blessing of the bird's-nest harvest the following day. These performances do not contain segments where a main character falls from a height or has been killed or has died in a war because it will be bad luck for the bird's-nest collectors or accidents might happen during collecting or the birds' nests will get stolen or there will be no birds' nests to harvest.

These traditional rituals have been held through many generations that the embassy named Kiai Surti of King Kartasura, Mataram Kingdom who was assigned to find medicine for Queen Permaisuri, who had been sick for a long time. Finally Kiai Surti came to Karang Bolong beach and he meditated to observe religious precepts. A member of the retinue of Nyi Roro Kidul, named Suryawati, gave him *wangsit* (a supernatural mandate) and showed him the birds' nests from Gua Karang Bolong, and then he married Suryawati.

At the end of *acara syukuran* event there is the *tari tayub* dance show to worship the angels, for the benefit and the safety of nest-collectors to receive the blessing from Nyi Roro Kidul.[52]

These rituals and ceremonies are ambivalent in regards to Islamic beliefs and local traditions of the Javanese people.[53] These show the holy heresy that Islamic beliefs cannot provide to the local tradition.

The ritual named *doa peusijue* or *doa Teungku* ceremony is held at Guha Rayeak, Guha Siblah Mountain in the Kampung Meunasah, Lampuuk, Lhoknga District, Aceh Provinces. These rituals were a big party for orphans, widows and poor people and then they pray *doa* to Allah for the safety and blessing of the birds' nest harvest lead by *Teungku* or the *ulama*. These ceremonies are held twice a year, the first time before harvesting for safety and the second time after harvesting to be thankful to Allah.

The bird's-nest harvesters at Guha Rayeak in the Kampung Meunasah, Lampuuk, forbid women from entering the caves because it is a difficult journey and climbing *purih* and *ubangon* (bamboo ladders) to collect the birds' nests on high shelves in the dark caves is very risky. Also no outsider can enter the caves to protect the birds' nests from being stolen.[54]

Bird's-nest collectors at Kampung Meunasah, Lampuuk, when working in the cave will be very respectful to dangerous animals by calling them polite names such as calling tigers grandma or calling elephants father. It is forbidden for the pregnant wife of any bird's-nest collector, if they see turtle, to touch it; otherwise the husband will suffer an accident in the cave. This is a belief passed down to each generation.[55]

Concerning the Acehnese beliefs about swiftlet house farming, when building construction is completed, the owner will invite the *alim* who leads the blessing ceremony from Allah and give away food to orphans, widows and poor people. After the 2004 tsunami, more than a hundred of those people came to the party. This ceremony is to help bring swiftlets to the building and occurs about every six months.[56]

Women cannot be involved with harvesting in the natural caves because "This is a difficult task and climbing *purih* and *ubangon* (bamboo ladders) to collect the nests on high cliffs in the dark caves is risky".[57]

Concerning the ritual to the guardian spirits at Gua Karang Bolong, Karang Bolong village in Gombong, Kebumen District the south of middle Java, it is to a female spirit named Nyi Roro Kidul, who is the queen of the south sea and patron goddess of swiftlets. However, most of the workers in the birds'-nests business, including in the cleaning factories and sales positions, are women.

Belief and Truth in Nest Collection

This story had been told that nests were first eaten after the leader of Sadrana village discovered the Gua Karang Bolong Cave 300 years ago. He gave a bird's nest to Raja Kartasusa and the king's chef made a dish from it. It became the king's favorite food and became a high class food later on.[58]

A local legend explains that birds' nests can function as medicine for good health.

In the present day, in Indonesia they use birds' nests in many foods such as boiled with coconut, steamed with crab eggs, with American ginseng, savory soup and soup with rock sugar[59] From the Nutrient Directorate of Indonesian Department of Health, they announced in 1979 birds' nest nutritional value:

Bird's nest 100 grams. Nutrition facts:

Calories : 291
Protein : 27.5 g
Carbohydrate : 32.1 g
Fat : 0.3 g
Water : 24.8 g
Calcium : 285 mg
Phosphorus : 18.0 g
Iron : 3.0 mg[60]

Resource: Nutrient Directorate of Indonesian Department of Health

In spite of the birds' nests being an ethnic food and a high class food, typically the ethnic people don't consume it much because of the high price.[61] Some of Acehnese Bird's-nest collectors don't believe that eating birds' nests will help with good health or cure erectile dysfunction.[62] So the local ethnic groups in Indonesia only harvest the birds' nests for sale, both from natural caves and swiftlet houses.

3.2 Equipment and Tools

In macroeconomics, bird's-nest business is categorised as residual market, which generates a high revenue.[63] These businesses in Indonesia were modeled after "The model of the swiftlet farming" that started more than 200 years ago in the north of Java.

There have been many developments such as building design, inventing tools for setting up the swiftlet farming environment for swiftlets, and inventing egg hatching machines. There were also devices to control temperature, humidity, light intensity, plastic birds' nests, swiftlet aroma, audio bird call CDs to attract swiftlets, the booklet on building a house farm and raising swiftlets. There are tools and detergent for bird's nest cleaning, and the bird's nest recipe based on the local sources. These inventions and tools have spread throughout Southeast Asia in Malaysia, Thailand, Vietnam, Burma, and Cambodia for the past 20 years.

The Acehnese bird nest-collectors, especially at Guha Rayeak in Kampung Meunasah, Lampuuk, Lhoknga District, invented the tools and equipment for bird's-nest harvesting from *trieng* or bamboo (*purih* and *ubangon*) to make the ladders to climb high and dark cave faces. They also devised metal tools called *Radak* that are used for collecting white bird's-nests and *radak kenueku* for collecting black bird's-nests. Through observation, they found out that getting rid of the black bird's-nests (also called *jang got jin*) from the caves caused other swiftlet species to leave the caves.[64]

3.3 Culture, Traditions and Wisdom of Ethnic Groups in the Birds'-Nests Business

There have been swiftlet houses in Indonesia for more than 200 years. They have developed knowledge to improve farming methods such as setting times for harvesting to not disrupt breeding, which could lead to swiftlet extinction. They discovered *Seriti* or *C. esculenta* would lead *C. fuciphaga* swiftlets to swiftlet houses and that using the Seriti to hatch other swiftlets' eggs helped the *C. fuciphaga* swiftlet population breed faster, which in turn helped the industry.

At the time, the harvesting rituals showed human belief in the supernatural powers of the swiftlet caves spirits. These beliefs transformed into animism from feelings of fear and sublimation. The rituals also were about fertility rites and the ceremonies focused on rituals to placate fear.

The ritual surrounding *Burung Walet* swiftlets in natural caves became part of tradition and culture in Indonesia more than 300 years ago. The indigenous people continue to perform this ritual today. An example is the traditional ritual at Gua Karang Bolong to offer sacrifices to Nyi Roro Kidul, which is the holy spirit of the swiftlet cave. There are 2 purposes: 1. For the nest-collectors' safety while working and 2. To bless the bird's-nest business.

In these rituals, they kill goats, cows or buffalos to offer to the spirit of the swiftlet caves. There is also the *wayang kulit* performance from the Java ethnic group which became the commoditized culture and is now a tourist attraction.

The harvesting in the Guha Rayeak at Guha Siblah Mountain in Aceh Province has a ritual called *doa peusijuek* or *doa Teungku* ceremony which the people perform twice a year. The first time before the harvest for the safety of the collectors and the second after harvesting to be thankful to Allah. They believe these rituals will help yield more birds' nests.

The ritual for swiftlets house farming in Java involve giving offerings to special spirits such as food, flowers, incense and other items because they believe these special spirits will attract swiftlets to the houses.

The rituals for swiftlet house farming in Aceh are led by *ulama*, who hosts a big party for ophans, widows and poor people so that Allah will bless the building and bring the swiftlets to stay at the houses.

4. RIGHTS AND LEGAL SYSTEMS IN INDONESIA

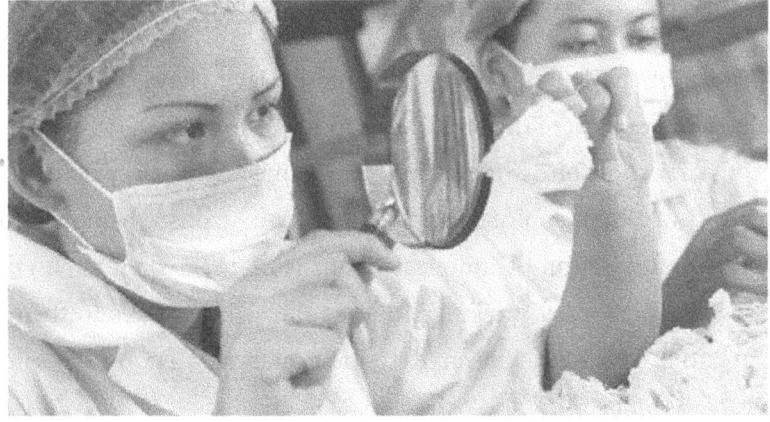

Bird's-nest cleaners in Medan city, Indonesia.

Indonesia's Island group contains more than 10,000 islands. There is a variety of ethnic groups and cultures. This country has been socially developed from ethnic society to Feudalism or Sultanate to colonized by the Dutch to the Indonesian National Revolution to guided democracy and to the dictatorship *Orde Baru* (New Order). After 2001 came democracy, with decentralization of government power.

Swiftlet harvesting in Indonesia was started by Java the dominant ethnic groups. They established the history of the bird's-nest business by sharing legends, so that other groups couldn't proclaim their own versions (geographies of exclusion). They claimed they found the swiftlet cave named Gua Karang Bolong in middle Java (Java Tengah) in 1720, which was the beginning of using birds' nests resources in Indonesia, which belonged to the Sultan.

Indonesia was colonized by the Dutch for a long period (1596–1945), and this influenced the people through Western hierarchies of power. These powers included the human value or the human right to participate in community activities and the right to access resources. These became the power relations of Indonesian society. Because Indonesia has many ethnic groups and a variety of cultures, the rights and laws concerning bird's-nest resources, the power of social stratification, and the hierarchies of power relations are complicated and unique issues that depend on the areas and the ethnic groups involved.

The rights and laws of using the birds' nests as a resource in Java started in 1720, when the leader of the Sadrana village in middle Java (Jawa Tengah) found Gua Karang Bolong and dedicated the birds' nests to Raja Kartasura.[65] This was the official beginning of harvesting birds' nests, which became high-priced goods for upper class groups and wealthy people.[66] The bird's nest as a resource belonged to the king until the Dutch colonization of Indonesia from 1596–1945, The Dutch government (*pemerintah Belanda*) forced the kings to lease the swiftlet caves to them and let a Chinese company from Karanganyar Kebumen take over, taxing the sale of birds' nests in Karang Bolong.

After Indonesia officially declared independence in 1949, the local government under the royal forest department announced that swiftlets and their caves were being taken care of. There was an auction system to allocate these resources. The local government named Kebumen and gave concessions to private companies, which earned a lot more money for the government than during Dutch colonization.[67] The local government in Karang Bolong focused on making more money from concessionaires, and rather than taking care of the swiftlet population, which affected breeding. However, the Indonesian government tried to decentralize to enable local governments manage their own resources.[68] There was an annual auction, following the order of the director-general of the department of forestry (*Direktur Jenderal Perlindungan Hutan dan Pelestarian Alam*) numbered 25/Kpts/DJ-VI/1997 and 73/Kpts/DJ-VI/1998 and also using community cooperatives (*KUD setempat*) to help bird's-nest harvest management.[69] Before that, the number of swiftlets and birds' nests in Karang Bolong had been decreasing because the concessionaire only focused profit without concern for the environment and preservation of the swiftlets. In 2005, in Kebumen, the local government canceled the auction system and handled the harvesting and selling the birds' nests themselves.[70]

In Middle Java, they employed inherited rights to the swiftlet caves, which shows the social stratification or hierarchies of power relations. They had been through a sultanate, colonial state regime, guided democracy, the New Order dictatorship, and directed democracy which demonstrates the relation to a monopoly of one family or specific department for managing the swiftlet resources.

These were the basics of resource management called the 'linear system of management' which was part of the 'linear concept of rights'. These rights obstruct and prevent others from using the resources. However, when Indonesia became a democracy, local government used the community cooperative (*KUD setempat*) to manage swiftlet resources. This shows the 'complexity of rights' or 'communal property' that allows people the right of access. These 'multiple systems of management' helped the community rights to manage and control the resources, especially the 'ethnic rights' of the local people.

In East Kalimantan, the Kenyah ethnic group obtained the rights to own the Long Peso Cave[71] and also the Aoheng or Penihing in Long Apari secured the cave rights through the family. They were able to sell birds' nests freely until 1978, when the regent of Kutai made a decree requiring swiftlet resources to be held by concession under the government. The local people rose up against these laws and did not follow them in Long Apari,[72] Long Peso and other places.

After 1940, the nest harvesting in many areas of East Kalimantan, such as Telang Teba and Sungai Peta area in Long Peso, held the rights through family (the *Ahli Waris*-inherited rights) and named the caves after the first groups who founded the caves. They also paid taxes to the local government.[73] They used a community cooperative called the *Koperasi Sarang Burung Walet* to manage the caves. Some families allowed others lease harvesting rights.[74]

At the same time, some areas in Muara Wahau and Berau Districts had a lot of Chinese businessmen[75] who became "concessionaires,"[76] called *Pahtar* (exclusive buyer), who got monopoly rights over the harvest.[77]

There was no law concerning swiftlet conservation in East Kalimantan, but there had been a decree by the Director-General of PHPA-*Perlindungan Hutan dan Pelestarian Alam* following the order numbered 73/Kpts/DJ-VI/1998.[78]

Concerning the rights and the laws of using birds' nests as resources in East Kalimantan, some parts were inherited rights which were private property regimes, while other parts were state property regimes. It shows the power relations of ethnic groups who have a monopoly of one person or local department over the local bird's-nest resources. These are the 'linear system of management' and 'linear concept of rights' which obstruct people from using the resources (exclusive rights). Even when Indonesia became a democracy, the rights to the swiftlet caves still followed the 'linear concept of rights' and were owned by families and government.

These rights of ownership of each ethnic family and the rights of the state were the 'complexity of rights' or 'communal property', which made the ethnic group claims the cave rights legal. It was also made 'ethnic rights' officially accepted.

In the past, the person who found a swiftlet cave would receive the rights of ownership in Aceh. Later, when the local government became aware of the cave, they also claimed rights along with the person who originally laid claim to it.

However, in the case of the Guha Rayeak at Kampung Meunasah, Lampuuk, Lhoknga District, before the tsunami of 2004, the government used an annual concession system. The Aceh local ethnic groups were the concessionaires and paid taxes to the state. These were called *Mukim*. After the tsunami and ensuing wildfires, the concession system was canceled because the bird's-nest harvesting had decreased significantly. Instead, they employed a community cooperative which allowed the local Aceh people to manage the harvesting. As of 2011, the Aceh ethnic group had the rights of ownership, and the bird's-nest collectors pay a fee to the village (*kampung*) committee.[79]

In Aceh, they had been using inherited rights to own the swiftlet caves which was a monopoly to one family or specific department. These were based on the 'linear system of management', obstructing unauthorized people from using the resources. However, when Indonesia became a democracy, the local government used the community cooperative to manage the resources. These 'multiple systems of management' helped the community to manage and control the resources, and led to the ethnic groups' rights being officially accepted.

In Indonesia there are several systems of rights and laws (legal pluralism) under the enclosure law and customary law. The inherited rights (the *Ahli Waris*) are also part of Indonesian society with only a few powerful people able to access those rights.

There are 3 types of regimes concerning the rights and law for managing the swiftlet resources in the natural caves:
1. Personal or family owned caves under private property regimes,
2. Common cave-Common regimes,
3. Cave tendering to private contractors-state property regimes.[80]

However, the law and rights that concern the power to access or obstruct the use of swiftlet resources in nature of Indonesian business demonstrate that there is a monopoly by the ethnic groups and local governments that have unequal relations. They both have inclusive and exclusive rights within their own groups. The local governments also centralize and monopolize to a single department that takes take control of these resources. These powers of management at the local government level 1—a 'linear system of management'—were devastated by the *Ahli Waris* or inherited rights. Also there were the caves, which by the law, had become common property; that is, they fell under the inclusive rights established by the government for anyone's use. This became legal pluralism—the 'complexity of rights' with multiple management systems.

Swiftlet-house owners, no matter which ethnic group they belonged to, were legally able to pass the rights down to their families.

5. BUSINESS AND MANAGEMENT SYSTEM OF THE BIRD'S-NEST BUSINESS IN INDONESIA

Swiftlet nest cleaners in Medan, Indonesia.

5.1 Bird's-Nest Business in Ancient Times – Conservative Society

During the conservative society, the *Sarang Burung Walet* swiftlet (also known as *Emas Putih* or white gold bird's nest) in Indonesia was collected using bamboo ladders to climb the cave walls. This is how the bird's-nest business first began.

Indonesia has harvested birds' nests for food and medicine for hundreds of years. Javanese is the dominant ethnic group involved in the business since before the 17th century. This group created and established their own history and society to block other groups from the business (geographies of exclusion) by spreading legends of the bird's-nest harvest at Gua Karang Bolong and building the bird's-nest collectors monument (cultural artifact) in Kebumen city, middle Java (Jawa Tengah).

In 1625 they started to sell birds' nests, and in February 1720, they found the Gua Karang Bolong Cave in Gombong Selatan and started harvesting white birds' nests.[81] The swiftlet cave belonged to the Sultan before being sold to the Dutch government (*pemerintah Belanda*) and then sold again to Chinese businessmen (*seorang Tionghoa*) in Karanganyar of Kebumen, who had the harvesting rights to the birds' nests on behalf of the Dutch government. They would then sell the birds' nests to other countries.

After Indonesia proclaimed independence (1949), the local governments granted concessions for harvesting. At the same time, the ethnic groups created and heightened beliefs in the value of the birds' nests and their special qualities through the culture and tradition, which made the ethnic groups in Indonesia accept it.[82] They claimed the birds' nests were a special food for kings and rich people. The birds' nests were the property of the Sultan or kings. These beliefs are very important to the bird's-nest value that supports the business. Especially during the time of Raja Kartasura, the bird's-nest collectors would pay taxes to the state with birds' nests.

These systems continued until Indonesia was colonized by the Dutch and then changed to a free trade system. The Chinese business group (*seorang Tionghoa*) in Karanganyar of Kebumen had rights to harvest the birds' nests. After 1949, the swiftlet caves belonged to the local governments, which used concession systems until 2005, when Kebumen (local state) canceled concessions and took over the harvesting and selling of the raw birds' nests.

5.2 Business of Birds' Nests in Food Sovereignty Time: Postmodern Society

After 2001, the Indonesian government had to adjust to modern business models because of strong competition in the business world. They did this by giving each province the power to manage their own swiftlet resources and local business. There then developed a lot more swiftlet house farming units and bird's-nest companies.

Since 1970, the bird's-nest price had continuously increased until in 1998, it had risen to USD 2,000 per kilogram in Indonesia and USD 3,000 per kilogram in Hong Kong.[83] The middle of 1990 saw even more market demand, which pushed the price from USD 400 per kilogram to about USD 3,000 per 120 birds' nests.[84]

Size of Indonesia Bird's-Nest Business

There are at least 25 provinces out of 33 in Indonesia that provide a swiftlet habitat both in nature and the farming houses.

Many of the ethnic groups in Indonesia harvest the birds' nests but do not eat them. Most nests are exported to Hong Kong by the Chinese groups in Indonesia and thus, the Chinese language is primarily used in the buying and selling process. The main market to export the birds' nests is Medan and other cities such as Jakrata, Surabaya, Semarang, Makassar Bandung. Medan's nests are flown directly to Hong Kong.[85]

Even though it's difficult to ascertain the official numbers of swiftlet-house units, since a lot of the farmers use the buildings' lower floors as shops or storage and the upstairs as swiftlet farms, in 2011 it was estimated that there were 250,000 swiftlet houses in the country.[86]

Registered bird's-nest export companies under the Department of Foreign Trade in Indonesia (*Departemen Perdagangan RI*) include CV. Sunda Kelapa Trading Co., CV. Bumi Jaya, Surabaya, CV. Metraco in Semarang city, CV. Walet Perdana, CV. Niaga Wira in Jakarta Pusat, CV. Dwi Karya Baru, CV. Dwi Jaya in Pasuruan,

CV. Sumber Bumi in Samarinda, CV Bintang Sakti, and Original Bird's Nest International (OBNI) in Medan.

Registered bird's-nest import companies under the Department of Foreign Trade in Indonesia (*Departemen Perdagangan RI*) include Kim Hing Co., Golden Swallow Co. PTE. Ltd., Sarang Mas (S) CORPN., Guan Sang Co. PTE Ltd, Horse Brand Bird's Nest in Singapore[87] and Original Bird's Nest International (OBNI) in Hong Kong.

In East Kalimantan, there is only CV. The Sumber Bumi company from Samarinda city, which exports 1,250 tons of black bird's-nests to Singapore and Hong Kong annually.[88]

In Medan of northern Sumatra, only Original Bird's Nest International (OBNI) company exports raw cleaned birds' nests to Hong Kong and China at 1,000 kilograms per month[89] or 12,000 kilograms each year.

In Jakarta 2010, bird's nest sellers from Aceh said that only one exporter sent nests to Hong Kong at around 100 kilograms per day[90] or 36,500 kilograms per year.

In Aceh, there is no known exact number of exported nests, but information from swiftlet-house companies and the wholesale dealers says that East Aceh was the biggest bird's-nest business in Indonesia. Yet the birds' nests from Aceh were packed with birds' nests from Sumatra.[91]

The growth of the business is reflected by figures for specific years. In 1927, they exported 109,310 kilograms,[92] in 1980, 62,000 kilograms, with a peak in 1987 at 86,000 kilograms. In 1996, they exported 110,000 kilograms from the natural caves,[93] and in 2009, there was a report showing the total income of USD 226,000,000.[94]

The main businessman in Hong Kong said that about 98 percent of birds' nests in Hong Kong come from Indonesia.[95] Based on that figure, 80 percent of the birds' nests around the world are from Indonesia. The Chinese businessmen in Indonesia said that in 2011, Indonesia exported 2,000 tons of nests.[96] The price averages about USD 1,500 per kilogram. So, Indonesia has an income from birds' nests of approximately USD 3 billion per year.

Table 2.1: Exports from Indonesia from 1981–91

Year	Destination Country	Amount (kg.)	Total (kg.)
1981	Hong Kong	33,999	70,886
	Singapore	35,772	
	Malaysia	1,115	
1982	Hong Kong	33,494	66,743
	Singapore	30,972	
	Malaysia	2,277	
1983	Hong Kong	35,259	62,685
	Singapore	24,455	
	Malaysia	2,971	
1984	Hong Kong	42,833	66,780
	Singapore	22,168	
	Malaysia	1,779	
1985	Hong Kong	59,165	87,947
	Singapore	26,569	
	Malaysia	2,213	
1986	Hong Kong	36,921	62,018
	Singapore	23,192	
	Malaysia	1,905	
1987	Japan	232	85,921
	Hong Kong	55,353	
	Singapore	29,713	
	Malaysia	623	
1988	Japan	281	68,589
	Hong Kong	41,171	
	Taiwan	95	
	Thai	150	
	Singapore	24,852	
	Malaysia	2,040	
1989	Hong Kong	31,278	64,216
	Singapore	31,935	
	Malaysia	1,003	
1990	Hong Kong	42,257	64,691
	Taiwan	30	
	Singapore	21,478	
	Malaysia	519	
	Poland	407	

Sources: Department of foreign Trade of Indonesia, 1991
(Sumber: Badan Pengembangan Ekspor Nasional, 1991)[97]

Table 2.2: The bird's-nest price in Indonesia in 2000–2002

Swiftlet Type	Price average each year (IDR per kg.)		
	2000	2001	2002
House nest			
White bird's nest	19,265,715	5,093,235	23,030,280
Seriti bird's nest	23,243,220	5,405,400	27,567,540
Blood bird's nest	20,956,320	4,989,600	25,446,960
Cave nest			
White bird's nest	16,386,930	5,536,547	20,372,940
Black bird's nest	19,459,440	6,486,480	24,864,840
Blood bird's nest	17,963,560	5,987,520	22,952,160[98]

Type and Price of Birds' Nests in the Indonesia Market

The bird's-nest types in the Indonesian market are divided by different qualities in a complex fashion.

1. The birds' nests are divided by color and harvest timing. There are 7 types:
   - Blood bird's nest (*mutu merah* or *sarang darah*): these are collected after the swiftlets lay their eggs. They have a complete shape, are clean, and the best quality. The average weight is 9 grams, they are 10 cm. In diameter and 100–130 pieces per kilogram.
   - White bird's nest (*mutu perak* or *mutu balkon*): these are collected after the swiftlets lay their eggs. They are clean, are not contaminated by feathers, and the average weight is 8 grams, at 10 cm. Diameter, with 110–140 pieces per kilogram.
   - Bird's nest with feathers (*mutu bulu*): These are the same as grade 2 but are bigger. They are collected after swiftlets lay eggs but are contaminated with feathers.
   - Bird's nest before egg-laying (*mutu sarang rampasan*): these are nests collected before swiftlets lay their eggs. They are white in color and without feather contamination, but they are not a good shape and are small and fragile.

- Broken bird's nest (*mutu sarang pecah*): these are nests collected before swiftlets finish building them. They are low in quality and either incomplete or broken.
- Bird's nest after hatching eggs (*mutu sarang tetasan*): these are collected after the eggs hatch and the baby birds can fly. These have good quality, white color, and are large. However, there is a lot of contamination, such as baby bird excrement, bedbugs, ants, and cockroaches that damage the nest.
- Bird's-nest biscuit (*mutu sarang hancuran*): these are the lowest quality nests.[99]

Table 2.3: Showing the birds' nest price in Aceh, 2010

Bird's-nest type	Quality per size	price average (IDR per kg.)
White bird's nest		
grade A	Big size, 130–140 pieces per kilogram	8,000,000–13,000,000
grade B	Same as grade A, depends on the shape of birds' nests	7,000,000–12,000,000
grade C	Small size, yellowish color	3,000,000–12,000,000
Black bird's nest		3,000,000

Remark: The fieldwork report from Aceh Province.
Exchange rate: IDR 10 to USD 1

2. Swiftlet nests are divided by quality and color. There are 3–5 different grades.

In 2010, prices in Aceh were between 8 million rupiah and 7 million rupiah for white bird's-nest. The average price was 6 million rupiah. Black bird's nest were priced at 3 million rupiah.[100]

There are 3 different grades of birds' nests in Sigli, Aceh Province.
- Grade A: white bird's nest, 3 inches in size and selling for 12.5 million rupiah.
- Grade B: 2 inches in size and maybe with broken pieces or contaminants, selling for 8 million rupiah.
- Grade C: small size and yellowish, selling for 3 million rupiah.[101]

In Bireuen city, the bird's-nest sellers and swiftlet farming owners divided nests into 5 different grades : A, B, C, D and E
- Grade A: 130–140 bird nests per kilo, 13 million rupiahs per kilogram.
- Grade B: about the same amount a grade A, depending on the quality of nests.[102]

In Samalanga city, the swiftlet house farming owners divided the birds' nests into three grades:
- Grade A, size 3 inches and 13 million rupiahs per kilogram. Bird's nest grade B and C selling together for 11–12 million rupiahs per kilogram.[103]

Incentive and Welfare System for Bird's Nest Collectors

The Intensive, welfare and lifestyle of bird's-nest collectors, the caves or swiftlet house owners, the sellers, the workers in bird's-nest factories, and the authorities who have the power over these businesses attempt to maintain secrecy. Here are some facts about these businesses in Indonesia.

Semarang, Middle Java

In February, at the mansion number 4, Indrabura road, Semarang Province there was a Chinese father and his son living in Indonesia interviewed by a researcher from Thailand. The veterinarian father was Elisa Nugroho, 77 years old. He wore a red-brown shirt and black glasses, and his businessman son was Harry Kusumo Nugroho, 40 years old. He was active and strong-willed. He wore a short black shirt and square-shaped glasses. The two men told the Thai researcher the story about the business in Indonesia:

> "… The swiftlet caves belong to the state of local governments and use concessions for harvesting. They only focused on making more money from concessionaires and there were no direct laws to control or manage the concessions.

Indonesia is the largest bird's-nest exporter in the world, or about 90 percent of the Hong Kong market. They clean the raw birds' nests, pack them into boxes, and carry them on a plane to sell in Hong Kong or ship them by boat if they know the buyer well enough. Anyway, mostly for the first time selling, it is better to ship by plane, because if shipped by boat, the buyer might trick you by saying the birds' nests were broken or not of good quality or switch them for bad ones and will either not pay or accept the condition of the birds' nests. The exporter also pays taxes to the Indonesian government.

There are a lot of birds'-nest agents in Medan, which is the biggest exporter in Indonesia. The bird's nest come from around Indonesia, including Medan, Jakarta, Surabaya, Semarang, Makassar, Bandung and Bali. The bird's-nest export cities are Medan, Jakarta, Surabaya and a small amount is exported from Semarang and Bali as well.

The reason the people of Aceh have to bring the birds' nests to Medan is to be able to fly them directly to Hong Kong themselves. When selling the bird's nest , you have to meet with buyers in person to discuss and bargain because the prices are very changeable depending on the quality of the bird's nest.

Actually, the China bird's-nest market is bigger than in Hong Kong and is growing faster too, but it's not easy to get into this market. There are Hong Kong businessmen who try to export birds' nests to China because if Hong Kong is the only market, then the price is lower.

Price wars are a problem in Hong Kong. In the past, there was a lot of demand for the bird's nest. The buyer would wait for you at the airport, but now the sellers have to go sell at each house and give the buyers cheaper prices.

During the bird flu outbreak in 2008–2009, the Chinese government banned birds' nests from Indonesia, which made prices drop to USD 1,000 or 6–8 million rupiahs per kilogram and for raw birds' nests, the prices decreased from USD 1,500 to USD 800.

Bird's-nest factories need a lot of raw birds' nests to produce bottled products, so it is mixed with *agar* to reduce the cost. They also use broken bird's nest from the caves, which are cheaper than the brown ones and keep longer in the liquid. They use dark bottles of brown or light brown to mask the contents. The bird's nest from swiftlet houses are mostly more white, dissolve in water and are more expensive. The price for black bird's nest after they are cleaned is 3–6 million rupiahs or USD 600 per kilogram, but the white bird's-nests from the farming houses are 120 bird's nest per kilogram, USD 12 each or 1440 Rupiah per kilogram.

There is no exact known number of nests exported from Indonesia but an estimate is around 2,000 tons. Even though this number is from Hong Kong, it is still hard to tell because the sellers can carry nests on their own private planes.

The Indonesian government lets each province take care of their own swiftlet resources under the royal forest department because swiftlets forage in the forest. Therefore, no one owns the swiftlet and you don't have to feed them. Just build the house for them, which is different from a chicken farm. Bird's-nest thieves in Indonesia smash the walls of the house farm units and steal the birds' nests ..."[104]

East Kalimantan
From books, research papers and internet content.

"... The business and management for bird's-nest business in East Kalimantan for both ethnic groups, Kenyah ethnic group who own the swiftlet caves in Long Peso[105] or the Aoheng (Penihing) ethnic group in Long Apari obtained the cave rights from their families or were the first one to find the cave. They are able to sell bird's nest to buyers in the market. For the swiftlet caves owned by the state, concessions are used[106] by private companies that pay taxes to the local government.[107]

Chinese businessmen acquire concessions from the local government.[108] Also, the swiftlet cave-owners and collectors use community cooperatives called the *Koperasi Sarang Burung Walet* to manage the caves. Sometimes, some families let other people rent the harvest rights.[109]

There is also no direct law for swiftlet conservation in East Kalimantan but there are decrees from the director-general of the royal forest department (Director General of PHPA-*Perlindungan Hutan dan Pelestarian Alam*) ..."[110]

Aceh

A 40-year-old big, dark man who lives close to the beach in Kampung Meunasah-an Aceh Besar. Mulia wore a blue shirt, gray pants and a black cap that read: "Let's Be United MANCHESTER UNITED". He appeared careful and contemplative. Another man, dark and chubby with short hair and a beard was named Mahya. He wore a white shirt and pale jeans ripped at the knees. The two men are bird's-nest collectors.

They were sitting at the table in green plastic chairs. Both of them smoked cigarettes while telling us their story over the loud noise from the tourist traffic.

> "… In the past, the first person who found swiftlet cave would own the cave, but if the local government knew about it, this cave would be shared. After the tsunami in 2004, there were no concessions anymore because the number of bird's nests had decreased, so they tried to increase the number of swiftlets by setting up a community cooperative for the local people to control and manage under the village committee.
>
> After the birds' nests are harvested, you must pay taxes to the local government. After the tsunami, the locals didn't have to pay taxes until the numbers increased. So they only had to pay for the management and the labor costs.
>
> Before the tsunami, the local people offered concessions to the local government (*mukim*) and whoever put in the highest bid would get them. This money would be given to the mosque in the community.
>
> This community had nine collectors so the concessionaires could hire as many as they wanted. They collected nests 4 times a year, every 3 months and they waited for the baby birds to be able to fly first. Before the harvest, they performed rituals and had a big party for poor people, widows and orphans.
>
> After each harvest season, the collectors would give money to the village (*mukim*) 12 villages at 2 million rupiah each.
>
> When I was very young, there were thousands of swiftlets but now not so many. The collectors only work during the harvesting season and are general workers for the rest of the year …"[111]

A 40-year-old big, dark man named Musakir has an oval face, chubby cheeks and a beard over his mouth and chin. He wore a cotton, short-sleeved white shirt and dark blue jeans. He used to be a truck driver in Malaysia-Singapore but went to jail in Singapore for selling illegal cigarettes. Now he is a bird's-nest collector, leader and the president of the bird's nest community cooperative of Lampuuk, Aceh. He sat comfortably in a blue plastic chair on the beach and smoked a cigarette while telling us his story:

"… The bird's-nest harvesting here started in 1970. The bird's-nest (*Burung Walet*) prices went up in 1980. There are many different grades of birds' nests depending on the market prices. The bird's-nest collectors had to give money to the family and workers and also give to every village around 2 million rupiah each, depending on the area.

Before the Aceh Indonesia conflict in 1980, the white bird's-nest harvest was over 200–300 kilograms per year and the black bird's-nest harvest was 800 kilograms per year. After the tsunami and the conflict, there were a lot of dead people and no one took care of the caves. After that, the state government tried to make concessions for 1 billion rupiah per year. Later, the concessions rose to 8 billion rupiah, but the swiftlets decreased, so the concessions were canceled. Then the state government let the local people manage it themselves.

There was a concession bid only once a year, and concessionaires had to be Acehnese, but the money could come from anywhere. There were two ways of collecting the birds' nests: before the egg hatched and after the fledglings birds could fly.

The buyers are the local people here and then they sell to Aceh people in Medan. The price varies because the collectors don't know the current prices, but whoever gives the best offer will get them. In 2010, the prices rose to the highest amount at 8 million rupiah. The lowest was 7 million rupiah, and the average price was 6 million rupiah. For black bird's-nests, the price was 3 million rupiah …"[112]

H. Fainal is a chubby young man with short hair and a mark on his cheek. He wore a short-sleeved black shirt. He owns a swiftlet house in Sigli, Aceh Pidie. He was sitting on a wooden bench underneath a mango tree. He carefully told us his story:

"… I tried building a swiftlet house, which I studied from the handbook of E. Nugroho from Jakarta. I spent 1,200 million rupiah for the land and my contractor friend made the building. I built this swiftlet house 5 years ago. I think the swiftlets are from the Seulawah mountains.

Aceh ethnic groups mostly own the swiftlet farming houses here in Sigli, and they sell birds' nests to the Aceh group in the city. Sometimes they come to pick them up here.

Banda Aceh city are important bird's-nest markets. The building-owners have to pay a flat rate of tax per kilogram.

There are about 200 swiftlet houses in Sigli. People are afraid to invest in new buildings because you might have to wait a long time until the swiftlets come in and the government doesn't really support having another job. The average harvest is 2 kilograms, once a month.

When I started to build, I prayed to the holy spirit and after it was finished, I had a party for over 100 orphans, widows and poor people at the house and also gave money to the poor. I had an Islamic ceremony led by the Ulama to bless the building, and then the swiftlets came to stay after six months had passed …"[113]

There was a 50-year-old man with tan skin, short hair and a chubby figure who wore a prayer cap and a short-sleeved gingham orange and blue shirt. He is the owner of a swiftlet farm house and an authorized seller of Suzuki motorcycles – Suzuki Bakri Samalanga – in Samalanga town. He told us the story at his office with the air conditioning on. He was friendly and confident.

"… I have been working in this business for over 20 years. I donate the money I make from this to poor people and Islamic schools.

I own three swiftlet house farming properties. I use the upstairs for swiftlet farming. The first time, I saw the swiftlet (*Burung Walet*) come stay at my building, I didn't know what kind of bird it was, and then I went to the meeting in Semarang. I learned about these birds and then I built more swiftlet houses. After five years there were many more swiftlets, and I made more money. I started helping more people and supporting the Islamic schools. I gave money to the Ulama, whom I respect very much. I donated money to 10 Islamic schools around this area and sponsor kids and adults who want to go to the Hajj ceremony to learn about the Quran on Thursdays and Sundays.

There are laws to control the swiftlet house farming industry here and you need permission papers from the District leaders. Every time you collect birds' nests, you have to pay taxes to the state. You also pay the fee for a building construction licence, factory permit and swiftlet house farming permit. The rate of the tax is unknown. It depends on the Revenue department. There are three different grades of birds' nests. Grade 1 is 3 inches in size and selling for 13 million rupiah per kilogram, and sell the rest in bulk for 11–12 million rupiahs.

Now I sell birds' nests better than motorcycles. It's not too complicated. Just hire two collectors, work from 7:30–10:00 AM once a month for 2 days. Each day, we collect 5 kilograms, so about 10 kilograms per month. The Aceh buyers come to my house, so it's pretty easy.

The birds' nests here are the best quality but birds' nests from Sumatra are mixed with nests from Aceh and packed into boxes from Sumatra-Aceh …"[114]

There was a 50-year-old big, light-skinned, mixed-blood, Chinese-Acehnese man with clean, white teeth named Zafril. He wore black glasses and a yellow shirt that looked very neat and clean. He sells birds' nests and owns a swiftlet house farm unit. He was sitting at a local restaurant named Kambali Lagi (Come Back Again) on the Banda Aceh-Medan. This restaurant was surrounded by green rice fields and mountains. He told us his story with pride in his voice.

"… I have been doing swiftlet house farming for 10 years in Beren District because this is a very good business and has a good future. In the past, I used to be a contractor but many people recommended I build a swiftlet farming house, which cost about 1 billion rupiah for the first building, which was a two-and-a-half stories.

I shipped birds' nests at about 100 kilograms per month to Medan and Jakarta before exporting to Hong Kong. I can't export to Hong Kong by myself even though I would make more money because my cleaning worker doesn't meet their cleaning standards. So I use the cleaning centers in Medan and Jakarta. Even in Jakarta, there is a big market for selling nests to the local Chinese from Medan.

There are a lot of buyers from Hong Kong who want to buy birds' nests from Indonesia. Only at Jakarta do they export birds' nests to Hong Kong at 100 kilograms per day. The price depends on the size. There are 5 grades: A B C D and E. Grade A birds' nests sell for 13 million rupiah for 130–140 nests per kilogram, grade B would be the same amount as grade A, but the price differs depending on the quality and the same goes for grade C or D. Bird's-nest sales are about trust, networking and the mafia. It is very difficult to export birds' nests to China; Hong Kong is easier. There are no export laws or mafia like in Indonesia but you have to pay the fee for disease inspection. However, the bird's-nest business is very sensitive and needs God's provision. You have to have faith in Allah …"[115]

Observation: Bird's-nest harvesting is not a permanent job but only a part-time during the harvest seasons. So bird's-nest collectors also do other jobs such as farming, fishing[116] or as general workers.[117]

Export Market

The most important bird's-nest market in Indonesia is the international market, where Chinese businessmen buy all the birds' nests in Indonesia and then export to Hong Kong, Singapore, China, Taiwan, Malaysia, Holland, Japan, Poland and Thailand.

Nest-Trade Relationships with the Birds' Nests as a Link to Ethnic Relations

Nest-Trade Relationships with Swiftlet's Nest as a Link for Ethnic Groups

The swiftlets' nests are unique. They are hierarchy of food which can be food as nature, food as culture or culture maker, food as medicine, healthy food, food as a commodity, food industry or food supplies industry, food as a gift and symbolic as a food denoting wealth.

Swiftlets produce edible birds' nests that are complex products. These products can fall under state property, private property, common or 'communal property' regimes, Res nullius or open access regimes.[118] In fact, the swiftlets are a state resource which is protected by law as are other state resources, and swiftlets, or at least the birds' nests they produce, can be considered as private property when they stay at people's houses. The swiftlet also belongs to the community which is the food source for swiftlets. Local people are able to access the birds' nests unless the birds' nests are built in someone's house – and humans can't completely control where swiftlets choose to stay and build nests.

The swiftlet as a resource is also a mediator, connecting the relationships within a given ethnic group as well as between groups. Even though Javanese is the dominant ethnicity in Indonesia, the Javanese are not the only group able to access and use swiftlet resources. There are many groups, such as the Chinese, Dayak, Kenyah, Aoheng (Penihing) and Acehnese. Each ethnic group has monopoly power to manage, control and access the natural swiftlet resources in their areas, including the power to manage the researcher, bird's-nest collectors, swiftlet cave guards, and the bird's-nest processing factories. Additionally, each ethnic group also manages the business relationships within the group, which is "inclusive into the group" and "exclusive out of the group". This demonstrates the inequality found in the natural resources within a given group.

These examples are about the inclusive business relationships that centralize the power to access the swiftlet resources such as in Bali, a mayor – despite holding an office only five years – gave a 20-year to a concessionaire without concern for any possible benefit his successor could get from a new concession.[119] In East Kalimantan, there are the *Ahli Waris*-inherited rights passed from generation to generation. They have joined together in a community cooperative (the *Koperasi Sarang Burung Walet*). Some areas such as Muara Wahau and Berau Districts have some Chinese concessionaires who were granted rights from the local government. In the Aceh Province, whoever finds a swiftlet cave has the right to harvest it. For the swiftlet cave at Guha Rayeak, Guha Siblah mountain in Aceh Besar uses a concession system and only Acehnese can be concessionaires.

These are examples of the exclusive business relationships in the same group to obstruct the use of swiftlet resources. The locals defying the local government on the control of swiftlet concessions in Long Apari, Long Peso and elsewhere. There were armed gangs fighting (last war) to protect the right of the Dayak swiftlet caves in East Kalimantan. CV Bintang Sejahtera company canceled concessions for birds' nests in Aceh Besar.[120]

Meanwhile, the same ethnic group obstructed by their own group from access to the swiftlet resources are considered "the outsiders." They resort to criticism, slander, and stealing birds' nests from caves and swiftlet houses. So the official owners have to protect their property, especially the swiftlet caves in Guha Rayeak at Guha Siblah mountain in Aceh Bear. They have guard dogs at the caves, which adheres to the Religious Law-Sharia of Islam.[121]

Nest-Trade Relationships Across the Ethnic Groups

The Chinese bird's-nest companies in Indonesia buy all the birds' nests from all the ethnic groups and export them to Hong Kong, Singapore, China, Taiwan, Malaysia, Holland, Japan, Poland and Thailand. At the same time, the Chinese bird's nest company in Medan buys swiftlet nests from Malaysia because they are cheaper due to the labor used for harvesting. They then send them to Jarkata or export to Hong Kong.[122] The relationships between buyer and seller of the same ethnic groups or different nationalities are deep and complicated in the bird's-nest business, be it in the country or in swiftlet farming houses in the cities. They have to trust each other and be honest. They must also be able to supply the products the market requires.

Home of Swallows Limited in Hong Kong and China is a company invested in the bird's-nest business and bird's-nest beverages. It exports from Indonesia, Malaysia, Vietnam and Thailand. Up to 98 percent of birds' nests in Hong Kong are from Indonesia and imported by plane.[123] However, the company's proprietor said that there was nothing obstructing ethnic groups in Indonesia from selling birds' nests. He claims, "any ethnic group who has money can do it."[124] However, the Chinese ethnic groups in the industry have proven the most powerful group who can set up the prices in Indonesia, Hong Kong and the world market.

So the Chinese ethnic group in Indonesia has a virtual monopoly on the swiftlet business internationally and as the go-between for Indonesian states exporting abroad. This demonstrates the inequality in the use of swiftlet resources linked to the power wielded by the government at the state and local level.

Though the world has changed rapidly, the harvest of birds' nests in Indonesia has continued as relatively unchanged. Harvesters still use bamboo to climb the cave faces as in the age of hunting and gathering societies. Even now for many locals the collection of the birds' nests is about food resources and food sovereignty more than anything else.

6. BIRDS' NESTS IN POLITICS AND SOCIETY

Sukarno and Mohammad Hatta declared Indonesian independence on the morning of August 17, 1945. They said, "We the people of Indonesia declare Indonesian independence right now. Everything must be done efficiently and with much urgency!" They also announced the official 1945 constitution.[125]

Chapter 2

A news article about the problem of bird's-nest concessions in Aceh Besar.

Indonesian society was Sukarno's Guided Democracy from the time he declared Indonesian independence from the Dutch government in 1945, up to 1966. The country then transitioned to the New Order under President Suharto from 1966–98. Now it is has been heading toward democracy again, starting in 2001. This means more democracy and freedom.

The bird's nest resource has actually influenced politics. The feedback from many ethnic groups in Indonesia shows the inclusive relationship with the centralized power of using bird's-nest resources, and the exclusive relationship that obstructs the same ethnic groups so that they cannot access bird's-nest resources. This shows the shift in political structure, connected with the rights to swiftlet caves, local politics, the bird's-nest concession committees, private companies' monopoly of bird's-nest concessions, and export companies. They strive to maintain these rights and powers exclusively within one group. At the same time, another part can open to the community, giving access and use of additional bird's-nest resources as a community cooperative for the sellers and using the law and ethnic traditions such as the following.

There are some Chinese ethnic groups in Muara Wahau and Berau Districts called *pahtar*—exclusive buyers who hold monopoly rights to concessions provided by the state government.[126] There have been some conflicts between them and indigenous ethnic groups.

In 1999, after President Suharto lost power, the Aoheng ethnic group was fighting for swiftlet cave rights and to stop the state government's use of concessions. Also government departments sued each other over bird's-nest concessions when there was a conflict of interest concerning the power of new areas, related to the law on Regional Autonomy (Law No. 22 of 1999) and the local party.[127]

In Aceh Province, in the past only Acehnese concessionaires were allowed to bid for harvesting rights. They would pay the fee to the local government (*mukim*), but during the Aceh – Indonesia conflict in 1976–2005, Indonesian soldiers set up military camps at the Rayeak Cave. They frightened off the swiftlets with gunfire and burned the swiftlet cave, because during the war, the Achenese sold birds' nests to buy weapons[128] and support GAM (Free Aceh movement).[129]

Then in 2005, the Indonesian government and GAM announced a peace deal to end the war. After that, there were conflicts between the local politicians (*Dewan Perwakilan Rakyat Kabupaten-DPRK*) in Aceh Besar and they canceled the contracts for bird's nest concessions for the CV Bintang Sejahtera company in Aceh Besar. The same thing happened to the swiftlet caves in Lhoknga, Lampuuk, and Desa Naga Umbang, where concessions were canceled, following the forest decree number Kpts II/2003, which was used to protect the swiftlet caves.

The committee for bird's-nests concessions had also been corrupted.[130] Rumor has it that local politicians in Mandailing Natal or Madina District, Sumatera Utara had corrupted their contract by illegally extending its bird's-nest concession duration with PT Cipta Karisma company in December of 2007.[131]

However, there were some ethnic groups or families who inherited rights to the swiftlet caves, and this demonstrates the government's willingness to accept local, 'ethnic rights'.

At the same time, the owners of swiftlet house farming units or the private companies of ethnic groups in Indonesia had more freedom to do business in the state or with other groups, but only wealthy people can afford the investment required.

The disadvantaged groups in the bird's-nest business, such as bird's-nest collectors, local politicians, businessmen and bird's-nest thieves have rebelled against the system, representing the politics of resistance against the unequal rights to bird's-nest resources. They employed silent protests such as stealing birds' nests (everyday life resistance). They don't want to get caught by the police or have big, public protests. Rather, they use the "weapons of the weak" to avoid big impact from powerful groups of people.[132] These groups deomstrated the resistance to the power the government holds over them.[133]

These resistance groups challenge the authorities with the power to access bird's-nest resources, another demonstration of the inequality of power management in Indonesia. Thus, the crimes and stealing related to 'The battle over bird's-nest resources" among ethnic groups are continuing.

7. ENVIRONMENT AND ECOLOGICAL FACTORS

After President Suharto (1921–2007) was elected president in 1966, he changed the system to the New Order (*Orde Baru*) system from March 11, 1966 to May 21, 1998, in response to rapid economic changes and pressures from the outside world. These factors, especially from the 1970s–1980s,[134] pushed Suharto to develop the country and spur economic growth by following a capitalist economic system. More than twenty years later, he was pressed to resign in 1998. From that time onward, Indonesia has moved away from the New Order system.[135]

Considering the effects on the environment and ecology in Indonesia, the runaway wildfires of 1997-98 were devastating. From September–November, 1997 a wildfire

Swiftlet house in Java, Indonesia.   Swiftlet house on countryside in Aceh, Indonesia.

started as a result of Suharto's policy supporting palm oil plantations since 1970. The government had written laws about deforestation to benefit palm oil plantations.

This led to out-of-control deforestation and rampant corruption in the government, especially burning down forests to expand palm oil plantations, because it was cheaper than cutting.

In 1984–86, the government also moved people from overcrowded Java and Bali, to the other islands which were deforested for agricultural purposes. This led to the conflict between the Dayak people and the palm oil companies who burned down their homes to clear space for palm oil plantations. Indonesia's government was too weak-willed to enforce the law, and wildfire-related poverty in the country increased.

Heavy smog from the fires also spread over parts of Indonesia, Malaysia, Singapore, Negara Brunei Darussalam, Philippines and Thailand.[136] From these cases, Indonesia can be considered at serious risk when projecting potential effects on climate change and on the decay of the natural environment.

There has been a study on swiftlet resources in relationship with the dimension of environmental ecology, specifically concerning the relationship between swiftlets and their habitats.

The case of cave swiftlets in Central Java found that the caves are the local government's property and the government grants concessions to those who want to harvest and sell birds' nests.

This system creates problems because the concessionaires do not care about the swiftlets' longterm preservation. The concessionaires collect birds' nests when the swiftlets are laying their eggs or at hatching time. They want only the nests, not the eggs, so they throw them away.[137]

In some areas of Indonesia, concessionaires who win the auction from local government worry about collecting enough birds' nests, or find they cannot collect according to the contract. They usually collect birds' nests without thinking of breeding and survival of the swiftlet population and simply collect as many birds' nests as they can. This disrupts the birds' laying and hatching cycle. Harvests have decreased since the state government started using this system. Theft also damages the swiftlet populations.[138]

For example, the swiftlet cave in Karang Bolong, Kebumen in Central Java used to produce birds' nests 1,400 kilograms annually, eventually decreasing to 400 kilograms.[139] Gua Sarai and Gua Tugung, which belong to the Dayak ethnic group of East Kalimantan, allowed Chinese and Malay businessmen to rent the caves, from which they collected birds' nests about once a month.[140]

In the case of the swiftlet caves in Lhoknga and Naga Umbang, Aceh Besar on October, 2008 used the forest decree number 100/Kpts II/2003 guidelines for harvesting birds' nests (Collocalia spp) to allow concessions with of at least three years but no more than five years. The *Balai Konservasi Sumber Daya Alam*-BKSDA investigation found that five-year concessions in two different villages caused a serious decline in swiftlet populations due to corruption in the agreement. Millions of fledgling birds died as a result.

Regarding the Naga Umbang Cave, 10 years ago the nest harvest was 700 kilograms per year but has dropped to 200 kilograms per year. The same thing has occurred at the swiftlet cave in Lampuuk, which has dropped from 50 kilograms per year to five kilograms.[141]

These cases make clear that swiftlet resources and environmental management directly impact each other.

In general, swiftlet resources in Indonesia are now managed by leaving them alone to breed naturally. The management of this process has many levels and directions and has proved unstable. Swiftlet populations in nature have been greatly reduced.

Meanwhile, there is a new method to preserve and nurture swiftlet populations. The use of swiftlet farming houses is a relatively new method in the industry, and it is quickly replacing the 200-year-old method of collecting birds' nests from natural caves. In the 1990s, especially in 1992, swiftlet-house expanded throughout the country. By 1995, there were dedicated buildings in every region. Now 75 percent of birds' nests are produced in these swiftlet houses, with only 25 percent still harvested from natural caves.[142]

In order to preserve and nurture swiftlets dwelling in unnatural habitats, the keepers will take *Seriti* or *Collocalia Esculenta* eggs out of their nests and replace them with the eggs of other swiftlet species, so that they hatch without the need for the original nests. This method has been in practice for more than 20 years, and swiftlet populations are increasing again.

Once the eggs hatch, the keepers will release them to live on their own. However, studies show that only two out of every 10 fledgling swiftlets released into the wild survive. The swiftlets cannot find food on their own because they are used to being fed by humans. More importantly, humans cannot force the swiftlets to live in complete submission to human will.[143]

The swiftlet house farming method in Indonesia also has hidden and severe impacts. There are around 250,000–300,000 swiftlet farming houses throughout Indonesia. In 25 provinces, business owners have converted their buildings into swiftlet farms. The more swiftlet house farming units increase, the fewer buildings are available for other human endeavors.

Since swiftlet house farming doesn't require much labor, there are fewer jobs for workers in the industry as well. Swiftlet farming houses need very little electricity, since the birds prefer dark places, but the houses also contain lots of water, which causes a mosquito problem. The owners sell their buildings to other business owners and move to other towns. Towns turn dark and become dead.[144] Due to these problems, municipal governors hate swiftlet house farming.

This problem has developed very quickly and is difficult to manage. Its has spread to villages as well, where the use of sonic waves to attract the birds disturbs the villagers. It becomes noise pollution that affects the health of the community. The birdhouse farming business is growing without direction or restriction. This is a problem that Indonesian authorities must deal with.

Haryoto Kusnoputratanto, ex-Minister of Natural Resources and Environment and Director of Environment Impact Assessment Development (BAPEDAL), has said that there are many principles and laws concerning environmental conservation, but that they cannot be enforced because most people are too selfish and have bad relationships with the government.[145] This is the state of the industry in Indonesia, and the ongoing issues it faces.

APPENDIX

The pictures of ethnic group and birds' nests resources in Indonesia

A swiftlet living in a house farm in Sermarang, Central Java, Indonesia.

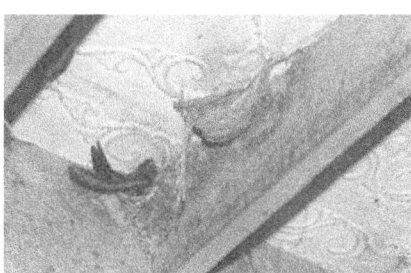

Seriti or *C. esculenta* living in a swiftlet house farm in Sermarang.

The security huts in front of Guha Rayeak, Meunasah Lumpuuk, Aceh.

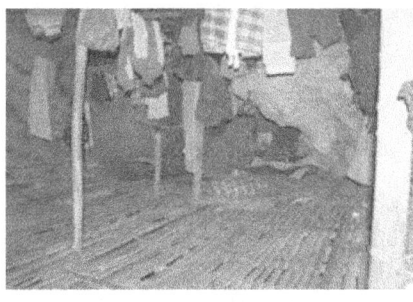

Inside a security hut swifltlet cave Guha Rayeak, Meunasah Lumpuuk, Aceh.

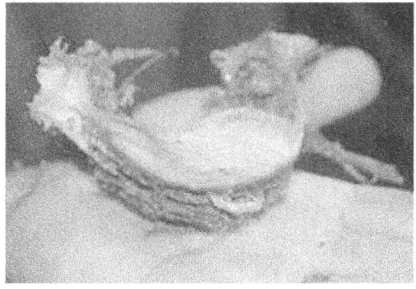

Seriti and white swiftlet built a nest together in Sermarang city.

Chapter 2

Ubangon made from bamboo to collect nests in Guha Rayaek.

Ubangon (bamboo ladder) high 50–60 meters in Guha Rayeak.

A birds' nests collector climbs a bamboo ladder for to harvest nests.

Bird's-nest collectors in Java using bamboo ladders to climbing the cave walls.

Ethnic Groups and Bird's-Nest Resources in Indonesia

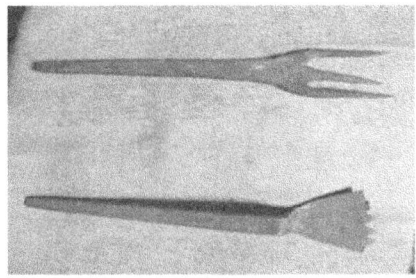

The tool for white nest collecting, called *Rada* and the tool for black nests called *Kennuku* from a cave in Aceh.

White birds' nests and black birds' nests and *Rada* which the tool to collect white bird's-nest in an Aceh cave.

The birds' nests collectors sorting nests from the cave into bags.

Some of white and black nests collected from Guha Rayeak.

The big swiftlet building in Java.

Swiftlet house in Java made from wood.

Swiftlet house in Java, Indonesia.

Swiftlet house in Bireuen city, Aceh, Indonesia.

The inside a swiftlet house in Sermarang, Indonesia.

A collector harvesting birds' nests in swiftlet house in Sermarang city.

Inside the birds' nest export factory in Medan, Indonesia.

A birds'nest cleaner in Medan city, Indonesia.

3

Ethnic Groups and Bird's-Nest Resources in Malaysia

INTRODUCTION

In an effort to connect its citizens with the government's policies and "One Malaysia" slogan (Satu Malaysia), Malaysia has been pursuing ways to promote cultural unity in the country. The Federation of Malaysia[1] is a country with a variety of ethnic and cultural groups. It is also rich in biological diversity and natural resources and has the oldest rainforest in the world.[2] Malaysia's important natural resources and minerals include tin, petroleum, teak, copper, iron, and natural gas. The country ranks 24th in the world in volume of crude oil; it is the 13th globally for natural gas;[3] it is the third largest natural gas producer in the world; and it is the world's largest producer and exporter of palm oil.[4] The country is geographically made up of two regions and is culturally home to a variety of ethnic groups. The people are conservative, free-spirited, intelligent, generous, and joyful. There are about 736 bird species[5] in Malaysia. The swiftlet is a very important natural resource that has had an impact on the country's historical, economic, social, political, cultural, environmental, and ecological spheres, and influences relations among various ethnic groups. A Chinese Malaysian businessman[6] once said, "As long as there are Chinese in the world, birds' nests will continue to be consumed."

Chapter 3

1. HISTORY OF THE INDIGENOUS PEOPLE'S USE OF BIRDS' NESTS RESOURCES

1.1 Swiftlets in Nature

There is no clear evidence as to which ethnic group in Malaysia first started to use birds' nests, but in Malacca there are various records pointing to the possible origins. Myths and stories about birds' nests as a resource have been attributed to Admiral Zheng He, the Chinese naval hero who traveled to Malacca in 1413.[7] It is said that once during Zheng He's journey through the islands of Malay Peninsula, the fleet experienced a storm. After avoiding the storms and waves for days without food and water, the Malay Islanders brought food to the crew. Many days later, the crew who ate that food felt refreshed and healthy. Zheng He found out that the food everyone ate was swiftlets' nests. When they returned to China, they offered the birds' nests to Emperor Yongle of the Ming Dynasty. Since then, birds' nests have been popular among the Chinese.[8] Similarly, according to a Chinese myth the first person who ate birds' nests was Zheng He, a Chinese mariner and fleet admiral during the Ming Dynasty who sailed to the South China Sea. While stopping near the Malay Islands, he saw birds' nests on the cliffs when the crew was running out of supplies. He sent the soldiers to retrieve them. They then cleaned them and ate them. Several days later, everyone's skin looked radiant. Zheng He then brought the birds' nests back to the Emperor.[9] However, these stories have not been supported by any written evidence from China.[10] The evidence of people using birds' nests in Malaysia in the early days was recorded by Mandelslo, a Westerner, in 1693. He wrote that birds' nests were found on the rocks by the seashore and were respected by the Chinese. The birds' nests were sold at a price of 3 to 4 crown[11] per pound.

It has been noted that when China reopened the marine trade in the late 16th century it encouraged traders to look for new products from overseas. According to records, places that produce birds' nests products, such as "The Ballad of Jerjezang," include Niah, Sarawak. These stories explain how the local Sarawakians saw little value in the birds' nests until they were made a valuable product by the Chinese traders.[12]

The Idahan people of Sabah on Madai hills in Lahad Datu District have long claimed the right to harvest edible birds' nests. It was assumed that the bird's-nests business here started in the early 15th century or around the time when Chinese people frequently traveled to this region in order to find birds' nests and traded them for pottery or porcelain.[13]

In Sarawak, the main bird's-nest resources are in Niah cave and the cave in the Bao area. The bird's-nest business has a long history and close ties with the community in Sarawak. Even though there is no written evidence of the bird's nest trade before 1840, stories from many communities have shown that swiftlet caves were found in Sarawak before 1800 in the middle of Baram, where the largest white-nest swiftlets' nest resource was discovered and exploited.

In 1851, Spenser St. John, the secretary of Rajah James Brooke recorded that birds' nests were considered a precious treasure for the people in the Kayan community. Harvesting birds' nests at Gumbang Cave near Bau District began in 1848. Hugh Low mentioned that bird's-nest harvesting and equipment for the business have been found in this area. In addition, birds' nests were also harvested in Sirih Cave and Mt. Rabang in the northern part of the Sarawak Kiri River. These confirm that the harvesting of birds' nests in Sarawak has been around since the mid-19th century.

Therefore, it has a history of over 150 years.[14] The demand for birds' nests among the Chinese dates back to the Ming Dynasty (1368–1644). It is believed that birds' nests have properties to "treat various diseases," such as helping with skin treatment, preventing influenza, detoxifying the body, and helping in digestion. It is also recommended for patients with lung problems such as bronchitis, tuberculosis, and asthma. The Chinese medicine book *Zhong Yau Da Ci Dian 1978* (Chinese Dictionary 1978) verified properties of birds' nests that help to nourish the blood and lungs. Serving birds' nests at parties represents a way of honoring guests. Birds' nests help activate the organs inside our bodies to work better andnourish our skin. In addition, Chinese people believe that bird's nest is a sexual stimulant.

Chapter 3

That is one of the factors explaining why the demand and price of birds' nests have increased.[15]

From the 17th century onwards, birds' nests have become increasingly valuable resources and among the more important products for trade between China and Nanyang. Although the birds' nests have been claimed by the local people under various managements, the Chinese merchants controlled the bird's-nest business and shipping on Chinese junk boats.[16]

During the past decade (1990–2000), the production of birds' nests in Sarawak has greatly declined. This is due to a decrease in the number of wild swiftlets mainly because of the uncontrolled birds nest harvesting. Due to the high price of the birds' nests resulting from the demand of the Hong Kong market in the 80's, the villagers were urged to harvest more and more birds' nests for sale. When the villagers started to receive more income from selling birds' nests, money became important in their lives. The villagers were living better as a result of the money from the business. The money was not only circulating in large cities but also spreading out to villagers in distant areas, such as in the inner part of Sarawak. Sometimes people were harvesting birds' nests every 30 days. High profits from bird's-nest harvesting had several side effects. Many caves weree opened for rent by third-party tenants who were granted rights from the cave-owners. Those tenants had to harvest the birds' nests within a limited rental period in order to realize maximum profits.

The acceleration of birds' nest harvesting led traditional harvesters to cease to exist. Harvests aimed to get the most birds' nests possible. As a result, the number of swiftlets rapidly dropped.[17] In Malaysia, noble families living near the Baram River Basin have been wealthy for generations because they owned bird's-nest caves.[18]

Information given by the owner of the birds' nest, a Penan in Batu Niah, states that Penan people like to eat birds' nests. They make bird's-nest soup, bird's-nest soup with chicken and boiled nest with rock sugar. They believe that eating birds' nests makes them strong and healthy, and helps with their sexual vitality.[19] An Iban merchant in Rumah Panjang, Kampung Chong, Batu Niah, said birds' nests are used as medicine. "If we are tired and eat birds' nests, we will be refreshed. If we eat them regularly, we will be strong. Because birds' nests are expensive, it is worth it to sell them rather than eat them. Iban people have their own recipe for making bird's-nest soup with chicken. Generally, Iban people do not eat birds' nests. They prefer selling them. If they are invited to eat them or someone treats them, they will eat them. However, they only sell their own birds' nests because they are expensive, and they see them as food for the rich."[20]

1.2 Swiftlets in Swiftlet House Farming Business

Development of Swiftlet House Farming Business in Malaysia

The edible swiftlet house farming business means the production process of birds' nests by preparing the building to be suitable for living and making nests for the swiftlets. This human intervention process has spread quickly. In the first phase of the new farming era, it was divided into two main types, namely, Java bird building and Sumatra bird building. The distinctive feature of the Java bird building is the small entrance with a size of 1–2 feet for flying into and out of the building. On the other hand, the Sumatra bird building is a large building with a large entrance. The Malaysian bird building has added other characteristics like a Malaysian style rowhouse. This style is not only different in size but also in its management. They can get high-quality birds' nests in limited areas such as rowhouses.[21] These commercial buildings are called the shophouse or shoplot.

The birdhouse industry has existed on the Malay peninsula for more than 50 years. There were not more than 100 birdhouses throughout Malaysia in the 1990s. Most of the birdhouses along the coast were abandoned before the war or during the Colonial period. Birds would come to live in these buildings. Only a few buildings needed adjustments or improvements in order to increase the amount of swiftlets. It was considered good fortune for the owner of the building when birds came to live there and make nests. No one knew about technology or how to lure birds into the buildings until society and politics in Indonesia were unstable and there was a riot in 1998. As a result, many Indonesian refugees and entrepreneurs invested in West

Malaysia. The swiftlet farming industry in the 1980s increased tremendously after 1997, after the financial crisis in Asia which caused many businesses to fail. Some entrepreneurs turned to invest in the swiftlet farming business.[22] In addition, the economic crisis in 1997 also lowered the price of real estate. Those Indonesian refugee entrepreneurs started joint investments with local investors. They adapted abandoned buildings and turned them into modern birdhouses. The knowledge and techniques of how to run bird farms were kept secret. In 2005, on the Malay peninsula, there were approximately 15,000–20,000 modern birdhouses, which are worth more than RM 4.5 billion.[23]

Swiftlet farming was a new industry in Malaysia compared to rubber, palm oil, oil, gas, and forestry. In the past, there were slightly more than 100 birdhouses and were most were found in the countryside. Before 2002, birds' nests were mostly taken fromcaves.

The swiftlet farming industry in Malaysia began partly due to the impact of the regional economic crisis in Asia in 1997–98, which caused many businesses to go bankrupt. Swiftlet farming gradually grew after 1999. Before 1998, around 900 bird buildings were found in Malaysia, and at the end of 2006, there were approximately 36,000 bird buildings all over the country. The rate has been increasing 35 percent per year since 2002.[24]

Development of Swiftlet House Farming Business on the Malay Peninsula

White-nest swiftlets started to build nests in the rowhouses from the early 1940s to the 1950s on the Malay Peninsula. This was similar to Javanese bird farming. The owner of the house did not create any enticements or modify the internal structure of the building for the birds to make nests, but they also did not chase them away.

In the second phase of edible swiftlet house farming, house owners began to improve the conditions of the building to increase the number of swiftlets. The first records by Nigel Langham mentioned the first edible swiftlet house farms in Penang in 1985.

In terms of new developments, the technical concept of intensive farming has spread in the Malay Peninsula during the past 10–15 years (1982–2006), for example, Nibong Tebal in Penang, Sitiawan and Taiping in Perak, and Terengganu, Pahang, Kelantan, Johor, and Malacca. It is estimated that in 1997 there were at least 150 houses on the Malay Peninsula that were inhabited by edible swiftlets. In 2000, the number of edible swiftlet houses increased to about 800 and continually increased to 5,000–8,000 houses in 2003. Part of this phenomenon is due to the increased number of swiftlets' rowhouses after the economic crisis in 1997. This was affected by a substantial decline in asset prices. In 2007, the number of bird buildings increased to 10,000–20,000 houses, and it is believed that only 30–40 percent of the birdhouse farming business was successful.

Meanwhile, there was a seminar on regional birds' nests in 2005. It was a collaboration between the Malaysian bird's-nest merchants and the Department of Wildlife and National Parks in Peninsular Malaysia. The seminar was held at the First World Hotel Genting Highlands Convention Center on August 14–15, 2005. There were 700 attendees from various agencies from both the national government and local governments, including speakers from various countries. At the seminar, there were group discussions for exchanging opinions and building understanding about the birdhouse farming industry.

In 2006, the issue of edible swiftlet house farming was set to be discussed in the cabinet by the Minister of Housing and Local Government, who has power over the city council and local government officials. Eventually, the government decided to promote and control this matter. Therefore, edible swiftlet house farming business became legal. As a result, the edible swiftlet house farming businesses in many states on the Malay Peninsula have worked closely with local governments. They started to require registrations for bird buildings and licenses for birdhouse farming.

Later, owners of edible swiftlet houses began to build the birdhouses out of town in agricultural areas or light industry areas. However, birdhouse farming outside urban area was only about 10 percentof the total because most people still preferred building their swiftlet houses in cities.

Development of Swiftlet House Farming Business in Sarawak

There is no indication when the first edible swiftlet house in Sarawak was built. It is assumed that the white-nest swiftlets first came into human houses in the city to make nests in Bintulu in 1996. Later in 1998, there were 2 birdhouses in Bintulu and Miri. People began to improve and modify their houses into edible swiftlet houses in Serikei, Sibu, Bintulu, Miri, and Kuching.[25] In 2008, there were about 1,500 bird buildings[26] scattered throughout Sarawak and there were about 5,000 bird buildings by the end of 2010.[27]

Development of Swiftlet House Farming Business in Sabah

In Sabah, there is a record mentioning that the nests of the white-nest swiftlets were first found in the urban community around in 1999, in Kota Kinabalu, where the edible swiftlets built their nests in the basement of a mall. After that, bird buildings were found in Tawau, Sandakan and Kota Kinabalu. The bird buildings must be built in the industrial areas or in the agricultural areas in order for a license for bird's nest farming[28] to be granted. In October 2012, there were 4,000 bird building businesses in Sabah.[29]

However, there were estimated to be more than 20,000 swiftlet farms in Malaysia in late 2007. There were 56,000 entrepreneurs and bird's-nest locations in 2011.[30] In the same year, the Malaysian government estimated that there were around 50,000 bird buildings in the country.[31]

2. THE NATURE OF SWIFTLETS

Birds' Nest Vocabulary and Ethnicity in Harvest Communities

Various ethnic groups in Malaysia call swiftlets in Bahasa Malay or the Malay language *layang-layang* or *lelayang*. If they build their nests in limestone caves, they are called *layang-layang gua*, while the Idahans in Sabah call them *kelimpisau*.[32] Nevertheless, swiftlets are commonly referred to as *Burung Walet* or *Burung Walit* and the nest is called *Sarang Burung Walet*. The white-nest is called *sarang putih*, the black-nest is called sarang hitam, the yellow-nest is called sarang kuning, and the red-nest is called sarang merah.

Swiftlets are a type of bird in the genus *Collocalia*. In Malaysia, there are 13 species[33] of swiftlets. In Sarawak, there are five species: White-nest Swiftlet—*Aerodramus fuciphagus*, Black-nest Swiftlet—*Aerodramus maximus*, Mossy-nest Swiftlet—*Aerodramus salanganus*, Glossy Swiftlet—*Collocalia esculenta*, and Giant Swiftlet—*Hydrochous gigas*[34] or Waterfall Swift.

Natural Characteristics

Edible-nest swiftlets play an important role in the economic system, particularly in swiftlet farming. In Malaysia, there are two species of edible-nest swiftlets:

1. White-nest Swiftlet or ***Walet Sarang Putih***; the scientific name is *Aerodramus fuciphagus*. It is a medium-sized bird, about 12 centimeters long. The plumage is blackish-brown. The upper part is also blackish-brown. The rump is slightly pale grey or light brown. It has brown irises, a black bill, and feet, living in high terrain more than 500 meters above sea level. The edible-nest swiftlet likes to build nests in caves along the coastal areas and limestone mountains. It feeds on flying insects. It dwells in the dark with 0.2 Lux light intensity. It can fly to find its own nest in the dark precisely by using its own rattling call for echolocation. The nest is white cup-shaped. It is built from the bird's saliva. The average weight of the nest is 8 grams. Both male and female swiftlets participate in building the nest. It takes 30–45 days. In the rainy season, when there are plenty of insects, the nest can be completed within 30 days. The nest is completed in September and April. Outside that period of time, it will take more than 80 days to build a nest. The breeding season starts after the nest is completed. The swiftlets breed 4–8 nights. After that, they will start laying eggs. They lay two eggs in one nest. They will lay the second egg three days after the first egg. The average weight of the egg is 1.2 grams for both male and female.

White-nest swiftlet or *Walet Sarang Putih* will start incubation after laying the first egg. It takes about 23 +/- three days. The first egg incubation period is 21–29 days, the second is 21–25 days. After two weeks, fledgling birds will hang on the edge of the nest while the parents find food for them until they have full-body feathers, which is 43 +/- six days. If the nest is not collected, it will be used during the next breeding season or the birds in the same group will use it for laying eggs. However, if the nest is collected, the bird will build a new nest. For the white-nest swiftlets that build their nests in buildings, they will build their nests in a room with 0–2 lux light intensity, 28 degrees Celsius, and relative 85 percent–95 percent humidity.[35]

2. Black-nest Swiftlet or *Walet Sarang Hitam*; the scientific name: *Aerodramus maximus / Lowi* (*A maximus / lowi*), is a medium-sized bird. It is about 12 centimeters long. The plumage is blackish-brown. The rump is grayish, which makes it look like it has feathers on the back legs. The tail is slightly incised. It is difficult to distinguish the black-nest swiftlet from the edible-nest swiftlet outdoor. The iris is dark brown. The bill and tail are black. The black-nest swiftlet likes to build nests along the coastal areas and in limestone caves. It feeds on small insects. The nest is made from its saliva and feathers, which comprise more than 80 percent. The nest is called "black nest." The price is cheaper than the white nest. It takes a lot of time and manpower to clean the nest and separate the feathers and other things out of it.[36]

Swiftlets Habitats

The habitats of the swiftlet in both natural habitats and bird's nest buildings are found in all 13 states of Malaysia: Kampong Tebing, Kampong Tasoh, Kampong Banat Bawah, Kangar, Kampung Jejawi Endol, Simpang Empat, Batu 20, Kaki Bukit, padang Besar,[37] **Perlis State**; Kampong Bakan, Kuala Nerang, Pokok Sena, Kampong Tanjung Radin, Kuala Ketil, Lunas, Kulim, Sungai Petani, Jitra, Kepala Batas, Legong, **Kedah State**; Bukit Mertajam, Nibong Tebal, Cangkat Kledang, **Penang State**; Jelai, Cangkat Jering, Bruas, Pantai Remis, Lumut, Teluk Intan, Bagan Serai, Parit Buntar, Selama, Tanjung Malim, Slim River,[38] Ipoh, Sitiawan, Taiping and Manjung, **Perak State**; Kuala Kubu Bahru, Rawang, Kepong, **Selangor State**; Cheras, Kampong Bahru Paro, Negeri **Sembilan State**; Alor Gajah, Ayer Pasir, Durian Tunggal, Melaka town, **Melaka State**; Kulai, Tangkok, Pagoh, Bukit Pasir, Kampong Machap, Ulu Tiram, Tai Hong Village,

Senai, Pontian Kecil, Jemaluang, Kampong Seri Pantai, Mersing, Kampong Sawah Datuk, Kampong Air Papan, Endau and Desaru, **Johor State**; Kuala Besut, Tok Soboh, Kampong Pinang, Kuala Terengganu,[39] Kemaman, Dungun, Marang, Kuala Berang, Jertih, Setiu,[40] Rantau Abang, Kampung Tirok and Pulau Redang,[41] **Terengganu State**; Rompin, Pekan, Kuantan, **Pahang State**; Pasir Mas, Kota Bahru, Tumpat, Rantau Panjang[42] and Pasir Puteh, **Kelantan State**; Bintulu, Mulu Cave, West Baram,[43] Kuching, Tatau, middle Baram, Miri,[44] Sibu Sarikei, Mukah,[45] Bukit Sarang – Tatau, Gua Niah Gunung Subis – Batu Niah, Gumbang Cave in Bau District, Baram District, Lubang Salai in middle Baram, Sirih cave and Mount Rabang on the Northern part of Sarawak Kiri River, Bahagian Sarikei, Sibu,[46] Tanjung Datu, Bako, Serian, Klingkang Range, Ulu Kakus, Suai & Nyalau, Ulu Baram, Gunung Buda,[47] **Sarawak State**; in Sepagaya Lahad Datu District, Balok Kajong in Madai, Gomantong, Kota Kinabalu, Tawau, Sandakan[48] Batu Punggul, Kuamut – Kinabatangan, Semporna Islands, Pulau Berhala – Sandakan and Pulau Mantanani[49] in **Sabah State**.

Birds' Nests Collecting Season

In Malaysia, the collecting of bird's nest from natural sources happens three to five times a year. It varies from region to region. For example, the Idahan of Madai hill in Lahad Datu District, Sabah State, collect the birds' nests three times a year. The first time or Papas is from April 20–May 5. The second time or Penangah or Penango is from August 15–September 10 and the third time or Ekor is from November 15–December 15.[50] In middle Baram, Sarawak State, they collect birds' nests five times a year and it has been decided that the closed season for nesting is from January–April so that it has at least one round[51] of egg incubation per year for the swiftlets. In Niah Cave (Gua Niah) – Batu Niah in Miri District, Sarawak, the authorities permit the nesting season for eight months, from September until March of the following year[52] and four months of the closed season from April to August.[53]

On the other hand, the collection of birds' nests in birdhouses or bird buildings depends on the number of birds. Generally, nesting is done once a month.

3. BELIEFS AND RITUALS RELATED TO SWIFTLETS

3.1 Beliefs and Rituals

Beliefs Related to Swiftlets

At Gua Niah, an old bird's-nest cave in Batu Niah, Sarawak, the Penan, Malays and Chinese are the owners of the cave. The Penan group, in particular, have inherited the customary rights for the cave for generations.[54] According to their beliefs related to swiftlets, the Penan have high respect for the swiftlets. In the past, most of the cave-owners were Muslims, but the Penan believe in animism. Before collecting birds' nests, the Penans used to carry out the *Semah*[55] ritual, offering chicken, alcohol, and nipa palm leaf cigarettes for the cave guardian spirits once a year. They stopped after 1970, after the Penan converted to be Muslims.

A Penan who inherited the birds' cave and a fifth generation bird's-nest collector at Lubang Perintah in Gua Niah of Niah National Park, relates his beliefs regarding swiftlets to his dream. In his dream, an old man said that he would discover something valuable, and that he must help the poor after that. Later, he found three vast bird's-nest caves (*Lubang*), and the old man, whom he saw in his dream, and a son and daughter. He recognized the old man's ring, which he had asked for in his dream. During Chinese New Year while guarding the cave, he heard sounds, 'Bang! Bang!' and didn't know where they came from. On the second day, he heard them again so he asked his master what the sound was. He answered that it could be the spirits of the cave, who were angry because there was no ritual held before collecting the birds' nests. He then did the *Semah* ritual himself, and the sounds stopped. These days, the Penan have stopped practicing this ritual. After the group became Muslim, they changed to *sembahyang – solat*, and practiced, *doa selama*, to ask for blessings from Allah, the Islamic God, yearly before collecting the nests.[56]

The Iban, of Rumah Panjang, Kampung Chong, Batu Niah, is an ethnic group, bird's-nest merchant, and collector for the Penan, Malay and Chinese, who own the bird's-nest caves. The Iban have no belief related to swiftlets because they only recently settled there in 1945. They regard the swiftlets as beneficial in making both medicine and money.[57] The Idahan of Lahad Datu, Sabah, believe the edible-nests from swiftlets are gifts from their great ancestors.[58]

Bird's-nest building-owners generally believe that birdhouse or building-owners are blessed by God or Allah. People, especially in Sandakan in Sabah, have shown how important the birds are to them by building a statue of a sleeping swiftlet in a nest, on the Bird's-Nest Roundabout on a road along the coast of the city. The Niah National Park, Batu Niah, an important bird's-nest resource in Sarawak, values the swiftlets and uses them as a symbol of the national park.

Belief and Ritual Related to Nest-Collecting

Bird's-nest collectors and those in some Malaysian ethnic groups have inherited beliefs and rituals towards the birds and the collecting of birds' nests in their natural habitat. It has always been a risky job to climb along steep cliffs in dark caves. Before collecting the nests, some collectors will perform a ceremony to pay homage to the guardian spirits of bird's-nest caves, asking for protection and courage and safety in collecting birds' nests so they may be used as medicine, food, and as special items for people in society.

In the past, the Penan of Batu Niah, Sarawak believed in animism, and would do Semah rituals before collecting birds' nests in the Gua Niah. The Penan stopped this ritual when they became Muslims in 1970.[59]

In the past, the Penan would bring food and desserts that they believed the guardian spirits favored. Everyone in a bird's-nest collector's family would attend the ritual in the bird's-nest cave. A white chicken would be released in the cave as an offering for the spirits, named Musang, or Harimau (tiger). If the Penan found out that someone killed the chicken, the person would have to pay a fine covering the expenses of the ritual, around RM 2,000–3,000. Therefore, the chicken often would be left untouched, as people believed it belonged to the spirits and would soon die.[60]

The Iban of Rumah Panjang, Kampung Chong, of Batu Niah, Sarawak believed in animism before becoming Christians. The most powerful spirit was Jakuibantara, as in a ritual called *Kirimu Shaman* or *Miring* would kill pigs and chickens and remove their internal organs to offer to the spirit. This ritual was conducted in front of a house (*medan*) where everyone would attend dressed in Iban costumes. Men would be shirtless but wear Ibanic *Chang kben* pants. This ritual was held around June, or at another time depending on the readiness of the villagers. After the ritual, there would be a celebration that involved hitting a gong to call the spirit to the offerings. A cooked 'pig's head' would be laid on a table for both the spirit and people to share. The ceremony stopped being practiced in 1996[61] after the Ibans became Christians, as Christianity prohibits worshipping spirits, other than the Christian God. The ceremony, however, currently is practiced only as a show for tourists in homestays.[62]

A former bird's-nest collector says that today it is noisy inside the cave, unlike in the past when everyone would remain silent for safety reasons. Concentration when collecting the birds' nests was needed to keep the collectors alive. Until today, collectors also have a special language they speak and some practices in caves The bird's-nest collectors will not get angry at each other, speak rudely or badly, and reject any food or other things offered to them. Not following these rules can upset the spirits, they believe, and they may be harmed by snakes or scorpions in the cave. The Iban also believed that the spirits and dangerous animals, such as crocodiles, are scared of tattoos; the Ibans have passed down these ideas regarding tattoos for generations.[63]

Even though some Chinese-Christian in Batu Niah, Sarawak do not practice any ritual, Muslim bird's-nest collectors (*Melayu*) are allowed to perform Islamic *sembahyang-solat* in a *doa selamat* ceremony to ask for blessings from Allah for opening caves[64] before birds' nest collecting season.

The Idahan bird's-nest collectors known as *tukang pungut*, in Lahad Datu, a capital on a peninsula in eastern Sabah, Borneo Island, use tools such as ropes, ladders, and bamboo to climb the cave walls. The collectors are very skillful climbers. Some cave walls are as high as 30 m. above ground, and they work in teams. One person climbs and the other holds the ladder to keep it balanced. It is a risky job that only skillful Idahan men can do, and so working in teams is always safer. People have different roles on the team, such as holding ladders for the climber, moving equipment, carrying baskets for gathering birds' nests.

The team members usually are relatives, such as father and son, brothers, relatives, and friends.

The Idahan bird's-nest collectors are trained at a young age to climb along the cliff to collect birds' nests. Their wages are based on difficulty and risk. In some areas, normal bird's-nest collecting teams will not be able to do the job, and so a team with more expertise, receiving much higher pay, will be required.

The Idahan regard the bird's-nest cave as a sacred place because it is the place of their ancestors' burial. Even though burials are now done in the Islamic style, the ancestral coffins are still there. As a result, the cave is undisturbed while the birds are laying and hatching eggs. The Idahan belief in prohibition related to collecting birds' nests is generally associated with the ancestral spirits that reside within the cave. There is a ritual offering of sacrifices involving yellow rice, white poultry, ceramic vases, and goats. At present, the Idahan do not perform the ceremony as strictly as before, but they still pay attention to their behavior when entering the cave. They show respect by saying to the ancestors' spirits that they, their children, have come to collect the birds' nests, and that their spirits will not interfere. Another important taboo they avoid is to wearing a hat, especially a hat made from pandanus plants, known as *Serawang* in Malay, or *tegawih* in Idahan language. Wearing a hat is believed to attack the ancestral spirits. In addition, the bird's-nest collectors are not allowed to speak rudely or to curse others. They talk to each other quietly. If someone on the team argues before the bird's-nest collection day, this will upset the ancestors' spirits, they believe. Besides behaving in the cave, the collectors need to pay attention to various signs, especially what does not happen normally. This can mean bad luck, and they may have to change the time period to avoid it. The most important sign is when if any collector sneezes in the cave, he must go home and not go out again the rest of the day. When working in a cave, language is also different from daily use. To say "Tomorrow", they will say "day after tomorrow," to say that one will "go home" he will say, "I will climb to Bu Bubun Derain."

Language is important among Malay natives. It symbolizes the respect they have for the spirit that lives in that place.

If death occurs in the community, there will be mourning for at least two days with no nests collected during the time. Likewise, if someone has an accident and falls while collecting the nests, the collection must be stopped for at least three days. The Idahan also do not have cats as pets in their house. Cats are not found near the cave, but dogs are common in the village area. The most sensible explanation ecologically is that cats are threats to the birds, especially during mating season.[65]

The collection of birds' nests in Malaysia is restricted by gender. At Niah Cave, Sarawak, the Iban of Rumah Panjang, Kampung Chong, Batu Niah, women are not forbidden to enter the cave. But within a masculine society where people's relatives are counted mainly on the fathers' side, "Collecting birds' nests is a dangerous task for men, not women. Women can enter the bird's-nest cave, but not while they are having menstruation. Women with menstruation may cause the cave to be filthy, and upset the ghosts. Women can only enter the bird's-nest cave to take care of their husbands."[66] However, in the bird's-nest industry, whether in department stores, companies or factories, people who clean or sell birds' nest products are mostly women.

Belief and Truth in Nest-Collection

According to written records, the trade and use of birds' nest in Malay Peninsula in 1693 have been ongoing for more than 300 years. Various ethnic groups also believe that the nests can be used as medicine. People in Kedah believe that it can help develop the baby's nervous systems and intelligence, as well as strengthen the baby's lungs. Pregnant women, by consuming birds' nests, believe it can reduce pain during childbirth, and accelerate the healing process afterwards.[67]

At present, various ethnic people in Malaysia consume edible birds' nests as food, including bird's-nest soup, bird's-nest soup with chicken, boiled birds' nests with rock sugar,[68] stewed birds' nest with American ginseng, birds' nest oatmeal, birds' nest simmering with dragon fruit, stewed birds' nests with papaya, stewed birds' nest with pandanus leaves, braised birds' nests with French roses, birds' nests ginseng, stewed birds' nests with Aloe vera[69] and birds' nests served with fresh fruits. Research from CEPP Laboratory Services, Faculty of Engineering, Malaysia University of Technology, in 2008 included the following findings:

Table 3.1: Shows amino acids in swiftlet's nests

Type of Amino Acid	Intensity (g/100g)	Type of Amino Acid	Intensity (g/100g)
Aspartic acid	4.87	Tyrosine	3.23
Glutamic acid	4.58	Valine	3.87
Serine	1.18	Methionine	1.36
Glycine	3.64	Cystine	0.95
Histidine	3.95	Isoleucine	2.27
Arginine	3.62	Leucine	4.66
Threonine	3.51	Phenylamine	3.88
Alanine	2.47	Lysine	3.57
Proline	3.71		

Table 3.2: Shows elements in swiftlet's nests

A Sample Nest Test Result			
Pb (ppm)	0.48	Co (ppm)	0.03
Hg (ppm)	0.09	Ti (ppm)	1.12
Cu (ppm)	2.90	Na (ppm)	4303.02
Zn (ppm)	4.41	p (ppm)	18.64
As (ppm)	0.64	se (ppm)	0.07
Fe (ppm)	50.03	Al (ppm)	4.02
mg (ppm)	556.73	Ag (ppm)	0.01
Ni (ppm)	1.53	Ba (ppm)	0.37
Cd (ppm)	0.01	K (ppm)	91.12
Cr (ppm)	0.78		

Source: CEPP Laboratory Services Chemical Engineering Pilot Plant University Technology Malaysia: 3/11/2008

The edible swiftlet nest is considered high class food and is popular among various ethnic groups in Malaysia, partly because it is expensive.[70] While the Iban and Penan communities in Batu Niah believe that edible birds' nests can help strengthen body and enhance sexual performance, other ethnic groups in Malaysia who collect nests do so only for trade.

3.2 Equipment and Tools in Collecting Birds' Nests and its Industry

Malaysia's bird building business has been influenced by Indonesia, 'Bird's Building business leader.' It is believed to have taken place in Malaysia's coastal areas around 50–60 years ago. Since then, many tools used in the bird's building/house have been developed, such as various designs of artificial bird building, devices to control conditions and atmosphere to suit the livelihood of the birds, egg incubators, temperature and humidity control devices, devices to measure intensity of light, plastic birds' nests, perfume, CD with sounds to attract the birds, textbooks to teach how to build a building like a bird's natural habitats, and bird breeding, also bird's-nests cleaning tools and chemicals, as well as cookbooks. These inventions have spread throughout the region in Thailand, Vietnam, Myanmar, Cambodia, and the Philippines over the past 20 years. In Gua Niah, Sarawak, the Iban community invented several tools for collecting nests from natural materials. The *'bulo yulo sarang'* (bird's-nest collecting tool) using in a high and dark cave wall is the tali punsung payan. It made of a bamboo trunk pole, stick on the ground, stretches with ropes in four directions. It is used to climb up or support a bamboo scaffold (*buluh*), with an iron tool called *lampong* to collect black bird's-nests. The bird's-nest collectors here found that, normally, the black bird's-nests here are very white in January and February. The bird that builds black nests also builds this white nest, and despite the feathers being mixed in with the nest, it still contains a lot of bird saliva. But in August, the bird's nest becomes black because more feathers are mixed in with the nest. Bird buildings in Malaysia are shophouses for selling the nests to customers; they also create different products such as healthy birds-nest drinks, instant bird's-nest coffee, and even beauty cosmetics made from bird's nest.

3.3 Culture, Traditions and Wisdom in Bird's-Nest Business of Ethnic Groups

Malaysia has developed its swiftlet farming businesses for 50 years and gained new knowledge in farming or building such as system and time in collecting birds' nests in ways that does not interrupt, or threaten the breeding of swiftlets, or promoting their extinction in any way, but rather to encourage conservation.

At the same time, rituals related to swiftlets and nest collection have arisen from the feeling of being overwhelmed and given in to supernatural powers, the spirits of the birds' nests cave. There is a belief in animism, where a ritual arises from feelings of fear and sublimation. It is both fertility rites and technological rituals to eliminate fear.

Tradition and culture about swiftlets (*Burung Walet*) in Malaysia were formed over 200 years ago. Despite this, it has become less conservative as it changed from spirit worshipers to faith in Christianity and Islam. Conservative practices still exist, such as the ritual of *Semah* of the Penan , which has changed to *doa selamat*, an Islamic ritual at Gua Niah. The sacrifices for ancestral spirits residing within the cave with yellow rice, white birds, ceramic vases, and goats as a group offering of the Idahan/Idaa'an community in Lahad Datu, Sabah. There is the use of polite language and the specific language when collecting the birds' nests of the Idahan/Idaa'an in Lahad Datu. The Iban of Rumah Panjang, Kampung Chong, Batu Niah, Sarawak worship and offer sacrifices to the guardian spirits, or God or Allah before collecting birds' nests once a year. These have two main objectives: 1) To ask for protection over the bird's-nest collectors to be safe during their work, and 2) To ask for great prosperity in the collection of birds' nests.

The Idahan (Idaa'an) in Lahad Datu, Sabah strongly believe that only the birds' nests should be removed from the cave, not the birds' droppings. Normally, the droppings are used to make fertilizer, but the Idahans have a few reasons to leave them in the cave. First, they believe that droppings, which have accumulated for hundreds of years, have filled up cave holes, making them shallower. Another reason is because these layers of droppings are thick and act like a soft cushion for anyone who accidentally falls while working. Many collectors survive because of these layers of dropping. Besides, some Idahan people alsowill not kill any insects or rats inside the caves.⁷¹

4. RIGHTS AND LEGAL SYSTEMS IN MALAYSIA

Malaysia is home to many different ethnicities, cultures, biodiversity, and natural resources, including bird's-nest resources. The collection of birds' nests in Malaysia has occurred for a long time. Even though the Malay ethnic group is the 'ruling,' or 'dominant ethnicity', it's the 'ruled ethnic groups' or 'minority ethnics' who have been producing history about the bird's-nest business. Each group creates its own history and legend in order to create its historical and social space. At the same time, it excludes other ethnic groups geographically. Even if there is no written evidence of a trade in birds' nests before 1840, there's evidence in the family of bird's-nest cave-owners, and people in various communities. They have provided consistent information that a bird's-nest cave in Sarawak had been identified since the early 1800s. In the middle of the Baram District, the largest source of white bird's-nests, the trade can be traced back two or three generations. In 1851 Spenser St. John, the secretary of Rajah James Brooke, recorded that the possession of the swiftlets' nests was considered a treasure by the Kayan. Bird's-nest collecting in Gumbang cave close to Bau began in 1848. Hugh Low mentioned the collection of birds' nests and equipment for storage in this area. In addition, the collection of birds' nests in Sirih cave, and the mountains in the northern part of the Sarawak Kiri River, confirms that the birds'-nest business has been operating for more than 150 years.⁷²

However, they were colonies under Portugal, Holland, and Great Britain for a long time (1786–1957) before Malaysia became independent on 16 September, 1963.⁷³ Malaysia has adopted the hierarchies of power relations from those colonies, at a certain level, in a fundamental value system: values for human dignity, powers through either traditional rules or laws, power in participating in various social activities, and rights in resources. The hierarchies of power relations are used in Malaysian society.

At the same time, Malaysia is a land with diverse ethnic cultures. It has developed from a tribal society to a feudal system with a sultan under the colonial powers, and now a democratic system. Rights system and laws regarding swiftlets is technology of power to rank social stratification, and hierarchies of power relations for access to the resources. This is complex and varies in accordance to characteristics of each territory and ethnic group.

Most caves in Sarawak are the habitat of the black nest swiftlet. People living around the caves are the ones with the right to collect birds' nests there. Generally, state laws on the control of the bird's-nest business are accepted as good laws, with clear standards, such as the Sarawak's Wildlife Protection Ordinance 1998, Wildlife Protection (Edible Birds' Nests) Rules 1998, where all edible-nest birds listed in the first group of protected animals. Wildlife protection law requires that the collection of birds' nests from natural caves must be approved by government agencies that take care of wildlife only.[74]

As for bird's-nest resources in national parks, the National Park will be the one that determines the beginning and end periods for collecting the nests. If the owner of the bird's-nest cave breaks the laws, the National Park has full authority to punish and terminate the ownership and the right to collect birds' nests.[75]

For 'nests' collecting to trade or 'running birds' houses or building business are rapidly expanding in the city area. The Sarawak government has changed the laws to facilitate the businesses in rural or remote agricultural areas or residential areas. At the same time, they recognize that with good management and sustainability principles, the benefits of birds' nests will be distributed to the local people, similar to how the birds' nest exports have generated a lot of income for the country. Edible-nest swiftlet farming is not allowed in the city areas because this will negatively affect both the quality of human life and the environment. Therefore, to modify a shophouse as a bird farm is to break the Building Ordinance 1994 and Local Authorities Ordinance 1997; meanwhile, the Sarawak government has amended the laws relating to the bird's-nest business. These include the amendment of Wild Life Protection 2003,

Section 33 (2) (b) prohibit anyone without authorization by the supervisor, to create or add any part of any structure or building that will lead to induce the Swiftlets to come to build nests. Also, any collection of birds' nests for sale or exchange is prohibited. The Amendment of the 2006 Wild Life Protection (Edible Birds' Nests)

Article 17 (2) Prohibited a license for any construction of the bird's nest farm issued by the supervisor, but is not approved by the State Planning Organization.

Article 18 refers to Article 17 prohibiting the use of land or buildings for a bird's nest farming if:

(a) Building has been categorized as building(s) in the urban area under Section 11 (1) of the Land Code, or

(b) In the area that has been declared to be the metropolitan area of the city under Section 11 (1) in accordance with the Land Code, except the land with special characteristics of agricultural land, which requires written permission from the manager of the Land Department and the survey for the construction of buildings for the swiftlet's farm.

At present, although local authorities in Sarawak do not strictly adhere to this regulation, they have been issued a warning letter from the authorities that control wildlife. As a result, a group of bird's-nest farmers around Sibu have tried to negotiate with the Sarawak government, but without progress.[76]

After Malaya officially gained independence (1957) the bird's-nest caves and other swiftlet resources belong to local governments and native ethnic groups, under the control of the Department of Forestry.

The findings of antique tools of native Penan in Gua Niah, in Batu Niah, Sarawak mean that most bird caves belong this ethnic group as well.

The rights and legal system for the bird's-nest resources in Gua Niah are inherited rights. The Penan, Malay and even the Chinese inherit the rights to the bird's-nest caves for their children. The owner of the cave has licenses which some sell their rights to Chinese. The Chinese often hire workers to collect the birds' nests for them.[77]

Society in Sarawak has a hierarchy ranking in which rights and monopoly power are linked to an individual or agency specifically in bird's-nest resources-management. These are basic characteristics of 'linear system of management', which is 'linear concept of rights' and Exclusive Rights. Those who found the bird's-nest caves have passed their ownership, with the inherited and customary rights, to their children. In the meantime, it is also complexity and dynamism of rights. They are 'communal property' which allow 'rights of access' and management and control, inclusive rights that opens for participation from any licensees, bird's-nest traders, cave guards, workers, Sarawak Forest Department (SFD)], Sarawak Forestry Corporation (SFC)], Bird Nest Entrepreneur Association of Niah Cave, Niah Special Park Committee (SPC), Cottage Bird Nest Processing Industry[78] in the resource management. This has contributed to 'multiple systems of management', leading towards sustainable bird's-nest resource-management.

The edible-nest swiftlets are the second group of reserved animals in the Sabah Wildlife Conservation Enactment in 1997. The granting of a permit for collecting birds' nests is defined under Article 85 of the same law. It also covers the case of applying for a swiftlet farm license, in order to receive license for constructing a birds' house. The bird farms must be built only either in light industrial or agricultural areas.[79]

As for the rights and legal systems in Lahad Datu, Sabah, the Idahan or Idaa'an communities have collected birds' nests in various limestone caves in Lahad Datu, east coast of Sabah, for a long time. Aware of high profits from bird's-nest trades, the Idahans have their own rules in sharing both 'rights of access' and they collect the birds' nests among the members in the community, in which most people are related.

According to the rules, the collection is allowed only after the fledgling birds are independent. They also use a rotation system where each family rotates in collecting the birds' nests, preventing monopoly of the resources. The bird's-nest area is controlled by the community.

The Idahan also claim the inherited rights in the Madai hill, in Lahad Datu as they believe the collection of birds' nests began in the early 15th century, at the time of the Chinese arrival in the region.[80]

The Idahans have inherited the rights in four areas: Madai, Baturong, Segarong, Tepadung; their rights were certified by the British government under Chartered Company of North Borneo, and by the Malaysian government later. In 1914, the Birds' Nest Act was enacted to supervise all of the bird's-nest collections in the state under the laws. (Sabah Chap. 14) This Act has verified the Idahan traditional claim in bird's-nest collecting in the cave since the British colonial period. The Lahad Datu District Office is the one to register these claims, while the Forestry Department supervises bird's-nest collection and taxes. In Madai, an estimated 1–1.5 metric tons of birds' nests are collected per year.

The Idahan are everywhere in Lahad Datu, but especially in Sepagaya village, the edge of Lahad Datu. Most who work in collecting the nests have a second house near the cave, and stay there only during the collecting season. The rest of the year, they often go back to the village and work other jobs. Only a few of them stay to guard the cave.

The Idahan have a kinship system that cares about relatives, both on the father and mother's sides, which enables a person to claim the rights repeatedly. Moreover, an Idahan who is married to non-Idahan person will not lose such rights. Each year, the rights to collect birds' nest in each area (*pesui*) will rotate among each group, that can prove its relationship with the ancestors. They were the ones who first laid the foundation in claiming the rights of bird's nest resource. Any group that can trace the connection either on the mother or father's side, is considered to have rights according to the ancestors. Each group has the right to collect birds' nests for one year at a time. The following year, the rights will belong to another group. Each group will join with another group with a different family, regrouping to claim the rights to collect birds' nests in other resources. They will do this until the rotation comes to their group again which usually takes around two to five years, depending on the number of groups in each area. These "founder ancestors" are the first group of people who found the bird's-nest resources. It is never only one founder who found a cave, because the danger of exploring caves and cliffs. They worked in a big group in exploring new caves without any ownership, and once they found one, the rights belonged to the "Discoverers" and were passed down to their children. There was no clear detail about the determination of who will get the rights first among the ancestors, but they are guaranteed a share in the rotation. The Idahan adhere to the pattern that has been done since the "ancestral times." The elders in the clan determine and deliver the right to collect the birds' nests to the heirs. The elders thus have played the most important role in determining the landmark since the British colonial period. The claim to collect the birds' nests are recorded in government documents. This rotation confirms the collaboration of the Idahan in the same clan, thus preventing a monopoly. Although each group has the rights when it is their turn, the bird's-nest resources are 'communal property'. The number of people in each clan, and the clan with the rights in each resource determine which group will get the rights. In any clan with many family members, each member will receive a small profit from collecting, such as RM 3-4 or USD 1-1.20 only.

Due to the different sizes of the bird's-nest areas, the quantities of nests that each line can collect will be also different. Therefore, the rotation is a method that ensures that each group has equal opportunity to benefit from the resources, regardless of size and ability in collection of each clan. In Madai Cave, which is a complex cave with at least 116 areas in which the birds build their nests, or the three mountains: Baturung, Segarong, Tepadung, have hundreds of bird nesting areas, so each year all clans have an opportunity to collect the birds' nests. On the other hand, a clan may get more than one right from different bird's-nest areas. All of the bird's-nest resources are claimed to be common property or usufruct, for the Idahan by the elders of the tribe. The leadership is on the senior system in the order of kinship. The elders are also the judge of any dispute. Their best knowledge of complex family clans always can terminate the case, when investigating the exercise of rights in any bird's-nest area. At the same time the committees sometimes mediate when there is a complaint about intrusiveness to collect birds' nests in adjacent areas. These "Inherited Birds'-Nests

Chapter 3

Committees of Baturung, Segarong, Tepadung" contain 15 people whose jobs are to care for an overall benefit of the Idahan related to ecology management of the caves.

They also determine time periods of bird's-nest collection and assign heads of bird's-nest collectors, which is a delicate matter. They also protect any intrusiveness to the caves; especially during mating season many tough Idahan men will be guarding and patrolling around the caves.[81]

The rights and legal system in Lahad Datu in Sabah are based on inherited rights, which are private property regimes. It is in line with the society of Lahad Datu that relationships are organized power and social relations in tribal or ethnic systems; the monopoly of rights and power are tied to individuals or agencies to manage bird's-nest resources. It is a primary characteristic of the 'linear system of management' and 'linear concept of rights', which are Exclusive Rights that block participation. Though the bird's-nest caves' rights system is also the 'linear concept of rights', it belongs to ethnic group families. From the local government or state perspective, individuals or families' ownership rights are the 'complexity of rights' or 'communal property' that grants 'rights of access' to the resources and accepts the 'ethnic rights'.

Although there are no important natural sources of birds' nests in the Malay Peninsula (*Semenanjung Melayu*) or western Malaysia, there are artificial birds' nest habitats, with a total of about 50,000–60,000 birdhouses and buildings. In 2012, Swiftlets were protected under the Protection of Wild Life Act 1972 by the Department of Wildlife and National Parks of Malaysia – PERHILITAN, Ministry of Natural Resources and Environment, to support the growing bird building business. The wildlife protection programs have adjusted the status of swiftlets, by reducing the level of protection from Totally Protected to Protected animal.

Since 2006, the government has come to promote and control the bird building business, and make bird farming legal. The local government has opened the registration of the birdhouse, and provided licenses for bird farming.[82]

The Malay Peninsula rights and legal systems are directly involved with the birdhouse business that ethnic groups, including Chinese, Malay, and Indonesians, join with the locals. There are characteristics of monopolizing rights to specific groups, which is also 'linear system of management', 'linear concept of rights', and also Exclusive Rights. However, it is also 'complexity of rights' or 'communal property' that grant 'rights of access' to the resource, and inclusive rights that open for participation. It has 'multiple systems of management' of resources, with 'dynamism of rights' and has resulted in 'rights of management and control' to sustainable management of bird's-nest resource and accept 'ethnic rights' at the same time.

In Malaysia, the rights and legal systems have 'legal pluralism,' both enclosure and customary law in passing down the rights in family lines or inherited rights. It is in line with the bird's-nest collectors in some areas that pass down their knowledge to their children.

In Malaysia, the rights and legal systems related to bird's-nests in natural resources are divided into three groups:

1. Personal or family owned caves – private property regimes
2. Common cave – Common regimes
3. Caves tender to private contractors-state property regimes[83]

Modern law allows each state to directly control bird buildings and the swiftlet's natural resources, with the power to enforce regulations and laws.

However, the law and right system as technology in Malaysian bird's-nest natural resources, among owners of the bird's-nest caves, buildings, and the local government found the monopoly of resources. Among the cave-owners and local government, there is an overlapping power level of those in the center of power and others in the margins. Power is centralized in the local government, monopolized with individuals or agencies in managing the bird's-nest resources. There is both exclusion and blocking of participation, as well as openings for participation in the management and use of bird's-nest resources. Social class hierarchy and the arrangement of historical social power relations are the key in verifying inherited rights of bird's-nest caves, and the bird's-nest-collectors to their children. The bird's nest is an individual or family treasure (Exclusive Rights) as well as 'communal property', which a common property legal system applied. The owners of the bird buildings, regardless of their ethnicity, have the legal right to bequeath the bird building business to their children.

5. BUSINESS AND MANAGEMENT SYSTEM OF THE BIRD'S-NEST BUSINESS IN MALAYSIA

5.1 Bird's-Nest Business in Ancient Time – Conservative Society

Sarang Burung Walet or Edible-Nest Swiftlets are known as *Sarang emas* meaning, "Gold Nests" in Malaysia. Bird's-nest collecting in the hunting-gathering time used bamboo scaffolding as an important tool.

Malaysia has two similarly sized regions: Peninsular Malaysia and Malaysia Borneo. Birds' nests have been special resources in Malaysia for hundreds of years, and used as food and medicine. In East Malaysia, there is evidence that the Idahan, Bidayuh, Kayan, Kenyah, and Penan have been bird's-nest collectors in Sabah and Sarawak before the 15th century. Despite this, the Malay are the 'dominant ethnicity,' creating a history of the bird's-nest business as a set of perceptions to create historical and social identity for their group, and to exclude other groups geographically. Legends regarding the collection of birds' nests created in Malaysia are various, such as a myth in Malacca. The myth was built to be associated with Admiral Zheng He, China's great naval hero who had traveled to Malacca in 1413. The fleet had experienced a storm and the crews were fasting for many days. The Malay Islanders brought swiftlets' nests to the crew, and they were fresh and strong. When Zheng He returned, he brought the birds' nests to the Emperor Yongle in Ming Dynasty. Mandelslo recorded around 319 years ago that the birds' nests on Malaysia beach was highly admired by the Chinese, and they were collected for trade. Spenser St. John, Rajah James Brooke's secretary, recorded in 1851 that for the Kayan community, the possession of birds' nests was valuable. The Penan ownership of Niah caves in Batu Niah, Sarawak is as a result of the artifacts found in the cave, which were the Penans' tools. Therefore, most bird's-nest caves belong to them as well. Similar to the creation myth of Idahan in Lahad

Datu, Sabah, they are descendants of Besai, and Apoi who were the ancestor bird's-nest caves discovery, and so the Idahan are the rightful heir of the caves for a long time, perhaps since the early 15th century.

These reflect Malaysian's bird's-nest business and business management, and the caves used to belong to the noble-class groups, sultans, or kings. It was before local governments had taken control after Malayan Independence in 1957, and allowed people and private businesses to compete in auction for bird's-nest concessions.

However, ethnic groups in Malaysia have created and reproduced the Chinese myth that birds' nests are a high-value specialty food.

The myth appears in social relations of people who share the same perception, and bird's-nest consumption is now a symbol of valuable and specialty food in the society.[84] These beliefs have strongly supported the bird's-nest industry.

Even though there is no clear detail about the nature of the bird's-nest business during the feudal era, there are resources of Gomantong Cave, Sabah was the property of Sultan of Sulu.[85] The bird's-nest business system continues in such a way. Even when the British ruled, it still maintained the rights of ethnic groups in collecting and accessing the resources. Before the local governments took over in 1957 and operated by opening for private business to compete in auction for concession until the present day.

Despite the popularity of ready-made birds' nest consumption in various forms, as a convenience of modern society, most people still prefer selling raw birds' nests in Malaysia.

5.2 Business of Birds' Nests in Food Sovereignty Time: Postmodern Society

During the period of 1971–90, the Malaysian government implemented the New Economic Policy (NEP), with "Wawasan 2020" or "Vision 2020" policy since February 1991[86] in order to develop Malaysia into an industrial country and a fully developed country by 2020, and adjust the social system to keep up with fast changes in global trade. The nature of the bird's-nest business-management system has changed accordingly. Besides, each state oversees its own natural bird's-nest resource and related businesses; from the 1990s onward, various ethnic groups in Malaysia have been active in bird's-nest building-business and setting up private companies. Private companies provide training courses for cleaning the birds' nests, such as Alga Prima Sdn. Bhd company in Kulim, Kedah, or AG Walit Training Center Company in Alor Gajah, Melaka; a one-stop service business for birds' houses such as Jonker birdhouse store; a hotel cum selling raw and ready-to-drink birds' nests shop such as Joon Onn Holdings Sdn. Bhd. company in Melaka Chinatown, which also provides bird's-nest cleaning services, restaurants, and learning resources in Ornithology of the Swiftlet. There are bird's-nest cave models for anyone interested. Nonetheless, since 1970, bird's-nest prices have always been on the rise. By the late 1980s, the prices in Malaysia had increased dramatically.[87] In 1975, the bird's-nest prices were USD 10 per kilogram, and continuously rising to USD 400 in 1995, and USD 1,600 (RM 5,600) in 2002[88] After the 1990s, as a result of high demand, the prices for unclean white bird's nests (90–120 nests) in 2006 were RM 4,500–6,000 per kg., while the clean white bird's nests were RM 15,000–25,000 per kg. in Hong Kong and China.[89] In 2008, one kilogram of unclean birds' nests were RM 4,000–6,000, and the clean ones were sold at RM 5,000–7,000 per kg.[90] In 2009, the prices went up to USD 2,700 (RM 9,450) per kg.[91] In 2011, the prices had gone up to USD 3,000 per kilogram.[92] This was before the impact from the seizure of Malaysian fake red birds' nests exports by the Zhejiang Industrial and Trade Department, China on 26 July, 2011.[93] The Chinese government stopped all imported birds' nests from Malaysia, resulting in the prices of unclean grade A birds' nest went down to only 1,500 from 4,000 (RM 4,000 per kg.)[94]

Size of Malaysia Bird's-Nest Business

Currently, swiftlets' habitats, both in nature and birds' buildings in Malaysia are scattered in each of the country's 13 states. However, for ethnic groups in Malaysia, who are producers of birds' nests, eating the birds' nests is not popular. It is Hong Kong as a middle market, and the Chinese who are the main consumers. Chinese is therefore the main language in the business; the bird's-nest exporters from Malaysia to China and Hong Kong are mostly Chinese.

There are great numbers of birds' houses that are adapted from shophouses, by using the ground floor as a store or storage, and the upper floor as the birds' house, and it is difficult to determine an official number. It is estimated that in 2012 in Malaysia there were about 50,000–63,000 bird buildings around the country.[95] If an average price of a bird building is RM 500,000, the birds' building would be worth up to RM 31,500,000,000. Campaign signs of the bird's-nest business groups, who had gathered to pressure the Malaysian government to negotiate with China on cancellation of imports in July 2012, revealed that at least 3,000,000 people were involved in the bird's-nest business in Malaysia.

Major companies in bird building production, construction materials and equipment manufacturers, raw & ready-to-drink birds' nest trading, and exports in Malaysia include Keko Manufacturing (M), Sdn. Bhd. in Pulau Pinang, Bio Research Center (M) Sdn. Bhd. in Perak; Nan Yang Nest Corporation Sdn. Bhd. in Puchong City.

In Klang there are: CCG Bird Nest Sdn. Bhd., Yenzheka birdhouse Design Specialist Yenzheka Technology Sdn. Bhd., Bumi Suria Development Sdn. Bhd., Dama Bird's Nest International Sdn. Bhd., Batu Caves City, Universal Cargo Group Sdn. Bhd., in Melaka, and Petaling Jaya, Sun Shine Region Sdn. Bhd. Shah Alam, Selangor; Sisiqing Healthcare Sdn. Bhd., Kulai City, Zakir Sdn. Bhd., Gelang Patah City, Chang Chung Chan Enterprises (M) Sdn. Bhd., Senai City, Jin Yan Wo Resources Development Sdn. Bhd., Kulai City, Sen Yang Enterprise Sdn. Bhd., Segamat City, Josing Enterprise Sdn. Bhd., Kulai City, and Ecolite Biotech Manufacturing Sdn. Bhd., Batu Pahat City.

Longevity Wellness Industries Sdn. Bhd. Johor Bahru, Diamond Brand Birds Nest, Skudai, Eseven Resources Sdn. Bhd., Johor Bahru City, White Bird Nest Enterprise, Skudai City, JB Bird Nest Resources Sdn. Bhd. Johor Bahru City, Nest Tech System Sdn Bhd. Johor Bahru City in Johor (Johor); Ag Walit Training Center (AWTC) Alor Gajah in Melaka; Nespure Birdnest Sdn. Bhd. Kota Bharu in Kelantan; AMG Advance ASSET (M) Sdn. Bhd. Sandakan in Sabah, and Dragon Brand Birdnest (Malaysia) Sdn. Bhd., Kuching in Sarawak.

Chapter 3

The only exporters of Malaysian birds' nest to China, announced by the Malaysian Division of Quality and Food Safety, Ministry of Public Health (Bahagian Keselamatan dan Kualiti Makanan, Kementerian Kesihatan Malaysia) in June 2012 are as follows:

Ecolite Biotech Manufacturing Sdn. Bhd., in Batu Pahat, White Bird Nest Enterprise in Skudai, Birds Nest Forest in Batu Pahat, Nest World Sdn. Bhd. in Kota Tinggi, Amity AKF Enterprise Sdn. Bhd. in Muar, Happy Health (M) Sdn. Bhd. in Batu Pahat (Johor); Aeries Pure Bird Nest (M) Sdn. Bhd. in Seremban (Negeri Sembilan); LP Birdnest Advantage Sdn. Bhd., Hutan Melintang, Moh Kee Birdnest Trading in Setiawan (Perak); Alga Prima Sdn. Bhd. in Kulim, SSCM Northen Sdn. Bhd. in Sungai Petani, Elixir World Sdn. Bhd., Jitra (Kedah); Evernest industries Sdn. Bhd. in Pulau Pinang, Fuciphagus Agritech Sdn. Bhd., Pulau Pinang, Glitter Summer Sdn. Bhd. in Butterworth, Kedai Ubat Sao Lim, Bukit Mertajam, Kelly Birdnests Sdn. Bhd. Prai Pulau Pinang, Swallow Palace Sdn. Bhd. in Penang, Agrowbionest Sdn. Bhd. in Butterworth (Penang); Yen Pao Lai (M) Sdn. Bhd. in Kuantan (Pahang); Tean Siong Trading in Kota Bharu, Tawang Nest & Agro Industry in Kota Bharu, Nespure Holdings Sdn. Bhd. in Kota Bharu (Kelantan); Herculean Food Industries Sdn. Bhd. in Ayer Keroh, Multiform Food Supply Co. Sdn. Bhd. in Melaka, Besfomec Industries Sdn. Bhd. in Dareah Alor Gajah (Melaka); Sunshine Region Sdn. Bhd. in Petaling Jaya, Steady Farm Sdn. Bhd. in Kuala Selangor, Mei Wen Birdnest Trading, Puchong, PT Swift Marketing Sdn. Bhd. in Puchong, Yan Fook Kee Enterprise, Seri Kembangan, Sai Kim Enterprise Sdn. Bhd., Genius Revolution Sdn. Bhd. in Batu Caves (Selangor); Wing Shen Food Industries Sdn. Bhd., Chang Fung Enterprise Company, Orient Union Bird Nest Sdn. Bhd., in Kuching, Seng Kee Food Product, Kuching, Swallow House Enterprise, Kuching, and Jia Cheng Trading in Bau (Sarawak).[96]

It is estimated that in 2010, Malaysia produced around 275 tons of birds' nests, worth RM 1.5 billion or USD 470 million. In addition, the government had a vision to increase the production to 500 tons by 2020. In October 2011, the birds' nest price was RM 4,000 per kg., four times higher than 20 years ago.[97] 90 percent of the nests were exported to China,[98] and only these exports alone is worth around RM 5 billion per year.[99] The ready-to-drink bird's-nest product exports are expected to increase

Ethnic Groups and Bird's-Nest Resources in Malaysia

from RM 1.7 billion in 2010 to RM 5.2 billion in 2020.[100] In 2011, it was determined that Malaysia exported around 600 tons of birds' nests per year.[101] If an average price of birds' nests is USD 1,500 per kg., this means that the country benefited from exports of around USD 900,000,000 per year.

Table 3.3: Shows the value of Malaysia bird's-nest agriculture and business from 2010–2020

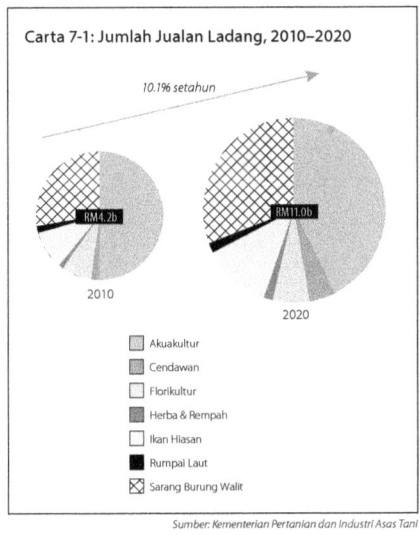

Table 3.4–3.5: Show the target value of Malaysia bird's-nest agriculture and business from 2010–2020

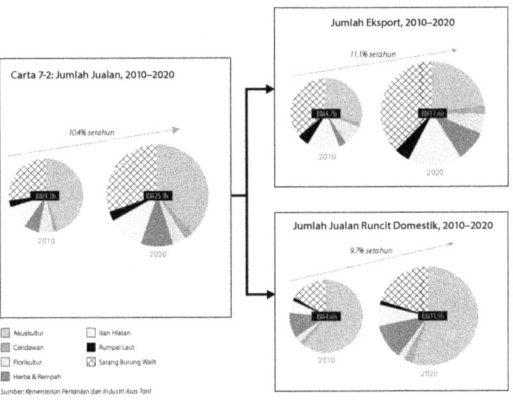
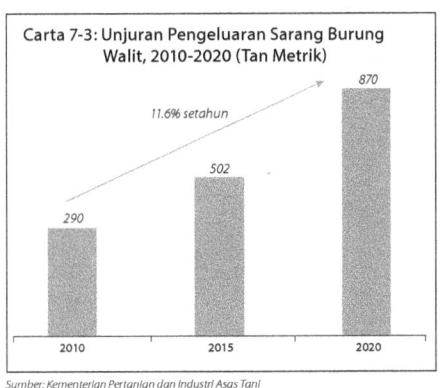

139

Type and Price of Birds' Nests in Malaysia

Birds' Nests Market Malaysia bird's-nest business market has divided the birds' nest by various criteria as follows:

1. Swiftlets' nest divided by color: there are normally 4–5 groups such as black (*sarang burung berwarna hitam*), price of RM 1,500 per kg., white (*berwarna putih*) price of RM 3,000 per kg., yellow (*kuning*), price of RM 25,000 per kg., and red (*merah*) price of RM 45,000 per kg.[102]

Table 3.6: Shows Malaysian bird's-nest prices in 1975–2012[103]

Year	Bird's-nest type	Price RM per kg.
1975	X	3 5
1980	X	320.50
1990	X	900
1994	X	6,454
1995	Black bird's nest	893.75
1995	White bird's nest	1,400–4,062.50
2001	X	4,566
2002	White bird's nest	5,600
2005	White bird's nest	4,000
2006	Clean white bird's nest (90–120 nests per kg.)	4,500–6,000
2008	White bird's nest (not clean)	4,000–6,000
2008	Clean the white bird's nest	5,000–7,000
2009	White bird's nest	4,000–16,000
2010	Black bird's Nest	1,500
2010	White bird's nest	3,000–4,000
2011	White bird's nest (not clean)	3,000–75,000
2011	Clean the white bird's nest	10,000–18,000
2012	White bird's nest (not clean)	4,000
2012	Clean white bird's nest	9,000

Table 3.7: Shows Malaysian bird's-nest prices according to colors in 2010

Bird's nest Color	Price RM per kg.
Black (sarang burung hitam)	1,500
White (sarang burung putih)	3,000
Yellow (sarang burung kuning)	25,000
Red (sarang burung merah)	45,000

2. Clean Birds' Nests from Birds' Houses or Buildings, in 2009, are divided into 5 groups as follows:

1. Birds' Nest Grade AAA, height of 38 mm++, price per kg. RM 16,000
2. Birds' Nest Grade AA, height of 32–37 mm, price per kg. RM 15,000
3. Birds' Nest Grade A, round-shape 135 degrees, price per kg. RM 14,000
4. Birds' Nest Grade B, 90 degrees, price per kg. RM 4,000–8,000
5. Birds' Nest Grade C, bits and strings, price per kg. RM 4,000–8,000[104]

Table 3.8: Shows prices and grades of clean birds' nests from Malaysian birdhouses in 2009

Type/Size	Height	Grade	Price RM per kg.
Complete nest	38 mm++	AAA	16,000
Complete nest	32–37 mm	AA	15,000
Round nest, 135 degrees		A	14,000
90 degree nest bits		B	
Birds' nest string		C	4,000–8,000[105]

Source: Persatuan Pengusaha Industri Sarang Burung Kulai Johor Baru, *China – Iskandar Malaysia & Bird Nest Business opportunity 2009*

3. Black Swiftlets' nest is divided into 3 groups according to quality and color:

According to an Iban birds' nest seller, a former Iban bird's-nest collector in Batu Niah, Sarawak in 2010, the birds' nest selling prices depended on grades or quality of the nest; fine quality of birds' nest had selling prices between RM 800–1,300 per kg. There are three different grades of black bird's nest:

Grade A, approximately 30 nests per kg. with price of RM 1,200–1,300

Grade B, 30 nests per kg., with price of RM 700–900

Grade C, 50–60 nests per kg., with price of RM 300–500

Good quality birds' nests, with price of RM 120 per gram, and RM 1,500 per kg.[106]

According to data from a Chinese bird's-nest seller, the best birds' nests are those which the birds build from December to February. Selling prices for the birds' nest middleman are RM 1,200–1,300 per kg., and normally sell at RM 1,500 to big traders in Miri Town. The lower quality birds' nests are collected in August-October, due to the time when the birds' shedding and so there are more feathers mixed in the nests, and less saliva. The selling prices in front of the cave are RM 500–700, and market price of RM 800. For clean red birds' nests are selling at RM 280 per tahil or RM 7,280 per kg. Clean white bird's-nests are 3 RM 50 per tahil or RM 9,100 per kg.[107]

Table 3.9: Shows prices of black bird's nests in Sarawak in 2010

Quality	Nest Amount per kg.	Price RM per kg.
Grade A	30 nests	1,200–1,500
Grade B	30 nests	700–900
Grade C	50–60 nests	300–500[108]

Note:
Grade A birds' nests are nests that the swiftlets build from December to February, mostly containing bird saliva, mixed with little plumage.
Grade B birds' nests are nests of the same size as Grade A birds' nests, but mostly contains plumage, and are incomplete.
Grade C birds' nests are nests that the swiftlets build from August to October, during the period when birds are fledgling birds, and mostly contain plumage, and little saliva.

Incentive and Welfare System for Nests Collectors

The welfare, compensation, and life of people in the bird's-nest Business, whether they are workers, concession holders, collectors, birdhouse-owners, traders, industrial workers in bird's-nest product manufacturers, or those with more authority, are working in the world of confidentiality.

The following 'true stories from different angles,' can probably present, 'different aspects,' of what exists in the corporate world of Malaysian birds' nests business.

Here Batu Niah, Sarawak!

Sunni Mahli, a 40-year-old male came in his uniform as staff of Batu Niah National Park, Sarawak. On the evening of November 10, 2008, bunches of bats started to fly out, and the swiftlets were coming home to the Niah Cave, where we sat, he started telling a story.

> "… Here at this cave, in Batu Niah National Park, there is only the Penan ethnic group who own the cave. The artifacts found here were the Penans' tools, so the cave belongs to them. There used to be 100 licensees of the cave in the past, now there are 40–50 people left. They have to register and pay a yearly fee to officials from the Sarawak Forestry Department.
>
> Each year, the National Park allows us to collect birds' nests for eight months, from September to March of the following year. They are only concerned about the baby birds, and there is a four-month break in which nest collection is prohibited. Each collector, after gathering, must bring all birds' nests to be counted and recorded at the National Park office.
>
> In the past, before collecting birds' nests, the collectors would make a ritual in line with their belief in animism. Later, they all stopped after they became Muslims. The Penan were last seen practicing the ritual in 1970, and 1996 for the Iban. Birds'-nests collectors age ranges from teenagers to over 40 years old. The families train their children from a young age ….."[109]

At 2.30 PM on November 11, 2008, we met Nuar Bin Haji Jaya, a 40 year-old-Penan man, Licensee of Lubang Perintah cave, in Niah National Park came with Haidar Bin Ali, an officer of the Conservation Executive Niah National Park Sarawak Forestry Corporation Malaysia, a 40-year-old man in his uniform. Haidar Bin Ali, walking with authority, was our Malay-English interpreter for Nuar Bin Haji Jaya at a noisy cafeteria at the National Park.

"... We started collecting birds' nests here in 1985. My great grandfather was the licensee and passed down the rights to my father. We are the fifth generation. Normally, the rights and profits are managed within the family fairly. My father, who is a leader, gets the most share. Women get their share too. There were around 1,000 Penan bird's-nest collectors at this cave in 1978. Later on, there were more than 100 licensees in the family.

The Iban's relation with the birds' nests is that they were the first group who stole the birds' nests. The bird's-nest prices went really low in 1988, and the Penans were not interested in collecting any. However, the prices went up quickly in the late 1980s, so the Ibans started to steal them. Normally, the Penans work in agriculture. They started to have conflicts within the group after the bird's-nest prices went up; people without any license started to steal. Selling birds' nests is a main income in families. We sell to Chinese friends in Batu Niah. I cannot say how much each family makes each year though. (laughed).

I do not know about the international pricing, but I think our current selling prices are fair. Sometimes, there is an argument with customers in negotiating prices. The prices depend on the quality. These days, a kilogram of raw birds' nests cost no more than RM 2,000. We share work in collecting birds' nests, including guarding the cave and gathering the birds' nests. There are also people who do both jobs.

In caring for and conservation of swiftlets, we try to have a close range of bird's-nest caves to increase the amount of birds, and comply with the laws of the national park. They guarantee the rights of the Penan community in collecting birds' nests, only prohibiting collecting from April to August. If anyone breaks the rules, there would be a penalty by cancelling the bird's-nest cave-ownership, and rights to collect birds' nests. (*lesen untuk memungut sarang burung*). There is no killing among the Penan ethnic groups resulted from birds' nest robbery. The Penans do not have conflicts with park officials because they follow the rules of the park. The park collects income from the cave licensees. A license fee is RM 100 per year. There are about 110 people who have rights to register for the license. There is no tax collected from the bird's-nest collectors, only from the licensees; I do not know how the Park manages or uses the money. The Ibans are only laboring in bird's-nest collection. In the past, they had conflicts about collecting but not anymore. When they arrived, they did not have any license so they were stealing, and later they worked for the Penans.

Women can enter the cave but men are the ones who collect the birds' nests. Women used to help pick up the nest on the cave ground, but now men do everything. Women are here to cook and clean the birds' nests.

Managing the cave is challenging and makes a great income. In the family, there is no problem being the manager of the cave. Most families will have a few leaders, and the clan will follow the leaders. In the past, I used to collect birds' nests in other places such as Kuching, Tatau, Bintutu and on the mountain. I make around RM 3,000 each time, depending on the location and time.

The rights system in Kuching is the same as here. The owner of the bird's-nest cave is the one with the license. They sell the rights to Chinese people (Baba). Then the Chinese hire workers to collect the birds' nests. Now some Penans in the village also collect the nests in other places, such as in Tatau working for the Chinese. The Chinese are the only ones setting the prices. During the 1980s, the largest bird's-nest business was here in Niah as we had most black bird's nests. They reduced in number as a result of too much collecting. Now, birds' nests collected are shipped to sell in the big cities like Batu Niah, Miri, Kuching and Bintulu, to the Chinese, who are major consumers...."[110]

Michael Bueng, a 64-year-old bird's-nest merchant, and former collector from the Iban community. He is a plump man who wears glasses, and only white cotton pants. He sat on a mat smoking waiting to meet with us, in a spacious room, on August 13, 2010. After 3 PM, the man, who is the owner of a homestay, Oil Palm plantation, and bird's-nest business, told us his story.

Chapter 3

"… I am an Iban Tulin, true Iban. We used to be called, 'Ibandayak'. I came from Du Labok Antu-Kuching, Kalimantan to be worker to overthrow the timber here. I met and married Pinak, the granddaughter of Ugop, Kampung Sungai Tangap, in Batu Niah, Miri. It used to be called Kampung Chong like Mr. Chang, who was a chief teacher. This village was founded in 1945. 65 years ago, these houses have changed into this. In each row, there is a house with 25 rooms, and one family lived in a room. 15 years ago, people became Christians, but before that they believed in Animism, worshiping the Jakuibantara, the most important Iban ancestral ghost. The reason that I became a bird's-nest collector in Niah cave was because an invitation from a Malay man around 25 years ago. He is a kind and honest Muslim person whom I have been working with until today. In the old days, here many owners were Penans, but not anymore. When a Penan who was the cave-owner died, the Malay and the Iban came to take over the ownership, not buying.

At present, the government must officially announce when it is the first day of a bird's-nest collection, and the last. The government registers all names of the licensees, and the head of the National Park will keep them. The licensee must pay 100 ringgit per year for his license. This bird's-nest cave rights are bequeathed to the son, not the daughter since this person must find and recruit bird's-nest collectors, and the job is better for men to do than women.

In the past, before collecting the birds' nests, the Penans would have a ritual to sacrifice food and things the ghosts favor in front of the cave. Everyone involved was required to attend this sacrificial ceremony.

The claim that the Ibans did not own any bird's-nest caves in the past is true. The Penan is the original ethnic group that lived here, whereas the Iban only migrated here in 1945. Currently, most of the cave-owners are Malay. They are good at climbing to gather birds' nests whereas the Ibans are not as brave. At present, there are about 30 licensees who are Iban compared to the past of around 100 licensees. This is due to the reduced numbers of birds' nests. It is presumably because of five to six months of drought, and birds may have died or moved elsewhere. Normally, black bird's-nests are found in this area, but in January to February, the birds' nests are very white. The same birds build white nests (with some feathers mixed, but mostly saliva). But in August, the nests are black because there is a lot of feathers mixed in the nests. We used to collect hundreds of kilograms of birds' nests in the past, but currently only 10–15 kg. Now, once you finish collecting, you must wait for one month to give time for the birds to build their nests before collecting again. When the authorities announce the closure of the caves, and you still go to collect the birds' nests, you can be charged and imprisoned from two weeks up to three months.

I sell birds' nests to the Chinese who also sell them outside. When I was young, I used to travel far to sell it myself. Now, there are middle men who come to buy birds' nests in Batu Niah and Miri. I had good selling prices in Kuching. There are now many Chinese who open big bird's-nest stores. They used to live here, but now those who are rich have moved to Miri.

Any profits from selling the birds' nests are shared fairly among the collectors. For example, if five birds' nests collectors made RM 1,000, they will get 200 each, and we pay for food and boats as well. If there is no collecting job here, the collectors can go work elsewhere. The Chinese know the collectors well, whether they work well or not. I used to be guarding the cave, now I am too old and my children do that instead.

There are about 10 Penan licensees, mostly they are Malay. The Malay are the Islamic Penans. 40 years ago, there were some conflicts between the Penans and Ibans on boundaries. But after the government came to manage the caves, the problem was solved. When they had conflicts, they would go back to the masters in their ethnic groups, then it was the masters' job to settle it down.

Government officials manage and supervise the collecting of swiftlet nests. It is prohibited for any licensee to sell the rights of the cave, as the registration certificates are kept to prevent the sale of the bird's-nest cave. When there is any selling of birds' nest such as in Miri, the seller must bring the registration certificate to show as well. Purchasing without any certificate is impossible. The authority can cancel the rights, and they will automatically become the government's property. However, with no official termination of rights, the owner still has the right to gather birds' nests in the cave. When it becomes government property, the department of forestry will recruit their own collectors.

I have no comment for any improvement in the bird's-nest collection process. It is the state's responsibility. I am satisfied to keep having a license, and continue to make money.

I think that the birds have decreased greatly compared to when I was a boy. There were more birds' nests ….[111]

After paying for his time, and taking pictures of the birds' nests, and his id card, Michael Bueng gave us a couple of birds' nests before saying good-bye.

Johnson Chew Hui Chiang, a 50-year-old Chinese man is both a bird's-nest merchant and the licensee of Niah bird's-nest cave. He met us at his shop in the national park around 8 PM of August 13, 2010. He seemed friendly and relaxed, as he sat with us at a dining table, and told a story.

"… My father and I were born here in Kumpung Niah but I believe that my great grandmother was born in China and died 100 years ago. My great grandfather and great grandmother lived here and used to trade birds' nests for things with the locals, the Lubang. We inherited the bird's-nest caves from our ancestors, and I have a license to collect edible birds' nests of 15 lubang or small caves and license to sell edible birds' nests as well.

I am the 6th from a total of 13 children; 11 men and two women. My oldest brother has moved to Canada and become a citizen. She only comes back once every five years. She is over 60 years old. I inherited the bird's-nest cave because I showed more interest than my siblings. I always followed my parents to the caves since I was 12. We collected birds' nests twice a year. My siblings do not know much about the cave so I inherited the cave; they did not have any questions.

There used to be a lot more birds' nests when I was 12, compared to these days. Not many people tried to find or collect the nests before, so there were plenty of birds' nests. Now, there are less. Maybe it is because people have cut down so many big trees for oil palm plantation. The plantation requires burning grasses, and smoke can disturb the swiftlets. They do not like smoke at all so they have left. It is the cause for decreased numbers of swiftlets. Fire from farms also destroys their food sources.

Problems in the bird's-nest business come from stealing too. A kilogram of birds' nests is around RM 1,000. In the past, it was RM 18 to hire one robber. It did not take long to steal birds' nests in different caves. At present, these thefts are by Indonesians who come by car. Some of them marry local women, and then turn into thieves, as well as the Iban and Malay. Even though he did not seem afraid, he asked us, "Please keep this confidential because I don't want to invite any troubles." He said, "None of the Chinese are thieves. The Chinese own big bird's-nest businesses, and the smaller ones belong to the Malay, Chinese, and Iban. There are less than 10 Chinese with licensees, but around 100 Penans.

I trust and hire the Malay and Iban ethnics to collect the birds' nests. I have been working with them for a long time. The wages depend on how they work. I need three collectors which if I can get RM 1,000 per kilogram, it will be divided by three. The licensee gets one, and the rest will go the collectors. This will make them stay with me long. The rest of nests belong to the licensee. If I can sell it for 500 then 120 will go to the collectors. There are not as many birds' nests so I use only one collector that I trust the most. I have 10 guards for 15 caves just to look out for any theft.

There are things people do not know about how to increase the of birds. While there is a four-month break for the birds to build nests, there are selfish people who sneak in and steal the nests when they actually build nests to lay eggs. The nest-stealing stops the birds from breeding. Also, deforestation destroys food sources for these birds. People are not aware of this. It is like if a hen lays an egg, and we eat it, then how can we have more chicks from that. Even that, there are still more than 1,000 kilograms of birds' nests in this one cave. Our government is trying to solve this problem."

Siri Bin Neng Bua, a 55-year-old Malaysian-Thai male interpreter, told us that Johnson Chew implied that there are corrupt government officials that secretly sell birds' nests. They are bribed to open some room for the robbers during the cave closure period. These officials are usually the ones with low positions and incomes.

"… In the past, there were those who fell to their death while gathering the birds' nests. It was a long time ago in such a hurry. Most of them were thieves," said Johnson Chew.

Siri Bin Neng Bua, called the officials who were bribed to open rooms for the robbers, "Corrupted! Corrupted! Corrupted!"

"I sell birds' nests to the Chinese businessman in Miri, and he sells them in Kuching. This man goes to Sabah to buy birds' nests," said Johnson Chew.

"I don't know how far these birds' nests go. The cleaned birds' nests are in strings and called Isy' or tissues. After they are cleaned, they will be put in A-Chuon (mould), then packed. Most cleaning jobs are held by Chinese and Iban women. In Niah, there are companies that produce ready-to-eat birds' nest, and that clean birds' nests. There are three or four companies that buy birds' nests. I only know that the Yong Tai company buys only ready-to-eat which are the cleaned birds' nests …."[112]

After we paid Johnson Chew for his time, and asked him to sign his name and id, we went back to our residence in the national park.

Table 3.10: Shows the amount of black-nest swiftlets in the Niah National Park, Sarawak, Malaysia in 1935–2002

Year	Amount of Black bird's-nests	Percentage reduced
1935	1,700,000	-
1958	1,500,000	12 percent
1962	1,500,000	12 percent
1974	1,300,000	25 percent
1987	450,000–610,000	64–73 percent
1989	290,000–295,000	83 percent
1990	150,000–298,000	83–91 percent
1996	200,000	88 percent
2002	65,000	96 percent

After we left, Siri told us that Johnson Chew said to him that the Iban do not have any license for collecting any birds' nests in Niah cave, not even for a single hole (*lubang*) of birds' nests. And how can they collect the birds' nests, unless they collaborate with the Chinese? The Chinese do not collect any birds' nests themselves, but would hire the Ibans to do so. The Ibans can steal the birds' nests from other people's caves. On the contrary, others do not have any chance to steal from them because they do not have any license! We both laughed at this fact together.

Here Lahad Datu Sabah!

Mohamed Yusoff Ismail, a 50-year-old professor and researcher in Social Anthropology, Faculty of Applied Social Sciences, Open University Malaysia, is the researcher of "The Sustainable Management of Birds' Nest Resource of the Idahan Ethnics in Sabah." He came down from an elegant stage in the UN conference in Bangkok at around 1 PM., October 29, 2007, and kindly talked to us about his research.

> "... Idahan is a local ethnic group in Sabah. They are a minority of Muslims, and have a closed social system. They stand out because they are involved with the economy of birds' nests. The Idahan collect birds' nests in many limestone caves in Lahad Datu area, which is on the east coast of Borneo. Since the birds' nests have been a source of income for a long time, the rotation system is used in order to prevent a monopoly of the resource. The rights in collecting birds' nests are shared and rotated within the same clan. The bird's-nest caves are supervised and managed by the whole community, not only one person.
>
> During the British colonial period, the Lahad Datu District Office registered people who claimed to have the rights to collect birds' nests. The Ministry of Forestry took care of the collection of birds' nests and was responsible for collecting bird's-nest taxes.
>
> The rights to collect birds' nests were shared among those who descended from "the discovers" or from the ancestors who found the source of the birds' nests. The number of family lines, and the number of members in each one, determines which clans are entitled to collect the birds' nests in each round. In cases where there are many members

in one clan, each member will receive a small share of income from the birds' nests. Sometimes one gets only RM 3–4.

The "Committee for Birds'-Nest Inheritance" was founded to take care of the overall benefits of the Idahans, in matters relating to management, ecology and collection schedules.

Each bird's-nest collector makes around RM 30–50 per day, depending on the difficulty of the collection. The Idahan community has rules related to these traditions that go back to the ancestral period. They are based on prioritizing the ecology of swiftlets and their nests. Even though the demand for birds' nests is growing rapidly, the Idahan will not collect birds' nests during the breeding season. The current economy cannot destroy their conservation approach. The Idahans organize their social systems on the foundation of a kinship social structure. The rotation of bird's-nest collection is an important mechanism for the swiftlets' survival, since the caves are a shared treasure among everyone in the community. The elders in the village determine who will get to collect the birds' nests. Their belief, that the cave is the home of their ancestor spirits, also serves to reduce disturbances during the birds' breeding season. The Idahan' ways of managing natural resources have been related to the economic systems for generations ..."[113]

Here Semenanjung Malaysia

Reviews of books, newspapers, research report, including online articles show that:

"... since the beginning of the 1940s–1950s, white-nest swiftlets began to build natural nests on the top floor of shophouses on the Malaysian Peninsula. There have been various business management systems. The bird's-nest merchants in peninsular Malaysia have established a Swiftlets' Nest Merchant Organization in order to assist in negotiations with government agencies and ministries, with objectives as follows:

(1) To gather bird's-nest merchants from every state in Malaysia with the common objective to produce quality birds' nests and the proper development of the bird's-nest business,

(2) To handle and interact with government policies relating to the members' bird's-nest businesses,

(3) To enhance relationships and mediate between members in issues related to the bird's-nest business, and

(4) To promote and execute studies and activities among disadvantaged members in the industry, community, and country. Modern bird farms are widely popular in peninsular Malaysia and spreading to Sabah and Sarawak.

There are many swiftlet houses that have been illegally adapted from shophouses. The use of bird calls to attract the swiftlets has led to complaints from the public. At the beginning, the local government or council had no other solution besides closing down the shophouses that were illegally modified. This has led to the gathering of business owners and operators as a group to protect their interests. There have been negotiations between the government and the business owners many times. The strictness in granting permission to do bird farming varies on the principles and rules of the council in each locality. The Malaysian government has shown that the law is stricter in Sabah than it is in peninsular Malaysia. Bird-farming businesses are encouraged in rural and agricultural areas..."[114]

The government requires bird building-owners to register and pay taxes. These customs vary. For example, the business license fee in Ipoh (Perak) is RM 120 yearly, and in Rompin, and Pahang, RM 1,200[115] In Kangar, in Perlis, the fee for the industry is RM 200 yearly.[116]

The Chinese Zhejiang government in the past examined and seized fake birds' nests imported from Malaysia. The nitrite in the birds' nests was higher than the standard on 26 July 2011, causing the Chinese government to suspend all imports of Edible Bird Nest-EBN from Malaysia. The Chinese authorities became much stricter with product inspection, announcing new standards for the birds' nest producers to proceed through the government agencies. All the bird's-nest businessmen, bird building owners, and companies that export birds' nests to China are required by law to register and rec*eive the Jabatan Perkhidmatan Veterinar* Certificate (JPV) from the Department of Veterinary Services (DVS).

They must have a certificate of Radio Frequency Identification (RFID) registered with the Malaysian Communications and Multimedia Commission (MCMC) to identify the source of the birds' nests to prevent fake birds' nests. They must have a license issued by the *Tanda Kesihatan Veterinar* – VHM from the Ministry of Public Health. Entrepreneurs must be certified with food safety under the Food Acts (*Akta Makanan*),[117] and with Radio Frequency Identification (RFID) from the Malaysian Communications and Multimedia Commission (MCMC) certified by Health Ministry.[118]

Companies with the Veterinary Health Mark-VHM will be permitted to export according to the Food Safety Standards of Malaysian Health Ministry, as all exported products are certified by DVS.[119] All certified companies will have 'the 1 Malaysia Best' logo as guarantees for export to China.[120] This standard requires that the nitrite level in "cleaned birds' nests must not exceed 30 parts per million (PPM),[121] and the "raw birds' nests which haven't been cleaned" nitrite level must not exceed 200 PPM.[122]

As for tourists, the Malaysian government allows each one to bring home a maximum of 1 kilogram of birds' nests.[123] Tourists who buy birds' nests from legitimate retailers cannot travel with them. They will be confiscated at the airport. In practice, they must request permission from the Department of Wildlife and National Parks of Peninsular Malaysia which takes four days, and pay a fee of RM 200 and export duty RM 100 per kg.[124] They have strict law enforcement, and even posted signage at the airport warning tourists not to smuggle birds' nests out of the country. In Malaysia, besides the birds' nest trading companies that sell in showrooms across the country, they also have developed another channel of marketing, direct sales through websites. This channel classifies purchasing power and implies the status of the customers, middle, upper class.

Keko Manufacturing (M), Sdn. Bhd., Ecolite Biotech Manufacturing Sdn. Bhd., and the Alga Prima Sdn. Bhd. in Shah Alam, Selangor produce various kinds of birds-nest products. The last one has branches in Kulim, Kedah, and in Kuantan, Pahang, and can produce 50,000 ready-to-drink bird's-nest bottles monthly.[125] Ecolite Biotech Manufacturing Sdn. Bhd. produces ready-to-drink birds' nest with rock sugar in (3 x 70 grams) boxes, with a selling price of RM 91, without rock sugar (30 g) bottle, RM 38 per bottle, and the 230 ml sells for RM 368.

Birds' nests in Malaysia cannot be collected throughout the year, but it is rather a seasonal job. During the four months that the caves are closed, bird's-nest collectors work on oil palm plantations,[126] run their own plantations or workers, and work as rice field laborers, among other jobs[127] that are not related to the bird's-nest industry.[128]

Exporting Market

The export market is most important in Malaysia. The Chinese buy local birds' nests, and export them to markets in China, Singapore, Negara Brunei Darussalam, Dubai,[129] Taiwan, Hong Kong,[130] India, Middle East,[131] Europe, USA, and Canada.[132]

Nest-Trade Relationships with the Birds' Nests as a Link for Ethnic Relations

Nest-Trade Relationships with Swiftlet's Nest as a Link for an Ethnic Group

Swiftlet nests have unique characteristics. They are both a natural and culturally important food; a form of medicine and health food; a commodity and supply for the industry; and a gift and symbolic food for the rich. Moreover, edible birds' nest products are also complex, contradictory, and fluid social property. They are both state and private property regimes as common and 'communal property' regimes, and Res nullius regimes and Open access regimes.[133] Swiftlets are state property, required by law to be protected similar to other state properties. Yet, they become private property when they enter private dwellings to live. Similarly, they are open access as they choose where to nest beyond human's absolute control. Swiftlets also fall into the category of 'communal property' as their food resources are within the human community.

In Malaysia, even though the Malay ethnic group is the 'dominant ethnicity,' the access and use of bird's-nest resources is not a monopoly. On the contrary, there are different ethnic groups that can access and use the resources, such as Idahan, Penan, Iban, Chinese, Malay, Bidayuh, Kayan or Kenyah. Each group has absolute authority in managing, accessing, and using bird's-nest resources as a licensee of the bird's-nest caves, a researcher, bird's-nest collectors, guards, and workers in various birds' nest industries.

In each of the same ethnic groups, there is a power relationship between access and use of resources that represent inequalities and differences, either 'including' in the center of power or 'excluding.' The 'inclusive' relationship examples are: the Sabah Government granted the concessions to collect birds' nests to only five to seven companies;[134] the inherited rights of birds' cave within the same Idahan clans in Sabah; the same practice also done within the Penan, Iban, Chinese, Malay, Bidayuh, Kayan in Sarawak.

People in various ethnic groups who are 'excluded' from such access have responded by criticizing, gossiping, and even stealing birds' nests both from natural caves and buildings. The robbers are from different ethnic groups, and the bird's-nest cave guards become a necessity such as the Idahan or Idaa'an in Lahad Datu, Sabah which organize 'guards' patrolling around the cave, the Iban that steal birds' nests from the Penan, the Indonesians who marry locals in Malaysia and turn out to be robbers, and the 11 Malay robbers, who had no licenses and had died. Precedents are the Indonesians who marry with the Iban, who moved from the Belipat and died on January 11, 2010 in Niah Cave, Sarawak, and the case of Chinese bird's-nest business owners in Lumut, Perak which criticized the government harshly for not supporting bird's-nest businesses, etc.

Nest-Trade Relationships Across Ethnic Groups

In Malaysia the Chinese companies buy local birds' nests from different ethnic groups, and export them to markets in China, Singapore, Negara Brunei Darussalam, Dubai, Taiwan, Hong Kong, India, Middle East, Europe, USA, and Canada. At the same time, a bird's-nest business owner in Bireven City, Aceh of Indonesia said that some Chinese private bird's-nest companies in Medan, Indonesia, buy birds' nests from Malaysia because they are cheaper than in Indonesia. And from Medan, they will be shipped to Jakarta or Hong Kong. The Malaysian people cannot buy birds' nests, but can sell them in Medan or Jakarta. This is because Malaysian birds' nests are very cheap as a result of the cheap labor.[135] A Malaysian news show on May 9, 2012 reported that Indonesia cannot sell birds' nests directly to the Chinese market, and so they ship them to the Malaysians to sell them for them.[136] Two factors that strengthen the business relationship in bird's-nest trading or birdhouse construction, whether within the same ethnic groups or different ethnic groups, domestically or internationally, are trust and sufficient supplies in quality and quantity.

The owner of the Home of Swallows Limited, a leading company of raw, ready-to-drink birds' nests in Hong Kong, operating both in Hong Kong and China, said that imported birds' nests in Hong Kong came from four sources: Indonesia, Malaysia, Vietnam, and Thailand. Malaysian bird's-nest prices are cheaper than in Thailand. They are also so popular that sometimes they claim they are Malaysian-imported nests for a fast sale. Most birds'-nests businesses in Malaysia are quite active and well-supported by the government. 80 percent of the exported birds' nests are carried by exporters on planes,[137] and 20 percent are by airfreight.[138]

Even though any ethnic group in Malaysia can participate in the birds'-nests business if they have the 'money' for investments, the Chinese are the most powerful in this business in the world. Hong Kong also is influential in setting prices both in Malaysia, and in the world market, especially after the 'Malaysian Bird's-Nests Incident in China on July, 2011.' Since then, China set regulations on quality and conditions for all imported birds' nests. As a result, all bird's-nest businesses run by Chinese and others have to follow Chinese's birds' nest regulations. Modern Chinese deregulation has affected the bird's-nest business in Malaysia, as well as other countries in Southeast Asia that are sources of birds'-nest production in the world. The Chinese monopolize the bird's-nest exporting business, as a result of the world bird's-nest business. Chinese ethnic groups in Malaysia monopolize international trade in birds' nests. In one dimension, this reflects conflicts of power, because the government has more power to access the bird's-nest resources. The birds' nests produced are mainly for export overseas.

However, even though the world has changed rapidly, the collection of birds' nests from natural sources in Malaysia is still based on a hunting and gathering society. Local tools, such as bamboo scaffolds, are still used along the cliffs to gather nests. Bird buildings are a source of birds' nest production parallel to the natural source, and are very active and developed at the present time. It is time for the world to pay attention to the importance of food sources and sovereignty.

6. BIRDS' NESTS IN POLITICS AND SOCIETY

Since the beginning of Malacca State in 1400, until becoming independent in 1957, Malaysia was under Western colonization for 557 years. The era in which it was a British colony affected the social structure by the influx of Chinese and Indian people and the integration of Sabah and Sarawak.[139]

The Legislative Council ratified the constitution on August 15, 1957 and the Federation of Malaya declared independence on August 31, 1957.[140] The Federation of Malaysia was officially established on September 16, 1963.

Malaysia is a modern state[141] that has experienced a more "traditional" society and economy. It has also seen a colonial governance which results in a pattern of new economic and political organizations. This caused extensive changes to local societies and traditional[142] communities through the effort of creating unity in the nation until. Malaysia has changed the social and political structure by continuously taking into account its being a multicultural society and having ethnic diversity.

In politics and social fields, the case of bird's-nests resources in nature is used as an intermediary of social practice in the Malaysian society. The 'over-harvesting' occurred because bird's-nest prices rose tremendously due to the demands of the Hong Kong market in the 1980s–1990s. This is one of the major causes of the decline in swiftlets in East Malaysia. This decline is responsible for social and political changes.

The information from various ethnic groups in Malaysia reflects the relationship style such as 'cliques' to access and use bird's-nest resources. It does not mean that people from the same ethnic group would get the same privilege as those in a close-knit group. These specific groups control all resources including the ownership rights of a local bird's-nest cave, a position in the committee in charge of bird's-nest harvesting auction, bird's-nest collectors, the monopoly of the state's birds' nest auctions from private birds' nests businesses, birds' nests export license, and the bird's-nest facts and knowledge.

Part of the changes made within the state's original power structure is that local governments declared a management plan for swiftlets' restoration and conservation allowing various groups in the community to participate in the management of bird's-nest caves. This includes details such as licensees, bird's-nest traders, cave guards or workers, the Bird Nest Entrepreneur Association, the Cottage Bird Nest Processing Industry, as well as respecting the rights and laws of the indigenous communities.

As for the bird building business, it was a new business that played an important role in the Malay peninsula. Many years ago, the development of bird's-nest farms in the Malay Peninsula started without rules or controls. There was a legal violation, modifying buildings into birdhouses, and installing devices like amplifiers at every corner of the building in order to lure swiftlets in to make nests. This caused a public nuisance. Bird buildings seemed like an outlaw business, so it attracted some influential groups to become involved.

When the government and local council responded to complaints from people in the community, they sought to dismantle and close the existing birds' nest farms in each city. This led to the establishment of *Persatuan Pedagang Sarang Burung Malaysia*—Malaysian Bird's Nest Merchants Association—MBNMA.

The MBNMA was found so that merchants could use official channels to negotiate with government agencies and related ministries. After 2006, the government came to promote and control the business, so swiftlet nest farming became legal. As a result, the group of bird-nest farms in various states of the Malay Peninsula has since worked closely with local governments. They started to have birds'-nest registrations and bird's-nest farming licenses.[143]

Through the Agro Bank, the Malaysian government began to support the birds' nest-building operators financially. Furthermore the Malaysian authorities have given the business priority by targeting 100,000 bird buildings in 2020, allowing the production of birds' nests to be 500 tons per year, worth RM 5 billion in the world market.[144]

China stopped the import of birds' nest products from Malaysia, with an event titled "Banning the Malaysian bird's-nest business in July 2011." Following the ban, datuk seri Najib Razak, the Prime Minister of Malaysia, traveled to negotiate with Guo Shengkun, the secretary of the Guangxi Province party, in order to find a solution to the problem. However, the result was not satisfactory. Malaysian businessmen from all over the country joined together to take a stand during April–August 2012 in Selangor, Penang, Putrajaya, and Johor in order to pressurize the government into solving the problem of low bird's-nest prices. Also, they wanted the government to negotiate to lift the ban on the import of the birds' nests from Malaysia as well as to negotiate standards for bird's-nest quality in Malaysia.

The Chinese authorities allow only Malaysia and Indonesia to sell birds' nests in the country, and most of the product is from Malaysia. Nevertheless, birds' nests in Malaysia at an international level saw a major turning point with the Chinese 'Blood bird's nest' culture, especially in the case of the "Banning the Malaysian Bird's-Nest Business in July 2011" in China. From that event, it became a hot political issue.

From the scandalous case of 'fake blood bird's nest' in Malaysia, the story spread through the cyber world in China. After detecting that the bloody birds' nests were counterfeit, the traders held a press conference with officials from Malaysia to address the situation.

The local government of Zhejiang Province said, "The press conference was held at a hotel in Hangzhou City on July 26, 2011. There were foreign men wearing colorful shirts, acting as officials from Malaysia. They claimed that they came from the Department of Import and Export of Malaysia's rare products, the Department of

Export Controls and the Department of Malaysian Quarantine Inspection Services." They also handed out documents to the press. However, the Xinhua news agency checked the list of names that were identified as Malaysian officials, and it appeared that the names did not match the actual names in those positions of the Malaysian government agencies. With this information, it was concluded that "the press conference was fake again."[145]

After the scandalous case of "Fake blood bird's nest" in July 2011, it was determined that China had passed the growth period of the traditional economy. If China still wanted to maintain the same growth, it would be necessary to increase the potential of industrial structure, increase the performance of workers, promote technological innovation and economic structural reforms as well.

For the past 30 years, China's rapid economic growth has depended on cheap labor and large savings and investments, which have led to an income gap and low consumption levels. That period has ended and the international economic crisis has caused China to accelerate the transition from depending on exports to promoting consumption in order to drive the economy with policies that stimulate domestic consumption. China will develop the consumption mechanisms and expand the demand for domestic consumption over a long period of time with six policies:

Promoting safe consumption, promoting environmentally friendly consumption, promoting consumption in the service industry, promoting brand-name products, online consumption control according to the system, and promoting consumption with financial instruments such as bank loans and credit cards.[146]

China seized the opportunity to issue new regulations on birds' nest product imports and other products. "The regulation on inspection and detention of people entering or leaving the city" became effective on November 1, 2012. Birds' nests (except canned birds' nests) were classified as prohibited products to import into China. This could result in consumers buying from companies that have standardized products, so it may lead to increased prices for birds' nests in China again.

The scandalous news of "Fake blood bird's nest" severely affected the birds' nest market in China. Bird's-nest products in shops were rarely sold. Throughout that period, online selling was the main channel for selling birds' nests. Although there were new regulations prohibiting birds' nest imports into the country, birds' nest shops and online bird's-nest shops were able to find ways to bring birds' nests from abroad into China.

Online stores required a channel for importing the products, so they did it via mail. However, the new regulation did not allow bringing birds' nests when entering the country and did not allow sending birds' nests via mail. Thus, it had a serious impact on businesses that imported the products outside the system into the country. On the contrary, this may have been good news for those companies that sold the products by following the standards because it may have led to the development of bird's-nest businesses in China.

Most birds' nest companies have to import raw materials from Southeast Asia. If there are fewer channels for purchasing outside the system, it will result in a decrease in the sales volume of the suppliers, and they may take advantage and increase the price. Meanwhile, the price of domestic birds' nests will also increase. This is related to what people in the tourism industry predicted: that forbidding bringing birds' nests into China would affect the foreign travel programs because Southeast Asian countries are popular tourist destinations for Chinese people, and birds' nests in those countries are popular among Chinese tourists. Therefore, the new regulation of banning birds' nests in China would affect the Chinese tourism business at some point.[147]

This latest regulation added a list of products that are prohibited for tourists to bring into China. Individuals traveling to China are not allowed to bring any genetically modified organisms, endangered wild animals, and wild plants, including all products made from endangered wild animals, and wild plants into China. The amendment of this regulation is changing the forbidden product list with more precise detail by adding birds' nests (except for canned birds nests) to the list of items being imported to China.[148]

Bird building-owners or private bird's-nest companies owned by ethnic groups in Malaysia have the opportunity to run the businesses both within the state, across states and across ethnic groups. The government valued research and development (R&D) in order to improve swiftlet farming to make it more sustainable and have better potential to compete in the market, and has greatly supported the business in all aspects.

In analyzing bird's-nest issues in politics and society, one could say it is symbolic of the country's politics. It is found that people who are inferior in the ethnic society of Malaysia, whether they are bird's-nest collectors, local politicians, bird's-nest businessmen or even birds' nest thieves from ethnic groups in Malaysia who steal birds' nests from caves or from buildings when the opportunity arose, have expressed their everyday life resistance in various forms such as gossiping, disobedience, and silent protests by stealing birds' nests. At one point, those who are oppressed or impeded from accessing and using bird's-nest resources do not want to openly stand up to protest. Instead they used a method called "Weapons of the Weak" to avoid being arrested by the authorities or losing help from those with power[149] including using the movement to show the power of bird's-nest businessmen in order to pressure the government to solve the problem of low prices and negotiate the conditions for bird's-nest quality from Malaysia to China. These actions are the hidden operations of the underprivileged used to criticize the state power system or power from different states that come to dominate. These are the gestures to express innocence, metaphor or concealment which have been used as tools to indicate criticism of being dominated.[150]

This kind of negotiation and retaliation is challenging in multiple dimensions; the power of the state, power across states, and those with power and authority to access and use bird's-nests resources because they are operating in the business in Malaysia and the People's Republic of China. There is inequality in managing power relations in access to bird's-nest resources.

Meanwhile, from the field data about thefts and crimes due to "The War of Bird's-Nests Resources", more violent crimes were not mentioned, but the birds' nest theft issue still existed in different communities in Malaysia.

Chapter 3

7. ENVIRONMENTAL AND ECOLOGICAL FACTORS

The Federation of Malaysia, or Malaysia, is a country with two lands that are divided into East Malaysia and West Malaysia. It is the land of the Indo-Malaysian rainforest, the world's oldest forest. It is one of 12 areas in the world that has a diversity of rare plants and animals. It has a tropical forest covering an area of approximately 46 percent of the country. It is the land with the world's most biological diversity. There are over 15,000 flowering plants (9 percent of the total on Earth), 185,000 animal species (16 percent), nearly 300 mammal species, 150,000 species of invertebrates, 736 bird species and 11 endemic birds.[151]

Malaysia has implemented the concept of Environmental Impact Assessment (EIA) and legislated it as a law in 1984. This shows that Malaysia attaches importance to the environment by having decentralization to the state governments, which have adopted the EIA since 1988. Having decentralization, the hearings were under the power of the local government in every state since 1995.[152] However, public participation was still low. In addition to the fact that Dr. Mahathir bin Mohamad became the 4th Prime Minister of Malaysia in 1981, it was the beginning of a new political era in the country for the next 20 years. His government aimed at developing Malaysia in terms of its politics, economy, trading, exporting, modernization, and basic infrastructure in the country since 1991. The Malaysian government has devoted a huge amount of its budget to infrastructure improvements in order to support foreign investment as well as preparing to become a fully developed country by 2020. Nevertheless, the new economic development policy for the better well-being of Malaysians has led to corruption problems. Some politicians sold their rights to others[153] because Malaysia's political culture is a patronage system or a system that supports the same party. This is due to the relationships between patrons and sponsors in various areas within the same ethnic groups.[154]

To illustrate, oil palm planting is the main cause of lthe loss the lowland forests. The amount of deforestation increased by 10 percent per year from 1970-92. The Department of Environment stated that chemical industries, food and beverage industries, textile industries, metal industries and livestock have contributed to a rise in pollution. There was a water quality check at 119 places in 1995. It found that 14 places were highly polluted, and 53 places were partially polluted.[155] The Department of Environment said that out of 31 rivers, 6 rivers were polluted, 16 rivers were moderately polluted and only 6 rivers were clean. The destruction of forests in Malaysia is comparable to Central America, the Amazon Basin and the "Great ages of clearance" during medieval Europe and early America.[156]

As for the environmental and ecological impacts, it can be said that the environmental and ecological systems in Malaysia have shifted toward degradation.

The specific case involving swiftlet resources in the ecological environment dimension relates to other living things, and the relationship between swiftlets and their habitats is the case of swiftlets in natural sources in Niah Cave, Niah National Park in Batu Niah, Sarawak. The 'over-harvesting' occurred because the price of birds' nests rose tremendously according to the demands of the Hong Kong market in the 1980s–1990s, which is one of the major reasons for the great decline in the number of swiftlets. In the past 40–50 years, there were a lot of swiftlets here and not many people to find or harvest birds' nests in the caves. But today, it is assumed that the result of pioneering in the forest in order to plant oil palm, forest clearing, or forest burning is causing big trees to disappear. Moreover, burning in the fields causes smoke to go into the caves. Swiftlets do not like smoke, so they migrate[157] elsewhere because their natural food sources are destroyed. In addition, some areas where local governments in Malaysia used to allow bidding for bird's-nest harvesting in the caves, including birds' nests, thefts are common causes for the population of swiftlets in natural sources to decrease substantially[158] each year. In 1935, in only Niah cave, there were 1,700,000 swiftlets, but the number was down to 65,000 in 2002.[159] This has also happened elsewhere in Sarawak, and in Sabah as well.

From that point, Sarawak started using a sustainable bird's-nests harvesting plan in 1998. They decided to close the bird's-nest caves for four months in order to have enough time for swiftlets to build their nests, lay eggs, hatch eggs, and let the baby birds grow[160] until they could fly.

Chapter 3

The current general condition of swiftlets in natural resources in Malaysia is well managed. There is swiftlet conservation, which allows swiftlets to live naturally. After 1998, the government agency by the Forest Department developed a research and development (R&D) and restoration plan for swiftlet conservation.

Moreover, allowing the community to participate in the management of the caves has gradually increased the number of swiftlets in nature.

In Malaysia, the birdhouse business became a new type of business instead of harvesting birds' nests from caves. It began in the early 1940s–1950s on the Malay Peninsula. After the economic crisis in 1997, the bird buildings for swiftlet farming became widespread in different regions all over Malaysia.

It was estimated that in 2012, there were 4,000 bird building businesses[161] in Sabah. At the end of 2010, there were about 5,000 bird buildings in Sarawak, and there were about 50,000 birdhouses in 2008.

Currently (2012), in the Malay Peninsula,[162] it is estimated that there are about 50,000–63,000 bird buildings all over the 13 states of the country. On average, if 1 pair of swiftlets build 1 nest, if calculated from 50 percent of 60,000 bird buildings, there will be 2 kilograms of birds' nests per month. There are about 120 nests per 1 kilogram. It is assumed that nowadays Malaysia has no less than 3,600,000 swiftlets not in natural sources.

As for swiftlet conservation in Malaysia, the private sector recognizes the importance of the swiftlets as *sarang emas* or gold nest. The government encourages research and development (R&D) which aims to create sustainable bird farming and to have potential for a competitive market. This is indeed a significant reflection of effective development and great potential.

However, the bird building business in Malaysia also has negative impacts on the environment.

In all 13 states, bird building farming and modifying shophouses into birdhouses are popular. Due to the fact that birdhouses or bird buildings are both in communities and outside communities, using sound to attract birds from birdhouses or bird building has become a noise pollution problem. It affects the health of the people in the community. The bird building business has become a contemporary issue Malaysia is facing which is difficult to control.

Malaysia has no less than 60,000 birdhouses and produces about 26 tons[163] of birds' nests per month. Although Malaysia learned this lesson from looking at Indonesia's rapid expansion of bird building business and their failure to manage it, Malaysia has created a law in order to manage the bird building business,[164] but there are contemporary complex problems which are difficult to control and have not been resolved.

For instance, the noise problem from the sound they use to attract the birds to the buildings causes a nuisance for the villagers. As a result, the Sandakan City Council in Sabah had to announce and give warnings to those merchants.[165]

In another case in Sarawak, farming is not allowed in the urban areas because having a large number of birds living in the city will negatively affect both the quality of life of the people and the environment of the city. Also, modifying shophouses into bird buildings is against the law, according to the 1994 Buildings Ordinance and 1997[166] Local Authorities Ordinance.

The case of bird nest farming in the Peninsular Malaysia includes modification of buildings for bird nest farming were against the 1974 Street, Drainage and Building Act and 1986 Uniform Building By-law Act. It was considered destroying the aesthetic value of the city, especially the use of bird sounds from amplifiers to lure birds into the building to make nests. It creates a nuisance to the public[167] as well.

China's deregulation during the new century is about the politics of international bird's-nest business in an event called "Breaking Malaysia bird's-nest business in July 2011" or the Malaysian media called "China clips wings of Malaysian bird's nest industry". This may be one of the factors leading the trend of bird building business management that involve human intervention to a more satisfactory direction.

The former Prime Minister of Malaysia, Mahathir bin Mohamad, once said with regret in early 2000, that despite the government's assistance to the *Bumiputera*, these people have not yet developed themselves to be as equal as Chinese or other ethnicities.[168] Even though it may be subjective and it reflects the reality that had always existed in the past, the people from various ethnic groups, both in the bird's-nest business and those who are not, cannot ignore that subjective viewpoint at present, especially as it currently impacts the environment and ecosystem.

APPENDIX

Pictures of ethnic groups and bird's-nest resource in Malaysia

Black-nest swiftlet in Niah cave, Sarawak.

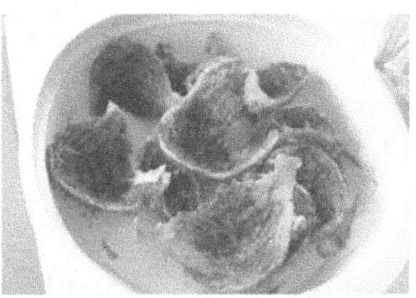

Black nests from Niah Cave, Sarawak.

White-nest swiftlet in an old building, middle of Melaka.

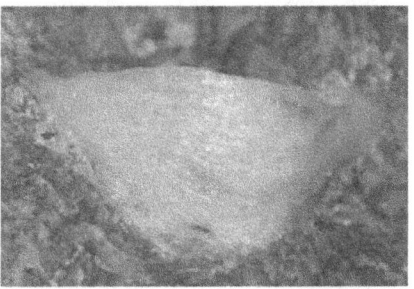

White nest in a cave near White Rock lighthouse, Sembilan Islands, Perak.

A cottage for birds' nests guard watch, Niah Cave, Batu Niah, Sarawak.

Chapter 3

Lampong, a tool for birds' nest harvesting, Niah Cave, Sarawak.

Iban bird's-nest collector with a *lampong*, a tool for bird's-nest harvesting, Niah Cave, Sarawak.

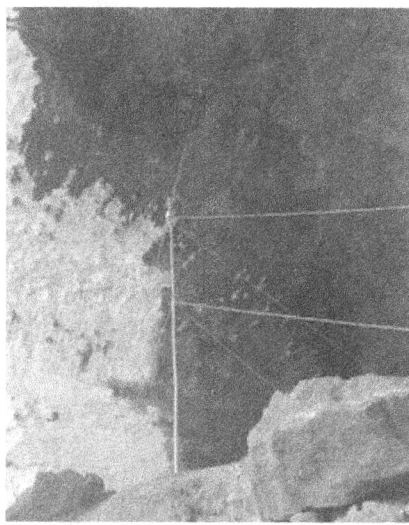

Iban birds' nests collector on Payan, Niah Cave.

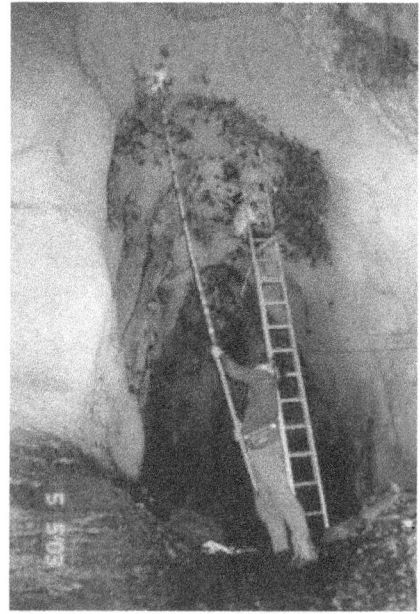

Iban bird's-nest collector in *Lubang* or mini cave in Niah Cave.

Ethnic Groups and Bird's-Nest Resources in Malaysia

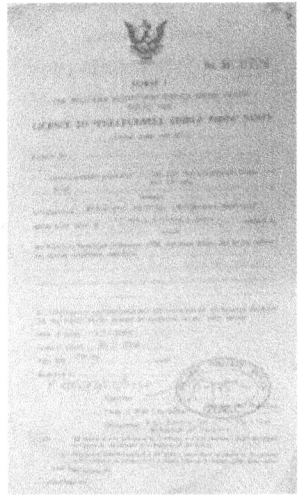

License to collect & sell birds' nests, Niah Cave, Niah National Park, Sarawak.

Iban bird's-nest collector weighting the birds' nests for the officials, Niah cave, Sarawak.

Bird's-nest business-owner cleaning black nests, National Park office, Sarawak.

Bird building: Swiftlet Eco Park, Shoplot style It was built for the market in Manjung, Perak.

Black swiftlet nests after being cleaned, packed in a box as a souvenir, Miri International Airport, Sarawak.

Bird building in the middle of the city, Lumut, Perak.

Chapter 3

Bird building in the midst of palm plantation, Mersing, Johor.

Bird buildings; completed and in process, on a seashore in Pahang.

Prayer Room: Dahimah's Guest house, on the seashore in Terengganu, modified into bird building.

Bird building from the colonial era, Kota Bharu, Kelantan.

Bird building in the middle of the field, Semerak, Pasir Puteh, Kelantan.

Swiftlets making nest on the lower floor at the back of Puri hotel, Melaka.

Ethnic Groups and Bird's-Nest Resources in Malaysia

Inside a bird building In Peranakan, Melaka.

A birdhouse owner in Jahor is collecting the nest.

Workers are cleaning birds' nests for Alga Prima company, Kulim, Kedah.

Machines for bottled birds' nest by Alga Prima, Shah Alam, Selangor.

Dragon brand's ready-to-drink bird's-nest bottles.

Bird's-nest products by Alga Prima Sdn. Bnd., Selangor.

4
Culture and Edible Birds' Nests in the Philippines

INTRODUCTION

After the flight was delayed twice for a total of three hours, it took a hundred passengers into the past. After moving through the land, the water, and the sky in the darkness for four and a half hours, in the dawn and the rain of the new day, the giant iron bird landed on the runway of the capital city of the islands. These islands are the homeland of cheerful, simple, and friendly people. It is a land rich in marine resources, the land of storms of Asia's first republic, the Republic of the Philippines.

Forty minutes south of Manila by plane is Francisco B. Reyes Airport on Busuanga Island, Palawan. This is the land of the Tagbanwa or Tagbanua, an ethnic group not well-known to the outside world.

These are communities that have inherited the trade of *'busyadors'*: men who gather the nests of *'balinsasayaw'* (the edible nest swiftlet) along the treacherous cliffs in the darkness of the caves.

The history of the *busyador* and the *balinsasayaw* dates back to the arrival of Chinese traders in the early Sung Dynasty before Magellan led the Spanish army to occupy the islands. The culture has possibly been active since the 11th century A.D. but is known for certain to have been operating for at least 400 years in the Republic.

The Palawan Islands are home to various ethnic groups living a traditional lifestyle, and often perceived as cheerful, simple, and friendly.

In Palawan, the swiftlet is a significant natural resource with importance nationally and internationally, influencing economics, history, politics, culture, the ecology, and relationships between ethnic groups.

1. HISTORY OF THE INDIGENOUS PEOPLE'S USE OF BIRD'S-NEST RESOURCES

A *busyador* from the Tagbanua ethnic group collecting nests from a cave in Palawan.

1.1 Swiftlets in Nature

Although there is no clear timeline as to the use of birds' nest from natural sources, there is considerable evidence about the communities that, "gather the bird's nest for sale" in the Palawan Islands of the Philippines in the early period of the country's history.

The Chinese writer Chao Ju-Kua wrote a book titled *Chu Fan Chi*, published in 1225 A.D.. The book noted three islands in the Philippines; Palawan, Busuanga, and

Calamiane Group.¹ He described the islands and the people of Calamianes and the goods exchanged with Chinese traders.

Fray Luis de Jesus, a Roman Catholic priest of the Augustinian Recollect Order, described that the Calamian Tagbanwas or Tagbanua of Coron Island in 1663 A.D., the place seemed sacred.²

In 1624, Fray Juan de la Concepcion wrote about Calamian Tagbanwas, saying that there were goods exchanged for the edible swiftlet nests or *luray* of Tagbanwa. The luray is a component of "the rare and expensive Chinese delicacy" called *nido* or bird's-nest soup. The *luray* of Tagbanwa were traded through a Chinese middleman. So, the Calamian Tagbanwa, or Tagbanua, has been selling nests internationally for at least 400 years.³

The El Nido Islands are the most important sources in Palawan. A Chinese trader made contact with these islands around 982 A.D., in the early period of the Sung Dynasty (960–1279 A.D.) because these islands are rich in swiftlet nests in numerous caves.⁴ The Chinese people call this land Pa-Lao-Yu or the Land of Beautiful Harbors, or El Nido which means "The Nest" in Spanish.⁵

It is believed that the name Palawan was coined by the Chinese people, meaning Land of Beautiful Harbors, where Chinese ethnic traders traveled by junk to make contact with the Palawan territory no later than the 11th century. But there are logs by Chinese traders who had come in contact with Pabellon or Pabillion Island in 1662 A.D.. The Indigenous Tagbanua people, the natives of the islands with bird's nest-gathering experience, enjoyed commercial success in trading with Chinese people by exchanging and trading local products of rubberwood, sea cucumber, and birds' nests in exchange for earthenware and brass gongs.⁶

Diokno Manlavi said in the history of Palawan that the cliffs of El Nido are steep like a house wall, as told in Chinese narratives in 1209 A.D.. At that time, Chinese traders came to the islands to trade for birds' nests, a long time before the Spaniards conquered the Philippine Islands.⁷

Today, at Coron Island, the cliffs are important to the Tagbanua's livelihood because the crevices and limestone caves are the habitat of swiftlets or *balinsasayaw*.

Tagbanua gather the edible nests, which can be cooked into bird's-nest soup. They sell the nests to Chinese middlemen in the Coron Town market who then export them to other Southeast Asian countries.

The historian claimed that as early as 1225 A.D., the Calamianes exchanged goods with the Chinese middlemen.[8]

Miguel de Loarca, a Spanish chronicler, recorded in 1582 A.D. that the Chinese middleman in Busuanga buys *nido* and *balat*, both sold by Tagbanua. Nowadays, the ancient tribe still talks about trading between their ancestors and the Chinese from hundreds of years ago.[9]

Tagbanua rules prescribe that those who find the caves have "exclusive rights" to harvesting them. These rights have been respected by other gatherers. All experts in the islands who gather the bird's nest in the Balinsasayaw Season are trained in the skill, handed down through generations. The training can be traced back to when the first group of Chinese middlemen came to the islands, before the arrival of Magellan.

The Tagbanuas have a longstanding practice for managing the nest resources with open season and closed season, to limit the impact on the bird population. The seasons differ on each island. In Banwang-Daan, the gathering begins in early December and ends in April. Yet in Cabugao, the bird's harvest begins in January and ends in April.[10]

According to the practices of Tagbanua, this philosophy derived from observing nature has been passed down for centuries, and the ethnic group continues following the ancient practices. The Tagbanua will gather the nests (*nido*) for only six months of the year. In each month of the open season, they have to ensure that it does not have any impact on the nesting and the propagation of the swiftlets. The bird's-nest cave will be cleaned after each harvest.

Normally, the bird's-nest collection is a burden reserved for men. Women may enter the caves but not for harvesting. For bird's-nest caves with relatively easy access, men who gather the nests will be shirtless and climb the rugged cliff with his bare feet.[11]

Climbing the cave cliff is considered a death-defying process, which is common in Coron.[12] In the past, the Tagbanuas lit torches made of rubber from the almaciga tree to illuminate the cave, but now use flashlights.

There was no permanent settlement in Coron until after World War II because the Tagbanua moved according to the seasons. They had moved for fishing, agriculture, and nest-gathering. The Tagbanua family living in Coron now are fishers and nest harvesters.

Tagbanua people engage in farming (*kaingin*: slash-and-burn) and gather nests when the wind from the northeast (*amihan*) makes the sea extremely dangerous for small fishing boats.[13]

In the early 1970s, the government of Kalamian municipality in Northern Palawan has used its authority to declare the caves of the Tagbanuas' ancestors, which are spread throughout the islands of northern Palawan, were co-opted as state properties. Then the municipal government auctioned exclusive rights to gather birds' nests from the cave. It eliminated traditional rights and a crucial income source for the Tagbanwa.

But it did not stop. The government of the municipality also issued orders taxing land inherited from ancestors, causing unrest among the Tagbanwa. The Tagbanuas fell into heavy debt because of low income from nest-gathering and excessive taxation by the local government. The policies impacted their livelihoods and effected a state of poverty.[14]

The Tagbanuas' community organization was founded in 1985, due to the municipal government demanding license registration. The government allowed outsiders to bid for nest collection rights to the Tagbanua clan cave, canceling all traditional rights to the caves. The municipal government focused on income from the natural resources in Coron only, with no concern for the local people.[15]

The situation of the Tagbanua grew worse every year at the hands of the municipal government. In 1990, there was an agreement voiding the taxation and returning the land rights to the Tagbanua, canceling the outsider's rights to gather the bird's nest. This also protected the community from various intruders, including illegal smugglers, loggers and fishermen.[16]

Many families in Coron Island and Tara gather nests from their clan caves, which are hidden within the steep cliffs. The clan caves have been cared for, ith successful harvests from generation to generation.[17]

At Pabellon Island in Taytay Bay, the northern of Palawan, the bird's-nest cave is the personal inheritance (guardianship of individual caves) which have been passed down from generation to generation.[18]

The *busyadors*—those who specialize in gathering nests—are local Cuyonon men from the Maytegued Islands. They freeclimb the cliffs to gather the nests, a technique passed down from father to son, generation to generation. Each family has to take care of the cave and take responsibility for their nest-gathering.[19]

Before this, the government granted harvesting concessions for Pabellon's nests for Chinese middlemen. But in the late 1990s, the nest-gatherers claimed they found blood in the nests, indicating that the bird population was stressed.

In 2004, the *busyadors* gathered together to reclaim the Pabellon's nests concessions from the local government in order to adopt a more sustainable system. The harvesters now have to pay PHP 2.6 million in taxes to the municipal government each year and the municipality sends police to oversee the island, and guard against thieves who moor their boats off the coast and swim to shore before pilfering the Swiftlet Cave.

Eduardo Guerera, Maytegued's community leader in the business since he was six years old said, "It's different from the Chinese concessionaires. At that time, they just tried to make as much money as they could, harvesting even when the birds are laying eggs. It caused a drop in the number of swiftlets. Some people tried to explain to them that gathering nests like this prevents the birds from hatching their eggs, but the concessionaires did not believe it and continued anyway."

After the *busyadors* united, the swiftlet population recovered, and they controlled the gathering and income depending on the market value. Each year, the birds had more time to breed in the Pabillion Islands. Nest-gatherers come to Pabellon Islands in early December. They clean the cave cliff to remove the decay from the past year, so the swiftlets can nest on clean cliffs, or it could take many years for swiftlets make its nests in that area again. This approach reflects the recognition of the symbiotic relationship between the *busyador* and the *balinsasayaw*.

In the 1950s, there were only 10 or 15 *busyadors* (compared to 50 in the present day) The nests were sold to ethnic Chinese people from Manila, who paid only PHP 0.12

per kilogram. The gatherers received around PHP 35 for each gathering, which they considered to be good revenue.

In those days, nest harvesting was a risky task. The nest-gatherers used only bare feet, bamboo poles, and ropes for climbing caves more than a hundred meters high.[20]

The owners of the bird's-nest caves, a Tagbanuas, the natives of barangay Panlaitan and Talampulan Island, confirmed that the nest harvesters could only be the Tagbanuas. The caves are their heritage. The bird's nest-gathering is an ancient's tradition. They inherited rights to the bird's-nest caves from their forefathers. Once collected, they would sell the nests to Ethnic Chinese people in Coron Town.[21]

The reconciliation of the Tagbanuas finally with the government was finally achieved when the Department of Environment and Natural Resources (DENR) accepted the Tagbanua's claim to cave rights on July 28, 1998. The Tagbanua were granted the rights to ancestral land. (The Certificate of Ancestral Domain Claim: CADC).[22] This allowed them to reclaim the caves, and also exempted them from the 50 pesos per year tax.[23]

The Tagbanua do not have an issue with the outside world. In the end, their lives depend on income from fishing and selling nests to the merchants. Cooperating with private organizations (NGOs) is yielding good results. And the agreement with the CADC process, although sometimes frustrating, has increased the harvest's value.[24]

The Tagbanua ethnic group has a firm sentiment concerning the bird's-nest business world of middlemen and merchants. As Floro Aguido, President of Barangay Turda, said, "They cannot get rich without us. We are the workers. We are the ones on the land."[25]

All of this shows the injustice that has remained hidden in the world of this business. The cross-border history linked to lifestyle and local history, confirmed that the bird's-nest trade from natural sources in Palawan, Philippines, has been in operation since the 11th century, nearly 1,000 years ago. The written evidence shows the relationship between local and Chinese populations has carried on for more than 400 years.

According to field data, the owners of the bird's-nest caves and the gatherers of the Tagbanua ethnic group of the Black Island and the Coron Island, Busuanga –

Palawan, noted that the Tagbanua people enjoy eating the nests. Some boil them[26] to make soup, mixed with coffee and milk.[27] They believe the nests are full of vitamins and a cure for many diseases.[28] Eating them makes the body stronger, healthier, and also strengthens sexual performance. The Tagbanuas eat the birds' nest scraps, while selling the good quality ones. The traders in Coron Town, Busuanga Island-Palawan, also say that eating nests makes the body stronger and is good for health.

The Tagbanua's income is used to buy rice, consumable products, and daily life tools, including boats for fishing.[29]

At the same time, the former Filipino gatherers from the Island of Cadlao, at the estuary of El Nido, said that in the Philippines, many nest caves are controlled by the state. In these cases, Filipino people can also be concessionaires for gathering nests.[30]

1.2 Swiftlets in Swiftlet House Farming Business

The business of nest-farm buildings involves producing the nests by preparing a building to suit swiftlet's preferred living conditions and attracting them to build nests inside them. This end of the business is still small and not widespread in the Philippines.

2. THE NATURE OF SWIFTLETS

 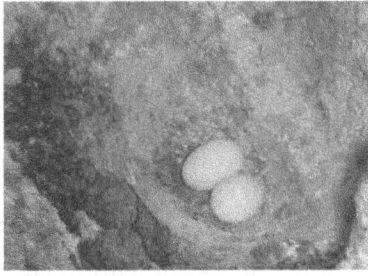

The characteristics of *Balinsasayaw*, Kola-Kola, or grass nest swiftlets in the caves of Codognun Island, Palawan, Philippines.

Chapter 4

The Birds of Ancestors and Life

The Tagbanua and various other ethnic groups in the Philippines call the swiftlets *balinsasayaw* in Tagalog language. They call the nests *luray* in the Tagbanua language, *Pugad ng Balinsasayaw* in Tagalog, and *El Nido* in Spanish.

2.1 Natural Characteristics

The natural characteristics of the Philippines swiftlet of the *Collocalia Fuciphaga* genus are as follows:

> Common name: Edible-nest swiftlet
> Scientific name: *Collocalia fuciphaga*
> Family: *Apodidae*
> Length: 12 cm.
> Weight: 15–18 grams

Characteristics: The birds are gray with a brown hairy band on the hips. They have dark brown eyes, with black beaks and feet. They have slender wings that enable fast flying, eating insects while in flight. They breed from July to November and are found in coastal, forest, and mountainous areas of the country.

The number of swiftlets is unknown.[31]

At Coron Island, Palawan, the *busyador* or Tagbanua gatherers, who are experts in bird's-nest collecting, along with researchers and naturalist scientists, have identified three species of *balinsasayaw*:

1. *Kola-Kola*, a swift with black-brown feathers. Its nest is mixed with wood scraps, grass scraps, and feathers.
2. *Kalipatpat*, a swift with full black feathers. It looks like the *Kola-Kola*
3. *Balinsasayaw*, white-skinned swiftlets with black-brown feathers and white hips.

Swiftlets are nesting birds that tend to nest repeatedly in the same location. But the number of swiftlets in a cave can change. The main enemy of the swiftlets at Coron Island, Busuanga – Palawan, is the people and also the Abwatt snake, a black snake one meter long that does not eat eggs or nests.[32] On Coron Island, there is also a bird called *kara-ut* which nests in the caves, but its nest is too dirty to be edible.[33]

On Pabellon Island, in Taytay Bay in the north of Palawan, it is the edible-nest swiftlet (*Aerodramus fuciphagus*). It lives in a cave from December to August, while breeding, nesting, and hatching in June–July.[34]

At El Nido, Palawan, a Filipino *busyador* said that there are two types of swiftlets: the *balinsasayaw* and *Kola-Kola* or grass-nest swiftlet (*Collocalia esculenta*). The two species are different: *Balinsasayaw* flies faster than the *kola-kola*, and *kola-kola* do nest with grass, wood scraps, or feathers. Its nest is inedible but Balinsasayaw's nest can be eaten.[35]

At Black Island, Busuanga, Palawan, the Tagbanua ethnic group said that there is only one species—the white-nest swiftlet. Each nest weighs only a few grams. Swiftlets lay eggs in May, so the nest will not be gathered until after the baby birds can fly. The breeding the swiftlets here is handled by nature. Each year, the nest-gatherers will wait for the eggs to hatch. This practice has been passed down from their ancestors. The enemy of the swiftlets here is the Abwatt, a cobra with a large and long body. It eats the swiftlets but does not eat eggs or nests.[36]

Another *busyador* said there is gathering seven months of the year, from December to June. Each month, nests are gathered in varying quantities. The enemy of the swiftlets are Palanakan snakes. This black snake is deadly poisonous, sufficient to kill a human being. This snake will eat both the bird and the nest. The swiftlet population here has not significantly varied over time.[37]

2.2 Swiftlet Habitat

From all of 79 provinces of the Philippines, the habitat of swiftlets in both natural and nest-farm buildings are in 17 provinces: Palawan, Cagayan, Sulu, Samar, Leyte, Bohol,

Mindoro, Bicol, Davao, Cotabato, Agusan, Misamis Oriental, Camiguin, Bukidnon, Surigao, Zamboanga, Cebu or Binondo.[38]

2.3 Birds' Nests Collecting Season

In the Philippines, bird's nests from natural sources are gathered 6–7 months per year, varying from region to region. The Tagbanua ethnic group on the Coron Island gathers nests from December to May.[39] If they are gathered after the end of January for around one month, or in April, or in May, or in June, they can be gathered every 15 days. In the last week of May, there is no harvesting. Outsiders are not allowed to enter the cave except by special permission, since it is considered a sacred place,[40] due to the close connection with Tagbanua's way of life since ancient times.

Previously, the collectors gather the nests once a month, for 6 months from December to May. The Tagbanua nowadays gather the nest the same way as their ancestors. In May, gathering is prohibited because the birds are hatching. If there is a violation, the community will punish them. The swiftlets numbers here have reduced somewhat.[41]

At Pabellon Island in Taytay Bay, in the north of Palawan, is the nesting habitat of edible-nest swiftlets called *Aerodramus fuciphagus*. Each year, the gathering takes place from December to June. During this period, the *busyadors* or Cuyunin or Cuyonon climb the caves every 15–20 days. In June to July, the swiftlets make a new nest and hatch their eggs.[42] The Filipino ethnic group at El Nido, Palawan, gathers the nests 6 months per year from December to May, every 15 days. *Busyadors* spray water on the nests pluck them by hand. Without water, the nest will crack easily.[43]

At Black Island, Busuanga, Palawan, people who control the caves and the gatherers of the Tagbanua ethnic group, said that nests are collected six months a year from December to April. They do not harvest in May when the birds are laying their eggs. But they will resume the harvest when the baby birds can fly. Some *busyadors* said they gather the nests seven months a year, from December to June, with quantities varying from month to month.[44]

Officials said that since the early 1990s, local governments have enacted laws to establish open and closed seasons for nest harvesting. The official season runs from December to June and the nest can be gathered only after the baby birds can fly.[45]

Swiftlet farm buildings meanwhile, where the harvesting is less cyclical and based on the bird population, are not popular or well established in the Philippines with only a few people doing it. These nests are usually gathered once a month.

3. BELIEFS AND RITUALS RELATED TO SWIFTLETS

The bird's-nest soup or Sopa de nido in Philippines.

3.1 Beliefs and Rituals

Beliefs Related to Swiftlets

According to the beliefs of people in Palawan, the Cuyonon are the cave-owners and the gatherers of the bird's nest sources on Pabellon Island.[46] The Busuanga and the Tagbanuas are the cave-owners and gatherers on Coron Island, and Black Island. If the bird's-nest cave belongs to a family, it is the guardian of the cave.[47] The ownership of the cave rights are inherited down the generations.

The Tagbanua ethnic group, the owners and the gatherers in the north of Palawan, believes that *balinsasayaw* is a sacred bird.[48] The people here have respect for swiftlets, considering important in their history because it provides benefits to their livelihood.[49] Not only does it generate income for the Tagbanua, it has become part of the Tagbanua identity.

Nest-gathering has been a way of life for Tagbanau from their ancestors to the present day.[50] They also believe that the nests (*balinsasayaw*) are valuable for vitamins and as medicines.[51]

Violeta Francisco, a Filipino woman who bought nests in Coron Town, Busuanga Island, said that the swiftlet (*balinsasayaw*) are delicious, but not often eaten.[52]

Many areas of the country that have swiftlet (*Collocalia fuciphaga*) nests call the swiftlets *Balinsasayaw* and the nests are *Nido*.[53] In El Nido, Palawan, the people ascribe great value to swiftlets. On June 17, 1954, the Republican Act no. 1140 was enacted, changing the name of the city to be Bacuit. It named a conservation area Kuapnit-Balinsasayaw National Park in Leyte Province. Padre Pupong, the contemporary Filipino poet, wrote a poem called "*Busyador*" (Bird's Nest Gatherers):

> Looking at the clouds in the middle of force
> between light and darkness at dawn.
>
> Mind is busy reminiscing the memories of the past
> the clouds overview seem like television
> of the happiest memories of love ones.
>
> Sitting on his nest Gasping the cool breeze of the air in the east,
> just like music and laughter of the happiest moments
> the surge of waves in the Pacific.
>
> Yet, he doesn't journey
> His mind and heart only move
> But the body is like a log waiting all day long
> in the nests of some playful swiftlets.

Eyes are watching the surroundings moment by moment
but not waiting for the arrival of his child nor his wife
Ready to defend against those who will attempt
To steal the nest when he alone has the authority to obtain.

Saliva is spoiled without any sense being used
to having a thin tone of voice due to being alone.

That is the opposite of the saliva of the bird being guarded.

Yet his feet and arms are strong day by day
And the nest that he can gather
Commensurate a penny, drinks to a bird's owner
The nests of a swiftlet which is so expensive
with no luck he may not be able to taste the broth.

He is nesting without a nestling
He who is in the nest that no one delivers love.

It has been years since he is away from his family,
The island that is monitored is like an Alcatraz just to make a dime.

Shining and setting the golden rays of the sun
Divides and embraces the wave of the ocean by it beams
Yet to all, he is alone having no companion
In the middle of vast and deepest ocean.

Beliefs and Rituals Related to the Gathering of Swiftlet's Nests: Sacred Heresies

Giving value and importance to swiftlets by the birds' nest-gatherers, their families, and communities involved, some ethnic groups in the Philippines have created, reproduced, and inherited the beliefs rituals for swiftlets and the gathering of swiftlets in the natural source.

With the deadly risk of gathering nests on the cliff face of dark caves, the constant danger of falling and the difficult access to the nests makes for an intense experience. Nature holds the power over humans, while humans cannot own nature. This gives rise to supernatural beliefs.

Before gathering the nests, some communities, especially Tagbanua pray to God to protect them and ask permission from the cave spirits.[54] They pray for a safe harvest.

In the past, the Tagbanua ethnic group in Coron Island, Black Island, and other places practiced animism. The cave-owners and gatherers performed rituals before harvesting the nests. This has faded as a regular practice, and now only takes place when they find a new cave.[55]

The present-day rituals have adapted to be simple and harmonious with everyday life by bringing pesos coins to the cave spirits at 1 peso per time. Due to fears of the spirits, known in the Tagbanua language as "Maleknor", the number of times the peso coins are offered depends on individual *busyadors*. Sometimes a *busyador* will just throw a peso coin into the cave to request permission and pray for blessings from God.[56]

Such practices are a ritualistic practice that runs counter to the belief in Christianity and the original beliefs of the indigenous people. The Tagbanua ethnic group considered it a sacred pagan practice. It is however off the path of Christianity.

One group of *busyadors* explained that the busyador must be a strong person who is flexible, stays alert, has a strong mind, is careful, and must have a commitment to the occupation. The *busyador* will kneel down and kiss the floor when entering the cave. They will not make loud noises because they believe that if they are loud, there will be no nests to harvest. They will not wear fragrance or use mosquito repellent. Neither will they drink alcohol in the cave because the birds flee from the smell it. They will not leave behind garbage or any other items.

When they finish the harvest, before leaving the cave, they must kneel down and kiss the floor to show their thanks to the cave spirits and God. The Tagbanua also prohibit women from entering the caves and only some *busyadors* can bring in the *sahing*.⁵⁷

The birds' nest-gatherers also spoke of the prohibition of entering the cave. They said if there is any swiftlet in the cave, they must be quiet and use the usual language to speak when working in the bird's-nest caves.⁵⁸ All of these are for prosperity allowing the gathering of birds' nests to be smooth and safe. The people who found a new bird's-nest cave will be respected people in their society.⁵⁹

Since the harvesting is a dangerous task, the Tagbanua in Palawan, have developed special skills in climbing the cave wall by using various equipment including ropes and bamboo ladders.

The Tagbanuas *busyadors* have been trained to climb the cliffs since childhood. The relationship of the gatherers is usually father and son or brothers or a group of relatives and friends that have accumulated experience over a lifetime.

Beliefs and contraindications related to the Tagbanuas nest-gathering, generally concerns the spirits they believe live in the cave. But nowadays, the people do not perform the ceremony strictly and have tempered its sacredness. But the Tagbanuas people are still concerned with how they behave when entering the caves.

In the northern area of Palawan on Pabillion Island, Cuyonon, the cave-owner and the nest-gatherers are exclusively male. In the case of Coron Island and Black Island, the Tagbanua ethnic group are patrilineal – and act in accordance with male-dominated beliefs. They believe women cannot gather nests because they don't how to enter the cave properly or how to climb. The duty of women is to trim, clean and sell the nests.⁶⁰

But one of the *busyador* wives on Black Island said she has been in the cave with her husband.⁶¹ Gracia Dennis, a Filipino young man, and a former nest-gatherer of Cadlao Island, El Nido, said that before harvesting at El Nido, there are no rituals. But they are careful not to wear any scent or lotion when entering the caves. Women go in the caves and some are even allowed to gather nests.⁶²

Chapter 4

Belief and Truth in the Consumption of the Swiftlet's Nest According to Local History

The consumption of the birds' nest from natural sources in Palawan, Philippines has been carried out over 400 years ago. The native people believe that the birds' nest (*balinsasayaw*) gives vitamins. It can be used to make medicine to cure a disease.[63] Eating the bird's nest makes the body become stronger and healthier. It can nourish or maintain the sexuality fitness of men. Especially in Coron Island, Tagbanuas prescribe Bird's-nest soup for recuperating women after childbirth. It also used for recuperating chronic patients according to the traditional treatment method.[64]

Nowadays, various ethnic people in the Philippines boil nests with hot water,[65] to make bird's-nest soup or *sopa de nido*, mixed with coffee and milk,[66] There is also soup with quail eggs, chicken pieces, crab meat, etc.

While in the view of an 'outsider', Christian Ward,* a famous British poet, wrote a poem called "Bird's-nest soup", reflecting the feeling by telling a story through *busyadors*:

Bird's Nest Soup

A *bangka*† beached, shushing waves
slapping its hull. Then busyadores jumped

out with rope and poles, making the sign
of the cross before lifting themselves

onto rocks while the birds gorged miles
away on mayflies, wasps and winged white ants.

Fernando moved quickly, feeling the frailty
of every limestone rock as he sprang from one

---

* Christian Ward (born 1980) is a UK-based poet. He earned an MA in Creative Writing at Royal Holloway, University of London and his work has appeared in Poetry Wales, *The Kenyon Review* and elsewhere. He hopes to release his first collection in near future.
† *bangka*=outrigger canoe; *busyadore*=skilled climber

position to another, judging if the crevice
could accommodate his foot. The sea hissed

like escaping oxygen. Gusts of wind recorded
him hitting the water like a funfair hammer.

Hacked off nests appreciated in value while
he sank; giant crickets chirped unscripted elegies

before swarming over tossed out chicks. The *busyadores*[†]
laid out their haul on a table at dusk and sorted it into first,

second and third class bundles before sleeping on bamboo
benches as swiftlets returned to their caves, one man

always waking to feathers running along an arm,
having dreamt of Icarus stealing flight and the sun taking

it back.[67]

Note: Results from scientific laboratories concerning the value and properties of the Philippines's nests are not yet widespread.

However, although birds' nest is an ethnic food resource and culture it is also considered high-class food. Yet, for various ethnic people in the Philippines, despite its popularity, it is prohibitively expensive. Regardless of whether the gatherers come from ethnic groups such as Cuyonon, Tagbanua, or Pinoy (Filipino or the Philippines), they have a deep and profound relationship between the world of experience and the world of the truth of swiftlet's nest. Though they hold the belief that eating nests has made them stronger and bestowed good sexual performance, various indigenous people who gather the nests from natural sources do so only for sale as a product.

3.2 Equipment, Tools and Inventions in the Bird's-Nest Industry

Despite the influence of bird farm buildings in Indonesia, a massive development in the business, there are only a few such farms in the Philippines.

The nest buildings are of rectangular building block design, with various devices employed to artificially control the conditions and atmosphere to make them suitable for swiftlet nesting – temperature, humidity, light, recorded bird calls, fragrances. The farming has also led to specialized harvesting and cleaning tools, and solutions.

These innovations were widespread throughout the Southeast Asian region for 20 years. There was an experiment to build a birdhouse according to the local characteristics of Davao del Sur. The building structure uses a nipa thatched roof, open space between the ceiling and the roof for cooling, and a wall partition with flat tiles.[68] But it is unclear whether the experiment was a success or not.

In the natural cave sources in Coron Island and Black Island, or at Busuanga, the Tagbanua nest-gatherers have fashioned equipment and tools as well as torches. [*sahing, sugpit, sapalung,* and *lebon*]. Sahing is a two-foot long herbal torch made from wood. Sahing's low smoke makes breathing comfortable when entering deep caves with little air. Sugpit is a bamboo prong for plucking the nests from the walls. If a cave has a high ceiling, *busyadors* will use a *sapalang*. A *lebon* or palm leaf basket is used to store gathered nests.

The *sugpit* can also be steel. Harvesters at Cadlao Island, El Nido, found over the years that it is easier to pluck the nests if they spray them with water first to prevent cracking.[69]

3.3 Culture, Traditions, and Wisdom in Bird's-Nest Business of Ethnic Groups

The development of expertise in bird-nest farming prevalent in other countries is not very active in the Philippines. However, nest-gathering in the natural caves by the Tagbanua and other ethnic groups has led to specific knowledge that has been passed down through generations.

This knowledge, particularly regarding nesting cycles prevents disrupting propagation, so that the swiftlets are not as risk of extinction. In the past, they used to gather nests once a month, only from December to the beginning of May. During the month of May, when the birds hatch, gathering is prohibited.[70]

This knowledge also gave rise to animist rituals, from a sense of devotion to supernatural powers in the form of the cave spirits. The are connected to feelings of fear and respect (sublimation), relate to abundance as fertility rites, and emphasize natural control as much as the technological practices.

The tradition and culture of the *Balinsasayaw* from natural sources date back 400 years. Despite the modifications and looser conservation style resulting from conversion to Christianity, these traditions are still passed down in areas that have bird's-nest resources.

The Tagbanua people throw a peso coin into the cave instead of putting out offerings for the cave spirits in Coron Island and Black Island, Busuanga. This shows respect and acceptance of the spirits' power, and represents a bargain for permission from the guardian spirits to harvest. It is also a blessing for the gatherers to keep them protected and safe while harvesting and ensuring a prosperous harvest.

In modern times, the caves, lifestyle, and/or the ritual practice of the nest-gatherers has become a product in Coron Town, Taytay, and El Nido, Palawan, to the point of advertising it to attract tourists.

4. RIGHTS AND LEGAL SYSTEMS: POWER TECHNOLOGY FOR ACCESS AND EXCLUSION OF NEST RESOURCES AND THE BUSINESS WORLD OF THE PHILIPPINES

The Philippines has a variety of communities, cultures, biodiversity, and a large variety of natural resources. The use of nest resources in the Philippines has a long history and the bird's-nest business and their usage are among the recognition processes in their history and social status and geographies of exclusion.

The nest resource use and history of the bird's nest business is owned by the country's ethnic minorities. There is evidence that Chinese merchants came into contact with the Palawan people during the early Sung Dynasty (960–1279 A.D.),

Chapter 4

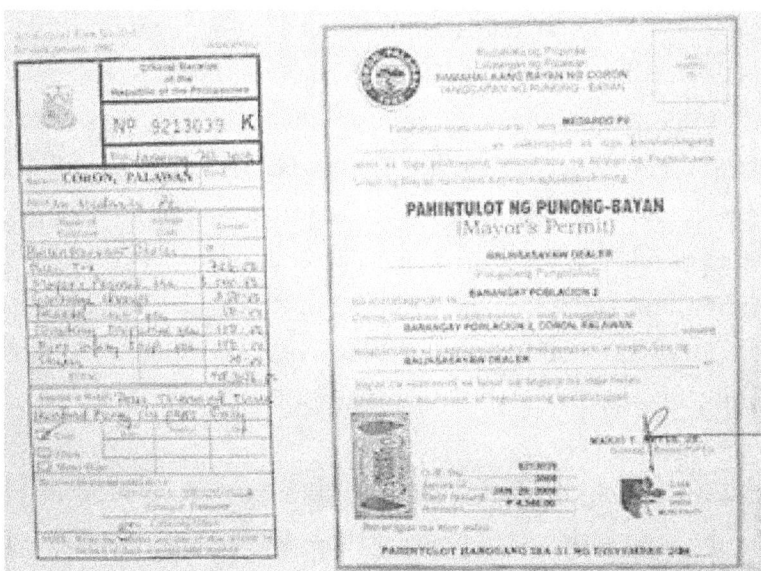

A license issued by the local government for nest merchants in Coron Town, Palawan.

about 982 A.D. in the late 10th century.[71] At that time, Palawan was rich in swiftlet nest resources and the Indigenous Tagbanua people were the original nest-gatherers. The Tagbanua traded nests and other local products for Chinese ceramic tiles and brass gongs.[72]

Later, the Philippines was under the authority of the Spanish colonists (1564–1899), the USA (1899–1946) and Japan (1941–44). It was under the authority of Spanish colonists for 335 years,[73] then the USA, before the Philippines finally gained its independence on July 4, 1946. At a certain level, Philippine society was influenced by the arrangement of social power relations (hierarchies of power relations) both the power of the system and the underlying value, and the power expressed in the form of rules or customary directives. The power of the system and the underlying value is the power and the value given to the importance of human dignity. The power expressed in the form of rules or customs is the power to participate in various activities of society or culture, and the rights to control and access resources. All of these powers and rights determined social power in Philippines society.

The Philippines is a land of diverse communities with equally diverse cultures and traditions. From a tribal society to a feudal system or the sultanate, its society developed to the colonial era until it became a democracy. Thus, the rights and laws system concerning the use of swiftlets nest resources from natural sources, which are the technology of power in social stratification and the hierarchies of power relations for access and use of the Philippines' resources.

The access and the use of swiftlet nesting resources differs according to the characteristics of the land and ethnic group. The Philippines does not have a national law relating to the management of bird's-nest resources. The central government has given local governments the authority to manage the resources with laws and regulations. All of these regulations, laws, and rights systems are written laws issued by the Palawan Council for Sustainable Development (PCSD), Palawan local government, and traditional laws (unwritten laws) of the descendants of various ethnic nest-gatherers. The ethnic groups holding significant rights to gather the nests are the Tagbanua, Cuyonon, and Tagalog.

In the case of Coron Island sources, this area has the most nesting caves and gathering nests is the main occupation of the Tagbanua people. They inherited the clan caves from their ancestors since ancient times. Both the clan caves and the newly discovered nesting caves have received the same attention.[74]

The Tagbanua clan caves can only be inherited by male heirs. A daughter cannot receive ownership rights of the nesting caves unless a new cave is discovered. However, each family shares the nest resources with both sons and daughters. While women can own new nesting caves they cannot enter them. Their brothers will gather and sell the nests. Women can clean and prepare the nests, but cannot be involved in the sale. After the sale, the women receive an equal share of the revenues.

The heritage and rights of the Tagbanuas to gather nests underwent problems until they fought a lengthy battle to legally claim indigenous rights. The result of this struggle was named the 'April Law' or The Indigenous People's Rights Act (IPRA). This recognizes the right of indigenous people to possess and use land inherited from their ancestors. These rights are called The Certificate of Ancestral Domain Claim

(CADC). The law named "The Indigenous People's Rights Act (RA.8371) of 1997" was issued in 1997 under President Fidel Ramos (1992–98).

In the early 1970s, the Kalamian municipality government, Northern Palawan, exercised its power to claim the Tagbanau nesting caves, spread throughout northern Palawan islands, making them the state property. The municipal government granted the highest bidder exclusive rights to gather nests. This cancellation violated longstanding tradition and stripped away a major income source of the Tagbanau people.

The municipal government also issued orders to collect taxes on inherited land.[75] The government claimed that the new trading schedule was to prevent the gathering of excessively large nests of inferior quality. The municipal governments implemented taxation plans over nest sales.

The Tagbanwa clan caves were confiscated under the rationale that the nests were public property and could not be held as personal wealth. When the caves were declared public property, the municipal government auctioned the rights with the winner paying the municipal government. Only winning bidders had the right to sell the nests.

This caused the Tagbanua, the original owners of the caves to become merely gatherers in their own clan caves. The winning bidder was officially the Tagbanwa *mestiza* backed by Chinese merchants from Coron Town. The Tagbanwa *mestiza* hired Cuyonon to guard the caves. This also prevented access to the largest of the sacred lakes, Awuyuk Dakulo.[76] The Tagbanuas on Coron Island considered this lake to be a vital part of the island's watershed, as well as shelter for the swiftlets' caves which is a sacred place (*panyaan*)[77] revered and cherished by all Tagbanua.

When the local governments confiscated the caves, Tagbanuas from Cabugao and Banwang-Daan underwent extreme oppression. The senior counsel of Cabugao stated, "We are experiencing the feeling of hunger till death." The clans rose up to protest the confiscations. Although desperation forced some families to gather nests in their own caves for the winning bidder, the protests of Tagbanuas on Coron Island grew.

In the mid-80s, 'Kudol' or Rodolfo 'Kudol' Aguilar, a member of the Cabugao Barangay Council who later became the president of the Tagbanwa Foundation of Coron Island (TFCI), coordinated with Tagbanuas in Lamani, Quezon, in central Palawan through the government's Community Forest Stewardship Agreement (CFSA) program.[78]

After four years of close monitoring by the TFCI, the public auctions of the clan caves was discontinued protect the swiftlet population. Permission for outsiders to visit Awuyuk lake was also terminated. Meanwhile, the CFSA was awarded final certification in 1990. Municipal tax collection was discontinued in Coron Island, so the Tagbanuas did not have to pay retroactive tax anymore. Life in the community has returned to the original laws of the Tagbanwa".[79]

In general, the Tagbanua ethnic group believes that whoever found the bird's-nest cave on the island, the community, and the other nest-gatherers would respect the exclusive rights to harvest swiftlets' nests of the cave discoverer. The practice has been passed down from generation to generation since the arrival of the Chinese traders.[80]

The above traditional practice is accepted among the Tagbanua ethnic groups. They agreed to keep secret about the caves and not allow any outsider to enter.[81]

The bird's nests the Tagbanuas gather belong to their family and revenues are shared within it. The clan and the family that found the caves must share with the community because they are a legacy of common ancestors, but those who found the caves will not tell where they are to prevent theft.

Tagbanuas people name each cave and grant inheritance rights to others. Inheritors of the cave are healthy *busyadors*, granted the rights from their father by a received a torch or *saleng*. Anyone allowed to enter the cave are acknowledged as family.[82]

Tagbanuas have clear rules for those who find a cave. They have exclusive rights to gather nests within that cave, and to pass down ownership through generations of their family. To maintain sustainability, Tagbanuas set open and closed seasons. During collection season, they have to inform the Ancestral Domain Management Plan, or ADMP.[83]

In the case of birds' nests at Black Island, which is part of Busuanga, Palawan, as well as Coron Island, a *busyador* revealed that there are about 700 nest caves in total. Approximately 200 are owned by minority Tagbanua, while the rest are in Barangay Panlita (BGY. Panlaitan). There are 20–30 gatherers who collect about 300–500 kilograms per year.

Although the Philippines has no national laws regarding bird's-nest resources, there has been a presidential decree on the rights of indigenous people [the Indigenous People's Rights Act 1997 (IPRA)].

One difference in more recent times is that the benefits of the nest resources does not provide a share for uncles, unlike in the past when the nests were more widely shared among the extended family. Currently, when gathering nests for sale, they earn money to share within the immediate family group, with men and women taking equal shares.

The *busyador* also said that before 1971, he had to pay 50 pesos in tax per year, but following the Indigenous People's Rights Act (IPRA), the state no longer collects the tax.

When there is a dispute, Tagbanuas will abide by a decision or judgment by the village committee. If nests are stolen, the thief must repay the cave-owner money equal to the price of the stolen nests. If it cannot be recovered, they must turn to the police to take the thieves to jail. But mostly, they handle their disputes internally.

On Black Island, the leader is the a village chairman, selected according to the law. Everyone respects and obeys him. When there is a problem on the island, the chairman manages and resolves all issues.[84]

The Tagbanuas will not sell their caves, even among relatives, since it is inherited from their ancestors, to be passed down so grandchildren and their descendants can continue to work as nest-gatherers.[85] Descendants start learning the skill at the age of 10–14 years old.[86]

In the case of nest sources at Pabellon / Pabillion Island, Palawan, all *busyadors* are Cuyonon. Rock climbing skills have been passed down from father to son, from generation to generation since ancient times.

The caves are a personal heritage, and those with the rights to them are more guardians than owners. They are obliged to look after the caves and ensure the nests are gathered.

Indigenous Tagbanua people are believed to have been gathering nests since Chinese merchants traveled by junk to Palawan land, not later than the 11th century. Chinese trader records say they came to Pabellon Island in 1662 and purchased nests and other local products with ceramics and brass gongs.

At one time, the local government gave the Chinese traders concessions to harvest Pabellon's nests, but in 2004, *busyadors* banded together to buy the Pabellon Island concession from the local government to re-establish a sustainable gathering system. Currently (2013), the haresters must pay a tax to the municipal government 2.6 million pesos per year (PHP 2.6 million).[87]

In the case of El Nido, Palawan, the indigenous peoples have ancestral domains among various islands. The municipal government has granted the nest-gathering licenses since the early 1990s. The local government has also set the seasons for nest harvesting. Open season is from December to June. The gatherers must wait until after the baby birds can fly.[88] Some of the caves are open to bidding for harvesting rights.[89]

A former Filipino bird nest-gatherer claimed that there are no concessions for the caves, but the gatherers must pay taxes to the local El Nido government. He also said that sometimes, when the nest-buyer has issued a loan to the gatherers, they have to sell them to that buyer.[90]

In the same way, the owner of the caves can claim inherited rights to ancestral caves but still have to pay tax to the municipality of El Nido.[91]

It can be said that, for the Tagbanua ethnic group, generally, if there is a conflict over the nests, whether between relatives or with outsiders, it is handled according to Tagbanua traditions, with community elders resolving the dispute. To protect the swiftlet population, nest-gathering is banned in May when the swiftlets hatch. Violators will be punished by the elders.[92]

As for the business of nest trading, according to field data on trading in Coron Town, the nest purchaser must have a license to buy nests. The one-year permit is issued by the local government for 4,346 pesos.[93]

Presently, the caves and the swiftlets are resources of local governments and indigenous groups, under the control of the Department of Environment and Natural Resources (DENR), the local government of Palawan, and the municipal government. In the case ownership rights to the caves at Coron Island and Black Island, Busuanga – Palawan, the Certificate of Ancestral Domain Claim (CADC) ensures the caves belong to the Tagbanua ethnic group.

In the case of rights and legal systems regarding nest resources at Coron Island and Black Island, which is part of Busuanga, or at Pabillion Island, Palawan, the indigenous ethnic groups, the Tagbanau and Cuyonon, inherit the caves in line with traditional practice.

The traditional and legal rights to inherit reflect the society in Palawan, which was initially a tribal system, then a feudal system, or Sultanate, through a colonial society and eventually a democratic society. There is a relationship between the monopoly rights and powers tied with a specific person or agency in the management of the nest resources.

This is the basic characteristic of single resource management ('linear system of management') which is a 'linear concept of rights' that involves exclusive rights. The person who found the bird's-nest caves pass the caves on to their descendants though inheritance – a customary right. But at the same time, they also have a 'complexity of rights' in the Dynamism of Rights as 'communal property' that gives rise to the 'rights of access' to resources. It opens to the rise of the 'rights of management and control', resulting in inclusive rights which gives the cave-owners the right to gather the nests in their caves.

This has led to a more complex nature of resource management ('multiple systems of management') in order to manage the nest resources sustainably. Even in the democratic era, most of the rights system is still a 'linear concept of rights' with the caves belonging to the families within their ethnic group. While at El Nido, there is a variety of rights systems. Both the inherited rights to ownership of the caves and the rights to gather the nest belong to the ethnic group, while the right to open nest-gathering concessions to public bidding belings to the local government.

But in another dimension, in the part of the ownership rights of a person or family, if viewed from the appearance of the state of the local, it implies openness to the 'complexity of rights' or the 'communal property' that allows 'rights of access' to the resources, and to the certification or acceptance in the 'ethnic rights' that overlap.

The rights and legal system relating to the management of birds'-nests in the Philippines can be classified into three types:

1. The bird's-nest cave-rights system which is owned by personal or family (personal or family-owned cave as private property)
2. The rights of the bird's-nest caves which are the community caves (Common cave – Common regimes)
3. The cave system is owned by the state and leases concessions to private contractors (caves tender to private contractors as state property).

Nonetheless, in modern laws related to swiftlet nest resources, the Philippines does not have both direct enforcement laws regarding nest-farm building-control and the natural cave resource of swiftlets. Each province that has natural sources of swiftlet's nests has the power to enforce laws and regulations according to their own local characteristics.

However, the law and rights system are a technology of power for access and discrimination of the use of such resources in the nest business world of the Philippines.

It can be said that the ethnic groups that can access and use the nest resources in natural sources whether it is monopolized by groups that own the caves, the owners of the birds' buildings, and the local government. The cave-owners and the local government, there is a relationship between the power to access and use the overlapping bird's-nest resources, both at the center of power and the edge of power. The power to manage the natural bird's-nest resources is centralized in the local government and tied to Absolute Rights. The power centralized in the local government is being monopolized and linked to individuals or agencies specializing in managing the nest resources. Though the characteristics of the power tied to the Absolute Rights discouraged and prevented participation; still, it is also opened to involvement to access the management and the use of nest resources. .

The social class hierarchy and the arrangement of historical, social power relations are one reason why the inheritance of swiftlet caves and the nest-gatherers has been passing down to the family's descendants. These reasons brought the bird's-nest caves under the exclusive rights of a person or clan. These caves are a 'communal property', and being the 'complexity of rights.' The 'Communal Property' has the rights and law system that opens up to participation as each group's inclusive rights. The 'Complexity of Rights' has the characteristics of 'multiple systems of management' under the complex legal management system, also known as Legal Pluralism. There is the significance of certifying the rights of ethnic groups ('ethnic rights').

The owners of the man-made nest-farm buildings, regardless of ethnic group, have the right to pass on the buildings and the business to their descendants, according to the law.

5. BUSINESS AND MANAGEMENT SYSTEM IN THE PHILIPPINES

5.1 Bird's Nest Business in Ancient Time – Conservative Society

Pugad ng Balinsasayaw or the Swiftlet's Nest is known as 'white gold'[94] or eastern caviar (the 'Caviar of the East').[95] In the Philippines, the gathering of nests from natural sources has primarily followed the ways of ancient times. The local technologies are the torch or *sahing*, ropes, and bamboo ladders used for climbing to gather the nests from the cliff.

Since the Philippines is a country comprising thousands of islands, it is called the "Eastern Islands" and the "Pearl of the Orient". It has for hundreds of years had

The two-arm scales for weighing nests, owned by traders in Coron Town, Palawan.

the potential to provide birds' nests for food and medicine as a special resource for certain communities in the Philippines society.

In the current awareness of communities involved in the nest business in in the Philippines, the Tagbanua, Cuyunin or Cuyonon, and Filipino ethnic groups have been the traditional gatherers and sellers in Palawan since the 11th century. Even though the Filipino or Tagalog is the dominant ethnic group, the history of the business reflects the history and social status of local ethnic groups, and the geographies of exclusion by producing a legendary history of the gathering of birds' nests in the Philippines.

There are a variety of historical perspectives on the gathering of birds' nests. On Coron Island, an important source of the nests in Palawan, the Tagbanua ethnic group has inherited and passed on the ownership of the bird's-nest caves and gathering rights for centuries. There are local myths concerning the bird's-nest resources and the name of the island.

One of them is the story of Calis Island. The name 'Calis' of Calis Island allegedly comes from 'Calee,' the Chinese merchant who found the swiftlet nests hidden inside dangerous caves. He is the one who educated the indigenous people on the value and the method of harvesting and trading the nests. One day he disappeared. After three days of searching, the natives found he had died. While searching for him, the natives shouted his name: 'Calee Calee!. So the island was named Calis Island.[96]

There is some ancient historical evidence of the bird's-nest resources at Coron Island and Black Island, Pabillion Island, or the islands in El Nido. Chao Ju-Kua, a Chinese chronicles writer, wrote a book called *Chu Fan Chi*, printed in 1225 A.D..[97] Miguel de Loarca, the Spanish chronicles writer, recorded the trade in his book in 1582 A.D..[98] The trade is also mentioned in Chinese narratives in early 1209 A.D..[99] The claims of the Calamianes about trade with Chinese middlemen can be traced back to 1225 A.D..[100] Local history says Chinese traders first got in contact around 982 A.D.,[101] during the early Sung Dynasty (960–1279 A.D.), just before the 11th century.

All of this evidence states that the Indigenous Tagbanua gathered birds' nests[102] to exchange with Chinese traders for their products.[103] This evidence also stated that the Tagbanua were trading in the global trade system not less than 400 years ago.[104]

Until the early 1970s, when President Ferdinand E. Marcos (1965–86) dominated the Philippines, the government of the Kalamian municipality used its power to legislate that the ancestral caves of the Tagbanuas, scattered throughout the islands of northern Palawan, belonged to the state. It also opened for auction the rights to gather the nests, which is a traditional way of life and source of income for the Tagbanuas.[105]

In 1990, the current agreement was announced. Government nest taxation was null and void. The rights to the land and the caves returned to the Tagbanuas. Outsiders were banned from gathering nests.[106]

The Indigenous People's Rights Act (IPRA) was issued in 1997, giving the rights to inherited land [The Certificate of Ancestral Domain Claim (CADC)].

In the 1920s, the local government of Taytay gave nest-gathering concessions in Pabellon (Harvesting Pabellon's nests) in Taytay Bay to Chinese merchants. Then, in 2004, the *busyadors* (nest-collectors) bought the concession from the local government to manage the system and ownership themselves.[107]

All of these reflect the nature of business systems and management of the bird's-nest business in the Philippines, where the caves are the property of local ethnic groups. The local government has used the system to allow various ethnic groups and some private bidders be the nest-gatherers. All the ethnic groups have a significant relationship with the Chinese.

Meanwhile, the country's ethnic groups have perpetuated beliefs about the consumption of birds' nests by Chinese through social process. This social process created the structure of awareness and importance in the value system that allowed various ethnic groups in the Philippines to believe in the value and the special features of birds' nests. Within the social relationship there is a consistent set of recognition processes, causing a symbolic capital that people recognized. These symbols were created with any specific sets of recognition processes that are created in various ways of thinking, allowing various ethnic groups in the Philippines to understand both values and beliefs in the value and special properties of the nests.[108] These beliefs gave both faith and importance to a value system that supports the nest business system by asserting that the bird's-nest is a special food of Chinese emperors, the nobility, and the rich in Chinese dynasties. It also reinforced the value by calling the bird's-nest soup "The Emperor's Soup," or "The Longevity Soup."[109]

There are however no clear details about the nature of the bird's-nest business in the Philippines' feudal or Sultanate era.

The bird's-nest business system has continued with its traditional momentum. Even when Spain, Japan, or the United States imposed colonial rule, they still certified the rights of various ethnic groups to – access nest resources. Then some caves were co-opted by the local government after the Philippines gained independence in 1946. From that time, some local governments still employed a bidding system for various ethnic groups and private concessionaires to gather nests until the present day (2013). Despite the popularity of the finished nests, consumption in various prepared forms is increasing in line with the convenience of modern society, but most are still selling them in raw nest form.

5.2 Business of Birds' Nests in Food Sovereignty Time: Postmodern Society

From the era of President Fidel Ramos, the Philippine government implements a foreign policy of Development Diplomacy, planning for economic development for the Philippines to become far more advanced by 2000 A.D., according to the 'Vision 2000' policy.

President Gloria Macapagal Arroyo (2001–2010) conducted the "Making the Republic of Stronger" policy (Strong Republic Vision) from 2004 onwards.[110] This policy was intended to develop the Philippines into an industrialized nation and adjust the social system to keep up with the global trade and business competition. Yet, the bird's-nest business-management system has changed little. Each province, especially Palawan province, which is the largest producer of natural nest resources, has overseen the bird's-nest business on their own terms.

The business of the nest-farm buildings is the production of nests by adapting a building to replicate the natural swiftlet habitat. Until now (2013), most ethnic groups in the Philippines still have only limited awareness of the nest-farm business.

Since 1970, birds' nests have had a consistently high price. During the 1980s, the price of the birds' nests in the Philippines was very expensive.[111] After the mid-1990s, consumption increased.[112] In 2009, the price rose to USD 2,700 per kilogram.[113] In 2011, the price reached USD 3,000 per kilogram.[114]

In July 2011, in China, the local government of Zhejiang, led by the Department of Industry and the Trading Chamber of Zhejiang Province, seized fake bird's nests from Malaysia. They claimed that the Malaysian nests contained 350 times the acceptable level of nitrite based on public health authority standards.[115] This event caused China to suspend the nest imports from Malaysia. The drop in consumer confidence also impacted the market with prices plummeting in the Philippines, Southeast Asia, and around the globe.

Size of the Philippines Bird's-Nest Business

Of the country's 79 provinces, only 17 feature natural swiftlet habitats, with Palawan Province as the major producer of bird's nests. There are few bird's-nest sources outside the natural habitats.

Ethnic groups in the Philippines are the primary nest producers. Hong Kong is the middle market to buy and sell the nests. Mainland China is a major consumer. Due to the buyers requiring Chinese language to conduct business, the bird's-nest exporters from the Philippines to China and Hong Kong come mostly from local ethnic Chinese.

The estimated amount of birds' nest production from various sources can give an overview of the size of the business in the Philippines. In 2008, the country produced about 5 tons of nests[116] worth the USD 7,500,000 for domestic consumption with some exported to the markets in China, Hong Kong, and Japan.[117]

If the average price is USD 1,500 per kilogram, the Philippines earns about USD 7,500,000 per year.

Type and Price of Birds' Nests in the Philippines Bird's-Nest Market

In the Philippines business, the nests are classified by color and characteristics into four types.

According to 2009 field data, nest merchants in Coron Town, Busuanga Island, Palawan, said there are three grades of white nests: Grade A at PHP 170 per gram, Grade B at PHP 120 per gram, Grade C at PHP 70 per gram. The black nests are PHP 30–40 per gram.

Table 4.1: Bird's nest price in Coron Town, Busuanga Island, Palawan, Philippines, 2009

The bird's nest quality	Price PHP per gram
White bird's-nest Grade A	170
White bird's-nest Grade B	120
White bird's-nest Grade C	70
Black bird's-nest	30–40[118]

Based on 2009 field data, the nest-gatherers in El Nido, Palawan, said that there are 3 grades of the white bird's-nest:
- Grade A at PHP 220 per gram, Grade B at PHP 140–160 per gram, Grade C at PHP 80 per gram. The black bird's-nests are PHP 80 per gram.

Table 4.2: Bird's-nest prices in El Nido, Palawan, Philippines, 2009

The Bird's nest quality	Price PHP per gram
White bird's-nest grade A	220
White bird's-nest grade B	140–160
White bbird's-nest grade C	80
Black bird's-nest	80[119]

Table 4.3: Bird's-nest price in the Philippines from the 1950s to 2011[120]

Year	The Birds' nest characteristic	Price PHP per kg.
1950s	X	0.12
1999	X	110,000
2005	X	135,000–180,000
2007	X	120,000–200,000
2008	Bird's nest grade A	144,675
2008	Bird's nest grade B	96,450–112,525
2008	Bird's nest grade C	64,300
2009	Bird's nest grade A	160,000–220,000
2009	Bird's nest grade B	140,000–160,000
2009	Bird's nest grade C and black bird's-nest	80,000
2010	X	20,000–200,000
2011	X	25,720–38,580

Incentive and Welfare Systems for the Bird's Nest Gatherers in the Philippines Bird's-Nest Business

There is some 'secret information' and concerning the welfare of bird's-nest workers, including the cave-owners, nest-gatherers, nest-traders, as well as people who have a position of authority and others in the business.

The following 'secret information' comprises selected stories that reveal the world of the bird's-nest business in the Philippines.

Here, Coron Island, Palawan

Fidel E. Mondragon Jr., a male figure with a meaty figure, wore black glasses, a denim shirt and round-necked sweater. This 40-year-old man was the advisor of the vice chairman of Saragpunta Federation from Barangay (Brgy.) Dobcauon I.

It is a clear sunlit morning on May 24, 2008, at the bamboo reception desk at Saragpunta Office, Coron Town, Busuanga Island.

Roy Abella, a young man with dark tan skin with straight hair, played with a flat mustache, and wore a white V-neck sweater with the crimson color on the shoulders and armpits.

Next to him is Aldrin G. Caballero, a tough and tanned young man, with a round chin, a nice-looking nose, and wearing a white Polo Shirt.

These three Tagbanua from Coron Island told us:

> "... Swiftlet in the Tagalog language is called *balinsasayaw*. Tagbanua calls the swiftlet's nest *luray*. The Tagbanua inherit the nest caves from their previous generations.
>
> On Coron Island, there are about 150 bird's-nest caves in Barangay, owned by 120 people. Only 29 people from five families are expert *busyadors*. They can gather nests from five caves in a single day.
>
> The nests are gathered between late January to June. They will not gather birds' nests during the last week of May. And from January to February, no swiftlets appear in the caves.
>
> The gathered nests will be divided within the families of the owner. If the *busyadors* manage the gathering well, they will be wealthy. The Tagbanua ethnic group knows nothing about the business or the prices in the global market. The gathered nests will be sold to well-known merchants in Coron Town and Manila. The merchants in Coron Town are Chinese such as two brothers, Dodoy Pe and Dodoc Pe.

Tagbanuas sell the nests in cash, using old pesos on the dual-arm scales. The scales have the shafts on each side of the scale, one for the nests, and another for the pesos. The price of Grade A nests sold in the local market in Coron Town, is about 162,000 pesos per kilogram.

In Coron Town, the nests are divided into three grades and prices. The Grade A is 4,500 pesos per ounce. Grade B is 3,000–3,500 pesos per ounce. Grade C is 2,000 pesos per ounce.

If weighing the birds' nest in the unit of grams, the price is around 700 pesos per 1 gram, with a 1 peso coin equal to 5 grams. And the government excludes the nest tax..."[121]

On the late morning of July 6, 2009, from a rectangular table in a low-ceiling house belonging to Mr. Medardo Pe located in a slum with Coron Island as the backdrop to the southeast side of Coron Town, Busuanga Island, Palawan. Violeta Francisco, ethnic Filipino is a 59-year-old nest buyer with short wavy hair, an oval face, rounded chin and thin lips. She is still beautiful, and wears a white T-shirt with blue stripes. With her refined personality, soft tone, and kind demeanor, she said:

"... on Coron Island, the birds nest caves are owned by the Tagbanua. I know the cave-owners and have had a friendly relationship with them since my father's generation. My father began to buy the nests when I was just eight years old, more than 50 years ago. My main career is as a bird's-nest seller. Each year, nests are gathered from December to May. I buy the nests with cash. Then I boards the boat to Manila, and sells them to Chinese people in Chinatown.

When the merchants transport the nests, they fear robbers because there are frequent robberies. The robbers are both Filipino and Tagbanua. They have often shot and killed each other.

In the Philippines, the law requires bird's-nest traders to have a permit issued by the local government. Each license has a 1-year validity. The merchants have to pay 4,346 pesos per year per license. Despite being known to government officials, there is a two-year waiting period for the license. In Coron town, there are five people licensed to buy nests.

Filipinos who like to eat the birds' nests are rich, high-class people because the nests are so expensive. In the Philippines, there are no ready-to-drink bottles of bird's-nest.

There are three grades of nest. Grade A is 170 pesos per gram. Grade B is 120 peso per gram. Grade C is 70 pesos per gram. If it is black nest, the price is 30–40 pesos per gram. For the wet nests, the price drops by half.

On Coron Island, there are swiftlet birds in nature. The number of swiftlets in Coron Island each year remains consistent. There are no bird's-nest imports from other countries.' She smiled before saying her last sentence, "I'm thinking to continue being a bird's-nest merchant, buying the nests …"[122]

On a peaceful day, Tuesday, July 7, 2009. One man sat on the bamboo reception chairs under the thatched roof of a bamboo building. This building is both the Saragpunta office and a shelter for the young Tagbanua who come to study in Coron Town.

Rodolfo Aguilar was a small man with dark skin, scarred and wrinkled face, big ears, thick lower lip and short chin. He was a cave-owner, and the president of the Foundation of Tagbanua for Coron Island. This 60-year-old guy wore a blue T-shirt with pink letters reading 'CORON ISLAND' on the chest. He also wore a small white towel decorated with orange tartan stripes, a metal necklace decorated with a dark heart-shaped pendant, a garnet gold ring on his right index finger, and a stainless steel watch on his right wrist. He chewed betel nut and spoke with a voice of authority:

"… On Coron Island, bird's nest-gathering is a way of life, the main occupation of the Tagbanua since ancient times. The caves have been inherited from their ancestors to the present day.

In the past, the nests were gathered once a month from December to May. But in May, when the bird's eggs are hatch, there is no harvesting. During the period, the *busyadors* here do other work, such as planting vegetables, fishing, and weaving mats. These days, the Tagbanua have more choices of earnings, and more opportunities for education too.

I used to gather nests in my youth. But now, there are many people in the family who gather the nests. I have three children, two sons and one daughter. I gave my children, including my daughter, the cave. Each family has many children so they must share the cave harvests among themselves.

The bird's nest-gathering business relates to local history. There is a story that nest-gathering started when Chinese people came to the island for the first time. At that time, the local people exchanged their birds' nests for items such as clothes, rice, and others with Chinese people. There is no record or evidence of which Chinese Dynasty.

On Coron Island, there are many bird's-nest caves. The population of two barangays is approximately 250 households. Only 1 percent of them are Tagbanua who have no caves. After gathering the nests the Tagbanua sell them to Chinese people in Coron Town.

On Coron Island, there is a nest-auction each month. I have has four caves and can gather about half a kilogram per month.

The nests are sold to Chinese merchants. One of them is Medardo Pe. Other bird's-nest merchants are Mintot Tae and Laksonik Tae, the Chinoys (Chinese-Filipino). The Tagbanua will sell to the merchant who offers the best price.

Recently, the Tagbanua people have killed each other, with four or five dead, over nest-theft. They have to guard the caves against theft, and sometimes when someone gets caught stealing, there is a gunshot. The conflicts can occur between relatives and with outsiders.

The Tagbanuas owners of the bird's-nest caves have no price conflicts with the buyers. They only have to clean the nests to get a high price from the ethnic Chinese buyers. Studies and research on the various aspects of birds' nests in the area, but the local has no access to the papers.

Now, there are plans to ensure that the cave resources inherited from the ancestors are sustainable. Some NGOs have claimed that the Tagbanua's nest-gathering has caused a decrease in the bird population due to poor care. Another study has said this is not correct.

There is a detailed plan to protect the cave resources, planned in collaboration with the government and NGOs. For example, in May, gathering will not be permitted because it is hatching time. If anyone violates this rule, they will be punished by the community elders. Now the number of birds may be reduced a little bit from before ..."

Rodolfo also said, 'After the research report is finished, we would like to have a copy of it. And we want the natives elsewhere to recognize the Tagbanua at Coron Island...'[123]

Black Island, Palawan

It is after 3.00 PM on July 6, 2009, on the bamboo chair of a thatched roof cabin, in front of Black Island, Busuanga – Palawan, is Uncle Bird-De Guia Merlindo Aguilar, *buysador* Tagbanua, 71. He wore a khaki cap black Ray Ban, a pale green long-sleeved T-shirt, and black wide-legged shorts. He crouched on one knee, in a good mood and with a soft tone. He said:

"... This area, both in Coron Island and Black Island, is part of the Busuanga. In each area, people who have rights to gather nests are the Tagbanua only because they inherit the rights passed down from their ancestors. The main jobs are fishing and gathering nests. Normally, they fish all year round, except during June–August storms.

At Black Island, there are about 700 bird's-nest caves. The nests are gathered from December to April. There is no nest-gathering during May because the eggs are hatching then.

In Coron, Grade A nests are 150 pesos per gram, or 150,000 pesos per kilogram. Each nest weighs around 1 gram. We cannot get the Chinese people to raise their prices. Currently, the money from the sales is shared within the family, divided equally between each child. There is sharing to extended family, unlike in the past. Each family earns around 7,000 pesos per month, divided within the family. Some months the family earns only 3,000 pesos and also have harvesting expenses.

Before 1971, the indigenous people had to pay a 50 peso annual tax. But after The Indigenous People's Rights Act (IPRA) was issued, the tax was cancelled.

Before being sold, nests must be cleaned and trimmed. After trimming, they are wrapped in paper bags. The nests are carried to Coron Town to sell to Chinese people. Normally, women (not men) will carry the nests.

Coron Town has many conflicts and killings but not Black Island. On Black Island, there are no nest-farm buildings. All swiftlets live in nature. Each year, the birds usually lay eggs once, two eggs per time. Gatherers allow the eggs to hatch.

The whole island has 700 bird's-nest caves, potentially yielding 50–100 kilograms per month. This island has 20–30 *busyadors*. They can gather 300–500 kilograms per year. Grade A nests cost around 500 pesos per piece, while grade C is around 200–300 pesos per piece.

Scholars from Palawan and NGOs have said that if the Tagbanua continue gathering nests as they do, it will eventually destroy the birds. I do not believe this because the bird population is increasing."[124]

It is before sunset on Monday, July 6, 2009, at the beachfront of Black Island, near the wreck of a Japanese World War II ship: Uncle June (Uncle June-Perfecto B. Dabuit Jr.) is a *busyador* who owns a nest-cave. This 63-year-old man has gray hair, a strong body, dark skin, an oval face, protruding cheeks, scar between his eyebrows, and sparse mustache. He wore a gray polo shirt with black and white stripes, black shorts, and slippers. He spoke with a soft, deep voice over the sound of the evening waves, while having Ton Ton (Ton Ton-Mark Anthony S. Blanco), a mixed-blood Filipino youth, translate from Tagbanua language to English.

"… The house is at Barangay Panlaitan, Busuanga Island. A family of five, including wife and children, lives in a native house built with a bamboo, thatched roof, and a cement floor. I began to gather nests at the age of 15. My grandfather was the owner of the cave, and my father inherited it. Later, I owned the cave, because I stayed here while my brothers and sisters moved to Manila. My siblings had normal careers. The monthly income from the nest harvest was about five thousand pesos. Sometimes, it was not enough for the family, so I also went fishing, but the income from the nests is better than fishing.

Around the 1980s, the nests became much more expensive. At that time, Grade A was 150 pesos per gram. Each nest weighs about 1.50–2 grams. It should be 200 pesos per gram.

One can only gather the nests seven months of the year, from December to June. The quantities vary month to month.

Most people who eat the nests are Chinese. I also eat the nest when I gather it. But I will not eat the Grade A because it is too expensive.

During the gathering, I was afraid of robbers as well. There were frequent robberies at the caves. The robbers were Tagbanua. Each time, they took lots of nests. The only protection was guns. When going to the cave, we took the gun too. Later we would sell the nests and buy food and household stuff."

Uncle June also said, 'I want to tell people that being a nest-gatherer is very difficult …'[125]

Mid-morning of Tuesday, July 7, 2009, after returning from Black Island to Barangay Panlaitan, Talampulan Island, Busuanga Island: In the native house of Uncle June (Perfecto B. Dubuit) which has bamboo walls, a thatched roof, and cement floor. His 66-year-old wife is thin, with dark skin, short wavy hair and an oval face. She wore a white T-shirt decorated with a small blue and olivegreen flowers and long synthetic pants. She sat on a long bench, next to the half-cement / half-brick wall. She spoke with a husky tone, and was enthusiastic and cheerful. She reported:

"… There are 10 children. Before marriage I was a small shop-owner selling general goods. He was handsome. Becoming a *busyador*'s wife is not so difficult. But we have to worry about the dangers when they go to gather the nests, as the caves are dangerous. I went into the cave once. I also helped him clean the nests, removing all residues. I also taught the children how to do this.

If I was to marry all over again, I would marry a *busyador*. When my husband went gather the nests, I prayed for his safety. He also fished but the main income comes from the nests. Caves are inhberited and not bought and sold. Tagbanua will not sell their caves, even to relatives, because they have a family bond to the cave. Our children continue to work as *busyadors* '… We eat a little boiled birds' nest, but only low grade.' "

Rey D. Dabuit is a young man, aged 21. He has an oval-shaped face with crew cut hairstyle. He wore a red vest, black shorts, and a colorful necklace. He sat in a wheelchair because of his damaged legs. He said:

"… I began to learn to gather at the age of 13–14. When I went to the cave for the first time, I climbed up a 12 meter ladder. Then ladder broke and I fell to the ground between two rocks. The first feeling was thinking of God. Then I was weeping.'

Rey said, 'I shouted to my brother to help. I fell at 8.00 in the morning. I went to the hospital at 3.00 PM and spent three weeks there. I feel sorry that I now cannot gather nests. I also dream about nest-gathering when I sleep. I want the nest price to rise. My family has rights to receive income from the nests. We get a share around 5,000 pesos per month as the family income."

Before leaving, he said, 'I still dream that someday I will walk again …'[126]

Pabellon Island, Palawan

From some articles on the internet, we can summarize:

"… at Pabellon Island in Taytay Bay, the north of Palawan. The bird's-nest caves are the personal heritage as guardianships of individual caves. They are inherited from generation to generation.

Busyadors who specialize in gathering nests here are local Cuyonon men. Each cave is taken care of by a family that is responsible for the gathering.

In 1920, the government gave the Chinese concessions to harvest Pabellon's nests. In the 1950s, there were only 10 or 15 nest-gatherers. Now, there are more than 50.

Previously, selling the nests to Chinese men from Manila, they sold for 0.12 pesos per gram. Each gathering would yield about 35 pesos (PHP 35), a good income at that time. Until 2004, *busyadors* joined together to buy the Pabellon concessions from the local government and the municipality has sent the police to take care of the island. Nowadays (2013), the climbers have to pay taxes to the municipal government of 2.6 million pesos per year (PHP 2.6 million) ...."[127]

El Nido, Palawan

It's 11:40 AM on July 9, 2009. The sky and the sea of the Pacific Ocean were full of black clouds and rainstorms. After three researchers from Thailand took a boat back from photographing grass-nest swiftlets [*kola-kola ibon* or grass-nest swiftlet (*Collocalia esculenta*)] in the Codognun Cave of El Nido – Palawan, Dennis Garcia sat on a bamboo seat in the pavilion of Codognan Resort. He is a 19-year-old Filipino ethnic boy with a large and dark-skinned body. He had short hair, an oval face, acne scars, an apple-shaped nose, thick lips, and nice white teeth. He wore black wide-legged sports shorts and no shirt. He was a former busyador from Cadlao Island, and the resort administrator of Codognan Island.

He said:

"... The gathering of nests here (in El Nido) is very common and there are a lot. The caves have no concessions but the gatherers pay taxes to the local government. Here, they gather the nest for 6 months each year from December to May, every 15 days. If there are many nests, there is some theft too.

I used to gather the birds' nests in Cadlao Island. There are lots of *busyadors* on the island because it is near El Nido town. At the age of 12–14, I was a *busyador*. My first gathering was with my father's siblings. They still gather nests, but my father is a tour guide. My relatives are at home in El Nido.

The basic equipment for gathering nests are torches and ropes. We spray water on the nests and our hands to make it easier to gather them. Without water, the delicate nests will break. Sometimes, the gatherer uses a fork tool.

Chapter 4

> We gather 30–50 grams per time. The workers divide up their duties. Sometimes a nest-gatherer will be a guard. Normally the *busyadors* will not sleep on the island, arriving in the morning and returning in the evening. Only guards sleep on the island to guard the caves.
>
> *Busyadors* gather the nests into a small bag and take it to their houses to dry. After the nests are graded, they are sold to the buyer. Sometimes, the buyer advances money for fuel to get to the island. Grade A is 220,000 pesos per kilogram. Grade B is 140,000–160,000 pesos per kilogram. Grade C and the black bird's nest is 80,000 pesos per kilogram. The buyer who is the big shot here is an old Chinese merchant."
>
> Then Dennis Garcia said, 'I have to go. I have business in the city...'[128]

In the Philippines, besides having the bird's-nest shops in the major cities, the Bird's-Nest Trading Company also has a direct internet sales system another marketing channel with the characteristic going directly to the middle class and the elites—the wealthy consumers.

Note: However, gathering nests from natural sources is not a job performed throughout the year, especially during the 5-month closed season. The nest-gatherers have to have other occupations, such as planting vegetables, fishing, and weaving mats.[129]

Export Market

The major market in the Philippines is domestic. Still, there are Chinese ethnic businessmen who gather buy the nests and send it them for sale in China, Hong Kong, Japan.[130]

Nest-Trade Relationships with Swiftlets as a Link for Ethnic Relations

Nest-Trade Relationships with Swiftlet's as a Link between Ethnic Groups

The unique characteristics of the swiftlet nest, which have their own hierarchy, are food as nature, food as the culture maker, food as a medicinal drug, healthy food,

food as commodity, food supplies industry, food as a gift, and a symbolic food of the wealthy. It is complicated, contradictory, and can flow within itself. It may be said that it is the social property system which can be the state property regime, – private property regime, 'communal property' regime, the *res nullius* regimes, or the open-access regimes[131] at the same time. It can simultaneously be a resource that is state property under laws requiring the protection of swiftlets as a resource like other state resources. It is a resource that is private property when the swiftlets make their nests in private dwellings. It is joint property or community property. It is an open asset that anyone can access when swiftlets build their nests in a purpose-made building. All of these are brought about by the fact that humans cannot control where the swiftlets choose to stay or not stay.

In the Philippines, the bird's-nest business world with resources as intermediaries (mediator) forges a relationship of people in the state, both within the ethnic group and across ethnic groups. Although the Filipino or Tagalog ethnic group is the dominant ethnicity in the Philippines, however, they are not the only ethnic group holding access and the use of nest resources. The access to nest resources is diverse, since many ethnic groups, such as Tagbanua, Cuyonon, and Chinese, participate in the business. Certain ethnic groups have monopoly power to manage the access and the use of the bird's-nest resources from the natural environment. The power is in both the authority level which has the power to manage and control, and the gatherers' level, which includes the cave-owners, the nest-gatherers, and the guards.

Within each ethnic group, there is a power hierarchy to manage the access and use of the resource. The power has both 'within the group' as the center of power, and 'blockade' keeping most outside of the center of power. The power is the access and the use of bird's-nest resources.

An example of the 'within the group' relationship is the case of the inherited rights from generation to generation in the clan of the Tagbanua and Cuyonon in Palawan, and elsewhere.

On the other hand, the relationship between ethnic groups called 'blockade' both prevents people from the same ethnic groups from holding power, while also excluding people from other ethnic groups.

The bird's nest robbery happens when there is an opportunity with no guards at the nest caves. The example of these cases are both the Tagbanua people and Filipino people who have had no caves robbed.[132]

Nest-Trade Relations Across Ethnic Groups

In the nest business, there is a private bird's-nest business company owned by Chinese-Filipino people. The Chinese merchants purchase the bird's nest from various ethnic groups, then export it for sale in China, Hong Kong, Japan.

In conducting the trade, both within or between ethnic groups, the company-owners, sellers, and buyers will have a strong relationship. They must have mutual trust in both the quantity of the raw nest as the product and the continuous supply to meet demand.

The owner of Home of Swallows Limited, the top company that sells raw nests and ready-to-consume bird's-nest drinks in Hong Kong, supplied to both Hong Kong and China, said that nests imported for sale in Hong Kong come from four sources: Indonesia, Malaysia, Vietnam, and Thailand. The quality nests from Malaysia are popular and most are transported to Hong Kong by airplane.

The Philippines have been instructed to export nests in small amounts[133] because the quality is not up to the standard desired by the market. In the Philippines, although consumption is popular within various ethnic groups, there seems to be no exclusion of ethnic groups in the business. Any ethnic group can enter the business in the Philippines, though the Chinese ethnic group holds most power in pricing, in the Philippines, China, and the Hong Kong world market. Hong Kong also has a significant influence on prices in the Philippine markets, especially following the scandalous event, "Fake Blood Bird's Nest in July 2011" in China led to unnegotiable import regulations.

That event was where China announced the import conditions and quality of nests from all exporting countries. This had an impact on the bird's-nest business for various ethnic groups. The Mestizos, Philippine Chinese (or Chinoy) ethnic groups must comply with stipulations and the business requirements of the new open business in China.

The opening of China in the new century has caused a ripple effect on the nest business in the Philippines, and other producing countries.

The ethnic Chinese group in the Philippines is now essentially a monopoly in the nest trade across the states. Since the nest business at the international level or across the state level is monopolized by Chinese, it reflects the conflict that is based on the arrangement of power relations with inequality in access to nest resources in the state and the nests produced for internal consumption and export to the international market.

However, even though global society has changed rapidly, the nest-gathering from natural sources in the Philippines still bears the characteristics of a hunter-gatherer society. Local—unchanged for centuries—technologies are torches, the ropes, and bamboo ladders. These are used for climbing and gathering the nests during the harvest season. This somewhat primitive method and system is at odds with an era when global society places great importance on food production and food sovereignty.

6. BIRDS' NESTS IN POLITICS AND SOCIETY

Long after the Philippines was named after King Phillip II of Spain by Ruy Lopez de Villalobos, a Spanish explorer in 1543,[134] the establishment of the first Philippine Republic (Biak-ng-Bato Republic) began on June 12, 1898. It was about 115 years after the beginning of the 16th century when these islands were encountered for the first time by Spanish navigator, Ferdinand Magellan. In 1521, the Spanish colonial government took possession of the island group and held it for more than 343 years before native rebellion in 1898. In the late 19th century, the Spanish colonial government in the Philippines employed a strict and brutal regime, for the benefit of the marine traders using 'Manila Galleons'.[135] When it finally gained full independence on July 4, 1946, the period under a colonial regime totaled 425 years. Being a Western

Chapter 4

Officers inspect bird's-nest sellers in the stores of Palawan.

Colony, especially in the Spanish (1564-1899) and American (1899-1946) eras had an impact on the country's social structure, creating a blend of Eastern and Western cultures. This was arrived at primarily through religious influence from Spain and the democratic political culture of the United States.[136]

The Philippines is a modern state[137] that has processed the social and economic aspects of "traditional" society through the colonial regimes. It created a new model of political and economic organization, resulting in massives changes to local societies and the traditional communities in an attempt to create a unified nation. Until now (2013), the Philippines has had to change the social and political structure while taking the multicultural society and ethnic diversity into account.

From the socio-political perspective, nest resources from natural sources, nest-collecting is 'beyond its size'[138] due to the high price of nests since the 1980s.[139] It is in fact one of the major causes of the decline in swiftlet populations. This has driven changes in social and political conditions.

The reflections from many perspectives of ethnic groups in the Philippines show the changes in the relationship. Both 'bringing into the group' to be in the center of power, and 'blockading' from the center of power have changed in the details of access to nest resources as the social and political resources. Whether it is ownership rights local politicians, the auction committee, monopolizing the nest-auction from the private nest business of some ethnic groups in the Philippines, the data reserves and the implementation of authority on nest resources are provided only to certain groups of people.

This caused changes in the details of the original state power structure for both ethnic groups with cave-ownership inheritance and the local governments. Its effects altered the traditional laws and regulations, the laws for restoration and conservation of the swiftlet species, and the openness of the community to participate in the nest management from the guardianships of individual caves. This along with the nest dealer, the winning bidder, the Palawan Council for Sustainable Development (PCSD), and the respect for indigenous laws and practice.

In the case of the caves at Coron Island, Palawan, however, the nest-gathering has been inherited for many generations.[140] In the early 1970s, the Philippines fell under the dictatorship of President Marcos, from 1972–86, which was a period of the patronage system over the local government.[141] The Kalamian Municipality, Northern Palawan, used the power to legislate and seize the Tagbanwa clan caves, nullifying the rights of the Tagbanua to inherit clan caves according to the their traditions. The municipality seized ancestral caves as state properties and opened bidding the rights to gather nests, granting exclusive rights. The municipal government also also issued an order to collect inheritance tax from the caves inherited from their ancestors.[142]

By specifying a trade schedule to prevent excessive gathering of nests and a lowering of quality, only the winning bidder had the right to sell the birds' nests. The Tagbanuas, who had been the owners of the caves and the sellers became the only gatherers to collect the nests from their clan caves. The winning bidder was the Tagbanua *mestiza*, backed by Chinese traders from Coron Town. The mixed-blood Tagbanua hired Cuyonons to guard the caves.[143]

When the municipal governments seized the clan caves, Tagbanuas from Cabugao and Banwang-Daan rose in protest against this. Until the mid-80s, under the leadership of 'Kudol' or Rodolfo 'Kudol' Aguilar, the Government's Community

Forest Stewardship Agreement (CFSA) was issued in 1990, canceling orders for municipal taxes on Coron Island. There was no payment required for retroactive tax and everything was returned to the original way of the Tagbanua.[144]

Caves being owned by the Tagbanua are recognized within the ethnic group as traditional practice. So the caves are kept secret. Others cannot enter, because since the cave is received from ancestors, others are not allowed to participate.[145] This is a measure to prevent nest-theft.[146]

In the case of Black Island in Busuanga, Palawan, the caves and the right to gather the birds' nest heres belong to the Tugbanua. They also inherit the rights without dispute.

When there is a problem, the Tagbanua go to the barangay, the village committee. If nests are stolen, the thief must return the money equal to the price of what they stole. If it is not paid, the official judicial system becomes involved.[147]

In the case of Pabillion Island, Palawan, *busyadors* from Cuyunon likewise inherit the rights from father to son.

In El Nido, Palawan, the municipal government is authorized to license the rights. The indigenous people have the right to inherit their ancestral domain on some islands,[148] but some caves are open to bidding for the rights.[149] They also pay taxes to the local government.[150] Similarly, the *busyadors* can claim inherited caves from their ancestors but have to pay tax to the municipal government of El Nido.[151]

However in one conflict several people were shot to death and lawyers were enlisted to assist the tribe whose members were shot. A family of businessmen had lobbied through local politicians in an attempt to own the rights on the island and intended to block the local people from inheriting the ancestral rights as on other islands.

Though nest-farm buildings have been greatly contributing to nest-production in other Southeast Asian countries, most notably Indonesia, the method is not widely used in the Philippines.

The scandal of fake blood birds' nests from Malaysia in July 2011, brought a halt to the business in Malaysia, as China stopped importing – from Malaysia, and other countries. It became international political issue for Southeast Asia. China issuing the inspection and quarantine regulations, taking effect from November 1, 2012, prohibiting people from bringing into China modified organisms, agricultural genetics, wildlife and endangered wild plants, and products made from wild animals and wild plants that are nearly extinct.

The amendment of this regulation added birds' nests (except ready-made nests), blocking them from importation into China.[152]

With nest-farm buildings, the owners are free to conduct business within the state, across states, and across ethnic groups. Because of the costs, the business is limited to people with ready capital, usually of Filipino ethnicity.

Considering birds' nests from the socio-political point, the everyday life's struggle within the ethnic communities is symbolic. People are disadvantaged in ethnic society in the Philippines, whether they are nest-gatherers, local politicians, bird nest businessmen, or even nest robbers in Filipino ethnic groups who steal nests from the caves.

They expressed everyday life resistance through gossip, intimidation, silent protests, and stealing the nests. All of this occurs quietly in everyday life because those who have been blocked or prohibited access to nest resources do not stand up and protest. They have been using the method called "Weapons of the Weak" to avoid being suppressed by the authorities or losing assistance from the authorities.[153] In some areas, especially in Coron Island in early 2009, Tagbanuas have killed each other due to conflict of interest and theft, resulting in 4–5 deaths.[154] These characteristics are the operation of the powerless that conceals criticizing the state power system or power across the state within the states that came to dominate. These characteristics are verbal expressions that indicate the innocence metaphor or concealment, which has been used as a tool to show the criticism of the dominance of the bird's-nest trafficking.[155]

One example is a report from the Palawan Wildlife Report Rescue and Conservation Center (PWRCC) which arrested a person who violated the Environmental law, the Republic Act No. 9147 (Wildlife Act) or Republic Act No. 9072 (Caves Act) in Palawan by smuggling nests without permission into Puerto Princesa Airport

(PPC Airport) El Nido from March to September 2012, with a total weight of 36.7 kilograms.[156]

In the late 1990s, local *busyadors* claimed that they had found blood marks on the nests. They claimed the blood means the bird population is under stress to make their nests because the Chinese concessionaires were granted the license by the local government of Taytay Bay Cuyunon, Pabellon Island – were over-harvesting. To earn as much money as possible, the Chinese concessionaires gathered the nests even when the birds were laying eggs, causing a drop in the population. The Chinese concessionaires were told that their actions harmed the bird population and long term production, but they did not care. In 2004, *busyadors* joined together to purchase the Pabellon Islands concessions from the local governments to employ their nest-gathering system, which they claimed to be more sustainable (2013).[157]

In another case from field data, the observation of one of the merchants in Coron Town said nest-smuggling was detected in early July 2009, meaning the nests were being gathered during the closed season (July–November).

The nature of these activities are considered to be multi-dimensional challenging of state power, cross-state power and authority in the unequal access to nest resources.

From both field data and official document data, theft and crime due to the "war of the bird's-nest resources", smuggling and theft appear to exist within the ethnic communities of the Philippines.

7. ENVIRONMENTAL AND ECOLOGICAL FACTORS

The Philippines and its 7,100 islands,[158] is a country with great biological diversity. There are over 12,000 plant species, over 8,000 flower species, 250 reptile species, 180 mammal species.[159] It is the habitat of 576 bird species, 195 endemic bird species. It is one of the top ranking countries where endemic species of birds are threatened.[160]

Before becoming a Spanish colony, the Philippines had abundant forests. In 1575, the total forest area was approximately 27.5 million hectares or almost 92 percent of the country's total area. But in 2010, the environmental group predicted that it could

A cabin guarding the bird's-nest caves on the cliff located in El Nido, Palawan.

be reduced to only 7 percent. These problems are becoming more violent, causing changes in the environmental management direction in the Philippines by changing from a state-to-public deal to a more and more globalized or universal concept of sustainable development. This change began being adopted in the country through the Philippines Agenda 21: PA 21[161] in 1992, in the days of President Ramos. The concept is that natural resources can be developed alongside the economy, principles accepted from the UN "Earth Summit."[162]

From the days of Ramos there was a period of economic development, that Filipinos believe arises from democracy. Democracy gives people the power to make decisions, contributing the people's ideas to help national development. According to Ramos's "Vision 2000" policy, the first policy is 'Empowerment,' which has been a great success. This policy enables empowerment to analyze problems, and join in developing one's community while petitioning the government for assistance.

The second policy is 'Development Diplomacy' which is establishing diplomatic negotiations to attract trade and investment to the country. The third policy is 'Entrepreneurial,' encouraging SME entrepreneurs to cooperate with foreign investors in trade and investment. The fourth policy is to open a naval base at Subic Bay as an Export Processing Zone, encouraging foreign investors to invest, and giving them special tax privileges. This is the basis for the economic development plan according to the 'Vision 2000' policy, which opens the Philippines to the outside world. President Gloria Macapagal Arroyo inherited this policy and continued opening the country to multinational relationships, raising economic growth to 7.5 percent[163] even though the economic development policy meets obstacles in law enforcement, with both government officials who ignored corruption and local influencers.[164]

As for environmental and ecological impacts in the Philippines, the changes have been mainly negative. Focusing on swiftlet resources, due to the ever-rising price of birds' nests, due to the increasing demands of the Hong Kong market since the 1980s, the harvesting in Palawan has reduced the swiftlet population.

The nest-gathering concessions granted by the local government in some areas of the Philippines, the over-harvesting of nests in Palawan, the 'traditional practice for the bird's-nest gathering' of some ethnic groups, and theft have been causing an ongoing reduction in the swiftlet population.

At Coron Island and in other areas, there has been a recent movement, because the swiftlet population has decreased rapidly. Due to ill-planned harvesting, young birds fell to their deaths in the caves. A marine biologist based in El Nido[165] Tagbanua people in Coron Island and Black Island, and the owners of bird's-nest caves, all assert that the swiftlet, all say the swiftlet population in Palawan has dropped.[166]

As a result, in 2004, the local government of Palawan through the Palawan Council for Sustainable Development (PCSD), approved PCSD Resolution No. 05-246, [167] PCSD Resolution No. 04-224,[168] and PCSD Resolution No. 04-225[169] on sustainable bird's-nest gathering. These regulations give the swiftlets sufficient time to build nests, lay and hatch eggs, and raise the young until they can fly.

In the current general condition of nest resources in the Philippines, there is now swiftlet resource management through preserving the species naturally.[170] Although the local communities, especially ethnic groups that own the caves, have authority and an important role in managing them, the swiftlet population is still declining.

At the same time, house-farm buildings, the new and growing method employed instead of gathering the nests from caves, aids the conservation of nest resources. The private sector in the Philippines still lacks the awareness of its significance as 'White Gold' or the 'Caviar of the East', a reflection of the inefficiency and potential that will take time to improve.

The environmental damage caused by the house-farming business is hidden. The Philippines has a few birds' buildings, but the pre-recorded sounds used to attract swiftlets to the buildings still does not match the noise problems that affect the health of the community as it has other Southeast Asian countries, where the swiftlet house business has boomed and proven to be difficult to control.

Chapter 4

APPENDIX

Ethnic Images and The Philippines Birds' Nest Resource

The characteristics of *balinsasayaw* or edible-nest swiftlets in Palawan, Philippines.

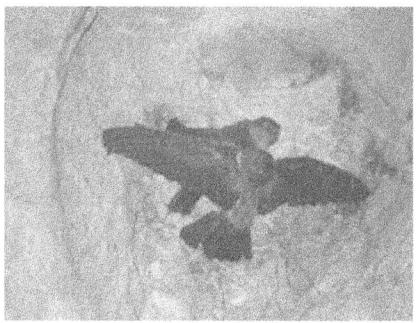

Kola-Kola or grass-nest swiftlets.

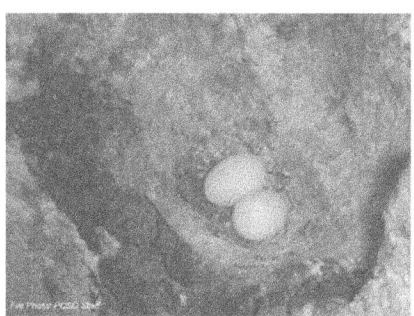

The eggs and the nest of edible-nest swiftlets in Palawan, Philippines.

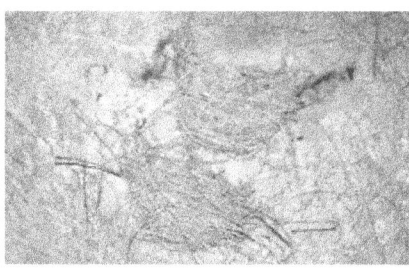

The nest of *Kola-Kola* in the caves of Codognan Island, Palawan, Philippines.

Busyador or bird's-nest gatherers of the Cuyonon ethnic group, with the nest at Pabellon Island in Taytay Bay, the Northern of Palawan.

Culture and Edible Birds' Nests in the Philippines

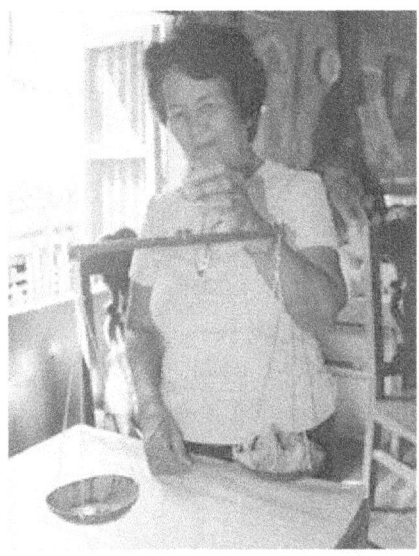

The old peso coins for weighing nests, owned by a bird's-nest trader in Coron Town, Palawan.

The two-arm scales for the bird's-nest weighing, owned by the bird's-nest traders in Coron Town, Palawan.

The bird's-nest gathering equipment of the *busyador* on the bird's nest island, Black Island.

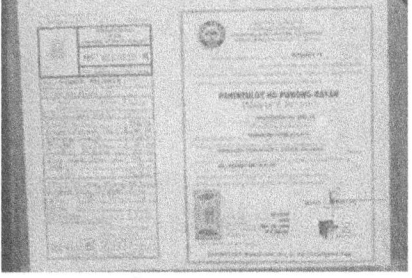

Sugpit, the bird's nest gathering tools owned by *busyadors* on the bird's-nest island, Black Island.

A license issued by the local government for bird's-nest traders in Coron Town, Palawan.

Chapter 4

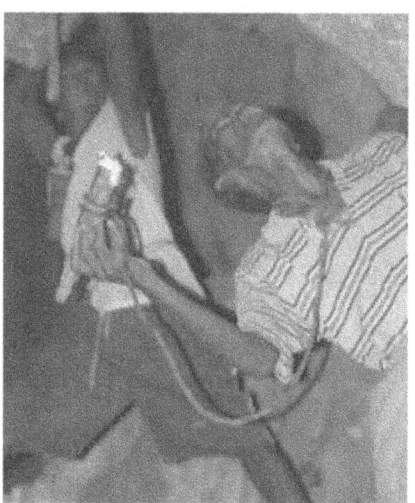

Busyador gather nests on Black Island.

When gathering nests in deep caves, a natural material torch or *sahing* helps make breathing easier.

A *busyador* climbs a cliff to gather birds' nests on Black Island.

Busyadors, Cuyunon ethnic group, climbing a bamboo ladder to gather the nest in the bird's-nest cave on Pabillion Island.

Inside a Tagbanua busyador's house in Barangay, Talampulan Island, Palawan.

Culture and Edible Birds' Nests in the Philippines

The scraps of *balinsasayaw* that the *busyador*'s family keep for their own consumption at Barangay Panlaitan.

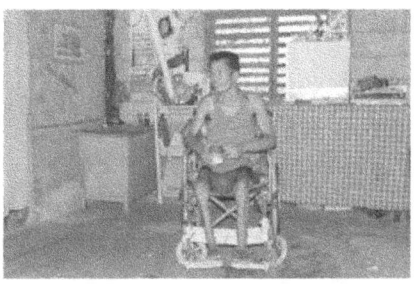

Rey, disabled young *busyador* who fell off a cliff while gathering bird's nests.

The researcher interviews the wife of a Tagbanua *busyador* at Barangay Panlaitan.

Busyadors of the Tagbanua ethnic group, help each other with ropes in a bird's-nest cave at Coron Island, Palawan.

The researcher interviews Rodolfo Aguilar, the chairman of Barangay, the chairman of the Tagbanua Foundation and a cave-owner at Coron Town.

The guest house of Tagbanua nest-gatherers on Black Island.

Chapter 4

A hut for guarding the bird's-nest caves on a cliff in El Nido, Palawan.

Nests in a cardboard box, brought for sale from El Nido to Puerto Princess, Palawan.

A test birdhouse in Davao del Sur, built according to the characteristics of the local area.

The cleaned bird's nest is ready to sell to tourists in Manila.

Bird's-nest soup with quail eggs at the high-class restaurant in Manila.

An advertisement board for nests in a high-class restaurant, located at Puerto Princess Town, Palawan.

Bird's-nest soup on the menu of the high-class restaurant in Manila.

5

Ethnic Groups and Bird's-Nest Resources in Thailand

INTRODUCTION

In a land on a peninsula just above the equator on the eastern hemisphere, there is a modern state with such a diversity of people and modern lifestyles. Yet, breathing underneath is an ancient kingdom where people of all races are welcomed but with a dominating ethnicity ideology. An old slogan portrays Thailand as a land of abundance, "... in the water, there are fish, and in the fields there's rice ...", bringing the pride of an ideal nation to the people.

It's also where, "[A]ny fellow walks with his own cattle to trade, rides horses to sell. Who would like to trade can trade freely, whether it's an elephant or a horse or gold ... the citizens are happy...." Among anthropologists, Thailand was once defined as a society with a "loosely structured social system,"[1] a notion that blended easily with a national pride at being called the Land of Smiles, before being spoiled by the Tom Yum Kung Financial Crisis in 1997, and political turmoil in early 2014.

Seafarers along Thailand's dual coasts—the Gulf of Thailand and the Andaman Sea—have for centuries explored the islands with limestone topography, home to swiftlets and their highly valued nests. Myths and histories about those who collect the nests often link to particular ethnic groups. Evidence buried underground and under the sea portray the arrival of Chinese merchants from the Sung Dynasty Period to Thailand's Ayutthaya Kingdom more than 500 years ago in pursuit of the nests.

Here, where thousands of islands are lying along the coasts, especially in the Southern Thailand, more than 170 islands play host to the swiftlets. Their nests form one of the most essential natural resources domestically and internationally, in terms of history, economy, society, culture, environment and ecological system, as well as the relationships between ethnic groups.

1. HISTORY OF THE INDIGENOUS PEOPLE AND BIRDS' NESTS

1.1 Swiftlets in Nature

Archaeological evidence found in the bird's-nest collectors community at the Koh Si Koh Ha Islands in Phatthalung Province include pottery from the Song Dynasty (1503–1822 B.E.), Ming Dynasty (1911–2187 B.E.), and Qing Dynasty (1636–1911 B.E.), along with ceramics from the Sukhothai Period (1792–1981 B.E.). This reflects an exchange system in both the domestic and foreign trades for the last 500 years, perhaps beginning in the Sukhothai Period.

Written evidence appears in the memoirs of French ambassador Simon de La Loubère (1686), who, during the reign of King Narai, noted that the Thai state collected swiftlet nests for sale in both the Gulf of Thailand and the Andaman Sea.

The harvest of birds' nests has played an important role in Thai society, economy, politics and culture for a long time, and we can divide the development of bird's-nest resources into these four periods:

Communal Collection (before 1792 B.E.)

For local populations, swiftlet nest consumption as a food was not very popular, but served rather as a component of natural medicine. From the 5th century B.C. onward,[2] Chinese traders traveled to southern Thailand to exchange Chinese goods for the nests, as indicated by the presence of Chinese pottery from the Song Dynasty (1503–1822 B.E.) found in Koh Si Koh Ha Islands, at Wat Rattanawararam, Bang Kaeo village, Bang Kaeo District[3] in Phatthalung Province. Around 10 pieces of colored pottery from the Ming Dynasty (1911–2187 B.E.) were also found at Wat Ban Laem Kruat, Koh Mak, and we also see small pieces of pottery from the Qing Dynasty (2179–2454 B.E.) in Ban Ao Tha Yang, Pak Phayun District, Phatthalung Province.[4] Chinese ceremonial art, such as statues of angels, found on Koh Si Koh Ha Island are believed to have been introduced to encourage the bird's-nest collectors at the start of the annual harvest season.[5]

Present-day worship of 'Ho Thao' and 'Ho Kae' or the ancestors among the collector community implies that they once had rights in both collecting and trading the birds' nests freely, with no one party presiding over the practice. A Phatthalung Provincial Court document chronicles the case of two people who were charged with an attempt to steal birds' nests. The judge dismissed the case, noting that the birds' nests were a natural resource, and could not be owned.[6]

Feudal Property System (1792–2482 B.E.)

At the end of the 18th century of the Buddhist Era (around 1792 B.E.), Sukhothai became the power center for Thais in the upper Chao Phraya River Basin, while

Nakhon Si Thammarat served as the center of power for southern Thailand and the Thai-Malay Peninsula. A clear relationship based on religion and trade developed between the two powers, with the swiftlet nests of the Thai-Malay Peninsula occupying a significant position in the latter. On the Koh Si Koh Ha Islands, then the main source of birds' nests, three ceramic[7] jars found in Tha Yang, Pak Phayun District of Phatthalung Province are thought to be related to this trade.

Later, as Nakhon Si Thammarat was annexed to the Ayutthaya Kingdom, it remained a center of international trade[8] and power on the southern peninsula, collecting taxes on goods traded among all cities of the south and sent to the Ayutthaya treasury.[9] This included taxation on bird's-nest resources on both sides of the Thai-Malay Peninsula, sent to Nakhon Si Thammarat, and sent to Ayutthaya as tribute.

The importance of the became apparent when Siam's ambassador Kosa Pan traveled to France in 1686, carrying a royal missive from Ayutthaya's King Narai the Great to France's King Louis XIV. French history records that, when the brother of Louis XIV, Duke of Orleans fell ill, Kosa Pan offered a present of swiftlet nests for the Duke as a cure. Likewise, when French ambassador de la Loubère arrived in Ayutthaya, he recorded that nests from Siam were traded freely as far away as Tonkin and Vietnam.[10]

During the Ayutthaya Period, we see no evidence of bidding on monopoly rights for swiftlet nests, although some historians believe that the nests were collected as tax.[11]

Nevertheless, the nests were valued very highly, and the Thai crown maintained absolute rights over the resource. "Bird nest taxpayers",[12] that is, the experienced nest-collectors, were ordered to present nests as tax to the local royal representative or royal tax collector. These nest taxpayers were found only in southern Siam.

In 1769, Siam's King Taksin traveled with his army to the south, he appointed rulers in Songkhla and Nakhon Si Thammarat.[13] The Siamese king appointed Hao Yieng, a Chinese man from Hokkien (Fujian) Province,[14] as head of Chinese immigrants[15] who were farming and fishing[16] in Songkhla in 1750. Hao Yieng evidently harbored vision about the nest trade, because he collated a list of valuables, including his wife, children, slaves and five boxes of Chinese red tobaccos, and presented these to King

Taksin in exchange for the right to collect birds' nests on Koh Si Koh Ha Island.[17] He also offered 50 *chang* (around USD 125) per year. The king received these gifts, and appointed Hao Yieng as tax collector. In 1775, the king bestowed the Chinese trader with a royal title and he was thereafter called Phra Songkhla (Yieng).[18]

Thus began the era of private rights for swiftlet nest concession holders in Thailand.

In 1782, after the crowning of the new Siamese King Rama I (1782–1810), the royal capital was moved across the Chao Phraya River from Thonburi to Rattanakosin (early Bangkok) and a new palace was built. With these changes[19] came changes in the south, beginning in 1791, when Songkhla began reporting directly to Bangkok. Rama I promoted Songkhla's Phraya Songkhla (Boon Hui) to the rank of Chao Phraya in charge of Pattani, Kelantan and Terengganu,[20] replacing Phraya Songkhla (Yieng), who had been close to the previous Siamese king.[21]

Boon Hui was granted the power to collect certain taxes, including birds' nest taxes. After he passed away in 1811, Siamese King Rama II (1809–1824) appointed Tien Chong, Boon Hui's grandson, to serve as Phraya Songkhla, and gave him control over Satun and La-ngu. He ruled over Songkhla and monopolized the nest trade in Songkhla for only three years, after which his brother Phraya Sunthonnurak (Thian Seng) replaced him as ruler of Songkhla. In the following year Thian Seng became tax collector for birds' nests until his death in 1847. Rama III (1781–1851) then invited Phra Sunthonnurak (Boon Sang) to serve as Songkhla governor. In 1861, under Siamese King Rama IV (1851–1868) Boon Sang also became birds' nest tax collector for Songkhla.

In 1865, Boon Sang died, and Phraya Sunthonnurak (Men), was promoted to Phraya Wichienkhiri became ruler and the birds' nest tax collector for Songkhla. He was succeeded by his son Chum under the reigh of King Rama V (1868–1910), who served until his death in 1888. Rama V then appointed Phraya Sunthonnurak (Chom) to rule and collect birds' nest tax in Songkhla for three years.

After that, nest taxation in Songkhla changed over from a city charter system to a system in which the rulers of Songkhla and families shared the nest profits, with periodic allocations that were sent to the central government.[22] This created great wealth for Songkhla rulers, especially the governor and assistant governor, for the next 130 years.[23]

Similarly, the rulers of Nakhon Si Thammarat, those who bore the family name Na Nakhon, were collecting bird's-nest taxes in Phang-nga, Krabi, and Trang cities for 71 years,[24] while Saiburi rulers took over the taxation of the birds' nests in Satun for 100 years.

From 1767 to 1891, rulers with concessions in the south—namely the families Na Nakhon, Na Songkhla, and Saiburi—were the only ones authorized to collect taxes for the central Siamese government. They passed these family monopolies down from generation to generation. At the turn of the 20th century, the Siamese royal government began taking a closer look at bird's-nest taxation, and in 1892 changed the nest-taxation over to a concession system for all bird's-nest areas in the south.[25]

The person who won the first concession auction was Luang Udomphakdi (Pun Na Songkhla), son of Phraya Wichiankhiri (Chum), a noble who was close to the governor of Nakhon Si Thammarat. Later from 1901 to 1905, he invited Chiang Soon, also close to the governor, to share the taxation concession in Chumphon.[26]

In 1927, Luang Phakdiphattrathon or Ko Hui Jia, son of a Chinese immigrant from Guangdong Province, won the auction and become the bird nest tax collector for Chumphon and Nakhon Si Thammarat, before transferring it to Lim Yim Ko, his shareholder. This Penang man was tax collector from 1930 to 1932, until Siamese military junta seized power from Rama VII and changed Siam from absolute monarchy to a titular democracy in 1932.

The junta established a committee to solve the country's economic problems by administering tax collection in a strict and systematic manner. Lim Yim Ko lost his nest tax concession for not paying the correct amount of tax, after which the finance ministry auctioned the concessions for Chumphon and Nakhon Si Thammarat Provinces in September 1932. Although Kang Liang Hung filed the highest bid, the ministry appointed Meng Tansacha as birds'nest tax collector for Chumphon and Nakhon Si Thammarat Provinces until 1935.

In 1935, the ministry re-opened the auction for Chumphon and Nakhon Si Thammarat Provinces again, and Chia Ha won the concession for 1935–37.

In 1938, another auction was held, but the winner never finished his three-year concession, because the government of Field Marshal Pibulsongkram enacted the Bird's-Nest Acts in 1939.[27]

Chinese Company Monopolies (1939–1992)

After 1939, private companies were in charge of bird's nest taxation.[28] The concession holder on Koh Si Koh Ha Islands, for example, was Rang Nok Tai Company Limited, a company in which it was rumored that Chief Marshal Thawee Chulasap had stock.[29] In 1956, the company sold out to Laem Thong Birds'-Nest (Siam) Company Limited,[30] a joint venture with a registered capital of THB 100,000,000 shared among ML Thawiwat Sanitwongse, Mr. Kamol Iamsakulrak, Mrs. Sumana Tangchitnop, Mr. Yui-tae Sae Ng, Mr. Yanyong Tangchit, Mr. Chu-meng Sae Ngung, Mr. Toh Sae Ngow, with Mr. Mongkhon Kanjanapas as chairman of the board of directors. Also involved was Dilok Mahadamrongkun, a businessman of Chinese descent who owned the largest watch manufacturing and distribution business in Thailand.

From 1959 to 2003, Hainan-born Mr. Ngow Yin and his company monopolized birds' nest concessions in Prachuap Khiri Khan, Chumphon, Surat Thani, and Koh Si Koh Ha Islands of Phatthalung.

Globalized Capitalism (1992–2014)

The Thai government response to communist insurgency in the south during the 1970s and early 1980s stifled trade with mainland China until 1992. After this, relations between the Thai and Chinese governments improved, which boosted the swiftlet nest business as direct trade between Thailand and China regained traction. China was, and remains, the most significant market for birds' nests consumption, and as the price of nests rose, the trade attracted crime and even violence, especially on the Koh Si Koh Ha Islands of Songkhla Lake in Phatthalung.

The general Thai public was largely unaware of the importance of these islands until a security guard at Laem Thong Birds' Nest (Siam) Co., Ltd. killed 10 nest thieves in the 1990s. After the same company killed another group of four bandits, there was a public call for an end to the violence.[31]

Finally, on 12 May 1993, members of the House of Representatives from the southern provinces proposed a new law under the government of Chavalit Yongchaiyut. The new law, Duties on Bird's-Nest Act B.E. 2540, was approved on 15 October 1997. The previous law was seen as too weak in protecting concessions from thievery. The old law also encourage secret renewals of contracts for the same company, for five years each time for up to nearly 50 consecutive years, propping up monopoly bidding.

At the same time, the localities benefited very little from the trade, and locals had no sense of ownership or participation in the nest economy. Therefore they felt justified in stealing the birds' nests to sell on the black market.

The new law authorized a committee made up of seven civil servants, six experts from local government, and the provincial governor, to grant contracts and terminate them if a company was not complying with the contract.[32]

In 2003, Chumphon, Phatthalung, Surat Thani, and Prachuap Khiri Khan together hosted an open tax auction covering the swiftlet nesting areas in the Gulf of Thailand Another auction was held for all provinces bordering the Andaman Sea – Phang-nga, Krabi, Trang and Satun – in 2007.

A similar auction was held for 2003–2008 concessions for the Koh Si Koh Ha Islands in Phatthalung Province, and seven other islands: Na Tewada, Ru Sim, Thai Tham-Dam, Kantang, Ta So, Yai So, and Rok Islands. Siam Nest won the Phatthalung auction with a final bid of THB 500 million on 23 July 2003.[33]

In late 2008, when this contract expired, the Phatthalung committee opened a new round of bidding, but after only one bid was received, Best Nest Company Limited filed a lawsuit against the Administrative Court of Songkhla Province charging that concession contracts for swiftlet nesting in Phatthalung Province were neither fair nor helpful for interested companies. The Songkhla court ordered a temporary ban on nest-collecting in the province while it considered the case.

Phatthalung nest-collectors and traders lost considerable revenue in the meantime, and had to continue paying for security surveillance on swiftlet nest islands. Finally after several months, a Supreme Administrative Court judge accepted an appeal from Phatthalung Province to cancel the temporary ban, thus re-opening the opportunity for the provincial committee to auction concessions, according to new procedures specified by the board.

The board adjusted the middle price for nest concessions from THB 270 million for five years to THB 627 million for seven years, and mandated that bidders use cash or securities insurance for 75 percent of the actual auction price. However, after only two days of bids, the court ordered the Songkhla Province to comply with the lawsuit. Phatthalung therefore had to close the auction, delaying new concessions another six months.[34]

Finally in 2009 Phatthalung tried again and this time the auction went through, with K.O.C. Import-Export winning the bid and taking on the concession for storing bird's-nests. An extension of the period of concessions – for storing birds' nests at Koh Si Koh Ha of Phatthalung Province – from around five years to seven years was considered for the first time in history. However, later on, the Siam Rang Nok Thalay Tai Company Limited got the license.

Later, in 2008, the concession business group collected the birds'-nests on both sides of the Thai peninsula in 9 provinces containing no fewer than 170 islands with birds'-nests. The concession holders for bird nest collection were as follows.

Along the Gulf of Thailand coast:

1. Trat has 4 islands, concession granted to W.T. Company Limited, concession fee THB 4.58 million,
2. Prachuap Khiri Khan has 3 islands concession granted to BY Business Company Limited, concession fee of THB 151 million,
3. Chumphon has 17 islands, concession granted to (1) BY Business Company Limited (THB 221 million), (2) Golden State Company Limited (THB 228 million), (3) MV Civil Company Limited (THB 71.6 million), (4) Southern Andaman Company (THB 893 million) before the concession

will be owned by A.J.K. Business Company Limited. (THB 240 million), (5) Golden State Company Limited (THB 515 million), total concession fee THB 1,928.6 million (2008),

4. Surat Thani has 15 islands, concession granted to (1) Petro Bangkok Company Limited (THB 565 million), (2) Nam Sing Bird's Nest Company Limited (THB 43 million 1 hundred thousand), total concession fee THB 608.1 million,

5. Phatthalung has 7 islands concession granted, first to Siam Nest Company Limited (THB 500 million), but later K.O.C. Import won the concession auction with THB 709 million offer.

Bird's Nests collection business groups in four provinces bordering the Andaman Sea, more than 130 islands. (1) Phang-nga has 40 islands, concessions granted to Chok Kitti Oil and Service Company Limited (THB 490 million), (2) Krabi has 61 islands, concessions granted to Best Nest Company Limited (THB 255.5 million), (3) Trang has 17 islands, concessions granted to JETA Corporation Limited (THB 135 million), (4) Satun has 11 islands, concessions granted to Rang Nok Satun Company Limited (THB 76 million).

1.2 Swiftlets in Swiftlet House Farming Business

Collecting birds' nests outside their natural limestone cave and crevice habitats, that is in abandoned buildings or purpose-built structures, has gradually become more important.

Collectors began preparing buildings to suit the swiftlets' nesting habits some 80 years ago after it was noticed that swiftlets were nesting in house number 3 in Pattani's Chinatown. In Nakhon Si Thammarat, the first such building to host nests was Ue Jin Guang in Pak Phanang, now known as the "Chinatown Building" in Nakhon Si Thammarat Province, beginning around 1937.

This type of nest 'farming' spread to all provinces in the south and other regions of the country as people learned how to build structures that would attract nesting swiftlets. Much local wisdom derives from techniques used in Malaysia and Indonesia. At first, such techniques were kept secret among households,[35] known only to the wealthy.

In the case of the Pak Phanang house, around 50 years later in 1987, so many birds came to nest that the owner had to move out and put his business on hold, leaving the swiftlets to occupy all three floors.[36] The house owners sold birds' nests at THB 500 per kilogram,[37] and continued to do so quietly.

By 1998, the price of birds' nests had reached THB 80,000 to 100,000 per kilogram. The "Swiftlet's Condominium" boomed in order to serve the biggest market for birds' nests in the world after China became member of the World Trade Organization in 2001.

More investment poured into nest-farming in pursuit of these high profits. A single two-to seven-story building 23 meters high sold for up to THB 20 million. Investments came from everywhere: local and regional funding from Hat Yai District, Songkhla Province, Phuket, and national capital from Laemnok Laemthong Co., Ltd., as well as from multinational capitals in China, Hong Kong, Taiwan, Singapore, Malaysia and Indonesia.[38] Some traders who started off as middlemen, buying birds' nests for THB 80,000–90,000 per kilogram, eventually invested in bird's-nest buildings, and then the value-added, ready-to-eat bird's-nest industry.[39]

By 2007 there were around 600 birds'-nest buildings in operation, while in 2014, at least 42 provinces in Thailand boasted nesting habitats. Throughout the 14 southern provinces, there were in 2014 approximately 4,410 nest buildings. In the eight provinces of the eastern region, namely Trat, Chanthaburi, Rayong, Samut Prakan, Prachinburi, Chachoengsao, Sa Kaeo and Chon Buri, there were about 3,000. In central Thailand, there are around 2,500 buildings in Phichit, Saraburi, Nonthaburi, Bangkok, Phetchaburi, Ratchaburi, Samut Songkhram, Samut Sakhon, Samut Prakan, Nakhon Pathom, and Prachuap Khiri Khan. In Northeastern Thailand around a hundred nest buildings were found in Nakhon Ratchasima, Khon Kaen, Loei, Nong Khai, Bueng Kan and Udon Thani, and in the north at least 10 buildings distributed among Lampang, Chiang Mai, and Chiang Rai. The number of such buildings in Thailand thus totaled, in 2014, approximately 10,020 houses, hosting 2,000,000 birds throughout the country. Nationwide the average collection for commercial purposes reached 4,000 kilograms per month.

2. THE NATURE OF SWIFTLETS

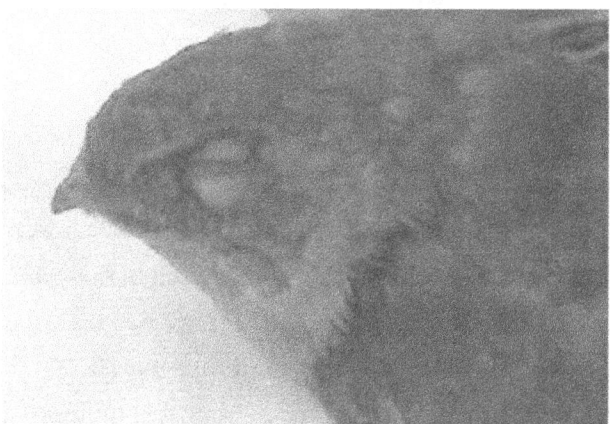

In ancient times, people in southern Thailand knew edible-nest swiftlets used their saliva to build nests but they believed the birds only fed while airborne.[40] As today, they collected the nests both for food and medicine.

There are three species of edible-nest swiftlets in Thailand: Edible-Nest Swiftlet (*Aerodramus fuciphagus*), White-Rumped swiftlet (*Aerodramus germani Oustalet*), and Black-Nest swiftlet (*Aerodramus maximus*).

2.1 Swiftet Natural Characteristics

Edible-Nest Swiftlet
Scientific name: *Aerodramus fuciphagus*.[41] Family: *Apodidae General*.

The bird is as tiny as a sparrow, with an average body length of 12 cm, wingspan of 11–12 cm, beak length averaging 0.5 cm, legs to around 0.9 cm. The top part of the body displays black and brown hues, while the rump is gray, the belly is brown, the iris is black and brown, and the beak is black. Its legs are reddish brown, with long curved blackish brown nails. The wings are sickle-shaped. Male and female birds are very similar, the only difference being that a female bird has a wider pelvis.[42]

The swiftlet's nest, which appears white from a distance, is made of the bird's translucent mucus, containing glycoproteins synthesized from its saliva gland.

Swiftlets build nests on walls whether in caves on coastal islands, or in abandoned buildings. In search of food they fly in the early morning to open areas such as forests or fields. The swiftlets flitter their wings to hover and feed on high-flying insects, such as flying ants. They also eat beetles, mosquitos, aphids, and flies both on land and in water. In the evening, they fly back to their homes, where in buildings or in subterranean dark caves, with ease and familiarity, with the help of echolocation, that is, emitting calls so that they can hear echoes of their high frequency sound waves, just like bats, to judge distances and geography. What distinguishes swiftlets from other swifts, and indeed almost all other birds, is their ability to use a simple but effective form of echolocation. This enables them to navigate within the breeding and roosting caves.

Swiftlets can fly at speeds of 89–100 kmh, and continuously for 40 hours, which means they can cover 90–100 sq km. However, they usually fly within a 25-km radius of their nests to seek food [43] and go right back to the nests without stopping.

They usually build nests at night. If necessary, they will rebuild their nests at the same location. The birds lay two eggs per nest. It is believed that long slim eggs hatch into female birds, while short and round eggs hatch into male birds.[44] A swiftlets can build their first nest when they reach nine to 12 months old, but their best nest-building comes when they reach three years old. the typical swiftlet lifespan is 10 to 15 years. After the nesting season, swiftlets gather in large groups.[45] Breeding season occurs January to April every year.

In general, the swiftlets' first nest is white or off-white. The next one will be yellowish, and the third nest will have a reddish tinge. The myth is that they suffer from building the nests, and spit out blood. In fact, the nests are always white, but iron ore along cave walls absorbs into the nests over time, and turn them red. Sometimes the red hue also comes from certain insects the bird has eaten.

During the breeding season, January–April, swiftlets build nests for laying eggs by excreting mucin from their saliva glands.[46] In general, these glands develop from December to June, and then disappear from July to August.[47] However, mating seasons and nest-building periods may vary in different areas.

Swiftlets are the only bird species with 're-nest' behavior, that is, they rebuild any nest that has been collected, or damaged, before spawning. However, after laying eggs, they will not rebuild even if the nests are damaged or collected. Swiftlets build their first nests around January, taking 30–40 days. The second round comes in mid-March, taking 20–25 days, and then the third is in mid-April, taking 15–17 days to finish. Some birds will build a fourth round of nests, and if this is collected, then they'll continue to build fifth and sixth nests.[48]

The nests are built at night. A swiftlet will grip a cave or building wall, then shake its head, spitting out threads of saliva. This weaves into a cup that dries to become a thin, translucent nest that is glued to the wall. Normally, female birds build the first two nests, and for the third both husband and wife build together.

The birds lay two eggs per nest, three times per year in nature,[49] hatching the eggs at night. White-nest swiftlets, which live in buildings, usually build nests throughout the year.

The swiftlets have a habit of recreating nests at the same location as their first nests. Only when they find that the location has an unusual smell, or is disturbed, or when they're attracted by recorded bird calls from a building, will build their nests somewhere else.

White-Rumped Swift or Germain's Swiftlet
Scientific name: *Aerodramus germani*. Family: *Apodidae*.[50]

General Characteristics: Germain's swiftlets are small birds that were considered the same species as edible-nest swiftlets in the past. They measure 115 to 130 mm.

long, and weigh 15 to 18 grams, both male and female. Their long and narrow wings typically measure 110–125 mm. in length. When perched on their nests, they hold their wings close together and tightly aligned. The tails are short and slightly forked, with rough-textured feathers. The longest tail is between 50 and 55 mm long, while shortest is between 43 and 46 mm.

The birds have tiny black feet that are not strong enough to cling to tree branches like those of other birds. Toes are anisodactyl, that is, having the first toe directed backwards and the other three toes directed forwards, and are featherless. Nails are black, curvy and sharp. Their black small beaks can open wide to form a triangle shape seen from the side. The culmen is black and slightly curved. The rictus, from behind, also looks like a triangle. The plumage is blackish-brown on top, but much paler on the underparts.

Germain's swiftlets can flap one wing faster than the other because feathers on their tails are short compared to the bird's body size. Thus they can control flight direction with the help of their wings.

In Thailand, the birds lay eggs from February to April. White-rumped swifts will build a replacement nest for any loss or damaged ones. This replacement process, though, would gradually by the end of June. The replacement nest usually takes one of two days.

Breeding season lasts from February to May as the birds build their nests February to mid-March, and lay eggs and care for their young until May. A new-born bird usually stays in the nest for around 65 to 69 days before it can fly.

Using fluid from their salivary glands, the swiftlets create nests that look like tiny half-cups that adhere to cave or building walls. In size, the nests are generally 4 cm. wide, 6.50 cm. long, and 3 cm. deep, and weigh around 7.08 grams.

A swiftlet usually takes around 39 days to build its first nest, 33 days for the second, and 25 days for the third nest-building. A swiftlet egg is white in color, with an average size of 13.73–21.14 mm., weighing 2.2 g. The birds lay two eggs per nest, usually take three to four days apart. The first and second hatches take 27 and 24 days respectively. If an egg is lost, the bird will lay another egg within 16 days[51] on average.

Black-Nest Swiftlet

Scientific name: *Aerodramus maximus*. Family: *Apodidae*.[52]

Natural historians who study the southern Thai peninsula classify the swiftlet into two types: black bird or black-nest swiftlet and "white bird" which is the edible-nest swiftlet.

The black-nest swiftlet has a larger head than the edible-nest swiftlet. The male and female look very similar. Feathers grow on the legs. Their nests are black, because they include feathers as part of the nest.

Enemies of the swiftlets include geckos, owls, pythons, cobras, cockroaches, bedbugs, monkeys, green snakes, rats, bats, lizards, and hawks. But human interference in the life cycle is the biggest danger of all.

Swiftlets wander for food, but always go back to their own nest in a cave or building. They will fly far on sunny days, but on cloudy or rainy day, they circulate near their habitat. When there are enemies, especially hawks, they fly in formation to defend against such enemies. In 2004, it was estimated that in Thailand there were around 1.09 million swiftlets nesting in nature, and 160,000 in buildings.

In Pak Phanang District, Nakhon Si Thammarat was believed to have the most swiftlets, around 80,000–100,000.[53] In 2008, it's estimated that there might be around 400,000–500,000 swiftlets there.[54]

2.2 Habitat

The main natural habitats for Thailand's edible-nest swiftlet are found in Trat, Prachuap Khiri Khan, Chumphon, Surat Thani, Phatthalung, Krabi, Phang-nga, Trang, and Satun. The 2014 estimation of swiftlet houses all over Thailand was about 10,000.[55]

2.3 Collecting Season

The collection of birds' nests from natural sources varies in each area of the Gulf of Thailand. At present, the official collection of birds' nests is in accordance with the contract for collecting nests between each concession company and the provincial committee. The nests may be collected three times a year, during the first and second lunar months, from the fourth day of the sixth waxing moon until 15th day of the sixth waxing moon.

The third time is from the 10th waxing moon until the last day of the 10th waning moon. This third time, the nests can be collected only when the fledgling birds in the nests have flown away. In terms of the solar calendar, the first collection is around March, and called Taeng Hua, the 'head' of the season. The second harvest falls around May, and is called Taeng Tor, the 'stubble' of the season, while the third and last harvest falls around September, and is called Taeng Hang, the 'tail' of the season.

The collection of swiftlet's nests on the Andaman Sea coast takes place first in the third month, the second collection in the fourth month, and then 20 days after the end of the fourth month, the third collection occurs in the fifth month. It takes 20 days to collect.

After that, there's a 90-day break, since the birds will start laying eggs again within 15 days. After these 15 days, the eggs will hatch and it'll be around three months before the yong birds can fly.

A fourth nest harvest, which falls outside the concession contract, is a collection of any remaining birds' nests. This is known as 'cave clearing,' or *balai* in the local dialect[56] of some areas.

In some places, this birds' nests are collected throughout the year; others only twice a year. However, the birds' nest harvest must fall in line with the signed agreements between the concession-holding company and the Provincial Bird's-Nest Taxation Committee. Generally, the contract permits three collections per year. As for the nest collection from buildings serving as artificial nesting habitats, it depends on the numbers of birds in each place, but it most often takes place monthly in Thailand.

3. BELIEF, WISDOM AND CULTURE RELATED TO SWIFTLETS

3.1 Belief and Ritual

Beliefs Related to the Swiftlet

In Thailand, beliefs related to the swiftlet revolve around wealth, power, and superstition. Since people never see swiftlets clinging to tree or wires like other birds, it was easy to believe the myth that swiftlets are fed by the wind, and that their nest-building saliva is therefore 'pure'.

A nest collector at Wat Khong Khasawat, and an owner of a 'swiftlet's condo' in Pak Phanang, Nakhon Si Thammarat, believes that swiftlets are sacred and powerful animals, and they can either bless or curse the lives of people related to them. Before each collection, he will pray and "ask for forgiveness and permission to collect the nest," to the Father and Mother Swiftlet spirits, the protectors of all swiftlets. The collector will promise the mysterious spirits that he'll not destroy any bird's eggs, or hurt any of the birds.[57]

Meanwhile, some of those who own nesting buildings believe that whether the birds will come to live in their buildings or not depends on supernatural circumstances. If such power grants their wish, the birds will come and live in the 'condo'.[58] Therefore, before building a 'condo', some nest traders will consult a spirit medium or 'bird fortune-teller', who is able to foresee when and where to build the structures.

Some Thai-Malay Muslims on the Andaman Coast believe that the swiftlets were born of Nabi Ibrahim (Abraham), a prophet and messenger of Allah in Islam. Before he created them, the birds promised that they would serve humans with their nests. At the same time, the prophet commanded humans not to hurt or eat them.[59]

However, Southern Thai Nest-collectors from both sides of the peninsula harbor different beliefs. They believe that eating baby swiftlets will boost libido or improve sexual performance. After cleaning the birds, they'll marinate the birds in liquor, and then eat them fried or grilled.[60]

Ethnic Thais in the southern region value the swiftlets so highly that even lullabys tell stories of the bird, passed down from generation to generation, such as the following:

> *Ah er* swiftlets, you fly so high
> you nest on Koh Si Koh Ha
> and killed you, so your nests were taken to sell ...
> on Koh Si Koh Ha birds' nests the merchandise ...
> (Khoom Thanyaudon)
>
> **Swiftlets**
> *Ah er* swiftlets, you fly so high
> you nest on Koh Si Koh Ha Island
> your eggs are found, then eaten
> your nests sell for high prices
> nesting on Koh Si Koh Ha, you give human a profit
> (Old verse from Phatthalung)

Tad Tada, a contemporary poet from southern Thailand, has written '*Bismillah*,' a poem that reflects the way of life and attitudes of the bird Nest-collectors and local society towards the swiftlet and the nest-collecting process:

Chapter 5

Bismillah

Jade-coloured wavelets race each other to the shore
    Lapping against the islands of the south, blurred in the distance
The islands appear still, whether in broiling heat or cold
    Covered by sea spray, as if hidden by a mantra
The bird's promise as pledged to the Prophet Ibrahim
    And recorded in the scriptures
To help humanity. To save them from killing each other. That is their rule.
From a bead of sweat of the Prophet
    Suddenly, a life is born, as if from a dream
Its curved wings created like an archer's bow
    Carry it ceaselessly through the air
Without perching on any branch in the world
    When ready to stop flying it lets out its call
Before speeding into an ancient passageway
    Of the dark cave of legend, and clutching to its nest
The edge of the nest is white as snow
    Built with such effort from its magical saliva
Its head moving to and fro all night with all its energy
    To build a home where it can procreate
Such is the image through the hidden eyes of a grey cobra
    Shadowed by dark stripes from head to tail
Flickering its tongue to listen, day and night
    Until the building of the nest is finished, in one month

The words of the prayer *"Bismillah ir-Rahman ir-Rahim"* sound
    Spoken from the heart, before he shakes
The bamboo ladder and vine to check them
    Then uses the *rada* to scrape off the bird's nest
On the 12th day of the waxing moon in the 3rd month
    Following the *Pu Ya* rituals each year
After the *Panlaema* chooses the first nest for luck
    In the candlelight the nests of dreams then begin to disappear

The musty smell of the cave fills the senses
    A heavy smell in a darkness that is full of white flowers
These nests are full of stories and tales. Well-known to all
The fishermen relate the news. Of dozens of people brutally killed
The repeated echo of the sound of gunfire
    When the caves are robbed, full of the smell of gun-smoke
Amidst the orders of the *Panglaema*
    "Hey! don't let the nests fall and break all over the place!"
He repeats, "Don't leave any nests uncollected!"
    To the nest collectors, while they use the *rada* to scrape off the nests

Jade-coloured wavelets race each other to the shore
    From the first and second months of collection, and the next
Until the third collection in the 9th lunar month, the red-stained nests
    Both birds use their saliva to build the nest
The male swiftlet helps the female
    Their wounded hearts, hoping only to produce their young
Their nests built in exchange with life
    They hope to lay two eggs to reproduce themselves

The sound of the words, *"Bismillah ir-Rahman ir-Rahim"*
    Spoken amidst dreams
In the forbidden cave where they look after each other
    The pain felt by both birds never ends
"Hey! Don't let the nests fall and break all over the place!"
    The order of the *Panglaema* fires out
His words, "Don't leave any nests uncollected!" resound
    While the uncomprehending grey cobra flickers its tongue
Mix witht the shrill cries of the birds filled with sadness
    In a place of sad solitude, the hatchling, born in hope
Falls, powerless, onto the cave floor
    The birds recall their original pledge

From the early morning the swiftlets flock from the cave
    Until dusk, when they return
To their beloved nests that they must continually build
    Through their tears they see only darkness
How many times, on this cave wall
    How many times in their lives, with no success
How many times their beloved has tried so hard
    With such patience, yet their nest disappears - no children
Oh! Prophet Ibrahim
    From their first pledge, made so long ago
Born out of His compassion from a bead of sweat
    By the *Hadith*, what sin did the swiftlets commit?

Jade-coloured wavelets roll frothing onto the shore
    Continue washing onto the islands, in the waves of time
Through both the broiling heat and cool scent of the sea
    At the same time the bloody curse continues

9 May 2003
Noen Tawan, Phromkhiri, Nakhon Si Thammarat. Translated by Patrick Jory.
28 October 2007

Sacred Norms

Regarding the swiftlet as more special, more magical, than other birds, nest-collectors and other ethnic Thais associated with them have reproduced and inherited beliefs and rituals towards the birds, and the harvesting of the nests in the natural habitat. It's always been a dangerous job to climb along steep cliffs in dark caves, risking missing a step and falling onto rocks or into the sea. Thais realize they can't know every aspect of the creature's life and habitat, and it is beyond human's control. As a result, belief in the supernatural is a way for them to accept that nature is more powerful than they are.

Before harvesting the birds' nests, Thai-Vietnamese collectors on islands in Trat Province, Southern Thais at Koh Si Koh Ha, Phatthalung, Thai-Malay Muslims in Koh

Thalu, Krabi (Phang-nga), on Koh Phetra in Trang, and Koh Laetong in Satun on the Andaman coast, all participate in a ceremony paying to homage to goddess Chailai. This *Puya Koh* or 'island ceremony' asks the spirits for protection. The ceremony also ask for permission from the spirits for courage and safety in collecting nests to use as medicine and food for society.

Harvesting birds' nests requires a great skill and expertise inherited over generations as well as a knowledge of the proper ceremonies. On Koh Rang Noi, in Trat Province, for example, Thai-Vietnamese collectors perform a simple ritual in which they offer food to goddess Chailai near the cave they intend to climb in exchange for protecting them from harm, and provide more nests to collect.

In Chumphon Province, collectors will pray at a sacred shrine to boost confidence and courage before the island is opened for nest harvesting each season.

Among other beliefs, a climber is strictly forbidden to scream if he falls to the ground while collecting nests. Not even a python found in the cave is to be harmed.[61]

In Koh Si Koh Ha, Phatthalung Province, before every harvest, the nest-collectors perform a simple ritual with candles and incense to ask for permission from ancestral spirits to enter the cave. The spirits, Ho Thao and Ho Kae, are propitiated during a ritual called Kad Thewada on Na Ko Thewada.

In the past, an annual island festival organized not only rituals but also Talung Manohra, southern Thailand's historic shadow play, and festive boats cruised Songkhla Lake. Nowadays the festival is only held once every five years when the company's concession is renewed.

The moral code for bird's-nest collectors mandate that while in the birds' habitat, they refrain from all profanity, verbal or physical, and to careful not to insult or challenge the spirits. In some communities, wives of the collectors refrain from having their hair cut while their husbands are at work in nesting areas.

On the Andaman Sea coast, beliefs associated with the nest collection culture tend to be related to Islamic doctrine since most of the collectors are Thai Muslims of Thai-Malay descent. Muslim collectors will break for prayer on Fridays.

Among non-Muslims, a common ritual for Andaman-based Thais is *Puya Koh*, a ceremony performed before the start of collecting season[62] to pay respect to the spirits who protect the islands, and asks for permission to collect. Thai Muslims won't attend this cermoney as worshipping spirits is forbidden in Islam.[63] The ritual is led by an experienced elder, called *Pang-li-mo* or *Pang-lae-ma*, and involves offerings that may include one whole grilled male buffalo, 12 kinds of sweets, seven candles, five portions of white and dark chicken, one fish curry, one minced buffalo-meat salad, seven small white flags,[64] seven portions of rice crackers, some bread, and one model house[65] placed on a low table.

The *Pang-lae-ma* drapes his head with a long white cloth, showing only his face. He stands before the offerings on the table, and prays quietly for the spirits to protect the bird's-nest collectors, using such phrases as "Here are the offerings we prepared for you, please protect these subordinates in their work collecting the nests, so that they will be encouraged to carry on the work." Then he shouts, "Oh ... Ahh", while mentioning the spirit's names three times. This ritual takes around 20 minutes, and the offerings will be stored for three days.[66]

After the ceremony, he or someone else who is capable will be asked to collect birds' nests from the cave, but only in odd numbers such as 3, 5, 7 or 9, to bring good luck.[67] This ceremony is held only once a year.

Another ritual, called *Tang Wap*, is held for every collecting season throughout the year. This ritual also involves offerings, and is led by *Pang-lae-ma*. The main difference is that he does not use the white cloth and doesn't shout to the spirits, but engages only in silent prayer.

There also are some taboos for both the collectors and their families, on the Andaman Sea Coasts. For example, any bird's-nest collectors' wives, even when at home, are prohibited from using body powder and from combing their using a comb (finger-combing is permitted).

At present, during the days when the husbands go, 'down to the island,' to collect the birds' nests, the wives are forbidden to use any oil on their bodies or hair because the oil is slippery, so it's believed it might make the men slip and fall. Bird's-nest collectors are also forbidden from taking a mistress or cheating on their spouses.

Women are not allowed to collect birds' nests. At home, they must refrain from fluffing pillows, washing them or putting them in the sunlight to air out. It is best if pillows remain in one spot. Children must also leave pillows alone. House-cleaning during daytime is prohibited during collecting season.

If a wife cheats on her husband, it is believed to bring harm or even death to the husband. Everything returns to normal after the collecting period is completed.

Collectors are prohibited from sitting on any knots in ropes or vines binding bamboo scaffolds to the cave walls, since the knots are believed to harbor sacred ancestral spirits.

The language that collectors use while on site differs from the language used in everyday life, to avoid misfortune or dangerous consequences caused by their works. Some examples of vocabulary for which substitutions must be made are buffalo (*ai rom*), cow (*aimo*), goat (*bae rae*), blood (*yang*), snake (*cheuak*), centipedes (*thao lay*) fall or slip (*long pai*), chicken (*ai yong*), lizard (*bae wa*), and slippery (*piak*). Alcohol (*na daeng*) is forbidden in the caves.

Such ritualistic practices have their roots in both Buddhist and Islamic beliefs, as well as the original animistic beliefs of peoples indigenous to southern Thailand.

Rituals associated with the collecting of nests in artificial structures is much less complex, and tends to be based on the convenience of each owner. Incense and candles may be lit out of respect for the "house spirit," or for ancestors in the property's separate spirit house, before collectors enter the buildings to harvest nests.

The collection of birds' nests from natural sites both around the Gulf of Thailand and the Andaman Sea, also relates to gender, following from the Thai social discourse norm that males are superior. Women are not allowed to enter the caves, but are expected to stay home because the work is considered unsuitable for women. The only tasks the women perform is trimming and cleaning nests.

Myth and Truth in Swiftlet's Nest Consumption

The bird's-nest culture has been part of Thai society for a very long time, perhaps inherited from the Chinese who started it over 1,000 years ago. Chinese people believe that the nests can treat respiratory diseases, sweating irregularly while sleeping, and chronic bronchitis, as well as strengthen the lungs and aid the recovery of patients with tuberculosis. They also believe that the nests, when mixed with Chinese ginseng, can dissolve blood clots. As a general health tonic, it's believed to be a good supplement for children, patients in rehabilitation, and the elderly. Women after childbirth consume the nests to boost their immune systems. Some Thais even believe it can resist the immune deficiency in HIV/AIDS.

There's evidence in Thai history that edible birds' nests were used in Thai cuisine for such dishes as Twelve [Ingredients] Curry, considered a health booster.

King Rama II wrote a poetic verse about edible birds' nests, likening it to romance:

> "I see this steamed bird's nest and it looks so delicious.
> The bird has been deprived from its nest, just as I was deprived of my beloved".

Thais generally prefer birds' nests as medicine, rather than cooked into food. They believe that medicine made from the nests can treat cough caused by tuberculosis. People on the birds'-nest islands of the Andaman Sea believe that mitigates sweating, and promotes longevity. Black bird's nest, when burned and mixed with coconut oil, is used to heal burns and prevent scars. On the Gulf of Thailand, people claim the nests cure allergies, sunburn, respiratory sickness, and cold sores. Other practitioners of Thai traditional medicine believe nests can improve sexual performance, relieve asthma, halt bloody vomiting and dysentery, and cure chronic malaria.

Pang-lae-ma, a third-generation nest-collector, tells the story of a Chinese ship that ran ashore on an uninhabited island in the Andaman Sea. "The survivors took shelter in a cave for 15 days. When they were finally found, searchers expected to find they had died without food or water. But they survived and looked well-nourished because they ate the swiftlet nests on the cave walls."[68]

At present, different ethnic groups in Thailand cook the birds' nests in various ways, including boiling with sugar,[69] and boiling with sugar and milk.[70]

Table 5.1: Nutrients found in edible birds' nests by the Thailand Institute of Scientific and Technological Research

Nutrients in birds' nests	Percentage
Protein	60.90 percent
water	5.11 percent
Calcium	0.85 percent
Potassium	0.05 percent
Phosphorus	0.03 percent

According to an analysis of proteins in the swiftlet nests in Thailand, 19 amino acids are found, as shown in table 5.2.

Nutritional analysis by the Food Research and Testing Laboratory, Faculty of Science, Chulalongkorn University, indicates that swiftlet nests contain up to 54 percent protein, 22.3 percent carbohydrate, 0.3 percent fat, 16.2 percent moisture, and 5.9 percent others compounds. The same researchers found that substances obtained from birds' nest extract show deterrent qualities with regard to red blood cell coagulation due to influenza, and an inhibitory effect on infection.[71]

From another perspective, Thien Limthanakul, managing director of Reading International, once posted a public sign saying, "Bird's-nest drinks contain only 1 percent bird's-nest," near an expressway in Thailand, after studying the nutritional contents of such drinks. His 90-year-old mother had drinking birds' nest tonics because she was ill, so he decided research the products at the Institute of Nutrition, Mahidol University. He found that the nutritional value of 26 bottles of the edible bird's-nest drinks contained an amount of protein equal to just one chicken egg. In other words, if you drank 34 bottles, you'd get the amount of protein equivalent to a small carton of milk.

Table 5.2: Amino acids in white swiftlet's nests in Thailand[72]

Type of Amino Acid	Quantity of Amino acid (mg. in 100 g. of dry sample of birds' nests)				
	A	B	C	D	E
Essential amino acids*					
Methionine + Cysteine	1,509.44	654.35	1,596.85	721.74	766.16
Methionine	5.13	4.78	4.67	5.63	4.48
Cysteine	1,504.31	649.57	1,592.18	716.11	761.68
Trionine	86.12	72.29	68.37	88.83	66.74
Valine	69.74	64.16	62.27	73.04	69.44
Phenylalanine + tyrosine	68.54	62.36	76.21	76.27	52.22
Isoleucine	64.50	66.60	64.32	78.38	63.99
Histidine	7.82	3.08	0.41	13.88	0.92
Lysine	50.01	48.52	52.44	48.58	49.20
Tryptophan	0.67	0.21	0.88	0.82	0.20
Livine	0.00	0.00	0.00	0.00	0.00
Inessential amino acids					
Glutamine	803.75	948.35	760.02	1,228.62	796.96
Asparagin	232.44	329.88	230.58	255.34	215.00
Serene	124.56	101.29	107.82	154.37	94.49
Glycine	112.96	82.50	88.66	108.92	76.85
Aspartic acid	76.68	77.61	73.53	82.58	83.69
Glutamate acid	65.31	66.09	68.28	65.83	71.86
Proline	58.14	57.02	62.90	65.00	61.17
Alanine	55.31	49.81	68.43	69.23	50.53
Cysteine	20.74	21.18	17.68	22.02	19.20
Hydroxyproline	0.00	0.00	0.00	0.00	0.00
Arginine	0.00	0.00	0.00	0.00	0.00

Note: A B C D and E are taken from samples of white swiftlet's nests from Trat, Phetchabun, Nakhon Si Thammarat, Satun and Narathiwat Province respectively.
* an essential amino acid type for adults (WHO, 2002)

Dr. Prapai Srisirikan, an associate professor at the Institute of Nutrition Research, Mahidol University, analyzed nutrient components in bird's-nest drink products, which on the label specified 1 percent edible birds' nests. When scientifically examined, it was found that one bottle of the bird's-nest product was only as nutritious as half a tablespoon of fresh milk, or two peanuts, or a quarter of a quail's egg. She urges consumers to use good judgment in deciding whether this product is worth the cost.[73]

Edible birds' nests also serve cultural purposes, especially as a status symbol. Ready-to-eat bird's-nest products thus remain popular among various communities in Thailand despite their relatively high cost. Opinions differ, however, depending on which ethnic group the collectors belong to, whether Thai-Vietnamese, Southern Thai, or Thai-Muslim Malay.

While Thai-Vietnamese say that the nests don't taste like something nutritious,[74] the Southern Thais believe it helps with cold sores.[75] Meanwhile, Thai-Muslim Malays say the nest products are useful in treating asthma, driving out sweat, strengthening the body,[76] helping someone near death to recover,[77] while some in this group say all it does is fill one;[78] and it doesn't seem to strengthen the body at all.[79]

3.2 Equipment, Tools and Inventions in Collecting Birds' Nests and the Bird's-Nest Industry

Thailand's building-centered bird's-nest trade is greatly influenced by trends in Malaysia and especially in Indonesia, which has been Thailand's prototype for trade of this kind. The business has been widely popular in Thailand since 1997, although evidence for birdhouses or bird's-nest buildings in the country can be traced to a 100-year-old house in Pattani's Chinatown. Thais in general perceive that such practices first took place at a shop distributing construction materials called Ue Jin Guang or *Hia* (brother) Waen in Pak Phanang Municipality in 1937.

Since then, various designs for artificials have been established, along with devices to control conditions for the birds, including egg incubators, temperature and humidity control devices, devices to measure light intensity, plastic birds' nest decoys, fragrances, and audio recordings to attract the birds. Textbooks teaching ways to build the structures so that they best imitate natural habitats, to manage bird breeding, and to clean the nests, have been published. Such aids have spread throughout Thailand, Malaysia, Vietnam, Myanmar, Cambodia and the Philippines over the past 20 years.

Thai-Vietnamese collectors in Rang Noi Island, Trat, invented a crescent-shaped metal tool called *kratai* used for collecting birds' nests in nature.[80] The Southern Thais in Koh Si Koh Ha, Phattalung, have also devised several tools, including flat-bottomed wooden boats suitable for collecting the nests. Bamboo is a favored material for tools used to collect birds' nests in caves, as well as for climbing cliffs. Thai-Malay Muslims along the Andaman Sea invented *kae,* bamboo sections used for climbing on both cliffs and cave walls, and *mai sua,* bamboo pieces that are laid atop the *kae* for a person to sit or stand on while harvesting nests. The same community has its own *ta chob* tool for hooking black birds' nests, as well as the *ta chan* (also called *ladak* or *rada*), a three-pronged harpoon used for collecting white birds' nests. The same tool is also used for spiritual protection due to the belief cave spirits fear it. During the *Puya Koh* ceremony, *rada* will be placed beside a bamboo stretcher, and under the stairs of miniature model house. When it isn't in use, the *rada* must be kept somewhere high, high enough that no one will walk over it, which could damage the tool's spiritual power.[81]

When collecting nests in artificial structures, some just use their hands to pull the nests from the walls, without using any equipment, while others use a knife or a *lek po*, a piece of metal forged with wide and flat ends.[82]

Thais have also created many recipes for a bird's-nest health tonics, medicines for burns and scars and so on, based on local ingredients. Nowadays most recipes have been turned into ready-made retail products that are advertised in print media and television. Thailand's well-known brands for bird's-nest products include Brand (Cerebos Thailand), Scott (Scott Industrial Thailand), and Bezz (C.P. Interfood Thailand, a subsidiary of C.P. Charoen Pokphand). There are also many smaller brands.

3.3 Cuture, Tradition and Wisdom in Bird's Nest Businesses of Ethnic Groups

Thailand's swiftlet nest farming has developed over 80 years in such a way that collectors have learned how to harvest nests in ways that don't interrupt or threaten the breeding of swiftlets, thus promoting conservation rather than extinction. At the same time, rituals associated with animism, Buddhism, and Islam are maintained to curb fear of the supernatural.

Many rituals are local to communities around natural swiftlet habitats. Thai-Vietnamese worship the goddess Chailai on Rang Noi Island, Trat, while Southern Thais pay homage to spirits on Koh Si Koh Ha, in Phatthalung. Meanwhile Muslim Thai-Malays always utter 'Bismillah' before taking a nest and collectors on Koh Thalu, Krabi, use a specific vocabulary while collecting the birds' nests. On Lae Tong Island, Satun, cave spirits are given offerings or, if strictly Muslim, request the blessings of Allah.

All of these actions are signs of respect towards supernatural powers or unseen spirits, basically bargaining with them in exchange for permission to collect the nests. At the same time, these spiritual entities are believed to protect the collectors, and bring prosperity for the work.

4. RIGHTS AND LEGAL SYSTEMS IN THAILAND BIRD'S-NEST BUSINESS

Thailand trades in swiftlet nests collected from natural locales in nine provinces: five in the Gulf of Thailand, namely, Trat, Prachuap Khiri Khan, Chumphon, Surat Thani and Phatthalung; and four provinces along the Andaman Sea, namely, Phang-nga, Krabi, Trang, and Satun.

Archaeological evidence found in the south, especially on Koh Si Koh Ha Islands, Pak Phayun District, Phatthalung include Chinese pottery from the Song Dynasty (960–1279 A.D.), Ming Dynasty (1368–1644 A.D.), and Qing Dynasty (1644–1911 A.D.),

along with Thai ceramics from the Sukhothai Period.[83] It may be assumed that Chinese merchants might have exchanged porcelain products for birds' nests directly with the local population, which would suggest that the nests have been associated with both domestic and international trade for more than 500 years.

On the other hand, written evidence appears in the records of French ambassador, Simon de la Loubère (A.D. 1686), who came to Ayutthaya during the reign of King Narai,[84] reported that there was no evidence of rights to birds' nests being auctioned during the Ayutthaya Period.

Sa-ngop Songmeuang, a historian in Thai history and Songkhla studies, believed that nest-collection during the time was in the form of tax collection[85] since the birds' nests were considered of high value and thus preserved for the state only. The state monopoly on birds' nests, 'Phrai Suai Rang Nok,'[86] or 'Lek Koh Rang Nok' referred to taxpayers who traded nests for exemption from state recruitment. Southern Thai nest-collectors would pay these taxes to the tax collectors who were authorized to represent the King, the center of the feudal system. This type of 'bird's-nest taxpayer' was found only in the south of Thailand.

The nest trade also comes up in an account from Songkhla in 1769, when King Taksin the Great raised his armies to subdue the southern city-state of Nakhon Si

Thammarat. Fearing for his life, Phraya Nakhon (Nu) fled to Pattani with Phraya Phatthalung and Luang Songkhla (Withian), when King Taksin's troops reached Songkhla, Phraya Tani turned in Phraya Phatthalung and Luang Songkhla (Withian), to the king."[87] During the time of these incidents, the bird's-nest concession system was developing further.

The right to trade in nests, once held in community as common owners, gradually gave way to a taxation system.

The tax-collectors in charge of bird's-nest duties in the southern region between 1767 and 1900 were well-connected to the authorities. These prominent families monopolized the nest trade were the Na Nakhon, Na Songkhla, and Saiburi families.

The tax collectors from Thailand's central region also benefited from the system, albeit over a shorter time, historically. Later on, in the reign of King Rama III, tax collection was given over to concessionaires, who would send the money as, "birds nest duty" to the state. The rulers of Songkhla, namely the Na Songkhla family, monopolized the production of birds' nests for over 130 years.[88] Meanwhile in Nakhon Si Thammarat, the Na Nakhon family monopolized production in Phang-nga, Krabi and Trang for about 71 years,[89] while rulers in Saiburi and Satun, who shared the same lineage, dominated the trade there for 100 years.

For tax Districts in the upper Gulf of Thailand, namely, Chaiya, Chumphon, Pa-thiew and Bang Nangrom, currently belonging to Surat Thani, Chumphon and Prachuap Khiri Khan Provinces, historical evidence shows that Luang Chamnan was in charge of the collecting duties in Chaiya, Koh Samui, and Koh Pha-ngan. Starting in 1852, Central Thais also competed for concessions in Chaiya, Chumphon, Pa-thio, and Bang Nangrom.

This system continued until a 1932 *coup d'état* in Bangkok seized power from King Prajadhipok and converted governance from an absolute monarchy to a democracy. The new military-dominated government managed taxation in a more systematic and rigorous manner.[90] In 1939, Field Marshal Plaek Phibunsongkhram's government issued the Duties on Birds' Nests Act B.E. 2482, considered to be the first modern law relating to bird's-nest resource-management. It was enacted on October 30, 1939.[91]

The Revenue Department, Ministry of Finance was given authority over allowing concessions to collect birds' nests.

A Thai-Chinese capital group, the Laem Thong Bird's Nests (Siam) Co. Ltd. operated a monopoly over bird's-nest concessions and developed a complex multinational business making huge profits in Prachuap Khiri Khan, Chumphon, Surat Thani and Phatthalung Provinces from February 21, 1959[92] until October 31, 2003.

From 1959 to 1963, Laem Thong Bird's Nest (Siam) Co., Ltd. held the concession for swiftlet nests in Satun Province. Birds' nests in the Gulf of Thailand, except in Trat Province, was collected by Thai-Vietnamese collectors. The Southern Thais and Thai-Malay Muslims collected birds' nests in the Andaman Sea for Thai-Chinese concession holders. The beliefs and rituals of the Nest-collectors from the past until 2014 reflected the historical relationship and rights system, especially in paying homage to ancestors of the Southern Thais and Thai-Chinese at Koh Si Koh Ha Islands in Phatthalung Province. This suggests that people in the community feel justified in trading birds' nests freely.

With respect to perceptions of bird's-nest robbers, Thai-Malay Muslims in the Andaman Sea generally believed that the birds' nests belong no one, but nature and God. When they steal birds' nests, they perform their own rituals, asking permission from Allah and ghost of the island.[93]

Thai bird nest resource access rights follows a system that inherited and adapted from the Thai feudal system, similar to the auction of the swiftlet nests along the west coast of the Andaman Sea in Phang-nga, Krabi, Trang and Satun Provinces.

Thai-Malay Muslims in the area of Satun Province only know that before Laem Thong Bird's Nest (Siam) Co. Ltd. became a concession holder, approximately 1959–1963, there was an owner from Malaysia who had been a concessionaire. His name was Je Abdullah Langpute, a southern Malay and former long-term Satun politician. He is thought to have been the bird's-nest tax-collector from 1927 to 1933. Chia Ha is also known to have been a concession holder, followed by *Ko* (uncle) Chui, from Satun, and then Ki Kong, owner of Satun Rien Tong Hotel. Next came Ko Chui, then Ko Chiew, and then Dr. Wirayut from Trang[94] an uncle of Sia Lek—Aphichat

Angsutharangkul, owner of Satun-Trang Birds' Nest,[95] Southern Birds' Nest[96] Co. Ltd., and Siamnest[97] company, which were a concession holder in Trang. They lost the concession to JETA Cooperation Co. Ltd. from Khlong Sam Wa, Bangkok in the mid-2003, before winning again from 2011 to 2015.

The bird's-nest concessions in Phang-nga, Krabi and Trang Provinces were monopolized by Pae Ching Gi and Ko Bin, whose a father-in-law of Ko Bun or Aphichat Kitprasan, the owner of APB Rang Nok Phuket Co. Ltd.[98]

Concessions in Trang and Krabi were controlled by APB Rang Nok Phuket Co. Ltd., while in Phang-nga Province, Aphichat Kitprasan was always the concessionaire. Sia Lek of Satun and Kamnun Daeng's bird nest company also had a turn winning auctions in Krabi and Trang Provinces, and becoming the concession holder instead of Aphichat Kitprasan from time to time.

In response to the Prime Minister's Office order no. 66/23 dated April 23, 1980, aka 66/23 Policy, which helped end the domestic conflict between the state and the Communist guerilla resistants in 1992, at the end of The Cold War. The Thai government, which had gone through a period of resisting trade with China, began to court better relations with China. This affected Thailand's bird's-nest commerce since China was such an important market with a high demand for swiftlet nests. The resulting price increases led to a series of nest-robberies in which the thieves were shot and killed, incidents that appeared often in Thai news media.

Thai bird's-nest resources had been controlled by feudal rulers since the Ayutthaya Period, and by concession systems since 1769. Still the income from bird's-nest duties remained part of the national budget.

Thailand's 1997 constitution gave local communities the right to maintain local natural resources. In the same year, the Chavalit Yongchaiyut government announced the Duties on Birds' Nests Act B.E. 2540 (A.D. 1997), which allowed requiring local governments to determine the granting of concessions, and allocation of income from bird nest concessions to benefit local businesses. It was the first time, in Thai history, that bird's-nest concessions were decentralized, and profits went directly to local communities.

Such communities were not used to taking responsibility for the protection and maintenance of the resources, partly as a result of exclusion from having a voice in either the old feudal system and more recent concession systems, and partly because they had little share in global data relating to nest sources, quantity, quality, and trade.

Such information was for the most part kept confidential by companies holding concession on islands in both the Gulf of Thailand and the Andaman Sea. Thus the image of such islands was they were places of cruelty and danger. People in general were afraid to approach such islands. The incredible amount of profits, especially from ready-to-eat bird's-nest businesses, meant that business turned a blind eye towards the concessionaires' outlaw power. The negative public image was in fact exploited in order to maintain power over bird's-nest resources, to make it seems as if lands related to the bird's-nest trade were 'prohibited' for locals who weren't collectors or traders.

In the case of birds' nests cultivated in artificial settings, although building-owners included Southern Thais, Thai-Malay Muslims, Central Thais and Northeastern Thais, most businesses belong to Chinese or Thai-Chinese. Profits were used to expand nest buildings in prime areas. In early 2012, when bird's-nest prices dropped, profits also dropped.[99] Business was controlled by close associates of the company families,[100] with functioning networks among sources, markets and investments.

Among newer laws related to swiftlet resources, none applies directly to the control of nest buildings, including the Reserve and Wildlife Protection Act B.E. 2535 (1992), and thus the general public has little voice concerning swiftlet natural resources, which aren't considered natural when they occur in man-made structures.

Also, the basic characteristics of a 'linear system of management' prevents participation[101] regarding access, management, and use bird's-nest resources. Moreover, as the biggest nest market is Hong Kong, and most consumers are Chinese, the main trading language is Chinese,[102] which also limits access by those who don't have the opportunity to learn Chinese.

Although rights elated to the nest trade might be suited to concepts of 'communal property', which grants right of access to such resources to the local community, in fact wealthy Chinese dominate nest concessions, including artificial bird's-nest buildings, and are also predominate as middlemen for the nest exports.

One might note that rights and legislation regarding nest resources, both natural and artificial follow the hierarchical order in Thai society. Some might say these relationships given ethnic Chinese special rights, in a de facto sense, if not by written law. This would be a difficult point to prove, however. It may just be common practice.

Historical power relations is a major contributor to the inheritance of rights to nest resources, superseding what might be supposed once were traditional rights systems, in which nest-collectors' families dominated. However, there is not significant data to prove this.

The data shows another dimension to the story, in that knowledge about the nest-collection and trade is passed on from one generation to the next.

In Pak Phanang District, Nakhon Si Thammarat Province and elsewhere where artificial structures support nest resources, local, regional, central government, and foreign capital has moved into the area. As artificial resources increase, so does competition among the nest-processing companies in both domestic and international markets.

Nonetheless, owners of the bird-nest buildings, regardless of ethnicity, have the lawful rights to pass on their businesses to their children.

5. THAILAND'S BIRD'S NEST TRADE AND MANAGEMENT SYSTEMS

5.1 Bird's Nest Trade During the Hunter-Gatherer Period

The collection of birds' nests in Thailand during this period relied on important local technologies, including bamboo scaffolding and other bamboo tools used for climbing the cliffs during nest harvest season.

Although the lines between different ethnic groups in Thai society is not always entirely clear, some evidence suggests that in the southern peninsula of Thailand, Southern Thais and Thai-Malay Muslims have been the traditional collectors prior to the 16th century.

Although the dominant political and economic region in Thailand has been Central Thailand and its inhabitants, traditionally they had little to do with the nest trade in the south. Legend has it that bird nest-collection pioneers were a southern Thai husband and wife on the Koh Si Koh Ha Islands, Phatthalung Province. A Songkhla chronicle mentions that in 1769, when King Taksin raised an army to subdue rebels in Nakhon Si Thammarat,[103] Hao Yieng, head of Chinese immigrant society in Songkhla, offered his wife, children, slaves and five boxes of Chinese red tobaccos for the king while asking permission to collect birds' nests in Koh Si Koh Ha Islands of Songkhla Lake. He offered to pay 50 Chang, or about THB 4,000 per year, but King Taksin returned all offerings, except the medicines. He then gave the Chinese man, the founder of the Na Songkhla family name, a new title, Laung Inkhirisombat Nai A-kon,[104] and granted the bird's nest concession for the islands.

Pang-lae-ma, the chief teacher of bird's-nest island Koh Thalu, Phang-nga Province on the Andaman Sea coast, tells a story about how a bird's-nest cave was discovered by an ancient Chinese shipwreck, in which the people were trapped in the cave for 15 days. With neither food nor water, they were expected to die, but everyone survived, and fared well, because they ate swiftlet nests adhering to the cave walls.[105]

Later, after the 1932 coup, when quasi-democratic military rule replaced absolute monarchy, the government still controlled its resources. Still, the appointed provincial administrative organizations were allowed to draft the regulations. After the announcement of a constitution (the first of many to come, each entirely replacing the last, without lasting legal power), administrative organizations in each province employed an auction system for private companies to compete for bird's-nest concessions.

Communities in Thailand have by and large copied Chinese beliefs about the exceptional value and attributes of bird's-nest consumption.[106] This value system forms a strong popular support for the nest trade by a convincing consumers that the nests were a delicacy for Chinese emperors, nobles and wealthy Chinese. Such a value sytem continues to the present day.

Although most Thais prefer to consume ready-to-eat bird's-nest products for their convenience, most of bird's-nest building-owners, as well as concession holders for bird nest caves, on the contrary, prefer to sell raw birds' nests.

5.2 The Bird's Nest Trade and Food Sovereignty in Postmodern Society

In 1961, the Thai government established the National Economic and Social Development Plan, and later in 1982, the government further instituted a policy to develop the nation into a 'newly-industrialized country' (NIC). After the 1997 economic crisis, a new constitution appeared to offer potential for Thai society to advance towards more decentralized forms of government, where local government organizations would have the power to manage community developments and preserve local resources. In addition to allowing each province to manage its own natural bird's-nest resources after 1997, various communities in Thailand established different kinds of professional bird's-nest services, for example, cleaning nests, holding companies for collecting birds' nests, nest building contracting, tool manufacture, construction materials for nest buildings, raw nest trading companies, ready-to-eat nest production, and exporting companies. Examples of these companies include:

A.P.B. Rang Nok Phuket, P.P. Cabana (1993), W.T. Co. Ltd., B.Y. Business Co. Ltd., Golden State, M.V. Civil Co. Ltd., Southern Andaman Company, A.J.K. Business Co. Ltd., Petro Bangkok Co. Ltd., Nam Xing Rang Nok Co. Ltd., Siam Nest Co. Ltd. (Natural Nest Co. Ltd.), Chok Kitti Oil and Service Co. Ltd., Best Nest Co. Ltd., JATA Corporation Co. Ltd., Rang Nok Satun Co. Ltd., Kwan Phetch (Siam) Co. Ltd., Siam Bird's Nest Southern Sea Co. Ltd., in Charoen Pokphand Capital Group, and Chia Tai Siam South Sea Bird's Nest Co. Ltd.

Finished bird's-nest product companies with substantial capital, and trade in both domestic and international markets include C.H. Farm Co. Ltd., Rang Nok P.P. Cerebos (Thailand) Co. Ltd., The Scott Industrial (Thailand) Co. Ltd., and C.P. Interfood (Thailand) Co. Ltd. As for smaller, family-run finished nest product industries whose markets are specifically in bird's-nest resource areas, such as Pak Phanang District, Nakhon Si Thammarat Province, brands include Sornsawan, Bird House, Pak Phanang Rang Nok, and Kwan Mui.

Since 1970, the bird's-nest prices have always been on the rise. In the late 1980s, the prices were increasing rapidly and consistently in Thailand. In 1979, the raw bird nest price was THB 15,000 per kg.[107] In 1991, the price went up to THB 25,000 per kg. In 1994, it was 50,000 and then in 1996, THB 70,000 per kg.[108] By 2003, the price had risen to THB 70,000–100,000 per kg.[109] After the mid-1990s, the bird nest were on high demands. In 2006, the raw bird's-nest price was THB 50,000–70,000 per kg.[110]

Meanwhile in Hong Kong and mainland China, retail prices in 2006 for cleaned nests was THB 150,000–250,000 per kg.[111] The minimum price for raw birds' nests stayed at THB 50,000 per kg. until 2011.[112]

The Zhejiang provincial government banned the importing of birds' nests directly from all Southeast Asian countries in 2011, after seizing fake red birds' nests imported from Malaysia because they contained up to 350 times more nitrite contamination than Chinese health standards permitted.[113] As a result, the price of raw birds' nests in Thailand dropped to THB 8,000–15,000 from THB 50,000–70,000 per kg. in 2013.

Size of Thailand's Bird Nest Trade

Out of Thailand's 77 provinces, natural habitats and artificial nests in birds' buildings are found in 42. Nest-consumption isn't very popular among the ethnic Thais who produce birds' nests. Hong Kong remains the biggest middle market in trading nests, while China is the biggest consumer market.

Because the primary market requires Chinese-language business contracts and Chinese networks, most of the exporters from Thailand to both regions are of Chinese descent. Although it is difficult to identify an official number of nested buildings because some shophouses have been converted into birds' houses with the ground floors used as shops and the upper floors for the birds, it's estimated that as of 2014 there were about 10,000 bird's-nest buildings in Thailand.[114] Figuring the average price for such buildings at THB 5 million per building, then the total property value would be as high as THB 50 billion.

Estimating bird's-nest productions of various sources suggest an overall bird's-nest business size in Thailand. In 2008, total income from the bird's-nest concessions in both the Gulf of Thailand and the Andaman Sea, was THB 3.5 billion, and THB 3.7 billion in 2010. In 2011, the Office of Agricultural Economics, Ministry of Agriculture and Cooperatives, indicated that Thai bird's-nest exports, of both major and small entrepreneurs, came to at least 80,000 kg. per year.[115] From 2007 to 2010, Thailand's exports steadily increased, with the total export volume in 2010 reaching more than 170,000 kg., valued at more than THB 270 million.[116]

In 2013, Mr. Aphichat Kitprasan, manager of Khwan Petch (Siam) Co., Ltd., stated that concession-holders in Thailand harvest approximately 18 tons of bird nest per year, with a total value of over THB 14 billion, most of which is exported to China.[117]

The nine major bird's-nest concession areas are found in Prachuap Khiri Khan, Surat Thani, Phatthalung, Krabi, Trang, Phang-nga, Satun, Trat and Chumphon Provinces. With concession periods of five years each, the yield from nest-duties amounted to approximately THB 3.1 billion per year.[118]

In the middle of 2014, nest-business operators valued Thailand's birds' nests, harvested from both natural and artificial resources, and both white and black birds' nests combined, at around 200 tons or 200,000 kg. per year.[119] Nests collected from a single artificial nesting structure average 3.5–4 kg. per month. Since there are about 10,020 nested buildings around the country, the total amount of harvested nests should be four tons per month, 48 tons per year or 48,000 kg. Since raw nests are priced at an average THB 20,000–45,000 per kg, the total value of raw birds' nests from buildings alone should be 960 million to THB 2.1 billion per year.

In 2007, the value of ready-to-eat nest products for industrial sectors was estimated to be approximately THB 1,300 million, with a projected market growth of 10–15 percent per year.[120]

In 2009, Mr. Toon Wongsupasawat, General Manager, Business and Marketing Management, Cerebos (Thailand) Co., Ltd., manufacturer and distributor of, Brand Rang Nok bird's-nest drinks, indicated that the market value of bird's-nest drinks was over THB 2 billion per year.[121]

In 2014, it was estimated that Thailand produced 200 tons or about 200,000 kg. of raw birds' nests. With an average price of USD 1,500 per kg, or about THB 45,000 per kg, the country earned approximately USD 300 million or about THB 9 billion that year. When combined with the market value of the bird's-nest beverage industry, Thailand's total nest market value would have been at least THB 10 billion per year.

Table 5.3: Showing the amount and value of the export of agricultural products and nests of the swiftlet in Thailand in 2010–2011

Quantity: Metric Ton Value: THB 1,000

Commodity	2010		2011	
	Quantity	Value	Quantity	Value
Animal fats	6,303	114,037	6,233	114,250
Margarine and edible mixtures	1,411	80,732	1,527	96,247
Human hair, hair and feathers	3,973	332,584	3,890	444,005
Natural honey and royal jelly	7,167	604,051	8,925	608,801
Swiftlets' nests	175	277,316	479	273,729

Source: Agricultural and Foreign Trade Statistics of Thailand 2011, Office of Agricultural Economics, Ministry of Agriculture and Cooperatives

Table 5.4: Shows amount and value of the exported Thai swiftlet nests from 2004–2007

Quantity: Kilogram Value: THB

country	2004		2005		2006		Jan–May 2007
	Quantity	Value	Quantity	Value	Quantity	Value	Value
Hong Kong	32,404	8,415,742	11,029	62,556,153	6,540	96,327,082	19,203,979
Australia	161	164,614	4,951	530,086	101	223,985	1,477,025
Singapore	5,716	10,462,954	1,200	804,885	2,543	16,869,442	1,073,869
Myanmar	5,894	5,023,600	5,815	3,101,661	3,277	2,470,582	851,710
India	-	-	-	-	-	-	824,601
Taiwan	51,537	7,553,158	32,538	3,282,001	12,124	1,593,048	540,492
Cambodia	19,717	1,769,335	728	409,255	1,272	597,570	257,780
China	-	-	24,610	2,238,012	34	1,688,064	89,880
Laos	-	-	82	75,260	3,030	1,613,363	22,044
Indonesia	-	-	-	-	-	-	12,782
New Zealand	-	-	172	17,800	517	53,400	3,202
Japanese	3,899	3,126,863	21,056	9,226,258	12,947	4,290,320	-
Malaysia	2,100	169,628	-	-	30	4,168	-
other	375	182,269	3,894	743,076	831	105,378	124,163
Total	121,803	36,868,163	106,075	82,984,447	43,888	126,503,543	24,481,527

Source: Department of Customs collected by Kasikorn Research Center Co., Ltd. Thailand.

Table 5.5: Shows amount and value of imported birds'-nests 2003–2007

Quantity: Kilogram Value: THB

country	2004		2005		2006		Jan–May 2007	
	Quantity	Value	Quantity	Value	Quantity	Value	Quantity	Value
Indonesia	17,225	731,365,991	17,362	840,840,702	19,340	936,501,739	8,728	402,320,086
Singapore	263	12,264,893	-	22,513	206	9,656,756	-	-
Malaysia	-	-	510	316,478	501	306,645	-	-
Hong Kong	60	2,324,911	100	5,554,369	*	21,145	-	-
other	-	-	60	28,015	39	131,311	-	-
Total	17,548	745,955,795	18,032	846,739,564	20,086	946,617,596	8,728	402,320,086

Source: Department of Customs collected by Kasikorn Research Center Co., Ltd. Thailand.

Types and Prices of birds' nests in Thailand

In the Thai bird nest market, the different types of birds' nests include:

1. **Swiftlets' nests categorized by color** are divided in 4–5 types: black, white, yellow, and golden. Prices vary depending on markets and economy.

Table 5.6: Shows Thai bird's-nest prices from 1937–2013[122]

Year	Type of birds' nests	Price THB per kg.
1937	White birds' nests	500
1961	White birds' nests Grade A	300
	White birds' nests Grade B	150
	Black birds' nests	N/A
1979	White birds' nests	15,000
1987	White birds' nests	7,000–8,000
1991	White birds' nests	25,000
1994	White birds' nests Grade A	65,000
	White birds' nests Grade B	48,000
	White birds' nests grade C	30,000
	Black birds' nests	2,000
1996	White birds' nests	70,000
2000	White birds' nests, 100 nests per kg.	60,000
2001	White birds' nests Grade A	70,000
	White birds' nests Grade B	60,000
	White birds' nests grade C	50,000
	Broken birds' nests and fragments	10,000
2003	White birds' nests Grade A	70,000–100,000
	White birds' nests Grade B	60,000
	White birds' nests grade C	30,000–50,000
	Black birds' nests	2,000–20,000
	Broken birds' nests and fragments	12,000–38,000
2004	White birds' nests Grade A	50,000
	Yellowish White birds' nests Grade B	25,000
	Yellowish White birds' nests grade C	15,000
	Yellow-red birds' nests and grade D birds' nests	8,000
	Black birds' nests	12,000
2006	White birds' nests	50,000–70,000
2007	White birds' nests	35,000–70,000
2009	White birds' nests	50,000
	Black birds' nests	6,000–30,000
2011	White birds' nests	30,000–50,000
2012	White birds' nests Grade A	40,000
	Low-grade white birds' nests	15,000
2013	Large White bell-shaped, less feather birds' nests Grade A	15,000
	White nest, cup-shaped	10,000
	White birds' nests, curved, less feather	6,000–13,000

2. **Swiftlet's nests from houses or buildings** in 2014 are divided into six types:
    1. AAA birds' nests, height 38 mm ++, 20,000–30,000 THB per kg.
    2. AA grade birds' nests, height 32–37 mm., 18,000–20,000 THB per kg.
    3. Bird nests Grade A, 135 degree round shape, 12,000–13,000 THB per kg.
    4. Bird nests Grade B, 90-degree angle, 10,000 THB per kg.
    5. Bird nests Grade C, fragment, 500–2,000 THB per kg.
    6. Bird nests string, 20,000–25,000 THB per kg.[123]

Table 5.7: Thai bird's-nest form houses/buildings prices and grades in 2014[124]

Style / Size	Height	Grade	Price THB per kg.
Bird nests, complete	38 mm++	AAA	20,000–30,000
Bird nests, complete	32–37 mm	AA	18,000–20,000
135 degree round birds' nests		A	12,000–13,000
90-degree angle birds' nests		B	10,000
Bird nests fragment		C	500–2,000
Bird nests string			20,000–25,000

Incentive and Welfare Factors among Bird's-Nest Business Organizations in Thailand

The welfare and compensation of people in the bird's-nest business, whether they are workers, concession-holders, collectors, birdhouse-owners, traders, industrial workers in bird's-nest product factories, or those with more authority, are working in a world of confidentiality.

The following 'true stories from different angles,' can presents different aspects of what exists in the corporate world of Thai bird nest business.

Koh Rang, Trat

On 14 May 2010, Uthit Kieokhachi, a Thai-Vietnamese bird's-nest collector on Rang Noi Island, Salak Phet village, Koh Chang Tai Sub-District, Koh Chang District, Trat Province, shared with us his story.

"… I am of Vietnamese descent. My grandfather was Vietnamese; I do not know where in Vietnam he is from, but I am certain I am a Vietnamese. My family is Khmer. My mother originally came from Koh Chang and married a Vietnamese. My grandfather was originally a bird's-nest collector, then handed the craft on to my father. My father is from Trat. I am a Thai citizen by birth. I am a Thai. The grandfather gave the son-in-law, my father, the right to collect, and that passed down to me, the third generation. Now, it comes to the fourth generation, to my son.

A hundred years ago, my grandparents used sailboats to travel for days. I did not know who found the first cave, but my grandparents were collecting nests for a long time because we had the concession over several generations. Thai-Vietnamese people have done this for a long time.

Before, Tookgae was a Chinese (bird's-nest) buyer in the (Chang) Island. For about 50 years the concession belonged to the Chinese-owned Hok Sia Tung Company. Mr. Uan's father used to buy the bird's-nests and then his son. It was transferred to WT Company, Mr. Chuengchai's company, about 10 years ago.

Then government officials dismantled the cabin here over the last 6–7 years. In fact, it should be my job mainly because I took care of this in the past.

This chief teacher came in and we have to ask permission. The company takes care of the collectors well. The salary is good. They help us in all aspects like my house has no entrance, they helped pave the way for THB 200,000.

I started to collect birds' nests for the first time when I was 30. At first, the number of nests was only about 100, but we allowed time for it to grow and collect only two to three times a year. Six to seven years ago, we collected 600–700 nests per month, and 300 nests per month last year.

The general market price that I know is roughly THB 80,000 per kilogram for prime grade nests, while second grade birds' nests sell for THB 30,000, or THB 20,000 for the third-grade ones.

For a sustainable number of birds, you must keep a close guard on them so that hawks do not disturb them. We are not allowed by law to shoot hawks with guns. If the law can be resolved, and we have a gun to subdue the hawk, the number of swiftlets will increase.

I don't think we'll continue to renew concessions. There are less birds, and the contract is expensive. My three to four employees receive a monthly remuneration of THB 10,000, and they get THB 6,000 each for collecting birds' nests for the company.

Tools needed in collecting the birds' nests are a flashlight, *kratai*, bag, and bamboo scaffolding that we make ourselves. One lasts for two years. There are five caves with lots of birds: Taphao, Muet, Prathun, Hinkhap, and Mai, among which Taphao and Muet have the most birds' nests.

These past two years, the number of swiftlets has reduced because no one has taken care of the forest. Those auction-winners should take care of the birds thoroughly, protect them, because there are less birds' nests. It's not good. The company doesn't provide insurance, when one is sick others have to care for him. But if the company paid well, I may think twice. The birds' nests have reduced dramatically in these two years. It was 5–6 kg. each time before, then it kept decreasing. I had a shelter on the island before, but it was taken apart six years ago. They said it was their property, but my grandparents used to live here. It's all gone now…"[125]

Koh Si Koh Ha, Phatthalung

On March 7, 2003, in front of his room in Si Yang Temple, Ranot District, Songkhla, Kra Praeng Phetchamrat, a 57-year-old monk and former resident of the bird's-nest island, told his story:

"…I was born in a farming family and grew up in the rice fields. I worked on farms and then lived in Jana District for four years selling things till I finished grade 7. When my father remarried, I moved to the bird's-nest island, and learned about way of life here. I moved to Koh Si Koh Ha because of Mr. Kluen who lived across the lake from Nangkam Island. He cooked for the island's workers before they worked. I agreed to go when I was around 14–15 years old. There was no car at the time so we had to walk from Ban Thahin to Pak Phayun, and got picked up by a boat on January 15. There were like 100 people from different places and regions. I didn't think much; I just went along.

At that time, the concession holder changed from Rang Nok Thai, Mr. Thawee Chulasap's company, to Laem Thong company. At first, we didn't do much, and had no shelter. The new shelter was under construction, though there were old ones but the new company took them apart.

The company gave us one ax each, which we signed for at their office on Thewada Island. They deducted our money for this afterwards. I prepared food, cutting so much wood with that ax that it lasted for a year.

I was too young to work in the cave, so I was a, 'patrol boy,' The patrol boy was like a house sitter. I was not officially a bird's-nest collector, but got paid THB 110 per month. This money I'd get before I returned home at the end of the year. We could ask for some advance money, and buy anything they had for sale at the company. However, they provided free rice and some food once every five days.

Later, I started to collect the birds' nests with *Jorhor* on the second year. I've never seen how they do this as I wasn't allowed during my first year. I was told in advance before going to the cave, as I had to light some candles and pray for blessings, saying things such as, "Please protect us," with some flowers and incense. After the ceremony, each of us carried a big candle.

The first day that I went down, there were large ropes called *chuek taphot*, and I was called, *luk cheuk*, which means someone who carries the ropes. We went in Kantang Cave, a large cave with many rooms. The first room was big, and each room had a unique name, such as Lap Jek Lee, a name of Chinese man who found that room. All the names started with *lap*, that means secret, and was a name of the person who first found it. The team on my first day consisted of people with three job titles, *Jorhor*, the head master, *Luk Tho*, his supporter, and *Luk Cheuk*.'

Jorhor is someone who knows all about where to find the nests, and how to find them. He must be very experienced. It takes years before anyone can get that position. This *Jorhor* was different from the rest in the team, he was good, courageous, and able to use all his staff well. If any *Luk Tho*, or *Luk Chuek*, was nervous or unable to pick a bird's-nest, he did it himself.

Chapter 5

Luk Cheuk's job was tying the ropes in four directions on bamboo staves. The ropes needed to be tied in pairs and knotted to strengthen the bamboo and *luktang*, which were four pieces of cut wood tied on top of each other to form a seat, with about half a meter long left on each side for a person to hold. The ropes are tied to its four corners, and when one rope was pulled, the sling would go in one direction and so this could go in four directions. For a much wider cave, this would be tied into six directions. For a smaller cave where the birds' nests are closer to the ground, the bamboo frame won't be necessary, and a long bamboo stick will be used instead.

For a very wide cave, a lot more ropes will be added to make the frame go in six different directions. In a place where climbing may be impossible, as for a cliff, then a *pha-ong*, will be used. There's another tool for picking the birds' nests called a *tor*. It's a piece of sharp but flat steel that looks like the '*kra-tai*,' a coconut grater. The birds' nests would be collected into big sacks to be carried back.

When I was a young man, I was promoted to *Chinteng* and allowed to carry a gun. This position was one down from manager. I had to supervise all of our workers, and if there were any theft or damages to the company, I had to report them. Everything was recorded, even personalities of each worker. I had to report and consult the manager, but I could fire any worker if I needed to. I supervised the workers collecting the nests, but I had to show them how sometimes to build credibility. Women on the island would be called three times a year to help cleaning up the birds' nests. They would sit in a line to work, and get paid every 14–15 days only 1,000 Baht. These days, it's 1,500 for 15 days.

An incident that still haunts me today, and caused me to resign was the murder of 10 people on the island.

At the time, someone came to tell me there were 10 people who sneaked into the cave and were shot dead. These men used to live there in 1994. I was frightened with the scenes of bloodshed, and so I quit not long after that.

A man named Uncle Yung-Phayung Khunsi was the manager, but Ko (uncle) Seng was the top manager. Uncle Seng came from China at 16 or 17 years old, and went to school in Bangkok. He had a Thai name so he could have a bank account. He was a very hot-tempered guy, and would fire any worker instantly if he got upset. The former manager, Uncle Toi, was the opposite. He was calmer. It was during Uncle Seng's management that those *Jorhor* were getting together to steal the birds' nests. In a year, there were hundreds of kilograms of birds' nests on Koh Si Koh Ha, and so there were 30–31 boxes, each box was 60 kg., and four to five boxes of bird's-nest scraps.

I don't know about the dark side of the concessionaire, but I know they avoided taxes. Sometimes we had to hide 20–30 sacks of birds' nests in a cave before the Revenue Department officers who would tell us in advance, came. They would come to the front of the island where people could see them arrive.

A *chinteng*'s salary used to be THB 3,000, and was THB 7,000 when I worked there. I could save up to THB 3 million because I worked there for a long time, and did not have to spend much. It was said that anyone could steal the birds' nests during the collecting season. In the past, there was no place to sell stolen nests, but just a few years ago, the bird's-nest price on the black market reached THB 1,000 per kg. These recent years, there has been a lot more stealing.

In the past, the company would call four police officers from Songkhla, and they did just a rough check. People didn't dare to steal at that time. But later, we had to check every day from early morning, unlike every 15–16 days as before, and if there was any loss, it would be reported immediately.

I decided to leave the job because it was difficult. The shootings made me unhappy. It's too dangerous. The bird's nest that people eat, I don't think it does anything, and Westerners have said the same thing. The only useful thing is that it helps with cold sores. The Chinese say to boil the birds' nests with rock sugar.

If anyone asked me to go back and work on the island, I'd say never...".[126]

Koh Thalu, Phang-nga

We arrived at the pier of Koh Yao Noi in the late afternoon, Abdul Rozak was a young person with light skin color. He seemed calm, polite and generous. He brought five guests to lunch at his relative's coastal fisherman's house. One of the researchers introduced himself by showing him his identity card. He seemed cautious but began to tell his story. He came from Ban Nam-chuet, Koh Yao Noi Sub-District, Ko Yao

Chapter 5

District, Phang-nga Province. He is the third of a total of five siblings. He was forty-three years old with four children, with his wife, Yaroh.

... About a hundred years ago, Tok Chai-at came from Satun to the bird's-nest island with four or five friends. Years later, he married someone there and worked as a bird's-nest collector while Pae (uncle) Jinkee, a Chinese man, was concessionaire. He gained the man's trust and became *Pang-lae-ma*, which means head of collectors on Thalu Island. Abdul Rozak's father also worked on the island, and he had to help Tok Chai-at in the Puya ceremony on Phi Phi Island, Krabi, when he was young.

His father began his work when Ko Bin was the concessionaire, and father-in-law of Ko Bun, also known as Aphichat for Eric Vally and Dial Summer, National Geographic writers.

Seventy ago, his father, was a bird's-nest collector on Thalu Island even before he was born. Now at 80, his father still worked on the island but only as a cook for the bird nest workers.

Abdul Rozak became a nest collector at 26 years old. Before that he worked in a rubber plantation and as a fisherman. When he was little, he was asked to go through a small hole in a cave. His dad was saying to him, "When you go in the hole, breathe gently and don't be afraid of anything," since it was a dark cave hole and frightening for a young kid. He ended up crying as he could hardly get out of it. Ten years after schooling in Koh Yao, he was invited to back to the island by Wachu Utchakan.

He hesitated since, at the time, there was violence on the island. Some bird's-nest thieves from Trang were shot dead on the island, while others got away but swore to come back for revenge. Though his father wasn't scared, he and his mother were. Finally, after talking to his parents, his dad said he could decide for himself, and his mom disagreed. He decided to ask his teacher, who said to him to go but be careful of the danger.

He took only a little luggage with him to start working on Kalat Island, where he found six people working there besides himself.

His work was to collect nests attached to the stone walls of the cave by climbing up a bamboo trunk called *khae*. Whether they were at Koh Kalat, which had more birds' nests, or any other island in the Andaman Sea, the collectors did the same thing: carrying about 500 bamboo sticks, about 500 thick ropes, 5,000 strands, a long flashlight, candles, and container for storing 2–3 kg. of the birds' nests. Each person had to bring their own *rada*, a three-pronged iron tool usually ordered from Phuket. When the work was done, the *rada* had to be stored in a high place and used on the *puya* ceremony. *Rada*, in addition to picking the birds' nests, are believed to also protect a person, because the ghost of the cave is afraid of *rada*.

The three-pronged *rada* is about one handspan long and has a casing similar to a sheath, to be worn with a bamboo handle that is 3–7 *wa* long (6–14 meters).

In some places, a four-to five-*wa*-long *rada* is used for harvesting nests, and everyone sits or stands on one of the bamboo frames.

Abdul Rozak was at first afraid of collecting nests in a wide and high cave, but he gradually got used to it. The collection starts from small to big birds' nests, and from the bottom to the top. The nests in the middle of the cave require a longer-handled *rada*. In case of a very wide and high cave, it must be done with a higher bamboo scaffold with a wood seat across the top, along with a support pole for balance.

He recalled that when he first began collecting, the number of nests harvested was uncertain. One person couldn't collect more than two kilograms, normally, and a skillful person usually harvested no more than three kilograms. Some nests might be broken, but any part that was dropped must be kept, otherwise there would be punishment. If anyone left nests behind or broke them, *Pang-lae-ma* would give a warning. He was head of all collectors.

On the island, one person was a cook, and the rest worked together with *Pang-lae-ma*. On some islands that had more birds' nests, there would be more workers, so some locations might employ 4–5 people, while others up to 15.

Outside of harvest season, we would patrol the island and report to a patrol speedboat or to island police. This was only at night, because in the daytime, the collection locations were clearly visible. At the same time, the fishermen near the island would tell us if they saw anything unusual. Collectors and fishermen had good relations. Abdul worked there for two years, and then returned to Koh Thalu, but still collected nests. After three years, he accepted an invitation to go back to Koh Kalat. This time he had to follow an agreement that he and other collectors signed with the concession-holding company. It stated that all workers, regardless of employment duration, must collect at least the same amount of birds' nests as the previous year, or more. For example, if 800 kg. of birds' nests were collected last season, the number couldn't be any less, or there would be a penalty. People from the concession company would visit once every few days.

Abdul Rozak, when he first became *Pang-lae-ma*, had five staff who were his relatives. The *Pang-lae-ma*, in his opinion, must be an honest, patient person with at least 10 years' experience. They are picked by either the concession holder or by senior nest-collectors, anonymously. Sometimes, an outsider could become *Pang-lae-ma* as well, though this was very seldom. He was the third generation in his family to occupy the position.

When asked if his own son was also a nest-collector, he said,

"No, I asked him when he was in 4th or 5th grade to go through a small hole in a cave before, and he collected about 1 kg. of birds' nests, or 100 nests. Now he's in 10th grade and helping only during school breaks."

When asked if a woman can enter the cave, he said,

"Yes, they can enter but not climb to collect nests, because it's too scary for them."

When asked if there were any more brave women who applied to be a nest-collector, and he replied,

"There have never been any female bird's nest-collectors. I believe that it's too nerve-wracking for them. Even if there was one who was capable of doing it, I'd not take her in. In the cave, the *Pang-lae-ma* knows the best, and knows how to read people well. I have to read people's minds before I can trust them. It's natural."

He told stories about his Tok (grandfather) having supernatural experiences. In places without any bamboo bunch, or high cliffs in deep valleys, he'd tell everyone to turn all the lights off, and then he appeared on the other side to get the birds' nests. His grandfather once had a fever, and came to the island in early morning which was about 20 km. away, without any sight of boat. He said that the person, who told him this story.

He said that as he gained confidence, he came to believe in his own supernatural senses, especially after Tokoh Aae, his teacher, chose him among many others to kill a buffalo in an important ceremony, even though he was only 26 years old at the time. The sacrifice was held to celebrate the fact the collectors had been able to exceed the required number of birds' nests to be collected. He said that he was more certain of his sixth sense when he could visualize the spirit of the island in a dream. It was an old man, with long white beard, and dressed like an Islamic teacher; wearing a sarong and long sleeves with cloth wrapped around his head. The spirit said to him that he should work on the island. He gained his confidence and authority to tell where the nests should be picked and who should pick them.

When asked whether he had ever tasted bird's nest, he said,

"Yes, it tastes just like Jell-O."

"The real story is that once there was a Chinese shipwreck, and people got stuck in the Viking Cave for 15 days, with no food or water. Everyone was fine because they ate the nests."

He started a new story "It's believed to be an antipyretic drug. You can notice that the swiftlets can fly all day without ever stopping anywhere, so people who eat what has come out of its body should gain some similar attributes, more or less. When eating nests, you will sweat a lot even if you exercise only a little. This can make you stronger."

When asked how often he eats the nests, he said,

"Once a year, the company prepares it for everybody. It's only the broken nests that cost THB 300 per nest. Still, it's expensive so they'd not let you taste it often, and I cannot afford it. Only a small nest, after it's soak in water, expands so much."

When asked what his belief about the swiftlet was, he said,

"The *puya* ceremony is the first priority. It's like you do it first, then let everything go naturally. If we didn't, I believe we cannot collect the nests."

When asked where he learned how to perform rituals, he said he learned from Tokoh Aae and Grandpa Chai-at's son, and his uncle. His teacher taught him all about the swiftlets, and all the names of the islands, and the spirits that own the islands, and even the names of the bamboo spirits; with the belief that people who knew these would be more protected.[127]

Koh Phetra, Trang

On October 29, 2009, Suwet Ketkaeo, 34-year-old man and former nest-collector, now living in Koh Sukon Sub-District, Palien District, Trang Province, told us his story.

"… The first time I learnt about the birds' nests I was 14 years old. I lived on Samran Beach and my parents split up. When I was in 6th grade in Koh Mu, I did not have money to go to school; so, I drove a boat for the fish pier owner, but the money was not good. Precha Siemmai, brother of Seri the concessionaire, invited me to drive a boat for the bird's-nest island. Before this, I didn't know much about the nests, aside from taking tourists by boat near the island. I only knew some people from Koh Mu who worked there. The first time I drove to transport supplies to various islands. In less than a year I became a collector by learning from a master. I saw a large python on my first trip, as if it was the owner at the mouth of the cave. The adventure began with entering the cave using a wrist's size rope into the cave for climbing. The only device I brought was a flashlight. Other tools were already in the cave, i.e., a stick, *rada, lam thaeng*, and the bag in which to keep the nests. There were some speaking taboos in which you used different vocabulary out of superstition, such as saying rope instead of snake, rubber for blood, broken rope for torn rope, rain falls for fallen rocks, and slippery is changed to bard. A nest-collector's wife isn't allowed to use oil as it may make the husband trip and fall in the caves.

On Friday, during the Islamic prayer times, the work stops, and we pray. In the cave, you say, "*ta bay tok ur*", if there is something that scares you. The first time, it took me a week to collect. In just the one large cave called Yai cave on the Island of Phetra, 1,000 kg. of nests were collected. I was 15 to 17 years old. All the nest-collectors here are Muslim Thais. People work in three groups; those who pick, collect, and gather. At first, there were no guards, but they were added as the nests became more expensive.

I collected sacks of birds' nests, tied and put them inside the cave. When the Revenue Department went to check the cave, we selected a large sample of nests to show them. They took a look at a couple of nests, and came only once a year. When I was a collector, the birds' nests were commonly sold for THB 20,000–25,000 per kilogram.

You can cheat by hiding up to 10 nests in a torch and carrying them out with you. Sometimes they're hidden in underpants and water bottles. If you successfully get them out, then you can sell to a middleman yourself. The middleman has his own boss, and they sell the stolen nests to Hat Yai, and split the profit or give the money to the 60 workers on the island.

According to the law, we were permitted to harvest nests twice a year, but we collected three times. The first round is in February. These are called 'sleeping nests' because the birds leave the cave at the time, so there's no birds, only the nest. These nests are full, thick, and at a good weight. We spend a month to collect them because there are many caves.

The second round comes around April. This time birds make the nests for laying eggs. If there's one egg, we take the nest because if the birds don't lay a second egg, then they'll build their nests again. But if they leave two eggs in their nests, they will not make another nest.

In the third round birds accelerate the building of nests while laying two eggs per nest. In August, when it rains, the birds feed their offspring insects that come with the rain. This time around 50 percent of the new-born birds will survive.

The fourth round is called "clear the cave". The birds that still make nests also lay eggs again but there are not so many nests.

Black nests are hard and found in dry places. The collector has to work hard, and must be strong. They collect the nests throughout the year as when they finish with the white nests, then the black swiftlets start to build right away. The black nests are relatively inexpensive at THB 6,000 per kilogram, and the company wasn't really interested at that time, but they are now fetching THB 20,000–30,000 per kg. Birds' nests have reduced in number by about 80 percent at Phetra Cave, with less than 200–300 kg. per year being collected now.

When I worked there, there were guards in front of the cave. There were also many police guarding caves that had many nests. They strictly prevented all outsiders from entering the area. Someone was shot once when he went into the cave while Sia Lek was the concessionaire.

I collected for JETA Corporation Limited, and got paid for THB 3,000 per kg. I would make THB 1,500–2,000 for the black birds' nests. The company conducted intense searches; they were afraid of theft. They learnt from Kamnan (Seri Siemmai). Birds began to decline and the nest numbers came down. People said it was because they did not worship the island and because they used solar cell panels, closed circuit television for surveillance. The technology that came in was though to cause birds to flee. There were bombs buried in the ground during Mr. Lek's concession period to prevent theft. I helped clearing them for JETA. Also, there were a few cans of pesticide found. It's believed that the company tried to avoid tax as they had a misunderstanding and though that there's only four years allowed before returning capital.

Most bird's-nest collectors are not rich. They earn a lot of money but usually spend for fun. Sometimes they deposit money with friends to take home, but get ripped off. So, they just keep going back and working. I think they should limit concessions to three or four years, but the provincial office profits from the bird's-nest auction. But I think the community should participate in management..."[87]

Kamnun (Head of Village – translator) Seri Siemmai started telling us his story:

"...I was born in 1946 on Koh Mu, and grew up here. In the past, there were more wild pigs (*mu pa*) than men, so it was called, "Pig Island (Koh Mu)". Now there's no more wild pigs left, because people on the shore killed and ate them all.

I left school at 14 years old, and helped my dad, Karim, to work in the bird nest business. He had been doing it for four or five years with a Phuket company belonging to Ko Bun (Aphichat Kitprasan), the concession holder at the time. They'd tell us how many birds' nests they wanted, and we'd collect that for them. In the past, there was rarely any collector. Prices for top-grade white birds' nests was THB 300 per kg., grade 2 was THB 150, and no one wanted black bird's-nest (grade 3).

Back around 1959, the caves was very dark; we didn't have any flashlight, only a fire torch and a three-pronged *rada*. We picked only from Koh Muk, Koh Waen, Koh Chuek, Koh Mah, Koh Lao, and the concession for these places was shared with Ko Bun's father-in-law's company.

In the past, there was no theft but we guarded the birds' nests anyway. It was difficult. We used a row boat, packed drinking water and slept in the cave. After my father died, I became the supervisor, and collected birds' nests on Phetra Island for a concession-holder; in 1989, they'd request like 150 kg. of birds' nests. At the time, I collected more like 200 to 300 kg. so, I sold the surplus to a middleman to sell in Tubtieng (Trang Province), and Bangkok. The buyers were also Muslims.

Around 30 years ago, in 1979, swiftlets were so plentiful that if you stood in front of a cave they would hit you flying in and out. We sold nests to the company for THB 700 per kg., and sometimes THB 12,000 per kg. for other customers. The concession company paid the Nest-collectors THB 1,000–2,000 per kg. We also made money from selling birds' nests we collected in excess of the contracted amount.

Later on, I joined with another person from Koh Mu, Sanit Chumkong, to enter an auction for the concession. We, along with six others who were my relatives, agreed to write 200 kg. in the contract, and we won. I had found a new cave, Takbai, but my competitors didn't know it yet. One day, four of us went on a boat for half an hour to Takbai Island, but only I went on the island. I was looking around carrying a 35-meter-long Manila rope. Although I never did anything like that on Phetra Island, I was strong enough to search for birds' nests from 11 AM to 3 PM Wherever there was a hole, I would drop the rope. I found two or three kilograms of birds' nests, and then I was picked up and left for Koh Phetra.

I went again the next morning because there were more holes to explore. This time, I dropped the rope to the water end, and I saw two bamboo poles (perhaps from other people exploring other caves) and around 40 to 50 birds' nests when I looked up. They were behind some rock curves. I used a flashlight, then tied long bamboo poles together with rattan. I used that for a scaffold, then climbed up by myself. (I was careless, no one should do this alone; you need someone else to help hold the scaffold.) Once I leaned forward and saw the cave wall, one side was full of white birds' nests. I used another bamboo and risked climbing up, and saw a cave full of birds' nests. I was so exhausted and brought only three kg. of birds' nests down, and sent them with my relatives to bring home. I thought about going again, but was also nervous to tell my team. Then I thought of a very good friend of mine, Bang Nuan.

He was a very good climber, and so we went by a boat to collect the birds' nests from the water source. We collected around 28 kilos about 50 nests per kilogram.

I gave some to him on our first time, and I took the rest home and sold them separately in bags only at my house. I was doing this for two or three years, with Bang Nuan and I sharing the nests we collected. We used blankets to wrap the nests in his boat, and took them home. At the time, the selling price was over THB 10,000 per kg. and cash only. I did it for four to five years before people figured it out because I was getting richer. That cave was named, 'Kamnun Cave.'

Later, I joined the next auction for Koh Phetra and Koh Lao Liang Islands. We increased the requirement to 250 kg. when the bird's-nest price at the time was THB 15,000 per kg.

My brother-in-law joined me and was responsible to collect 30 kg. only in Lao Liang, which was much easier than in Koh Phetra. There, I searched for three or four days but didn't find any. Four men on my team also searched at Serio (on the same island) and when I was at the hut someone told me about a treasure map. We followed it and found what's called, "smokestack," where we got two sacks (10 kg. per bag) of nests. There were five of us, and a 10-meters rope dropping from the top of the hole. Only in the upper part of that hole, it took us a year to collect the birds' nests. We collected four sacks at a time, and sold the nests in Tubtieng where we rented a house and dried the nests with five electric fans. Our buyer was Saenplern Shop. At the time, the price was THB 12,000 per kg. and four sacks would contain over 700 kg. of birds' nests.

We collected the nests twice a year because we did not want anybody to know. We put our truck on the boat to Laemyang hiding from people, but later on they became suspicious. At the time, we could collect over 1,000 kg. of birds' nests in that cave.

After doing this for four years, the concession was opened for auction again. A sergeant named Cheep, learnt about the secret island from my nephew. A competitor named Chao learnt only how to go from the back of the island. After negotiating with the sergeant, I could still collect around two sacks of nests. This was a three-story cave, so if we went early, we could collect up to four sacks of nests. There was only one person guarding the cave, and my competitor had conflicts within his team, so I ended up collecting there for another two to three years.

When Ko Boon lost in the auction, Sia Lek who was powerful at the time got the concession. I was the head of village at the time, so I did not get involved at all.

He had a big house used for running the nest business. He had his own staff from Libong Island, and hired Burmese guards. He ran this legally for five to six years, plus one year illegally. After that he won another 10 years of concession, and during that time anyone from Koh Mu was blocked from getting involved.

Later on, he let Ko Tong (Patchuban Angchotpan) run from the concession from 2546 B.E. to 2550 B.E. After that, the JETA Corporation took over, hiring my old staff from Koh Mu, but they lost THB 10 million per year. They were sued by the provincial office because they used insecticide. In Trang, the bird's nest committees did not inspect the island. Then, Sia Lek took over, and people were upset because they were not allowed to enter the island. They were accused of stealing the nests. Some were shot, and it scared everyone around. This wasn't a problem when the company was in charge.

According to a story told by the head of Koh Sukon District Administration office, a collector named Mee was locked up in a hotel room during an auction for concession. There were bribes paid to someone, who later was shot dead, from Libong Island. This would be investigated normally, but it wasn't.

When I had the concession, about 20 percent of the nests were left in the same cave that I used to collect up to 1,000 kg. At the time, I and 40 to 50 of my staff snuck at least two kg. each, and hid them on the beach.

> Six of us had so much money at the time. I'd carry THB 200,000 to 300,000 around in my wallet. One time, a young man asked me for THB 70,000 which I gave him in cash right away. We would reserve a famous restaurant in town for 2–3 nights straight, and spend like THB 100,000 each night. I carried a gun which was seized by a cop. I just got another cop to get it out for me. We traveled by plane often and it was fun. I once flew with a female singer to buy her clothes that cost like THB 70,000. If you worked in a rubber plantation, you would get paid THB 500 per day. When you collected the birds' nests, it's THB 20,000 a day, and it can change people.
>
> Every person involved benefitted: committees, governors, representatives, ministers, heads of provincial administration offices and District administration offices. The governor himself would receive around 800,000 after an auction ..."[128]

In Thailand, the company or shop's showrooms sell their bird's-nest products in cities in the south, and in Bangkok. They also have online direct sales systems. Marketing channels define purchasing power, implying consumer status for the middle class and the elite. This is true especially for the ready-to-drink bird's nest products of C.H. Farm, PP Bird's Nest Company, Cerebos (Thailand) Co., Ltd., Scott Industrial (Thailand) Co., Ltd., and CP Interfood (Thailand) Co., Ltd. Pak Phanang District in Nakhon Si Thammarat Province has its own brands of nest products, such as Son Sawan, Ban Nok, Pak Phanang Rang Nok, Kwan Mui, and more.

However, the collection of birds' nests from natural locations in Thailand is not something people do throughout the year. It is rather temporary work that takes place during nesting seasons only. When the cave-closing season comes, the collectors take other kinds of work that are not related to the bird's nest industry, such as working on rubber plantations or rice farms, or doing general labor.

Export Markets

The most important nest foreign markets are for the most part served by Thai-Chinese business interests exporting to China, Hong Kong, Taiwan, Vietnam. China and Hong Kong, as mentioned before, remain the largest two markets. According to

Customs Department data, companies from Thailand have also been exporting both raw and ready-to-eat birds'-nest products to China, Hong Kong, Taiwan, Singapore, Myanmar, Malaysia, India, Iran, France, Italy, Belgium, Denmark, England, Brazil, Negara Brunei Darussalam, Cambodia, Egypt, Indonesia, Japan, America, Australia, Germany, South Korea, Nepal, Netherlands, South Africa, Sweden, Ivory Coast, Cyprus, Ecuador, Philippines, Spain, Sri Lanka, UAE, Bangladesh and Pakistan.

Nest-Trade Relationships

Nest-Trade Relationships as a Link for Ethnic Relations

Nests of the swiftlet occupy a unique place in food hierarchies. They are a natural and cultural food; a health food and a medicine; a trade commodity; and a symbolic food for the those of wealth and/or high social status.

The nests also represent a complex, contradictory, and fluid social property. They have belonged to both state and private property regimes as common and 'communal property' regimes, and *res nullius* regimes and open-access regimes[129] at the same time.

Swiftlets are ultimately considered state property and must be protected as such. Yet, they become private property when they enter private dwellings to live. Similarly, they're open-access as they choose where to nest beyond human's absolute control. swiftlets also fall into the category of 'communal property' as their food resources are within the human community.

Even though Thais from Central Thailand have dominated the business world of birds' nests, they have not monopolized access to the resources. On the contrary, other ethnic groups such as Southern Thais, Thai-Malay Muslims, Central Thais, Northeastern Thais, Chinese-Thais, and Thai-Vietnamese also share access and use of the resources. Each maintains its own monopoly over managing bird's-nest resources both in nature and in buildings as supervising authorities, nest-building owners, concessionaire companies, nest-collectors, guards on nest islands, and workers in nest-product manufacturing facilities.

In each of these ethnic groups, there is a power relationship between access and use of resources that exhibit differences of power, broadly divided between being either included or excluded from the center of power.

Examples of an inclusive relationship are when concessions to collect birds' nests are rotated among a limited number of family-owned companies. It also includes rights for collecting birds' nests in natural sources that are passed on within nest-collecting families among Southern Thais, Thai-Malay Muslims, Thai-Vietnamese, and other communities.

People in various communities who are excluded from such access often respond by criticizing, gossiping, and even stealing birds' nests both from natural caves and buildings. Such thieves may come from any ethnic group but predominantly they are Southern Thais and Thai-Malay Muslims. The nest thefts have become so serious that it has become necessary to install guards at nest caves, and CCTV cameras in nest buildings.

Nest-collectors and concession holders in Trang Province also criticize the government officials for corruption scandals involving the illegal auction of bird nest concessions. Shares of the profits are taken by the provincial governor, the minister, the president of the Provincial Administrative Organization, and the president of the Provincial Administrative Organization. Money earned by the provincial governor at each auction totals around THB 800,000. Penalties for corruption cases that are prosecuted can including the halting of a company concession for three to four years, allowing a community to participate in the management.[130]

Nest-Trade Relationships Across Ethnic Groups in Thailand

Whether nests are traded within the same ethnic group domestically, or internationally between different ethnic groups, all parties seem to enjoy relatively good relations in terms of maintaining the flow of raw nests provided to purchaser companies in sufficient quantities.

The owner of the Home of Swallows Limited, a leading company of both raw nests and ready-to-drink nest beverages in Hong Kong, says that birds' nests imported into

Hong Kong come from four sources: Indonesia, Malaysia, Vietnam, and Thailand. Malaysian nest prices are on average 98 percent lower than in Thailand. It is popular to claim sometimes that nests come from Malaysia to ensure a quick sale. Most nest businesses in Malaysia are quite active, and well-supported by the government. The exporters mostly carry the nests on planes by themselves.

Thai bird nest-quality is considered to rank second after those from Vietnam. Taiwanese customers prefer Thai and Vietnamese birds' nests for better quality, regardless of higher prices. Thai nest prices are also higher than prices for Indonesian nests. For the company to import more Thai nests, the prices would need to be lower.[131] Twenty percent of nests are shipped by airmail, while 80 percent are carried across borders by the sellers themselves.[132]

Even though any community in Thailand can start up a bird's nest business when they have the money for investment, the reality is that businesspeople of Chinese descent tend to have more financial clout. Hong Kong is influential in setting prices for the Thai supply, especially after the, Malaysian bird nest incident in China in July 2011, when fakes were alleged to have been exported.

Since that time, China has set rigorous regulations on quality and conditions for all imported birds' nests, and this affects the nest trade throughout Southeast Asia, the major source for edible bird's nest products. The Thai-Chinese monopoly on exporting conflicts with the power of government to access to nest resources.

Despite the ways in which our world has modernized rapidly, the collection of birds' nests from natural sources in Thailand still comes out of a hunter-gatherer society. Local tools used along the cliffs to gather nests haven't changed in a century. Likewise in artificial structures hosting nests, more or less the same applies, with the addition of audio recordings to attract birds.

6. BIRDS' NESTS IN POLITICS AND SOCIETY

The formation of the modern state in Siam under King Chulalongkorn (Rama V) in 1892 was also the beginning of centralized power for the kingdom. A new state power gradually replaced traditional power, and accumulating influence throughout the country.

In Rama V's reign, when two great powers, England and France, expanded their political and economic might in Southeast Asia, it meant that the Thai kingdom needed to end its system of tributary relations between the monarchy and satellite states. By centralizing administration under Bangkok's control, Thailand moved into modern state development.[133]

During the late 19th century and early 20th century, Siam began to emphasize capitalist over feudalist economics along with expanding government administrative power to local areas via a centralized bureaucracy.[134] The kingdom more or less adopted a colonial state-governing model to replace traditional feudal governance, adhering to the rule of land for the rule of manpower, accepting the principle of determining borders by using maps, using regional management, prioritizing central power, and giving people on the outer edges of the kingdom lower power roles, and thus distributing benefits more unfairly.[135]

Siam made even more significant political and administrative changes following the 1932 *coup d'état* in 1932 which replaced an absolute monarchy with a quasi-democratic, military-dominated system. Ever since then, the Thai political system has been stuck in a vicious circle that moves from coup to elections, which are then protested by the opposition, leading to street violence and an excuse for another military coup. Hence periods of long military dictatorships have alternated with short democratic periods.[136] There seems to be no end in sight to this pattern. Thai military culture believes it 'owns' democracy in Thailand and may take whatever steps it chooses to ensure that vision is kept 'pure'.

The Thai economic system in the past 40 years has been closely linked to and dependent on the global economy. Nowadays even slight changes in the world economy has impact on the country's economy.[137] After the Cold War, which ended with the consolidation of Germany in 1989, the collapse of the Soviet Union in 1991, the old bipolar system of a US bloc versus a Russian bloc has changed.

Thailand aims towards globalization to be able to compete in international trade. Motivated by rising prices, natural nest harvests have increased considerably since the 1980s. The government has not paid much attention to conservation or properly managed resources with regards to the swiftlets and their nests. Community voices in Thailand reflect the relationships between groups that are included or excluded in access to the resources and their value.

Despite legal changes in government power structures, not much access has been granted for local community participation.

This can be seen from the following examples.

In On Koh Rang (Trat Province), Hok Sia Tung company held the concession for bird nest collection for 50 years, and before that W.T. Co. Ltd. owned the concession for 10 years. Although Thai-Vietnamese communities have been collecting birds' nests here for generations, the companies are owned by Thai-Chinese.[138]

On Koh Si Koh Ha (Phatthalung Province) the Revenue Department of the Ministry of Finance renewed the concession for collecting birds' nests for another Thai-Chinese company, Laem Thong Bird's Nest (Siam) Co., Ltd., continuously from 21 February 1959 to 31 October 2003. At this location, it has been Southern Thais who have inherited rights from ancestors to collect the nests.

As can be seen, rights in both cases fall along ethnic lines.

At Koh Thalu, Phang-nga Province Thai-Malay Muslims have been collecting birds' nests for generations. As well, here only a few Chinese companies take turns winning the auction to collect the birds' nests.

On Koh Phetra (Trang Province) the nest-collectors are also Thai-Malay Muslims. From 1994 to 2003, when there was an open auction, an important and powerful bidder submitted two bidding envelopes. This meant that if he lost, he could submit the case again when others could not. He finally received a five- to six-year concession legally, and one more year only by agreement with the provincial office. Then he later won another 10 years at auction. The Collection of Swiftlet-Nest Taxes Committee, and those involved were detained in the hotel during this auction. It was called, 'special treats'. According to legal regulations, they are supposed to check on the bird's nest island, but didn't do so. Instead, they checked the nests at the hotel.[139]

Birds' nests from artificial sources are a newer and increasingly important business in Southeast Asia. In Thailand, the first artificial birds' nests were cultivated in Chinatown at the Lim Ko Niao Shrine in Pattani Province, and at the Chinatown Building in Pak Phanang town, Nakhon Si Thammarat Province, about 80 years ago.

The nest-building business rapidly expanded after the so-called Tom Yum Kung financial crisis in July 1997. By 2007, there were approximately 600 nest buildings in the country, and by 2014, they totaled around 10,020 in 42 provinces, worth up to THB 50 billion. Just the raw nests collected from the buildings were worth THB 960–2.1 billion yearly. However, the Thai government still considers nests from buildings as 'foreign-illegitimate business' or 'business outside the state,' which means they are technically illegal.

In November 2012, a group of nest-building entrepreneurs from Eastern and Central Thailand, led by Kitti Kittipinyo and friends, organized a rally to visit other nest-building owners, and traders. A meeting was held at K Park Hotel, Surat Thani Province, on the 14th before the group became the Association of Bird's-Nest Entrepreneurs (Thailand) on 26 March 2014. Kamolsak Lertphaiboon was the first president of the association, and led a movement to amend the laws solving the ministerial regulations issued under the Wildlife Protection Act 1992 to include the *Aerodramus fuciphagus* and *Aerodramus maximus* in a category of breedable wild animals. This was filed as an open letter to the National Council of Peace and Order (NCPO) through the Southern Economic Development Board, at the Thai Chamber of Commerce on 2 August, 2014, at Genting Hotel, Su-ngai Kolok District, Narathiwat Province.

The Association of Bird's-Nest Entrepreneur (Thailand) movement was eventually accepted by Thai authorities. The Director-General of the Department of Livestock said in an interview with *Thairath Newspaper* on August 13, 2014, that the Department of Livestock wanted to encourage Thai bird's nest exports to China, including those from the nest buildings as well.[140] *

The 'fake red birds' nests' scandal that occurred in Malaysia in July 2011, following which China suspended the import of birds' nests from Malaysia and other countries, developed into an international political conflict among the nest-producing countries of Southeast Asia.

A act called Administrative Measures on Quarantine of Entry-Exit Passengers' Belongings, made effective from 1 November 2012, prohibited people from bringing genetically modified organisms in agriculture. This revised regulation added more details on birds' nests, except canned nests, that would be prohibited to enter China.[141]

---

* Recent TPBS television documentary, "Tat Truoan Ban Nok Aen" (breaking chain the swiftlet-houses), broadcasting on 8 March 2021, featured the story related to the dated 8 March 2021, reported: after many years of lobbying, the Ministry of Natural Resources and Environment published The Notification of Ministry on permission to collect, dismantle, or take possession of the edible-nest swiftlets (*Aerodramus fuciphagus*), and the black-nest swiftlets (*Aerodramus maximus*) will become effective in May 2021. Together with the regulation issued by the Department of National Parks, Wildlife, and Plant Conservation on the application and issue the permit to collect, dismantle, or take possession of the wildland animals' nests. Both laws will allow the birds' nests farm-owners to export the birds'-nests to China. See: https://program.thaipbs.or.th/PerdPom/episodes/76679x

Chapter 5

Considering birds' nests in natural resources through the political-sociology, some ethnic groups in Thailand traditionally passed down professions of bird's-nest collecting. However, Thailand does not endorse or accept the 'ethnic rights' of those who have found the bird's-nest cave and ownership. Simultaneously, the artificial resources of birds buildings or private companies belong to ethnic groups in Thailand have more freedom to run their businesses, both within the country and across the border. This freedom is limited for Thai ethnics with a sound financial background, especially Thai-Chinese.

When considering nest resources from a socio-political perspective, there is a symbolic everyday life struggle. People who are disadvantaged in society in Thailand, whether they are Nest-collectors, local politicians, businessmen, or even a bird's-nest thief, all express themselves in various forms of everyday life resistance, such as gossip, silent protests, and secretly stealing bird's nests. These forms of resistance happen quietly. They won't stand up to fight, blatantly, but use the so-called, "Weapons of the Weak" to avoid being arrested, or losing support from their superiors.[142]

Nonetheless, in some areas, especially Koh Si Koh Ha Islands, Phatthalung, people are sometimes killed for disrupting the profits, as well as for nest-theft. This has led to the stigmatization of bird's-nest islands as being lawless. The nest trade is associated with cruelty, blood, and death, by both locals and foreigners. Powerful figures and politicians locally and at national levels stand behind the business, while those below criticize the powers that control them.[143]

Another example is of Koh Phetra (Trang Province) in which 40 to 50 nest-collectors hid at least two kilos of nests while working for a concession company by covering them with shoes on the beach.[144] Birds' nests from a secret cave were stolen, or from any cave with the word *lap* (meaning 'secret') in front of the name, indicating a recently found cave.[145]

There was one incident where the Chinese manager of a concession company on Koh Si Koh Ha fired many workers, and later contributed to groups of *Jorhor* (cave team leaders) to steal nests.[146] In the case of people on the Gulf of Thailand and Andaman Sea, ostensibly-legitimate Southern-Thai and Thai-Malay Muslim collectors have been stealing nests and selling them on the informal market. On

November 8, 2008, Pak Phayun Police arrested a group of 19 thieves, aged 15–50 years old, who lived in Koh Mak Sub-District, Pak Phayun District, Phattalung. They were charged with nest theft from Ruen Cave, on Koh Rusim, Koh Si Koh Ha, Phatthalung Province. Police found 1.7 kg. of nests, three bird dropping sacks, five flashlights, and three longtail boats. Five of the 19 robbers were close relatives of the Phatthalung nest-tax committee. The stolen items were black nests, priced at THB 15,000 per kilogram on the black market. Pak Phayun Provincial Police Officer charged them with collecting natural birds' nests without having received concessions from the Committee, and causing harm to protected wildlife in a strictly prohibited area.

Another case involved a concession auctioned off to Eastern Chanthaburi Bird's Nest Group for nests from artificial structures in Pattani, Krabi, Surat Thani, Chumphon, Hat Yai–Songkhla, when technically these products were still illegal. Thai-Chinese smuggled nests into China, and bribed Chinese authorities THB 5,000 per kg. to allow entry.

There is also the issue of conflict between the nest trade and those who are oppose to bird's-nest consumption, claiming that nest collection is harmful to the swiftlets. Bidhouse-owners responded by explaining the swiftlet's life cycle and how it's consistent with the nature and life cycle of the birds, unlike cutting shark fins, or killing pigs, cows and buffalo for their meat. Nests are a product derived from animals in a way similar to that of collecting eggs from hens and ducks, coffee beans from civets and milk from cows.[147]

This conflict is challenging both the state's power and power across states, as well as the authorities who access and use nest resources. Field data and official documents show that crime arising from the "war of the bird's-nest resources" occurs in every area that has a bird's-nest concession.

Rungradit Isara, a village headman in Pak Phayun District, Phatthalung, died in a gunfight with his business rival in front of Robinson Department Store, Pathum Thani on 13 May 2007. On 28 October 2007, Roj Krairat, president of Koh Mak Sub-District Administrative Organization, was shot and killed by someone wielding an M16 rifle. These reveal the nest trade to exist in a somewhat violent sphere in Thailand.

7. ENVIRONMENTAL AND ECOLOGICAL FACTORS

Thailand has a biodiverse ecosystem, with about 15,000 species of plants, which is 8 percent of the world's total.[148] Based on the data from the Thailand Development Research Institute in 1988, it is concluded that Thailand has around 20,000–25,000 species of perennial plants, 10,000–15,000 species of flowers, 4,253 species of animals, 282 terrestrial mammals, 298 species of reptiles, 616 species of birds, 638 species of birds that breed in the country, of which 190 may already extinct, and 93 species are endangered.[149]

In 1915, Thailand had about 70 percent forest cover. Later, trees were cut down for planting cash crops, and led to a rapid decline in forest and woods in Thailand. By 1967, Thailand had to import wood for the first time.[150] In 1988, Thailand had 89 million *rai* of forested land, or 28 percent forest cover. In 1989 all forest concessions were abolished.[151] In 1991, less than 25 percent natural forest remained, with only about 10 percent primeval forest.[152]

Mangrove forest fared even rose. In 1961, Thailand was estimated to have 3.7 million *rai* of mangrove. By 1986, less than half remained. At the time, Thai authorities encouraged people to farm black tiger prawns along the coast to take advantage of rising market rates. In 1990, Thais destroyed 300,000 *rai* of mangrove for prawn farming, approximately 38 percent of the total mangrove forest.[153]

This generated an environmental problem that was so severe that it changed the direction of environmental management in Thailand. The government started to fall in line with global trends in sustainable development, participating in Earth Summit 1992 in Rio de Janeiro, Brazil, and a Rare Plants and Wildlife International Trade conference in 1975. The latter listed 675 species of plants and animals in danger of extinction. Thailand issued the Wild Animal Reservation and Protection Act, B.E. 2535 (1992), prohibiting trade in wild animals or wild carcasses, except with government official permission[154] in line with the Convention on International Trade in Endangered Species of Wild Fauna and Flora (CITES).

Higher demand for birds' nests from Hong Kong increased nest prices considerably in the 1980s, and an excessive harvests of birds' nests took place in nine provinces: Trat, Prachuap Khiri Khan, Chumphon, Surat Thani, Phatthalung, Phang-nga, Krabi, Trang, and Satun, which is believed to have led to a decreasing number of swiftlets.

While harvesting, nest-collectors may stand on the floor of the cave, at the edge of rocks, or on a bamboo scaffold to pick nests off the walls. Sometimes, the nests sit so high up the walls that the collector cannot see whether the nests contained eggs or new-born birds. Thus, in each harvest season, an estimated 10 percent of the eggs and neo-natal birds fall to the ground and die.

Collectors also capture fledgling birds at times and remove them from natural homes. Sometimes a concession company might order workers to collect birds for the company. Some collectors also secretly take the birds to cook and eat, or to pickle them in liquor, believing that the concoction makes a nourishing tonic for enhancing libido and sexual performance.

According to some collectors in the Andaman Sea, 90 percent of black nests collected have new-borny birds inside. During the collection of black nests, young birds often fall to the cave floor.[155] Collecting methods that do not comply with laws and regulations related to the concession, or the communities on the Gulf of Thailand and Andaman has greatly reduced the number of swiftlets in natural habitat of Thailand compared with the past.

Collecting without concern for sustainability, leaving the birds insufficient time for building nests, laying eggs, hatching eggs, and allowing fledglings to grow and fly out before taking their nests, reflects an inverse relationship between the community's management of swiftlet resources and the surrounding ecosystem.

The overall outlook for edible-nest swiftlets in Thailand is that the numbers are in recession. Ironically, owners managing swiftlets and nests in artificial structures are considered to be doing a overall better job at preserving the swiftlet population. This may reflect an urge for more effective conservation of swiftlet resources on the part of the private owner, versus those in the concession business.

However, nest buildings controlled by their owners also have a negative environmental and social impact. First, there is impact on community health and welfare from bird droppings, which are repellant to tourists and residents alike. There is also substantial noise pollution from the automated bird call recording. Some communities now limit bird calling to twice a day, in the morning and evening, when the birds leave and return only.[156]

There is also a fear that drinking rainwater may become infected with avian flu among the Pak Phanang community, where people buy drinking water instead of using rainwater as per tradition.

This fear of avian flu also occurs among shrimp farmers concerned that swiftlet droppings will infect their farms. Nest-collectors also fear the disease. Buildings are not built in accordance with the usual laws for commercial or residential buildings.[157] Water that is used in both the dry and wet systems to create coolness and humidity in the nest buildings is not treated. The waste water is drained into the water table, where it mixes with other water sources without treatment.

Stakeholder communities are not given a voice in formulating regulations related to swiftlet resources or nest buildings. Because of a lack of government oversight, nest building-owners tend not to pay tax, so the money from the trade does not reach locals.[158]

The house near Lim Ko Niao Shrine, Pattani and Ue Jin Guang on Chainam Road in Pak Phanang Municipality, Nakhon Si Thammarat, was the first nest building, having been in operation nearly 90 years, and now there are many more such buildings in Thailand. Problems with mosquitoes have been reported, with the fear that a town's population could face mosquito-borne disease.[159]

APPENDIX

Ethnic Groups and Bird Nest Resources in Thailand

Black-nest swiftlet in Ruen Cave, Koh Si Koh Ha, Phatthalung Province.

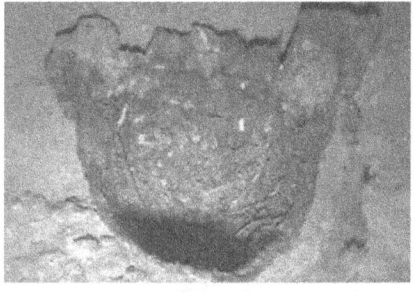

A black-nest swiftlet nest in Ruen Cave, Koh Si Koh Ha, Phatthalung Province.

A white-nest swiftlet, Koh Rang, Trat Province.

A nest and egg of white-nest swiftlet in Pak Panang District, Nakhon Si Thammarat.

A tool for collecting white swiftlet nests, Koh Si Koh Ha, Phatthalung Province.

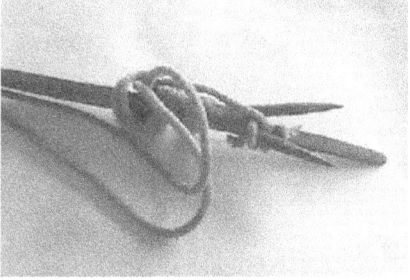

Rada, a tool for collecting the nests of white-nest swiftlets on bird's-nest islands in the Andaman Sea.

Chapter 5

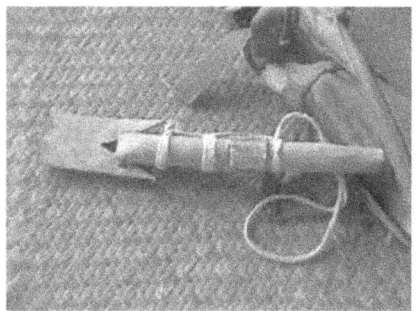

Ta chop, a tool for hooking black birds nests used by Andaman Coast collectors.

A miniature house used in the *puya koh ceremony* on islands in the Andaman Sea.

A statue of *Ho Thao* and *Ho Kae*, hero of nest-collectors, Koh Na Tay Wada, Phatthalung.

A hut used for guarding birds' nests on Koh Si Koh Ha, Phatthalung.

Kae, for climbing on to collect birds' nests, Koh Thalu, Phang-nga Province.

A hut used for guarding birds' nests in Koh Thalu, Phang-nga Province.

Ethnic Groups and Bird's-Nest Resources in Thailand

A Thai-Vietnamese nest collector harvesting nests in a cave, Koh Rang, Trat Province.

A female worker decorating bird nests in front of Tay Wada Cave, Koh Si Koh Ha, Phatthalung.

Ue Jin Kuang or Chinatown Building, the first nest building in Pak Phanang Municipality, Nakhon Si Thammarat.

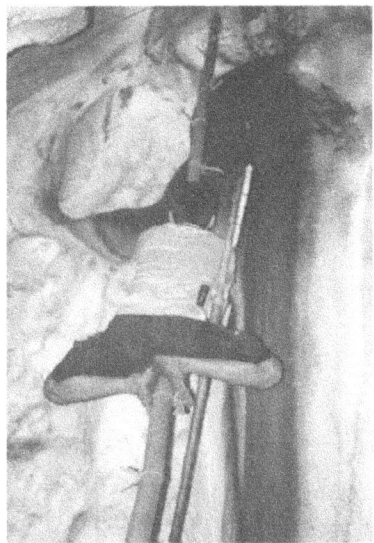

A collector harvesting nests in Ruen Cave, Koh Si Koh Ha, Phatthalung.

House no. 3, the first nest building near the Lim Ko Niao Goddess Shrine, Chinatown, Pattani Town, Pattani Province.

Nest buildings in Pak Phanang Municipality, Nakhon Si Thammarat.

Chapter 5

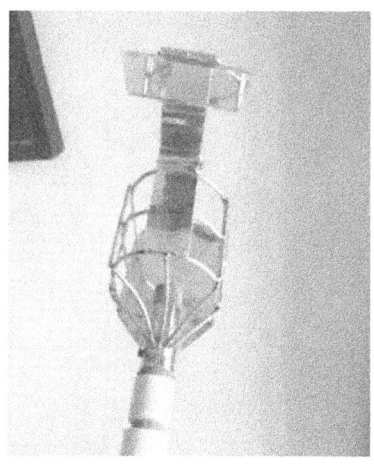

Birdwatching equipment and Nest-Collecting tools for a nest building.

A nest-building owner collecting nests.

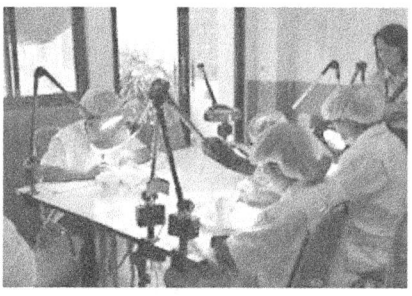

Workers are cleaning birds' nests in Kwan Mui Company, Pak Phanang Municipal area, Nakhon Si Thammarat.

Raw bird's-nest products, Thai House Thailand Bird Nest company, Chiang Mai.

Ready-to-drink bird's-nest products from a small business in Ban Laem District, Phetchburi.

Cosmetic products from bird's-nest by Kwan Mui Company, Pak Phanang District, Nakhon Si Thammarat.

A 4-story swiftlet-condo, 8 x 32 meters with a single-window on the top floor for the swiftlets to fly in and out.

A gutter filled with water is built around the building to prevent predators.

A high-temperature oven for destroying dead birds for hygiene purposes.

Bird's-nest collecting tools: a rounded-edge knife and a plastic basket.

A fog generator is set up inside the building, with a timer, for adjusting temperature and humidity.

© Sooksant Wongsearint, 2019.

Chapter 5

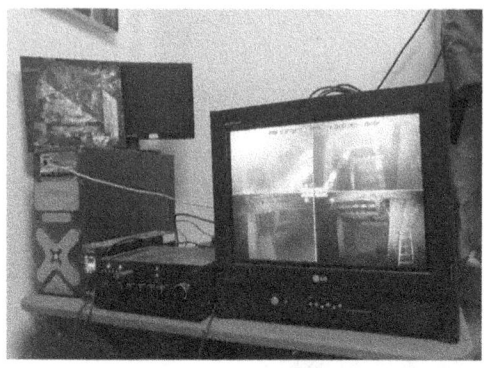

A sound control speaker for mimicking the call in the natural habitat and the protection system CCTV inside the building.

Woodworks inside a swiftlet-condo, the 14–20 cm wide grooved wood planks attached under the ceiling for the parent birds to build their nests.

A collector is collecting bird's nests.

The nest that parent birds are using to incubate their eggs beside the old one used during the previous season.

© Sooksant Wongsearint, 2019.

A full-grown swiftlet, ready to fly away.

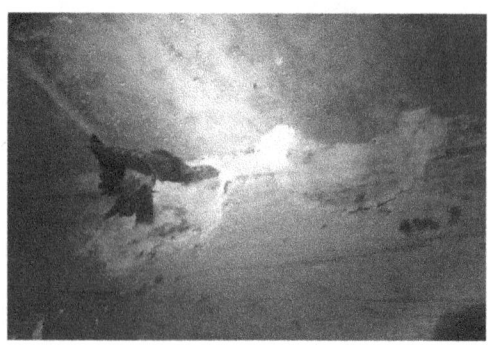

Ethnic Groups and Bird's-Nest Resources in Thailand

(*Top and middle*) The mother bird incubating the eggs in the nest. (*Below*) A swiftlet usually laid 2 eggs in one nest.

(*Top*) The new white nest was built over the uncollected yellow perch. (*Middle*) The feather layers in a nest are to provide comfort for the chicks. (*Below*) A perfectly-shaped nest.

© Sooksant Wongsearint, 2019.

6

Birds' Nests and Ethnic Groups in Hong Kong

INTRODUCTION

Hong Kong is a Special Administrative Region (SAR) with a population of approximately 7.3 million people crowded into an area of 1,092 square kilometers. It is a major center of financial markets and consumption. Even though Hong Kong is not the production source, it is a center of global modern and conventional products that are transported from around the world, especially from various ethnicities in the Southeast Asian region. One such product has been named 'White Gold' or 'The Caviar of the East', known in Hong Kong as 'Yan Wo' (燕 窩)—swiftlet birds' nests.

Hong Kong has functioned as the world market for birds' nest for centuries. The Hong Kong market has a powerful influence throughout the producing states, nationally and internationally, historically, economically, politically, culturally and in the relationships among various ethnic groups.

1. HISTORY OF BIRDS' NESTS IN HONG KONG

1.1 Bird's-Nest Consumption in the Old Society

The edible birds' nest is produced by a swiftlet called "*jīn sī yān*" in Chinese and the nests are called *yan wo*, *yen wuo*, *yen-ou* or *yin waw*.

From a description by Chinese naturalist, Wong Chi Men, in the middle of the 15th century, the focus was on the birds' nests as a nourishing food source with a delicious taste. It was considered a fine food that should not have oil flavoring or other poor ingredients added to it. It was written:

> "When the swiftlets fly over the ocean and feel tired, they will drop the nests they are carrying onto the sea and let them float like bowls. The swiftlets will leave the nests for a few moments and then pick them up again and continue to fly. Some nests are blown by the wind into caves where the natives will pick them for selling"[1]

The description in 1619 by Bont, the Dutch note taker (written in Latin as Bontius) was interpreted by John Ray, the English ornithologist, in *Hirundo Sinensis nido eduli Bontii* (the Chinese Swiftlets that build edible nests following the description of Bontius), stating:

> "On the coastal land of the Chinese kingdom in the exact time of year [of] the reproductive season, small birds with many colors on their bodies, [shaped like] swiftlets will fly out of the inner land to the rocky coastline. And from the wave bubbles caused by the sea water bouncing into the rocky coastline, they look for the viscous moist items which may be the sperms of the whales or other fish to be used to create the nests for laying their eggs and hatching larvae. Chinese people collect these nests from the rock formations and sell them to the East Indies in large quantities. They are well-known among consumers as a highly expensive food item. They are popularly mixed

into chicken or lamb soup and they are more acceptable in softness of taste than oysters, mushrooms, or any food. They are also credited with some properties of sexual arousal."

It is believed that mixing the birds' nests with Chinese ginseng, can help a dying person recover. In the north of China, where the weather is very cold in winter and people need to warm their bodies, it is generally believed that consuming the birds' nests can thin solid blood or it is possibly dissolved by drinking soup made from only birds' nests.[2]

It is believed that the nests have been consumed in China for more than 1,500 years. With the belief that consuming the nests boosts energy, Chinese people began to search for and trade birds' nests during the Tang Dynasty (A.D. 618–907).

During the years 1405–33 in the early Ming Dynasty (A.D. 1368–1644), Admiral Zheng He launched a fleet to explore Southeast Asia. The treasure fleet brought more than a hundred ships with more than a thousand soldiers to explore the land to the south.

Zheng He's shipping route traversed the nesting sites of swiftlets and it is said he brought the nests into China and presented them to the emperor. However, there are no data to support this.

The demand for birds' nests in China grew. The products became widely known and the price began to rise in the mid-17th century. Every year, at least six tons of birds' nests (about 4 million) were exported from Batavia (Jakarta) to China.[3]

There are similar descriptions in various local communities related to the collection and sale of birds' nests, such as the story of Hao Yieng entering into a lease contract by paying an annual fee to the Siamese king in the 18th century.[4] Since that time, the main market has been China, or Chinese overseas. However, apart from a small colony in Hainan, there is no evidence that there are swiftlets producing white edible nests within the borders of China. From Chinese evidence (that had already been translated into English), the activity appeared in Ming Dynasty records written in the 17th century. At that time, the birds' nests were an ingredient in traditional medicinal textbooks and consumed at royal celebrations.[5]

The Chinese traditional medicine textbook, "*Su U Yi Ji*" (食物 宜忌) mentions the properties of the birds' nest for "Empowering, stimulating the cravings, nourishing the mind and the bone marrow, moisturizing the lungs, treating chronic diarrhea, dissolving phlegm." The book "*Pen Chao Kang Mu Su Yee*" (本草纲目 拾遗) written by Chao Sia Min (赵学敏) in the Qing Dynasty (A.D. 1644–1911), mentioned the nests, "The birds' nests can be used to nourish the lungs very well (补肺养阴). It can dissolve phlegm, treat coughing, nourish, and cool. It is an excellent food and medicine to restore the unhealthy body. All diseases caused by depleted lung power or lung power that does not go down to the lower reaches (清肃下行) can be treated with birds' nests."

In Traditional Chinese Medicine (TCM), regular consumption of birds nests helps boost immunity and respiratory health. The balanced nature of a bird's-nest improves the lungs, spleen, and kidneys' function (补而能清). It also maintains the body's cooling effect and revitalizes the energy (补肺养阴, 滋阴补肾, 清肃下行, 补而能清).

The use of Chinese food and herbs cannot be determined from simply reciting the symptoms and prescribing the medicine to be used or a food to be eaten as a fixed formula, because the physical condition of the patients requires analysis. Patients with the same disease may have similar or differing physical conditions. The health treatment of traditional Chinese medicine aims to balance the symptoms that are expressed in each patient, which may have different reasons for the loss of balance.[6]

Until the Communist era, the major imported product to China was birds' nests, with Hong Kong as the largest market and consumer. Nests famed for their quality come from Thailand. Others come from Indonesia, Malaysia, Sabah, Sarawak, Singapore, Vietnam, and Myanmar.[7]

Restaurants in Hong Kong sell a bowl of bird's-nest soup for USD 50. The nests must first be left to soften, and are eventually eaten with noodles or mixed with chicken soup. There are many new recipes accepted under the term "birds' nests for health". A bird's nest cooked in chicken-broth makes an excellent soup.

Chapter 6

Bird's-nest soup with jujube.

"We eat bird's-nest soup whenever we can," said Dr. Yun Cheng Kong, Professor of Biochemistry from the Chinese University of Hong Kong, and an expert in history and chemistry concerning birds' nests for Chinese people. He also said that the Chinese believe eating swiftlets' nests promotes longevity. Various recipes have been devised to enhance the properties to treat lung-related diseases and to assist recovery. The elderly also eat birds' nests for energy. This is a tenet of traditional Chinese herbal medicine, perpetuated through a belief in the value and properties of birds' nests,[8] and the continuing culture of consumption by present-day Chinese ethnic groups.

1.2 Bird's-Nest Consumption Culture among Hong Kong Chinese Groups

Although there is no specific scientific evidence to support the supposed health properties of bird's nest, Chinese people in China and in Hong Kong choose to eat them and believe in the benefits.[9]

Ng Kar Man, a traditional Chinese medicine practitioner of Mahan Chan, New Territory, Hong Kong, who studies psychology in the treatment of cancer patients and has examined the use of birds' nests in treatment, states that birds' nests are not recognized as an official medicine. They are sometimes used in conjunction with herbs. After the patients have recovered, the traditional Chinese medicine practitioner will recommend the patients drink birds' nests as dietary supplement to restore health and help patients get better. It is believed that birds' nests have been used for a thousand years in China and throughout Asia.

Although expensive, the use of birds' nests in traditional Chinese medicine is deemed important. It is believed that the use of birds' nest will reduce bacterial growth. When a doctor is sure that a patient has recovered from a disease, he or she will recommend the patient consume birds' nest. For patients with diseases of internal organs such as kidneys, illnesses of the joints and tuberculosis caused by working too hard, eating birds' nest will help improve the function of internal organs.

The traditional Chinese medicine practitioner will write a prescription containing birds' nest in a medicinal recipe. The patients will purchase the medicine themselves. Eating birds' nests from childhood will help help the skin and internal system function well as it is the time when the body is growing.

Advertisement with a family eating birds' nests in Hong Kong
Red birds' nests and price tag in Hong Kong.

Hong Kong people like to eat red birds' nest but do not like cooking them. Since cooking raw birds' nests takes a lot of time and is complicated, Hong Kong people prefer to eat ready-made products.

Ng Kar Man, a young doctor, says the red birds' nest color comes from minerals the birds eat. The red bird's nest is associated with a system of ideas involving five colors and elements as part of a Chinese tradition. Green represents the element of wood. Red or purple represents fire. Yellow or brown represents earth, while white and gold represents iron. Black or dark blue represents water. Beliefs concerning color are also related to treating patients. For example, a red herb will cure diseases of the fire elements. Thus, colors are key in Chinese medicine.

With Yin and Yang and all five colors, each element is related in a cycle.

The white bird's nest is considered nourishing for the skin and lungs. The lungs are related to the large intestine. The red bird's nest is a fire element, used for treating heart disease and the small intestine. There is no study or research back up on the healing-quality differences of both types. Even the bird's nest is not in the official prescription; still, a TCM practitioner would recommend a recovered patient to consume birds' nests. Apart from ready-made birds' nests, they can also be mixed into rice porridge or used with rock sugar and seasoning as a dessert. They are also mixed with coconut to nourish the lungs and respiratory system.

Traditional Chinese medicine recommends patients eat birds' nests as dietary supplements only when really necessary. The financial condition of the patients must be considered as well due to the expense of the nests. The Chinese medicine treatment of patients makes no division between drugs and food and attempts to cure diseases through nutrition.

Traditional Chinese medicine will advise patients to use good quality raw birds' nest that has been dried naturally and has not been cooked. The recommended color depends upon what the patient can afford. If the patient is financially viable, the doctor will recommend good quality birds' nests. If the patients have problems with the heart or internal organs related to the fire element, the doctor will prescribe red birds' nest.[10]

2. BIRD'S-NEST CONSUMPTION BY HONG KONG ETHNIC CHINESE GROUPS UNDER CAPITALISM

In modern global capitalism, which has a consumer society with advertising messages via all media, the consumption of birds' nests is not limited to physical necessity, it has also become symbolic. This derives from a belief that birds' nest is a premium food of the rich and high class society. It has become an item of international consumption culture among ethnic Chinese and part of the universal culture of the oriental people. Modern birds' nest consumption has been modified to give new meaning and value to the birds' nest, using analytical data from laboratory research that supports the food's special properties. South East Asia, China and Hong Kong have similar societies.

Table 6.1: Nutrients in 100 grams of birds' nest from Pony Testing International Group, People's Republic of China (PRC)

Nutrients in birds' nest	Amount
Fat	0.34 percent
Protein	50.8 percent
Sodium (Na)	1.12×10^4 mg per kg.
Energy	310 kcal per 100 g
Sugar	0.01 percent
NO_2	<1.0 mg per kg.
Carbohydrate	25.9 percent

Source: Pony Testing International Group/The People's Republic of China/19 10 2010

In 1987, Yun-Cheng Kong, Professor of Biochemistry at the China University of Hong Kong, and an expert in the history and chemistry of birds' nests, found that they are formed of water soluble protein. This is believed to enhance the immune system cells. It is also possible that birds' nests help resist the negative effects of AZT drugs and also resist the development of AIDS. It is unfortunate that Chinese people often eat birds' nest needlessly because they have washed out the proteins and nutritional value in the process of cleaning them with water. Beneficial tiny particles in the birds' nests are thereby removed.[11]

In 2006 Chan Shun-Wan, Researcher, Applied Biology and Chemical Technology Department at Hong Kong Polytechnic University, studied whether the compound in birds' nest contributes to the growth of cancer cells. The study was conducted on people suffering from breast cancer and lung cancer. Chan Shun-Wan said that this research was not easy as some people believed that birds' nest produces negative effects on the body and might promote the growth of cancer cells. However, traditional Chinese medicine says that there are many nutrients in birds' nest that are beneficial to the body.

The research results do not contradict the traditional Chinese belief that birds' nests help strengthen the body and cause no harm. The research was specific to cancer cell growth, not to whether birds' nest strengthens the body. This is consistent with Chinese medicine believing that in the birds' nest, there are many kinds of nutrients that are beneficial. The main ingredients are protein and amino acids, varying according to quality. In general, there is about 30 percent protein. The percentage of amino acids depends to a large degree on the cooking process. The research results showed that birds' nest has no effect on the growth of cancer cells, so they can be consumed without concern.[12]

In 2012, Dr. Cheung Hon-yeung from the Department of Biology and Chemistry, City University of Hong Kong, studied birds' nest quality [Edible Bird's-Nest (EBN) or *Yen Wo* (燕窩)], including the physical and chemical bases, and biochemical properties. It was found that birds' nest contains high protein carbohydrate, has bioactive mucoid and epidermal growth factor (EGF), stimulating the skin and epithelium, helping to build good cells for cell replacement. This is why birds' nest is beneficial for young people, but not so much for people over 40 years old.

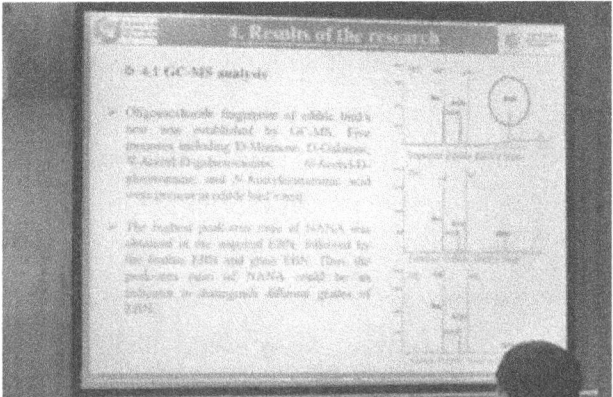

Power Point picture shows the nutrients contained in birds' nests by Dr. Cheung Hon-yeung, birds' nest researcher from City University of Hong Kong.

The research of Dr. Cheung Hon-yeung also discovered that birds' nest contains 5 monoses; D-Mannose, D-Galatose, N-Acetyl-D-galactosamine, N-Acetyl-D-glucosamine, and N-Acetylneuraminic acid[13] implying significant health benefits.

Ginseng drink mixed with birds' nest by a Hong Kong company.
(*Right*) Skin nourishing cream containing birds' nest.

In Hong Kong, there are companies that have many products made from birds' nests such as tea, fried potatoes, cookies, bottled birds' nest boiled with rock sugar[14] beauty facial masks, cosmetics, birds' nest cake, ginseng drink containing birds' nests, ready-made birds' nests drink, coffee, skin care cream, and more.

Local wisdom is used for incorporating birds' nests into modern food. Customers who buy raw birds' nests in Hong Kong, but are unsure how to cook them, can ask the supplier. The company selling the nests can explain the process to their customers. Companies ought to inform consumers, at the point of purchase, how to handle bird's-nest products. The bottled birds' nests have a specific recipe from each company.

In China and Hong Kong, people who consume birds' nests are well off. The market is very broad, especially for ready-made products. Both adults and teenagers frequently purchase ready-made birds' nests as gifts.[15]

3. CLASSIFICATION OF THE BIRD'S-NEST BUSINESS IN THE HONG KONG ETHNIC CHINESE MARKET

In June, 1998, according to Mohamed Yusoff Ismail's study, the moderate quality nests ranged in price from HKD 450–1,180 per 50 grams or HKD 9,000–23,000 per kilogram. A higher quality white nest is sold for HKD 21,000 per 600 grams or HKD 35,000 per kilogram.[16]

According to price data from a field survey in September and October 2009, it was found that the companies and stores have classifications and varying price levels of birds' nest based on specific characteristics of Hong Kong society's consumption. From the sample case of Eu Yan Sang and Home of Swallows Limited:

Raw bird's-nest types and various price levels in Hong Kong.

Eu Yan Sang divides the types and prices of birds' nests into 6 grades. Prices per tael (37.8 grams) are:

1. Special Grade red bird's nest cost HKD 1,950 per tael (50 grams)
2. Red bird's nest is HKD 1,700 per tael
3. Supreme bird's nest is HKD 1,350
4. Special Grade bird's nest is HKD 1,080
5. Special Grade bird's nest is HKD 1,030
6. Special Grade bird's nest is HKD 980

Home of Swallows Limited classifies the types and prices of birds' nests per tael (37.8 grams) into 12 grades:

1. Bloody-Red Bird's Nest/Grand Deluxe-Grade is HKD 1,380
2. Yellow Bird's Nest/Grand Deluxe-Grade is HKD 1,380
3. Yellow Bird's Nest/Grand Deluxe-Grade is HKD 1,250
4. White Bird's Nest/Grand Deluxe-Grade is HKD 1,250
5. White Bird's Nest/Grand Deluxe-Grade is HKD 1,180
6. White Bird's Nest/Grand Deluxe-Grade is HKD 1,080
7. Golden Bird's Nest/Grand Deluxe-Grade is HKD 1,250
8. Golden Bird's Nest/Grand Deluxe-Grade is HKD 980
9. Golden Bird's Nest Stripes/Deluxe-Grade is HKD 830
10. White Bird's Nest/Grand Deluxe-Grade is HKD 880
11. White Bird's Nest Strips/Deluxe-Grade is HKD 780
12. Ball-Shape Bird's Nest is HKD 620
13. Yellow Bird's Nest/Handmade Piece is HKD 620
14. Bird's Nest/Handmade Piece is HKD 580

The price of birds' nests is therefore HKD 21,924–36,514 per kilogram.

Notes:
1. The price of birds' nests sold at the Home of Swiftlets shop in Hong Kong on 12 October, 2009
2. 1 tael = 37.8 g
3. 1 kg. = 26.46 tael
4. 1 HKD = 3.85 THB (Nov. 2019)

Table 6.2: Shows types and prices at Home of Swallows Limited in Hong Kong in 2009

Types of birds' nests classified by colors	1 tael per HKD
1. Bloody-Red Bird's Nest/Grand Deluxe-Grade	1,380
2. Yellow Bird's Nest/Grand Deluxe-Grade	1,380
3. Yellow Bird's Nest/Grand Deluxe-Grade	1,250
4. Write Bird's Nest/Grand Deluxe-Grade	1,250
5. White Bird's Nest/Grand Deluxe-Grade	1,180
6. White Bird's Nest/Grand Deluxe-Grade	1,080
7. Golden Bird's Nest/Grand Deluxe-Grade	1,250
8. Golden Bird's Nest/Grand Deluxe-Grade	980
9. Golden Bird's Nest Stripes/Deluxe-Grade	830
10. White Bird's Nest/Grand Deluxe-Grade	880
11. White Bird's Nest strips/Deluxe-Grade	780
12. Ball Shape Bird's Nest	620
13. Yellow Bird's Nest/Hand Made Piece	620
14. Bird's Nest/Hand Made Piece	580

4. OUTPUT OF BIRD'S NEST PRODUCTS IN READY-TO-EAT CULTURE IN THE HONG KONG ETHNIC CHINESE COMMUNITY

From the field data (2009), Stella Blade, the manager of Home of Swallows Limited says that the company produces many products from the nests, such as bottled liquid, tea, ginseng drink mixed, fried birds' nests, cookies.

In this birds' nests company, there are more than 20 daily employees, working from 8.30 AM to 5.00 PM. The workers must be clean, possess expertise, and be trained.

The production of bird's-nest products requires human labor. Machines are not appropriate because it is delicate work. Most workers are women. Men are generally responsible for transport and cleaning the nests using equipment such as pots, enamelware, and pliers. Better cleaning tools do not exist yet.

The process of producing merchandise ready. for consumption involves steaming the cleaned nests and boiling them with rock sugar before bottling. Cooking is performed in the glass bottles by combining the nests and sugar at a temperature of about 100°c. After cooling, the nests will be tightly sealed. The products cannot be exposed to sunlight as this may cause bacterial growth. The ready-made birds' nests will be kept refrigerated before selling.

Stella Blade added that she could not describe in words how the best birds' nests are selected. They must be sampled. Most important is the raw material, reliability, and network.[17]

The power and gender issues in the world of Hong Kong bird's-nest business world – despite Hong Kong was under British's Crown colony from 1843–1997 – are based on traditional Chinese culture, assimilation into the unique culture of Hong Kong people. This leads to self-definition and a discourse on ethnicity, establishing the ethnic identities as Hong Kong people. However, in a society in which males are considered superior and the paternal relatives are held to be more important, the production of birds' nests products "is delicate work with most of the workers being women …" Even in the production of birds' nests products ready for consumption, it is open to women to be a manager or assistant to the marketing manager of a company. In bird's-nests shops, Hong Kong Chinese women are saleswomen of bird's-nests products as well as staff for cleaning the birds' nests.

5. THE SIZE OF THE BIRD'S-NEST BUSINESS OF THE HONG KONG ETHNIC CHINESE COMMUNITY

The bird's-nests business in Hong Kong is almost entirely operated by Hong Kong Cantonese, with only a single Singaporean company. As most major customers are in China, companies belonging to Chinese people enjoy an advantage in the business. Some bird's-nest companies in Hong Kong have their own bird's-nests building with a bird's-nest building partner. Additionally, in Hong Kong, there are no specific laws governing the bird's-nest business as Hong Kong considers the nests as a type of food. There is no nest tax and most are imported.

Female workers are cleaning birds' nests at the bird's-nest shop on Wing Lok Road, Hong Kong. (*Right*) Refrigerated ready-to-eat bird's-nest products display at the shop front of a Hong Kong bird's-nest shop.

The Hong Kong business is a gray market, not a black one. Or if it is a black market, it still has a large gray area, because Hong Kong has no special laws governing the trade. Those in this business know internally that all parties benefit from it. They all accept the chain of bird's-nest consumption. Three groups benefit from this system. The first group is the sellers who come from Southeast Asia. The second group consists of middlemen who resell them to transform the raw materials into finished products for sale. The last group comprises consumers who can buy birds' nest at a reasonable prices because of low taxes.[18]

On Wing Lok Road, Hong Kong, both sides are lined with bird's-nest shops for a kilometer.

Of birds' nests originating in Southeast Asia, 95 percent are from Indonesia. 20 percent of raw nests are delivered by plane. 80 percent are carried in bags. However, if they are imported by someone not known in the network, they cannot be sold. Everything depends on established mutual trust. Confidence is paramount in trading birds' nests to maintain price and quality. The industry must also beware of fake nests. If you do not know each other, when buying nests, there is the problem of not being able to track their origin.[19]

The nests imported for sale in Hong Kong come from four major sources; Malaysia, Vietnam, Thailand and Indonesia, and, to a lesser extent, from Palawan. The quality from the Philippines is not of a high standard and those from Myanmar are not popular.[20]

The business experiences seasonal demand such as during New Year. Maintaining a stable supply and quality is a difficult aspect of this business. The trade relies on a network of trust to maintain that stable supply.

In Hong Kong there are more than 100 bird's-nest shops, classified into two types; traditional medicine shops selling only raw birds' nests and modern shops selling both dry birds' nests and finished products.[21]

The island has about 10 brands. Among the five biggest brands, the largest Cantonese company is Wai Yuen Tong.[22]

It is noteworthy that no one can definitively state the exact size of the bird's-nest business in Hong Kong. The figures are based only on statistical data. However, the quantity of import and export of the Hong Kong market can be ascertained by other methods of importing the raw materials into Hong Kong, such as tourists traveling from Southeast Asia and bringing birds' nests as gifts for friends in Hong Kong.

Birds' nests are fragile, so must be carefully transported. If damaged when sent by mail, no one is responsible. Air transportation is safe and does not destroy the goods. With DHL Express delivery, the nests are placed in a plastic box with protective wrapping paper.[23] Even though there are no official import and export numbers for Hong Kong, some people try to calculate the size of the trade as follows:

> Eric Valli, Diane Summers and Jeanine MacKay stated, "Hong Kong is the largest consumer of birds' nests. They import about 100 tons per year with a value of USD 25 million".[24] Amy S.M. Lau and David S. Melville wrote in *International Trade in Swiftlet Nests with Special Reference to Hong Kong* (1994) "The import of birds' nests into Hong Kong has significantly increased since 1949. The total value increased 48 times between 1975 and 1991 from HKD 9.5 million to HKD 459 million".[25]
>
> Lim Chan Koon and the Earl of Cranbrook wrote in *Swiftlets of Borneo: Builders of Edible Nests* (2002) "Hong Kong is the largest bird's-nest market in the world. From 1980 to 1989, Hong Kong imported 81,000–160,000 kilograms of birds' nests per year with a value of HKD 40–300 million."[26]
>
> Chan Shun-Wan ("Review of Scientific Research on Edible Birds'-Nests", 2009) states: "Even though *Collocalia* are small swiftlets, they have created a huge market. It was estimated that the value of the market in Hong Kong in 2004 was about HKD 3 billion."[27]
>
> Journalist Andrew Marshall wrote an article titled 'Natural Bird Bonanza' in *Time* magazine's July 2009 issue, stating that "Hong Kong is the main consumer importing birds' nests worth USD 204 million in 2006 and USD 276 million in 2008".[28]

Table 6.3: Estimated value of birds' nests imported into Hong Kong from 1975–2008. The value is in USD and HKD.

Year	Million USD / HKD
1975	9.5 (HKD)
1980	40 (HKD)
1989	300 (HKD)
1991	459 (HKD)
2004	3,000 (HKD)
2006	204 (USD)
2008	276 (USD)

In 2009, Allen Pang, the head of product quality control at Home of Swallows Limited, estimated that the imported raw nests totaled approximately 1,000 tons per year, and that the business in Hong Kong has a value of at least 10 billion HKD per year.[29]

Frank Pak, the manager of Home of Swallows Limited, estimated the entire picture of the business operation at present (2009), The Hong Kong market grew more than China's. This was because the market in China grew significantly after Hong Kong's with the exact figures unknown. He said that most of the nests are transported by human carriers and the trade in Hong Kong is approximately HKD 2 billion.[30]

6. THE ORGANIZATION OF DISCOURSE RELATING TO THE BIRD'S-NEST BUSINESS IN HONG KONG'S ETHNIC CHINESE COMMUNITY

Apart from the shops or companies operating the birds' nests business in Hong Kong, there are also both public and private sector organizations involved in the business, such as the Chinese University of Hong Kong, Hong Kong Polytechnic University and City University of Hong Kong, researching various aspects of the trade and consumption.

A plaque of the Hong Kong Traditional Chinese Medicine-Merchants Association will be shown at the birds' nests shops in Hong Kong.

The Hong Kong Chinese Medicine Merchants Association (專業燕窩商), established in 1928, is the oldest Chinese medicine organization in Hong Kong covering various Chinese medicine industries. It plays a role in holding seminars, public relations and marketing involving Chinese medicine.[31]

The bird's-nest traders in Hong Kong are mostly members of the Association of Traditional Chinese Medicine. A non-member can do the business. However, the Association would like the traders to be harmonized even though these associations do not play a particularly important role in the business.

The Hong Kong Trade Development Council (TDC) is an NGO helping to develop the business and assisting in public relations for Hong Kong companies. Its working team operates worldwide.[32]

This especially involves the Centre for Food Safety which is part of the Government of the Hong Kong Special Administrative Region. When a scandal arose over fake red birds' nests from Malaysia in July 2011, this organization responded to business operators in Hong Kong that the accusation of staining birds' nests with nitrite to replicate the red birds' nests lacked clear facts.[33]

The belief in the value of consuming birds' nests is passed down through a social process that creates a structure of awareness and the importance of the value system that enables the Chinese people to acknowledge and believe in the special qualities of the nests. This appears in the social relationships that have a corresponding set of awareness processes created in various ways, to cause the ethnic Chinese to understand, accept, and believe in the nests' value. It also supports the bird's-nest business system in Hong Kong's ethnic Chinese community.

7. ANTS ARMY: THE ARMY RESPONDS TO BIRD'S-NEST SMUGGLING FROM HONG KONG TO CHINA

Sheung Wan District or the so-called Victoria City is one of the oldest baron Districts in Hong Kong since colonization by the British according to the Treaty of Nanjing in 1842.[34]

For 174 years, this District was the biggest sales area for the Chinese. Bonham Strand West and Wing Lok Road became the epicenter of Chinese and Asian products with merchants from various regions in China setting up numerous shops. At present, this is still the main area for traditional Chinese products such as sun-dried seafood, birds' nests, and ginseng.[35]

Wing Lok Street and Yongle Jie or Dried Seafood Street, host the world's largest specialist edible bird's-nest market. A large number of birds' nests from Southeast Asia and all regions are imported and re-exported to ethnic Chinese communities around the world, especially China, the market with the most consumers.

Wing Lok Road, Ginseng and Bird's-Nest Road in Sheung Wan, Hong Kong, with bird's-nest shops on both sides of the road.

Chapter 6

Due to Mao Zedong's Regime (1949–76),[36] birds' nests are still considered a luxury product. The Chinese authorities are not happy about the consumption of the product, but cannot stop it, despite declaring transport illegal.

With the flurry of controversy over China's internal political role under the Deng Xiaoping policy of one country, two systems,[37] the movement of the Ants Army originated in Wing Lok Street, transporting the birds' nests, which were "products not approved by Chinese law but favored by the Chinese people", into mainland China throughout this time. The high taxes and the laws governing the bird flu in China[38] became additional factors in the transport method of the Ants Army transporting nests.

It was known inside the business that the Ants-Army smugglers from Hong Kong to Mainland China were paid 500 yuan per kilogram. As it was very profitable, a lot of people were prepared to take the risk. The problems did not occur in Hong Kong, but in China, because China was strict on the illegal transportation of certain goods. It was a complicated problem. Although Chinese law was very strict on one level, it could also be negotiable.

Another reason for the secrecy of the Ants Army transportation of birds' nests by was because the business depends on trust between networks. It was estimated that the Ants Army carried more than 1,000 tons per year into mainland China. The main cities these birds' nests were smuggled into were powerful, with high purchasing power, such as Shanghai, Zhejiang and China's southeast coastal cities.[39]

8. COUNTERPOINTS OF BIRD'S-NEST CONSUMPTION BELIEFS BETWEEN MYTHOLOGY AND MODERN HEALTH-SCIENCE IN HONG KONG'S ETHNIC CHINESE COMMUNITY

The consumption of birds' nests is a complex subject, having evolved into a culture of consumption across borders, society, culture and ethnicity, becoming a cultural heritage through food and oriental international culture. But in local Hong Kong society, there has been a check and response in consumer discretion between the mythology and modern health science.

The bird's-nest businessmen and the birdhouse-owners say that in the production of bird's-nests products that a lot of raw birds' nests are needed. As the quantity of available nests cannot meet the needs of the canned and bottled products, broken birds' nests are used and adulterated with jelly. As using pure birds' nests is very expensive and one canned birds' nest can be sold for small change, it is impossible to use the birds' nests in large quantities. Most of the manufacturing companies package the products in brown bottles so that consumers will not see the contents clearly. Also, black bird's-nests are used due to the cheaper price.[40]

In the report "Composition of Foods Used in Far Eastern Countries" published in the US Department of Agriculture's journal, analysis showed that birds' nests consist of 16.2 percent water, 54.3 percent protein, 0.3 percent fat, 23.3 percent carbohydrate, and 5.9 percent ash or carbon. 100 grams of birds' nests will contain 32 milligrams of phosphorus. In the protein, there were insufficient amino acids. It especially lacks lysine, an element of saliva and digestion. The carbohydrate in birds' nests are difficult to digest. From this analysis, it is clear that the bird's nests contain insufficient nutrients for the demands of the body. Besides, there are unnecessary compounds such as carbon, while the existing nutrients are also not of good quality.[41]

Regarding the July 2011 scandal in China from faked red birds' nests from Malaysia, apart from revealing that there was a merchant dyeing the birds' nests and also indicated that the blood birds' nests being sold were 100 percent fake.[42] Such an event was considered a historical turning point significantly affecting the consumption culture of Chinese people for the blood birds' nests.

The website Centre for Food Safety of the Government of Hong Kong Special Administrative Region (SAR).

The feedback of the Centre for Food Safety on the dyeing of blood-red birds' nests lack of clear facts[43] refers to the conclusion of the fundamental truth from the research studies and from scientific and tests throughout long-term consumption. The preparation steps were correct and proper. The Chinese medicine in Hong Kong confirmed that there is a strong belief in the consumption of red birds' nests in China and Hong Kong and that the blood nest is safe for consumption.[44] People still believe that red birds' nests are better than other varieties.[45]

9. THE INFLUENCE OF HONG KONG ETHNIC CHINESE GROUPS IN THE BIRD'S-NEST GLOBAL MARKET

The business relationship has the swiftlet's-nest as a link across states and ethnic groups. The bird's nests is a resource for for various ethnic groups in Southeast Asia, China, Hong Kong, and Taiwan.

There are several ethnic groups in bird's-nest consumption in countries around the world. Especially in Hong Kong – the world's bird's-nest – the Cantonese or Chinese Hong Kong has the most influence over the nest's price.

This is especially the influence of the birds' nests price. Following the incident of fake birds' nests from Malaysia in July 2011, China *Suddenly Stop the Bird's-nest business"*. China defined import and quality standards for birds' nests from Malaysia and all other countries that export to China. This strongly affected the bird's-nests business in Malaysia and every other supplier.

9.1 Influence of Hong Kong Ethnic Chinese Groups on the Countries Producing Birds' Nests in Southeast Asia

The countries that are important sources of bird's-nests production in Southeast Asia are Vietnam, Indonesia, Malaysia, Philippines and Thailand with almost the entire production exported. Only Vietnam and the Philippines have much of a domestic market. Thailand's domestic market only consumes ready-to-drink birds' nests in bottles.

In Vietnam, a private Vietnamese company auctions birds' nests from the provincial government bird's-nest company. 90 percent of the collected birds' nests are exported to Hong Kong, Taiwan, China, Singapore. In the Hong Kong market, the Vietnamese nests are considered of top quality and priced accordingly, despite the small quantities compared to imports from Indonesia and Malaysia.[46] Hong Kong's global hub market has significant influence and ethnic Chinese are the most powerful in determining prices within the Vietnamese market.

Indonesia is the world's largest producer of birds' nests. The important markets of Indonesia are the foreign. Ethnic Chinese businessmen collect and purchase nests in the country, then export them to Hong Kong, Singapore, China, Taiwan, Malaysia, Holland, Japan, Poland, Thailand and other destinations. About 98 percent of Indonesian nests are transported by plane.[47] The Chinese traders in the Hong Kong market also have significant influence in Indonesia's market.

In Malaysia, ethnic Chinese businesses purchase birds' nests from various ethnic groups in the country for export abroad. Malaysia's major bird's-nest markets include China, Singapore, Negara Brunei Darussalam, Dubai, Taiwan, Hong Kong, India, the Middle East, Europe, the USA and Canada. The quality and price of Malaysian nests have made them popular in Hong Kong's market.[48] Chinese ethnic groups therefore have the greatest influence over the Malaysia's, China's and Hong Kong's birds' nests markets.

The Philippines has small production of birds' nests and various ethnic groups in the Philippines consume them. The most important nest market in the Philippines is domestic. However, there is a Chinese-Filipino private company and ethnic Chinese businessmen gather to buy birds' nests in the country. Ethnic Chinese collect and purchase birds' nests from various ethnic groups, especially from the Tagbanua for export to markets in China, Hong Kong and Japan. As with Malaysia, ethnic Chinese exert a powerful influence. All countries that send birds' nests into China were impacted by the *"Suddenly Stop the World Birds'-Nests Business"* in July 2011 scandal. This hit various ethnic groups whether mestizos, Chinese-Filipino or Chinoy.

In Thailand, the people do not popularly consume birds' nests except as bottled ready-to-drink products. Thus, most bird's-nest markets are abroad. Thai-Chinese businessmen purchase nests for export to the usual markets, but predominantly China and Hong Kong. The quality of Thai birds' nests is second only to Vietnam's, so they are priced higher than those from Malaysia.[49] The ethnic Chinese are again the most powerful in establishing prices for Thai nests in that market, China and Hong Kong.

9.2 New-Century Power of the People's Republic of China Under the Bird's-Nest Protocols for Trading-Partner Countries and Hong Kong's Global Market

In early 2012, the General Administration of Quality Supervision, Inspection and Quarantine of the PRC (国家质检总局), or AQSIQ temporarily prohibited the import of birds' nests from various countries due to the discovery of nitrites exceeding the standard of 30 ppm in nests imported from Malaysia. This affected the business and consumption of common bird's-nests. Especially in the source countries. China set the import system by proposing a draft protocol for each country to conform to. The protocol included quarantine requirements and hygiene inspection for the export of birds' nests from the source countries to China.

China's new protocols covered various measures such as requiring the source countries to register production sources, collection sources and exporters. These were to be checked and hygiene certificates issued before nests would be cleared for export. This meant establishing a traceability system including monitoring measures for quality control, diseases and labeling, as well as requiring the responsible agencies of the exporting countries to provide a list of production sources and exporters of birds' nests products following approval and registration by dedicated agencies each producing and exporting country. This was required for registration with CNCA (Certificate and Accreditation Administration of the People's Republic of China).

The source countries had to submit the information, laws, regulations, standards of production and processing of birds' nests products, a list of quarantine inspection measures, export procedures and processes. The packaging of bird's-nests products exported to China required the relevant information in both Chinese and English. According to China's requirements, there had to be a production-source registration number , list of exporters, production date and storage standards.

Animal health certificates and certificates of origin had to be attached to the shipment exported to China. Meanwhile, China imposed additional measures in the event of problems such as bird-flu outbreaks or residue detection cases. A group of experts from China travel to inspect the hygiene-control systems, production sites and nest-collection sites.

Only after satisfying the processes as specified by China and signing the protocol, the source countries and General Administration of Quality Supervision, Inspection and Quarantine of the PRC (国家质检总局 or AQSIQ) would allow the export of birds' nests to China.

After the source-countries has sent the information for consideration, China despatches two teams team of experts to inspect the hygiene control systems of the country. The first group evaluates the sanitation system. The second group inspects the caves, the bird's-nest collection sites, and the processing plant of operators who have applied to register as accredited exporters.

The operators submit an application form requesting permission to export to China with the responsible agency of the source country to the Certification and Accreditation Administration of PRC (中国国家认证认可监督管理委员会 or CNCA)

The bird's-nest source-countries have implemented system-wide traceability to solve problems promptly in case of quality and safety issues. In case of collecting / processing sources, they were required to be improved according to China's Good Manufacturing Practice GMP standards.

Chapter 6

Historical day that affected the bird's-nest business around the world, when the officials claiming to be from Malaysia held a press conference to protect the honor and dignity of blood birds' nests products in Hangzhou on July 26, 2011. Later, the Xinhua News Agency found that these officials were imposters.
(Picture from *South China Morning Post*)

In addition, companies or shops selling birds' nests in Hong Kong will observe the people from Southeast Asia who come to sell nests in Hong Kong. The owners of the bird's-nests shops will observe closely because they cannot be certain that they are genuine traders or want to find information about the prices. This is a common precaution because most customers are not from Southeast Asia but are from Hong Kong, China and Korea.[50]

Conclusion: Trend of Bird's-Nest Business under the Power of the Hong Kong Chinese Empire

Regarding the overview of the current bird's-nest business (2011), the birds's-nests market in Hong Kong grows more than in China. The new bird's-nest market in China grows after Hong Kong. The future of the birds' nests market, and especially the Chinese market will definitely mature, but this also depends on the economy.[51]

As the bird's-nests consumption of the Hong Kong market is already saturated, the traders are preparing to invest to meet the China market demand. It is estimated that the bird's-nests market in China is worth about USD 1.3 billion dollars.[52]

Related to China's rapid economic growth over the past 30 years, the market depends on cheap labor, savings, and investments. These growth features have caused an income gap and low consumption levels including the international economic crisis that spurred China to shift from dependency on exports to expanding the demand for consumption in the country in the long term. There are 6 policies; promoting safe consumption, promoting environmentally friendly consumption, promoting consumption in the service business, promoting brand name product consumption, systemized online consumption control, promoting consumption with financial instruments such as bank loans, using credit cards[53] and / or issuing *"Regulations for inspection and quarantine of things carried by people entering or leaving the country"*. This was enforced beginning November 1, 2012. The birds' nests (except for canned ones) were considered forbidden items if carried by individuals into China. This forced consumers to buy bird's-nest products from companies that adhere to the standards. This is one of China's economic strategies. Allowing Hong Kong to dominate the world bird's-nest market since the Communist ruling from 1949 is a strategy to legalize the 'illegal birds' nests' products. The world bird's nest market is moving from Hong Kong to China.

The consumption of birds' nests in the cultural roots of the eastern world, originate in beliefs related to supernatural mysteries, wealth, power and eternal life. The bird's-nest resources are a unique medium of ethnic relationships due to being popularly consumed only by Asian people.

Ethnic Chinese play an essential role as the middleman in the ongoing business of birds' nests. They collect the nests from various ethnic groups' sources and export them to Chinese around the world. The same group also plays a crucial role as consumers in China and the global Chinese communities, especially Hong Kong. China is the new center of power in the 21st century with countless new millionaires.

Chinese ethnicity is "a cultural empire in the bird's-nests consumption." The price of birds' nests is only a trade negotiation as stated:

> "As long as there are Chinese in the world, bird's nests will be eaten."[54] This reflects the social and cultural space with the negotiation and management of a powerful relationship in the fields of the cross-border trade among the ethnic owners or producers of birds' nests in the Southeast Asia. For the Chinese ethnicity both in Hong Kong and the Chinese community around the world, no matter how the culture of birds' nests consumption is developed and complicated in the form of "cycling development", the current culture of globalized consumerism penetrates dynamically to the society and the people.[55]

APPENDIX

Image of ethnic, consumption and Birds'-Nests Business of Chinese Hong Kong ethnic groups

Wing Lok Street sign, Ginseng and bird's nest street, Sheung Wan, Hong Kong.

Hong Kong Traditional Chinese Medicine Merchants Association sign in front of the bird's-nest shop in Hong Kong.

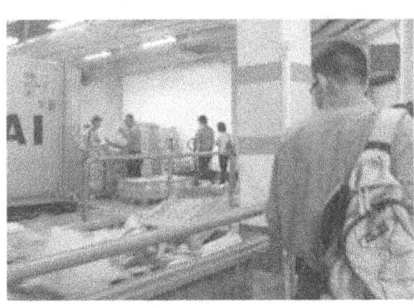

Birds' nests from Southeast Asia that have been transported to a bird's-nest product company in Hong Kong.

Boxes and bags containing birds' nests from Southeast Asia that a vendor brought to a bird's-nest shop in Hong Kong.

Chapter 6

Chinese Hong Kong women cleaning white bird's-nests in the bird's-nest shop, Wing Lok Road, Hong Kong.

Bird's-nest shops at the airport in Hong Kong.

Bird's-nest shops at the subway station in Hong Kong.

On Wing Lok Road, Hong Kong, both sides of the road in a kilometer are lined with the bird's-nest shops.

Chinese Hong Kong women are cleaning red birds' nests in a nest shop, Wing Lok Road, Hong Kong.

Advertisement of the company selling birds' nests at the subway station in Hong Kong.

Birds' Nests and Ethnic Groups in Hong Kong

Advertisement of a Hong Kong family eating birds' nest.

Bird's-nest shop of Wai Yuen Tong, the most important company selling birds' nests in Hong Kong.

Ready-to-consumed bird's-nest products in the freezer in front of the bird's-nest shop in Hong Kong.

Ready-to-be-consumed birds' nests products in front of the bird's-nests shop.

Raw birds nests of varying type and price level.

Chapter 6

Ginseng drink mixed with birds' nests in Hong Kong.

Raw birds' nests in a pharmacy in Hong Kong.

Facial beauty mask made from birds' nests in Hong Kong.

Various cosmetics made from birds' nests.

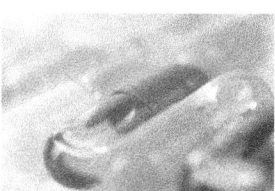

Encapsulated birds' nests for body nourishment.

Skin Lotion made from birds' nests.

ENDNOTES

Notes to Chapter 1

1. The World Factbook - Central Intelligence Agency. Vietnam. https://www.cia.gov/library/publications/the-world-factbook/geos/vm.html.
2. Sopharat Charusombat. *Enviromental Management in Southest Asia*. Bangkok: Faculty of Political Science, Thammasat University and Kobfai Publisher Project, 2003, p. 506.
3. Department of Trade Negotiations, ASEAN office. op. cit., p. 1.
4. Earl of Cranbrook. "Swiftlets with Edible Nests: Past and Future." Introduction to *Exposing the Billion-Dollar Bird's-nest Business World* edited by Patrick Jori and Jirawat Saengthong. Nakhon Si Thammarat: Research Fund and Regional Project Study Bureau, Art Academic Office, Walailak University, 2007, pp. 32–33.
5. Nguyen Duc Vinh, a former nest-collector, Cu Lao Cham Island. Interview, 26 October 2008.
6. Nguyen Van Hung, a boat driver in Thu Bon River, Hoi An, Quang Nam. Interview, 27 October 2008.
7. http://www.tienphong.vn/tianyon/Index.aspx?ArticleID=161548&ChannelID=2, (June 2010).
8. http://www.yensaonhatrang.com, (May 2009).
9. http://www.yensaonhatrang.com/Quy NHon, (May 2009).
10. http://www.tienphong.vn/tianyon/Index.aspx?ArticleID=161548&ChannelID=2, (June 2010).
11. http://www.yensao.vn/, (May 2009).
12. Vu Ngoc Phuong. *Khanh Hoa mot tiềm nang mot hiện thực*. Ha Noi: Nha Xuất Ban Chính Tri Quoc Gia, 2004, pp. 393–95.
13. Inscriptions at Noi Swiftlet Island, Nha Trang, Khanh Hoa, Vietnam.
14. http://www.yensaokhanhhoa.com.vn, (May 2009).
15. http://www.yensaokhanhhoa.com.vn, (May 2009).
16. http://www.yensaokhanhhoa.com.vn, (May 2009).
17. http://www.yensaokhanhhoa.com.vn, (May 2009).
18. "The Great Indoor", *Timeout*. http//72.14.235.104/search?q=cache:zFISSuFa7NcJ: www.vir.com.vn/Client/…(December 2007)
19. http://www.yensaokhanhhoa.com.vn, (May 2009).
20. Vo Thai Lam, owner of the bird's-nest building business and ready-to-eat bird's-nest industry, Yenviet Company, Ninh Thuan Province. Interview, 10 January 2011.
21. Hoang Ha, "Ấp nở nhan tao va nuoi chim yen hang bằng cong nghệ moi", http://www. ddddn.com.vn, (May 2009).
22. Ibid.
23. http://www.yensaonhatrang.com, (May 2009).
24. http://www.ddddn.com.vn, (July 2010).
25. http://www.yensaonhatrang.com/Quy Nhon, (May 2009).
26. http://www.yensaokhanhhoa.com.vn, (May 2009).
27. Nguyen Tan Tuan, Yen Sao Binh Dinh, http://www.baobinhdinh.com.vn/tiemnang-trienvong/2005/2/5394/, (May 2009).
28. http://www.yensaokhanhhoa.com.vn, (May 2009).
29. http://www.yensaokhanhhoa.com.vn, (May 2009).
30. Anonymous. Interviews, 26 February 2010 and 10 January 2011.
31. Vo Quang Yen, Huyen dieu, Yen sao. http://vietsciences.free.fr/timhieu/khoahoc/biologie/huyendieu yensao.htm, (May 2009).
32. Nguyen Quang, P., Vo Quang, Y. & Voisin, J–F., 2002. *The White-nest Swiftlet and the Black-nest Swiftlet: A Monograph*. Paris, Boubee, p. 242.
33. http://www.yensaokhanhhoa.com.vn, (May 2009).
34. Nguyen Tan Tuan, op. cit.
35. http://www.yensao.vn, (May 2009).
36. Nguyen Tan Tuan, op. cit.

37. http://www.ekavietnam.com, (May 2009).
38. http://www.yensaokhanhhoa.com.vn, (May 2009).
39. Vo Quang Yen, op. cit.
40. http://www.yensaonhatrang.com/Quy Nhon, (May 2009).
41. http://www.yensaokhanhhoa.com.vn, (May 2009).
42. Vo Quang Yen, op. cit.
43. http://www.ekavietnam.com, (May 2009).
44. Inscription at Noi Swiftlet Island, op. cit.
45. http://www.yensaokhanhhoa.com.vn, (May 2009).
46. Classified by the Characteristics of Different fur Colors on the Head, Chest and at the Back of the Bird.
47. Vo Quang Yen, op. cit.
48. http://yenvietnhatrang.com.vn/index.php?option=com_content&view=article&id=25:cac-loi-n&catid=3:t-vn-yn-sao&Itemid=4, (August 2010).
49. http://www.yensaokhanhhoa.com.vn, (May 2009).
50. http://www.ekavietnam.com, (May 2009).
51. Vo Quang Yen, op. cit.
52. http://www.yensaonhatrang.com, (May 2009).
53. Nguyen Tan Tuan, op. cit.
54. http://www.yensaonhatrang.com/Quy NHon, (May 2009).
55. http://www.ddddn.com.vn, (May 2009).
56. Inscriptions at Noi Swiftlet Island, op. cit.
57. Vo Quang Yen, op. cit.
58. http://www.ekavietnam.com, (May 2009).
59. Vo Quang Yen, op. cit.
60. Nguyen Duc Vinh. Interview, 26 October 2008.
61. Nguyen Nhuu Tri, a tour guide of Sanest Khanh Hoa-Nha Trang Company on the tour boat Sanest 2. Interview, 1 June 2009.
62. http://www.yensaokhanhhoa.com.vn, (May 2009).
63. Nguyen Tan Tuan, op. cit.
64. http://www.yensaonhatrang.com/Quy NHon, (May 2009).
65. Nguyen Duc Vinh. Interview, 26 October 2008.
66. Vo Quang Yen, op. cit.
67. Vu Ngoc Phuong, op. cit., p. 394.
68. Vo Quang Yen, op. cit.
69. Anan Ganjanapan. "Community Rights in Development." *The Community Dimension: Local Way of Thinking Regarding Rights, Power and Natural Resource Management.* Bangkok: Thailand Research Fund, 2001, p. 168.
70. Vo Quang Yen, ibid.
71. http://www.yensaokhanhhoa.com.vn, (May 2009).
72. A former bird's-nest collector in Cu Lao Cham said that there is no such ritual when he worked there between 1990–93.
73. Nguyen Duc Vinh. Interview, 26 October 2008.
74. Diab, bird's-nest collector for Sanest Company at Hon Noi Island, interview in front of the Le Thi Huyen Tram Shrine, interview, 1 June 2009.
75. Nguyen Nhuu Tri. Interview, 1 June 2009.
76. Nguyen Duc Vinh. Interview, 26 October 2008.
77. http://www.tienphong.vn/tianyon/Index.aspx?ArticleID=161548&ChannelID=2, (June 2010)., Võ Quang Yen, op. cit.
78. http://www.yensaokhanhhoa.com.vn, (May 2009).
79. http://www.tienphong.vn/tianyon/Index.aspx?ArticleID=161548&ChannelID=2, (June 2010).
80. Vo Quang Yen, op. cit.

81. http://www.ekavietnam.com, (May 2009).
82. http://www.yensaokhanhhoa.com.vn, (May 2009).
83. http://www.yensaokhanhhoa.com.vn, (May 2009).
84. A taxi driver in Nha Trang town, while leading the research team to see the Sanest Company bird's nest products at the factory. Interview, 2 June 2009.
85. http://www.yensao.vn, (May 2009).
86. Nguyen Duc Vinh. Interview, 26 October 2008.
87. http://www.yensaonhatrang.com/Quy NHon, (May 2009).
88. Sriprapha Petchrameesee, *Economic and Political Development of Vietnam*. Bangkok: Kobfai, 1999, pp. 214, 224.
89. Apinya Fuengfusakul, *Religious Anthropology, Basic Concepts and Theoretical Arguments*, (Chiang Mai: Department of Sociology and Anthropology, Faculty of Social Sciences, Chiang Mai University, 2008), pp. 49–53.
90. http://www.tienphong.vn/tianyon/Index.aspx?ArticleID=161548&ChannelID=2, (June 2010).
91. http://www.yensao.vn, (May 2009).
92. Nguyen Duc Vinh. Interview, 26 October 2008.
93. http://www.yensaonhatrang.com, (May 2009).
94. Nguyen Nhuu Tri. Interview, 1 June 2009.
95. Vu Ngoc Phuong, op. cit., pp. 393–95.
96. Dararat Mattariganond, *Vietnamese History Textbook in Elementary School*. Bangkok: Muang Boran, 2007, p. 26.
97. Santisuk Sophonsiri, referred to "Viriyanan", translator. *Collection of "Nam Cao" Short Story*. Bangkok: Sathirakoses-Nagapradipa Foundation, 1986, p. preface.
98. *Tự Nhien Va Xa Hoi* as cited in Dararat Mattariganond, op. cit., pp. 71–72.
99. Anan Ganjanapan, op. cit., pp. 168–69.
100. Thida Saraya as cited in Dararat Mattariganond, op. cit., p. 12.
101. Charles Keyes as cited in Pinkaew Laungaramsri. "The awkwardness of the ethnic conception", *Social Sciences* 19, 1 (2007), p. 201.
102. Anan Ganjanapan, op. cit., p. 219.
103. Sriprapha Petchrameesee, op. cit., pp. 86, 169–72, 203.
104. Vo Thai Lam. Interview, 10 January 2011.
105. Tran Duc Hung, Consultant of Nguyen Viet, Ninh Thuan Province. Interview, 10 January 2011.
106. Anonymous, Hoi An town. Interviews, 26–27 October 2008.
107. Anonymous, Nha Trang town. Interview, 2 June 2009.
108. Vo Quang Yen, op. cit.
109. Kasem Jandam. *Swiftlet Nest: Power, Conflict and Wealth*. Bangkok: Mahasarakham University Press, 2007, p. 56.
110. Bourdieu, Pierre. *Raisons pratiques. Sur la theorie de l'action (Economy of symbolic property)*. Translated by Chanida Sa-ngiam-phaisan, Bangkok: Kobfai Books, 2007, pp. 18, 20.
111. Vo Quang Yen, op. cit.
112. Anonymous. Interview, 28 October 2008.
113. http://www.yensaokhanhhoa.com.vn, (May 2009).
114. Vo Thai Lam. Interview, 10 January 2011.
115. Nguyen Quang, P., Vo Quang, Y. & Voisin, J-F., op. cit. p. 247.
116. Data from http://www.ddddn.com.vn, (July 2010), http://www.yensaokhanhhoa.com.vn, (May 2009), and Lau, Amy S. M. and David S. Melville, *International Trade in Swiftlet Nests with Special Reference to Hong Kong*, (n.p.: TRAFFIC International, 1994).
117. www.yensao.vn, bang gia (thong nhất tren toan quoc), (July 2010).
118. Nguyen Van Hung. Interview, 27 October 2008
119. Nguyen Van Hung. Interview, 27 October 2008
120. Nguyen Nhuu Tri. Interview, 1 June 2009.

121. Nguyen Tien Duong, a taxi driver in Nha Trang town, while driving the research team from the accommodation to the Sanest bird's-nest products shop. Interview, 2 June 2009.

122. A taxi driver in Nha Trang, interview, 2 June 2009.

123. The female owner of steamed duck shop in front of Sanest factory, Nguyen Sau Ngao house, the City of Nha Trang. Interview, 2 June 2009.

124. http://www.yensaokhanhhoa.com.vn, (May 2009).

125. http://www.sieuthihangchatluong.com/?Act=View&DoanhNghiep=yensaokhanhhoa&Id=EStore, (May 2009).

126. Pattamawadee Phonukul Suzuki and Chon Bunnag. "Power Structure for Natural Resources Allocation and Environment." www.econ.tu.ac.th/doc/seminar/120/sym50_paper3_pat.ppt, (March 2011).

127. Frank Pak, the owner of the bird's-nest business company "Home of Swiftlet", Hong Kong. Interview, 12 October 2009.

128. Thanyathip Sripana, "Vietnam: Politics, Economy and Foreign Affairs after the Economic Crisis (2540–2550)." In Srida Sornsri et al., *Southeast Asia: Politics, Economy and Foreign Affairs after the Economic Crisis (B.E. 2540-2550)*. Bangkok: Chulalongkorn University Printing House, 2009, pp. 504–86.

129. Scott, James C. Weapons of the Weak: Everyday Forms of Peasant Resistance. New Haven: Yale University Press, 1985. Cited by Anan Ganjanapan. "The social movement", in *The Fundamental Concepts of Society and Culture*, edited by The Faculty of Department of Sociology and Anthropology, Faculty of Social Science, Chiang Mai University, (n.p., n.d.), pp. 164, 167.

130. Scott, James C. *Domination and the Art of Resistance: Hidden Transcripts*. New Haven: Yale University Press, 1990, p. 14, as cited in Pathom Hongsuwan. "Mekong Giant Fish: The Sacred Food and the Competition of Symbolic Meaning in the Community in Thai-Laos Borders." In the *Documents of the 9th Annual Humanities Seminar, "Foods and Eating: Political Morals about Foods and Eating No. 3.*, Bangkok: Princess Maha Chakri Sirindhorn Anthropology Centre, 2010, p. 976.

131. Sopharat Charusombat, op. cit, p. 165.

132. Sopharat Charusombat, op. cit, pp. 154–55.

Notes to Chapter 2

1. The World Factbook – Central Intelligence Agency. Indonesia. https://www.cia.gov/library/publications/resources/the-world-factbook/geos/print_id.html.

2. Lim Chan Koon and Earl of Cranbrook. *Swiftlets of Borneo: Builders of Edible Nests*. Kota Kinabalu: Natural History Publications (Borneo), 2002, pp. 62–63.

3. Reny, Sawitri and R. Garsetiasih. "The Study of Population, Habitat, and Productivity of Thunberg's Swiftlet (*Collocalia fuciphaga*), in South Gombong, Central Java", http://library.forda-mof.org/libforda/data_pdf/620_3_2000.pdf (October, 2011), p. 37.

4. Goloubinoff, Marina. "Swiftlets, Edible Birds' Nests." In *Riches of the Forest: Food, Spices, Crafts and Resins of Asia*. Edited by Citlalli Lopez and Patricia Stanley. Desa Putra: Center for International Forestry Research, 2004, p. 35.

5. Reny, Sawitri and R. Garsetiasih, op. cit., p. 38.

6. Lau, Amy S. M. and David S. Melville. *International Trade in Swiftlet Nests with Special Reference to Hong Kong Species in Danger*. Cambridge: UK Traffic International, 1994, p. 6.

7. Lim Chan Koon and Earl of Cranbrook, op. cit., p. 63.

8. Ibid. pp. 88–90.

9. Oekan Abdoellah et al. "Communities and Forest Management in East Kalimantan: Pathway to Environmental Stability." *Research Network Report 3*. Berkeley: Center for Southeast Asian Studies, University of California, 1993, p. 50.

10. Lim Chan Koon and Earl of Cranbrook, op. cit., p. 63.

11. Swiftlet Bird Nests Harvest in East Kalimantan, http://swallow-nest.com/article/2006/10/02/swiftlet-bird-nests-harvest-in-east-kalimantan-2/ (November, 2009).

12. Michon, Genevieve et al. *Domesticating Forests: How Farmers Manage Forest Resources.* Jakarta: Center for International Forestry Research and the World Agroforestry Centre, 2005, pp. 58–59.

13. Aman Sitanggang, Indonesian worker of an oil company. Interview, 25 May 2008.

14. Mulia and Mahya, Acehnese bird's-nest collectors of Kampung Meunasah, Lampuuk, Lhoknga District, Aceh Province. Interview, 21 February 2010.

15. Muzakir, the Acehnese nest-collector leader of Kampung Meunasah, Lampuuk, Lhoknga District, Aceh Province. Interview, 22 February 2010.

16. *The Black Road: On the Front Line of Aceh's War*, Directed by William Nessen, 2005. 52 minutes. Film.

17. Special report of Trang swiftlet concession, http://77.nationchannel.com/playvideo.php?id=71936 (July, 2011).

18. Nugroho, E. *The Secrets of a Successful Swiftlet House.* Semarang: Eka Offset, 2001, p. 173.

19. There are many names for house-farming such as *hotel walet* or swiftlet hotels, swiftlet condos, swiftlet house or birdhouse or bird's-nest building, swiftlet farm or swiftlet farming or swiftlet farming house.

20. Goloubinoff, Marina, op. cit., p. 35.

21. Poole, Colin. "Swiftlet farming come to Cambodia," *BirdingASIA*, 13 (2010), p. 62.

22. Delaney, Daniel Vincent dan Fakultas Ilmu. *Budidaya Sarang Burung Walet Di Jawa Timur.* Malang: Universitas Muhammadiyah Malang, 2008, p. 3.

23. Boyle, Joe. "Welcome to Indonesia's bird nest soup factory town", http://www.bbc.co.uk/news/world-asia-pacific-12274825 (August, 2011).

24. Nugroho, E. and I. Whendrato. *The Farming of Edible-Nest Swiftlets Aerodramus fuciphagus in Indonesia.* Semarang: Indonesian Swiftlet Lovers Association, 1994, pp. 22–26.

25. Joe Boyle, op. cit.

26. Nugroho, E., op. cit., pp. 179–81.

27. Goloubinoff, Marina., op. cit., p. 36.

28. Nugroho, E. and I. Whendrato, op. cit., p. 36.

29. Nugroho, E. and I. Whendrato, op. cit., p. 45.

30. E. Nugroho, the researcher on swiftlet and swiftlet-house farming in Indonesia, President of The Indonesian Swiftlet Lover's Association. Interview, 23 February 2010.

31. Hary Kusumo Nugroho, swiftlet-house farming businessman in Sermarang and Jakarta. Interview, 23 February 2010.

32. Hary Kusumo Nugroho. Interview, 23 February 2010.

33. Indonesia has 14 swiftlet species; (1) *C. gigas*, (2) *C. lowi*, (3) *C. maxima*, (4) *C. fuciphaga*, (5) *C. salangana*, (6) *C. vestita* or *C. germani, Oustalet*, (7) *C. inexpectata*, (8) *C. spodyophyga*, (9) *C. vanikorensis*, (10) *C. hirundinacea*, (11) *C. papuensis*, (12) *C. nuditarsus*, (13) *C. linchi*, (14) *C. esculenta*.

34. Nugroho, E. and I. Whendrato, op. cit., p. 3.

35. Four type of Edible Swiftlet birds' nests; (1) *C. fuciphaga*, (2) *C. germani* or *vestita*, (3) *C. maxima*, (4) *C. unicolor*.

36. Nugroho, E. and I. Whendrato, op. cit., p. 13.

37. Michon, Genevieve et al., op. cit., p. 58.

38. Nugroho, E. and I. Whendrato, op. cit., pp. 16–19.

39. Nugroho, E., I. Whendrato and N. Kusomo. *The Farming of Edible-Nest Swiftlets Aerodramus fuciphagus in Indonesia.* Semarang: Eka Offset, 1996, p. 23.

40. Nugroho, E. and I. Whendrato, and N. Kusumo, op. cit., pp. 21–2.

41. Mulia and Mahya. Interview, 21 February 2010.

42. Nugroho, E. and I. Whendrato, op. cit., pp. 44–45.

43. This 30-years conflict began in 1976 when Aceh first sought independence from Indonesia. The demand was realized in 2005.

44. Mulia and Mahya. Interview, 21 February 2010.

45. http://www.kebumenkab.go.id/index.php?module=htmlpages&func=display&pid=62 (October 2011).

46. Nugroho, E. and I. Whendrato, op. cit., p. 175.

47. "Bird's-nest soup the Caviar of the East", http://indonesianow.blogspot.com/2006/08/ birds-nest-soup.html., (August 2011).

48. Mulia and Mahya. Interview, 21 February 2010.
49. H. Fainal, a swiftlet house farming owner at Sigli-Aceh. Interview, 23 February 2010.
50. Zafril, bird's-nest trader and swiftlet house farming owner at Bireuen-Aceh. Interview, 23 February 2010.
51. Arief Budiman dan TIM penulis PS. *Budidaya Dan Bisnis Sarang Walet.* Jakarta: Penebar Swadaya, 2008. p. 11.
52. http://www.kebumenkab.go.id/index.php?module=htmlpages&func=display&pid=62 (October 2011).
53. History about nyi roro kidul, http://iwansky82.blogspot.com/2010/08/history-about-nyi-roro-kidul.html. (October 2011).
54. Mulia and Mahya. Interview, February 21, 2010.
55. Muzakir. Interview, 22 February 2010.
56. H. Fainal. Interview, 23 February 2010
57. Mulia and Mahya. Interview, February 21, 2010.
58. Arief Budiman dan TIM penulis PS., op. cit., p. 10.
59. Delaney, Daniel Vincent dan Fakultas Ilmu., op. cit., pp. 44–6.
60. Nugroho, E. and I. Whendrato, op. cit., p. 17.
61. Muzakir. Interview, 22 February 2010, and E. Nugroho. Interview, 23 February 2010.
62. Mulia and Mahya. Interview, February 21, 2010. Muzakir. Interview, 22 February 2010.
63. Michon, Genevieve et al., op. cit., p. 58.
64. Muzakir. Interview, 22 February 2010.
65. Arief Budiman dan TIM penulis PS., op. cit., p. 10.
66. Delaney, Daniel Vincent dan Fakultas Ilmu., op. cit., p. 3.
67. Upacara Ngunduh Sarang Burung Walet di Karangbolong (Kebumen, Jawa Tengah), http://uunhalimah.blogspot.com/2008/12/upacara-ngunduh-sarang-burung-walet-di.html (November, 2011).
68. E. Nugroho. Interview, 23 February 2010. Hary Kusumo Nugroho. Interview, 23 February 2010.
69. Reny, Sawitri and R. Garsetiasih., op. cit., p. 43.
70. Upacara Ngunduh Sarang Burung Walet di Karangbolong (Kebumen, Jawa Tengah), http://uunhalimah.blogspot.com/2008/12/upacara-ngunduh-sarang-burung-walet-di.html (November, 2011).
71. Lim Chan Koon and Earl of Cranbrook, op. cit., p. 115.
72. Michon, Genevieve et al., op. cit., p. 59.
73. Swiftlet Bird's-Nest Harvest in East Kalimantan, http://swallow-nest.com/article/2006/10/02/ swiftlet-bird-nests-harvest-in-east-kalimantan-2/ (November, 2009).
74. Oekan Abdoellah et al., op. cit., p. 50.
75. There are 89 caves in Muara Wahau and the other 70 caves in Berau District.
76. Earle, Geoff. "Feature: Nest soup taxing Indonesian birds", http://swallow-nest.com/article/2006/03/01/feature-nest-soup-taxing-indonesian-birds/ (May, 2009).
77. Oekan Abdoellah et al., op. cit., p. 53.
78. Lim Chan Koon and Earl of Cranbrook, op. cit., p. 139.
79. Mulia and Mahya. Interview, February 21, 2010. Muzakir. Interview, 22 February 2010.
80. Lim Chan Koon and Earl of Cranbrook, op. cit., p. 103.
81. Reny Sawitri and R. Garsetiasih, op. cit., pp. 37–8.
82. Bourdieu, Pierre, op. cit. pp. 18, 20.
83. Goloubinoff, Marina, op. cit., p. 34.
84. Boyle, Joe, op. cit.
85. Hary Kusumo Nugroho. Interview, 23 February 2010.
86. E. Nugroho. Interview, 23 February 2010.
87. TIM Penulis PS. *Budi Daya Dan Bisnis Sarang Walet.* Jakarta: Penebar Swadaya, 2004, pp. 68–70.
88. *Investment Opportunities Study for Each Province of East, West, Central and South Kalimantan Executive Summary East Kalimantan.* (n.p.: PT. Pacific Consulindo International Indonesia, 2005), p. 63.
89. "Original Bird's Nest International (OBNI) Clean Good Shap and Chemical", http://www.originalnest.com/contact-us.html (September, 2011).

90. Zafril. Interview, 23 February 2010.
91. The swiftlet-house farming owner, Samalanga city, Aceh. Interview, 22 February 2010.
92. Lau, Amy S. M. and David S. Melville, op. cit., p. 6.
93. Lim Chan Koon and Earl of Cranbrook, op. cit., p. 91.
94. Boyle, Joe, op. cit.
95. Frank Pak. Interview, 12 October 2009.
96. Hary Kusumo Nugroho. Interview, 23 February 2010.
97. TIM Penulis PS, op. cit., p. 66.
98. Arief Budiman and TIM Penulis PS, op. cit., p. 77.
99. Ibid. pp. 80–81.
100. Muzakir. Interview 22 February 2010.
101. H. Fainal, Interview, 23 February 2010.
102. Zafril. Interview, 23 February 2010.
103. The swiftlet house farming owner, Samalanga city, Aceh, interview 22 February 2010.
104. E. Nugroho. Interview, 23 February 2010. Hary Kusumo Nugroho. Interview, 23 February 2010.
105. Lim Chan Koon and Earl of Cranbrook, op. cit., p. 115.
106. Michon, Genevieve et al., op. cit., p. 59.
107. "Swiftlet Bird Nests Harvest in East Kalimantan", http://swallow-nest.com/article/2006/10/02/swiftlet-bird-nests-harvest-in-east-kalimantan-2/ (November, 2009).
108. Geoff Earle. "Feature: Nest soup taxing Indonesian birds", http://swallow-nest.com/article/2006/03/01/feature-nest-soup-taxing-indonesian-birds/ (May, 2009).
109. Oekan Abdoellah et al., op. cit., p. 50.
110. Lim Chan Koon and Earl of Cranbrook, op. cit., p. 139.
111. Mulia and Mahya. Interview, February 21, 2010.
112. Muzakir. Interview, 22 February 2010.
113. H.Fainal, Interview, 23 February 2010.
114. The swiftlet house farming owner, Samalanga city, Aceh. Interview, 22 February 2010.
115. Zafril. Interview, 23 February 2010.
116. Arief Budiman and TIM Penulis PS, op. cit., p. 15.
117. Mulia and Mahya. Interview, February 21, 2010.
118. Pattamawadee Phonukul Suzuki and Chon Bunnag. "The power structure of natural resources and environment management", www.econ.tu.ac.th/doc/seminar/120/sym50_paper3_pat.ppt, (March, 2011).
119. E. Nugroho. Interview, 23 February 2010.
120. "Pengelolaan Sarang Walet tak Jelas," *Serambi*, 27 Oktober 2008, p. 3.
121. Muzakir. Interview 22 February 2010.
122. Zafril. Interview, 23 February 2010.
123. Frank Pak. Interview, 12 October 2009.
124. Hary Kusumo Nugroho. Interview, 23 February 2010.
125. Phuwadon Songprasert. *Indonesia: The Past and Present*. Bangkok: Chulalongkorn University Press, 2004, p. 292.
126. Earle, Geoff. op. cit.
127. Michon, Genevieve et. al., op. cit., p. 59.
128. *The Black Road: On the Front Line Of Aceh's War*, Directed by William Nessen, 2005. 52 minutes. Film.
129. Special report about Trang swiftlet concession, http://77.nationchannel.com/playvidephp?id=71936 (July, 2011).
130. "Pengelolaan Sarang Walet tak Jelas," *Serambi*, 27 Oktober 2008, p. 3.
131. "Panen Sarang Walet Madina Tak Dinikmati Rakyat," http://groups.yahoo.com/group/sa-roha/message/2465. (April, 2012).
132. Scott, James C. Cited by Anan Ganjanapan, op. cit, pp. 164, 167.
133. Scott, James C. Cited by Pathom Hongsuwan, op. cit., p. 976.

134. Oekan Abdoellah et al., op. cit., p. 1.
135. Vitaya Sujaritthanarak, "Indonesia: Political, Economic and Foreign Affairs after Economic Crisis (2540–2550)." In Srida Sornsri et al., op. cit., pp. 5, 17.
136. Sopharat Charusumbat, op.cit., pp. 220–25.
137. E. Nugroho. Interview, 23 February 2010.
138. Arief Budiman and TIM Penulis PS, op. cit., pp. 16–17.
139. Nugroho. E and I. Whendrato, op. cit., p. 13.
140. Lim Chan Koon and Earl of Cranbrook, op. cit., pp. 131–33.
141. "Pengelolaan Sarang Walet tak Jelas," *Serambi*, 27 Oktober 2008, p. 3.
142. Nugroho. E and I. Whendrato, op. cit., p. 45.
143. Hary Kusumo Nugroho. Interview, 23 February 2010.
144. Hary Kusumo Nugroho. Interview, 23 February 2010.
145. Sopharat Charusumbat, op. cit, p. 249.

Notes to Chapter 3

1. The Federation of Malaysia or Malaysia has a total land area of 329,758 square kilometers. It is divided into West Malaysia on the Malaya Peninsula, with 131,587 square kilometers, consisting of 11 states with the Sultan as the head of state. The other two states, Penang and Malacca, headed by the state governor. The capital city is Kuala Lumpur, and Labuan Island is under federal supervision.
   East Malaysia covers the north of Borneo, Sabah, and Sarawak, with 74,398 and 124,449 square kilometers. There is a state governor. The capital city is Kuala Lumpur, and Labuan Island is under federal supervision.
   Malaysia has a population of 32,652,083 (July 2020 est.) consisting of ethnic groups: Malay, Chinese, Indigenous, Indian, and other ethnicities. Religion: Islam, Buddhists, Christians, Hindus, and other believes. Overall, most population and prosperity are in western Malaysia. The various 69 ethnicities habituated in three regions: Semenanjung Malaysia 36 ethnic groups, Sarawak 16 ethnic groups, and Sabah 17 ethnic groups.
2. Jongjit Attayukti, editor. *Malaysia*. Bangkok: Window on The World Publishing, 2004, p. 55.
3. Data from PDF files of CP Malaysia.
4. http://www.boi.go.th/thai/asean/Malaysia/main.html (June, 2012).
5. Jongjit Attayukti, Ibid. p. 56.
6. Vincent Tiew, Managing Director of Meda Inc. Bhd.
7. Lim Chan Koon and Earl of Cranbrook, op. cit., p. 62.
8. Jonker Birdhouse Swiftlet Eco. "Thunder storm introduces Bird's Nest to Zheng He." Melaka: Joon Onn Holdings Sdn.Bhd., 2012, p. 1.
9. "Scandalous! Fake birds' nests from Malaysia cheated on Chinese people repeatedly", ASTV Manager Online, http://www.manager.co.th/China/ViewNews.aspx?NewsID=9540000103387&fb_source=message (August, 2011).
10. Lim Chan Koon and Earl of Cranbrook, op. cit., p. 62.
11. Giles, Francis H. "A Description of the Swifts (*Collocalia Francica* and *Collocalia Innominata*), The Birds Which Build Edible Nests." Translated by Sunalini Nikonthanon for the Commemoration of the Royal Funeral Ceremony of Luang Sawatdisansatphutthi (Sawat Sumit), Wat That Thong, Bangkok, February 25, 1973, p. 152.
12. Earl of Cranbrook, op. cit, p. 34.
13. Ismail Mohammed Yusoff. "Sustainable Bird Nest Resource Management of Idahan People in the State of Sabah." In *Exposing the Billion-Dollar Bird's-nest Business World*, edited by Patrick Jory and Jirawat Sangthong. Nakhon Si Thammarat: Research Fund and Regional Project Study Bureau, Art Academic Office, Walailak University, 2007, p. 87.
14. Lim Chan Koon. "Bird Nest Business and Bird Nest Farming Development in Malaysia." In *Exposing the Billion-Dollar Bird's-nest Business World*, edited by Patrick Jory and Jirawat Sangthong. Nakhon Si Thammarat: Research Fund and Regional Project Study Bureau, Art Academic Office, Walailak University, 2007, pp. 104–5.

15. Ismail Mohammed Yusoff, op. cit, pp. 87–88.
16. Lim Chan Koon and Earl of Cranbrook, op. cit., p. 63.
17. Lim Chan Kun, op. cit., pp. 104–5.
18. Earl of Cranbrook, op. cit, p. 42.
19. Nuar Bin Haji Jaya, the ethnic Pernan group, owner of welfare store and restaurant, at Niah National Park, Sarawak. Interview, 11 November 2008.
20. Michael Bueng, the Iban bird's-nest merchant, and the former bird's-nest harvester, Gua Niah Cave. Interview, 13 August 2010.
21. Lim Chan Kun, op. cit., p. 109.
22. Jegathesan, M. "Bird's Nest Boom has Malaysian Producers Drooling," http://www.thejakartaglobe.com/bisworld/birds-nest-boom-has-malaysian-producers-drooling/471393 (June, 2012).
23. Lim, David Y. C. Report on the Malaysia Swiftlet Nest Industry Issue. Federation of Malaysia Bird's Nest Merchants Association, 2002, rev. ed. 2008, pp. 6–7, http:/worldofswifletfarmimg.blogspot.com, (n.p: 2008).
24. Hameed Sultan Merican, "The 2007 Malaysian Swiftlet Farming Industry Report," http://www.smipenang.com/2006SwiftletFarmingReport.html (November, 2007).
25. Lim Chan Kun, op. cit., pp. 110–13.
26. Chan, Zora et al. "No Swiftlet Farms in Shophouses Says Naroden." *The Borneo Post*, Friday, 7 November 2008, p. 6.
27. "Birds Nests," http://www.cavesofmalaysia.com/photopage10.htm (December, 2012).
28. Lim Chan Kun, op. cit., p. 115.
29. Lajiun Jenne. "Swiftlet farms must move out," http://www.theborneopost.com/2012/10/05/swiftlet-farms-must-move-out/#ixzz2EBK5Zunt (October, 2012).
30. Ngah Haryani. "Walit Malaysia selamat untuk eksport," http://www.dvs.gov.my (September, 2011).
31. Jegathesan, M, op. cit..
32. Ismail Mohammed Yusoff, op. cit., p. 88.
33. "Kenapa Sarang Burung Dari Gua Niah?," http://budidayabirdnest.wordpress.com/2009/11/10/kenapa-sarang-burung-dari-gua-niah/ (July, 2012).
34. Sarawak Forestry. *Swiftlets*, Metal Signs Exhibition in Gua Niah cave Batu Niah, Miri, Sarawak Malaysia (13 August, 2010).
35. E. Nugroho and Whendrato, op. cit., pp. 16–19.
36. E. Nugroho, Whendrato, and Eko Kusumo N, op. cit., pp. 21–22.
37. Marzita Abdullah, "Sarang 'emas' cecah RM45,000 sekilo," http://www.utusan.com.my/utusan/info.asp?y=2010&dt=1126&pub=utusan_malaysia&sec=Utara&pg=wu_01.htm&arc=hive (May, 2012).
38. Hameed Sultan Merican. The 2007 Malaysian Swiftlet Farming Industry Report. Penang: SMI Association of Penang, 2007.
39. Hameed Sultan Merican. Ibid.
40. "Terengganu adalah tanah yang paling subur dan terbaik untuk industri burung walit di Malaysia," http://jahaniwalit.wordpress.com/2010/04/ (July, 2012).
41. Lim, Jessica and Wilson, "Swiftlet housing boom," http://www.jphpk.gov.my (October, 2007).
42. "Sarang burung Sumber ekonomi baru," http://www.utusan.com.my/utusan/info.asp?y=2008&dt=0725&pub=Utusan_Malaysia&sec=AgroBiz&pg=ag_03.htm (July, 2012).
43. Sunni Mahli, Gua Niah National Park staff, Gua Niah Cave, Sarawak. Interview, 10 November 2008.
44. Nuar Bin Haji Jaya. Interview, 11 November 2008.
45. Chan, Zora et al. "No Swiftlet Farms in Shophouses Says Naroden." *The Borneo Post*, Friday, 7 November 2008, p. 6.
46. Lim Chan Kun, op. cit., pp. 104–15.
47. Lim Chan Kun and Earl of Cranbrook, op. cit., p. 151
48. Lim Chan Kun, op. cit., pp. 104–15.
49. Lim Chan Koon and Earl of Cranbrook, op. cit., pp. 6, 151.
50. Ismail Mohammed Yusoff, op. cit., p. 95.

51. Lim Chan Kun, op. cit., p. 106.
52. Sunni Mahli. Interview, 10 November 2008.
53. Nuar Bin Haji Jaya and Haidar Bin Ali, the owners of Gua Niah cave, Peran ethnic group and the chief teacher. Interview, 11 November 2008.
54. Sunni Mahli. Interview, 10 November 2008.
55. Semah is a superstitious ritual to expel evil spirits and attract good spirits to come in.
56. Nuar Bin Haji Jaya, the ethnic group Pernan, the owner of Gua Niah Bird's-nest cave at welfare store and restaurant, Niah National Park, Sarawak, Malaysia. Interview, 11 November 2008.
57. Michael Bueng. Interview, 13 August 2010.
58. Ismail Mohamed Yusoff, op. cit., p. 3.
59. Earl of Cranbrook, Swallow's-Nest Researcher, interviewed at the Welfare Store and Restaurant in Niah National Park, 11 November 2008.
60. Michael Bueng. Interview, 13 August 2010.
61. Earl of Cranbrook. Interview, 11 November 2008.
62. Michael Bueng. Interview, 13 August 2010.
63. Michael Bueng, Interview, 13 August 2010.
64. Johnson Chew, a concessionaire of Niah Great Cave, Niah National Park, and bird's nest merchant, and the ethnic group of Batunah, Sarawak, Malaysia. Interview, 13 August 2010.
65. Ismail Mohamed Yusoff, op. cit., pp. 94–97.
66. Michael Bueng. Interview, 12 August 2010.
67. Isa Faten Saphilla Mohamed. "Burung Walit Import telur burung Indonesia," http://keluarga82.wordpress.com/2011/04/05/burung-walit/ (July, 2012).
68. Nuar Bin Haji Jaya. Interview, 11 November 2008.
69. http://www.facebook.com/ccgbirdnest (November, 2012).
70. Michael Bueng. Interview 13 August 2010.
71. Ismail Mohamed Yusoff, op. cit., pp. 94–97.
72. Lim Chan Koon, op. cit., p. 104.
73. Patcharin Suanthitapanya. *Malaysia: Unity and Education*. Bangkok: Thailand Research Fund, 1998, p. 69.
74. Lim Chan Koon, op. cit., p. 113.
75. Nuar Bin Haji Jaya and Haidar Bin Ali, the chief teacher Nahar Sarawak National Park Office, interview, 11 November 2008; Michael Bueng, interview, 13 August 2010.
76. Lim Chan Koon, op. cit., pp. 113–15.
77. Nuar Bin Haji Jaya. Interview, 11 November 2008.
78. Sarawak Forestry. *Swiftlets*, Metal Signs Exhibition in Gua Niah, Batu Niah, Miri, Sarawak Malaysia (13 August, 2010).
79. Lim Chan Koon, op. cit., p. 115.
80. Ismail Mohamed Yusoff, op. cit., pp. 86–7.
81. Ibid. pp. 90–4.
82. Lim Chan Koon, op. cit., pp. 112–13.
83. Lim Chan Koon and Earl of Cranbrook, op. cit., p. 103.
84. Bourdieu, Pierre, op. cit., pp. 18, 20.
85. Lim Chan Koon and Earl of Cranbrook, op. cit., p. 126.
86. Nantawan Yotphichit. "Dr. Mahathir and His Role in National Development." Paper presented at a Seminar on "The Story of Malaysia after the Mahathir Era," Regional Studies Program, School of Liberal Art, Grand Park Hotel, Mueang District, Nakhon Si Thammarat Province, October 18–19, 2003, pp. 13–14.
87. Nuar Bin Haji Jaya and Haidar Bin Ali. Interview, 11 November 2008.
88. Chin Mui Yoon. "Swift fortunes await," *The Star online*, Sunday, 23 August 2009
89. Hameed Sultann Merica, op. cit., p. 4.
90. Simon, Alina. "Rich pickings from swiftlet rearing," *New Straits Times, Nation*; April 24, 2008.
91. Chin Mui Yoon, op. cit.

NOTES TO CHAPTER 3

92. Boyle, Joe. op. cit.
93. "Scandalous! Fake birds' nests from Malaysia cheated on Chinese people repeatedly," op. cit.
94. Ngo, Edmund. "Bird's-nest business between China and Malaysia to resume soon," http://thestar.com.my/news/story.asp?file=/2012/4/26/metroperak/11175322&sec=metroperak and "Bird's nest traders rally for help over import ban," http://thestar.com.my/news/story.asp?file=/2012/7/22/nation/11710464&sec=nation. (September, 2012).
95. Dasar Agromakanan Negara (2011–2020) [PDF], http://www.moa.gov.my/c/document_library/get_file?uuid=346e790a-64f1-4589-ba72-0f22d9a445d0&groupId=10149 (July, 2012).
96. Bahagian Keselamatan dan Kualiti Makanan, Kementerian Kesihatan Malaysia, "Senarai Premis Pemprosesan Sarang Burung Walit Yang Mematuhi Keselamatan Makanan Bagi Tujuan Pengeksportan Sarang Burung Walit Ke China (Dikemaskini Sehingga 26 Jun 2012)," http://fsq.moh.gov.my/v3/images/filepicker_users/5ec35272cb-78/Aktiviti/Eksport/Sarang percent20 Burung percent20Walit/Senarai-Premis-Pemprosesan-Mematuhi.pdf (October, 2012).
97. Jegathesan, M. op. cit..
98. "Scandalous! Fake birds' nests from Malaysia cheated on Chinese people repeatedly," op. cit.
99. Haryani Ngah. "Walit Malaysia selamat untuk eksport," http://www.dvs.gov.my (September, 2011).
100. Dasar Agromakanan Negara (2011–2020) [PDF], http://www.moa.gov.my/c/ document_library/get_file?uuid=346e790a-64f1-4589-ba72-0f22d9a445d0&groupId=10149 (July, 2012).
101. "Scandalous! Fake birds' nests from Malaysia cheated on Chinese people repeatedly," op. cit.
102. Marzita Abdullah. op. cit.
103. Data from Chin Mui Yoon. op. cit.; Ismail Mohamed Yusoff., op. cit, p. 6; Lim David Y. C., op. cit. p. 6; Hameed Sultan Merican, op. cit., p. 4; Simon, Alina., op. cit.; Persatuan Pengusaha Industri Sarang Burung Kulai Johor Baru, China–Iskandar Malaysia & Bird Nest Business opportunity 2009, Johor Baru: Persatuan Pengusaha Industri Sarang Burung Kulai Johor Baru, 2009, p. 21; Marzita Abdullah., op. cit.; Ngah Haryani., op. cit.; Nazrul Azim Sharuddin. "Nilai hasilan sarang burung," Mega Utusan Malaysia, isnin 7 mei 2012, p. 3; and "Pemasaran SBW," http://agwalittrainingcentre.blogspot.com/search/label/Sarang percent20Burung percent20Walit percent20 percent28SBW percent29 (October, 2012)..
104. Persatuan Pengusaha Industri Sarang Burung Kulai Johor Baru. op. cit., p. 21.
105. Ibid. p. 21.
106. Michael Bueng. Interview, 13 August 2010.
107. Johnson Chew. Interview, 13 August 2010.
108. Michael Bueng. Interview, 13 August 2010.
109. Sunni Mahli. Interview, 10 November 2008.
110. Nuar Bin Haji Jaya and Haidar Bin Ali. Interview, 11 November 2008.
111. Michael Bueng. Interview, 13 August 2010.
112. Johnson Chew. Interview, 13 August 2010.
113. Ismail Mohamed Yusoff, op. cit., pp. 86–98.
114. Lim Chan Koon, op. cit., pp. 110–16.
115. Chin Mui Yoon, op. cit.
116. Marzita Abdullah, op. cit.
117. Zulhisham Isahak, "Pantau kualiti produk sarang burung walet," http://www.jpvpp.gov.my/index.php?option=com_content&view=article&id=396percent3Apantau-kualiti-produk-sarang-burung-walet&catid=61 percent3Aakhbar&Itemid=136&lang=bm (April, 2012).
118. "EBN palsu turut jadi ancaman." *Mega Utusan Malaysia*, 7 mei 2012, p. 10.
119. Haryani Ngah, op. cit.
120. "Nurhidayah Ramli, "1kg bird's nest limit for tourists," http://thestar.com.my/news/story.asp?file=/2012/1/17/nation/10275151&sec=nation (January, 2012).
121. "China may lift import ban on bird's nests," http://www.nst.com.my/nation/general/china-may-lift-import-ban-on-bird-s-nests-1.69626 (April, 2012).
122. "Bird's nest traders rally for help over import ban," http://drmat-ismail.blogspot.com/2012/08/birds-nest-trading-who-is-more.html (July, 2012).

NOTES TO CHAPTER 3

123. Nurhidayah Ramli, op. cit.
124. Chin Mui Yoon, op. cit.
125. Nazrul Azim Sharuddin. "Kursus cuci sarang burung," *mega Utusan Malaysia*, 7 mei 2012, p.2.
126. Nuar Bin Haji Jaya and Haidar Bin Ali. Interview, 11 November 2008.
127. Michael Bueng. Interview, 13 August 2010.
128. Ismail Mohamed Yusoff, op. cit., p. 90.
129. Nazrul Azim Sharuddin. "Nilai hasilan sarang burung," *mega Utusan Malaysia*, 7 mei 2012, p. 3.
130. Haryani Ngah, op. cit.
131. Jegathesan, M., op. cit.
132. http://www.amgadvance.com (June, 2012).
133. Pattamawadee Phonukul Suzuki and Chon Bunnag, "Power Structure for Natural Resources Allocation and Environment." www.econ.tu.ac.th/doc/seminar/120/sym50_paper3_pat.ppt, (March 2011).
134. Lim Chan Koon and Earl of Cranbrook, op. cit., 128.
135. Zafril. Interview, 23 February 2010.
136. Siri Bin Neng Buah, a Thai ethnicity, lives in Kelantan State, former senior officer of the Department of Culture, National Ministry of Culture, Malaysia. Interview, 10 May 2012.
137. Frank Pak. Interview. 12 October 2009.
138. Allen Pang, Product Quality Control Department, Home of Swallow Company. Hong Kong. Interview, 12 October 2009.
139. Najmee Madmarn and Numan Hayimasae. "Discourse on the nation, The Creation of the Nation and the Heroes of Malaysia: Study through the History of Secondary Education," *The TRF Forum* 2, 5 (January–March 2011), p. 21.
140. Andaya, Barbara Watson and Leonard Y. Andaya., op. cit., p. 462.
141. Under Abdul Rahman's three terms premiership, 31 August 1957 to 22 September 1970. Then the Abdul Razak's government took over from 22 September 1970 to 14 January 1976. After the five years of Hussein Onn's administration from 16 January, 1976 to 16 July 1981, Mahathir Mohamad's six consecutive terms came from 16 July 1981 to 31 October 2003. Mahathir's successor, Abdullah Ahmad Badawi, was the prime minister from 31 October 2003 to 3 April 2009. Badawi's successor was Najib Razak from 3 April 2009 to 10 May 2018. From 10 May 2018, Mahathir returned to power until 1 March 2020 before replaced by Muhyiddin Yassin.
142. Andaya, Barbara Watson and Leonard Y. Andaya, op. cit., p. (14).
143. Lim Chan Koon, op. cit., p. 111.
144. "The Birds Nest Standards, an overview of Malaysian standards related to edible birds nests," *Standards & Quality News* 18, 2 (February 2010), p. 14.
145. "Scandalous! Fake birds' nests from Malaysia cheated on Chinese people repeatedly," op. cit.
146. Bussakorn Lee. "The perspective from the 18th meeting of the Chinese Communist Party: Chinese economy will grow gradually, continuously, and stably in the next ten years," http://www.thaibizchina.com/thaibizchina/th/china-economic-business/result.php?IBLOCK_ID=69&SECTION_ID=442&ELEMENT_ID=11655 (November, 2012).
147. Nichakan Qin. "China bars bird's-nest import may affect the bird's-nest price raising." This may result in a new round of increasing price of bird's nest. http://www.thaibizchina.com/thaibizchina/th/china-economic-business/result.php?IBLOCK_ID=69&SECTION_ID=460&ELEMENT_ID=11519 (November, 2012).
148. Nichakan Qin. "From Nov. 1, China prohibits importing genetic-modified fruits, vegetables." http://www.thaibizchina.com/thaibizchina/th/china-economic-business/result. php?IBLOCK_ID=69&SECTION_ID=464&ELEMENT_ID=11495 (October, 2012).
149. Scott, James C. 1985, cited in Anan Ganjanapan, n.d., op. cit.pp. 164, 167.r
150. Scott, James C., 1990, op. cit., p. 14.
151. Jongjit Attayukti, op. cit., pp. 55–56, 61.
152. Sopharat Charusombat, op. cit., pp. 117, 136–37.
153. Nantawan Yotphichit, op. cit., pp. 14–16.

154. Chayachoke Chulasiriwongs. "The competition between UMNO and PAS to Compete for the People (UMNO-PAS Rivalry and Malay Electorate)." Paper presented at a Seminar on "The Story of Malaysia after the Mahathir Era," Regional Studies Program, School of Liberal Art, Grand Park Hotel, Mueang District, Nakhon Si Thammarat Province, October 18–19, 2003. p. 72.

155. Jongjit Attayukti, op. cit., p. 61.
156. Andaya, Barbara Watson and Leonard Y. Andaya. op. cit., pp. 532–33.
157. Johnson Chew. Interview, 13 August 2010.
158. Michael Bueng. Interview, 13 August 2010.
159. Haidar Bin Ali, "Welcome to Niah National Park Delegation of International Heritage Poetry Festival 9th November 2008 (Microsoft PowerPoint)," Niah National Park Sarawak Malaysia, 9 November 2008.
160. Lim Chan Koon, op. cit., p. 106.
161. Lajiun, Jenne, op. cit.
162. "Birds Nests," http://www.cavesofmalaysia.com/photopage10.htm (December, 2012).
163. Tan Boon Siong, researcher, bird's-nest business owner, Longevity Wellness Industries Sdn. Bhd. Johor Malaysia. Interview, 7 April 2010.
164. Hary Kusumo Nugroho. Interview, 23 February 2010.
165. Lim Chan Koon, op. cit., p. 115.
166. Ibid. p. 114.
167. Ibid. p. 111.
168. Chayachoke Chulasiriwongs, op. cit., p. 72.

Notes to Chapter 4

1. Coronel, Sheila S. *Memory of Dances*. Manila: Philippine Center for Investigative Journalism, 2002. p. 21.
2. Saragpunta Foundation and PAFID. "Mapping Ancestral Lands and Waters." *Indigenous Perspective* 2001, 4, No. 2, (December 2001), pp. 5–6.
3. Zingapan, Kail M. and Dave E. De Vera. "Mapping the Ancestral Lands and Waters of the Calamian Tagbanwa of Coron, Northern Palawan." Philippine Association for Intercultural Development (PAFID), March 10, 1999, p. 2.
4. "Saliva Soup," http://yapakyakap.blogspot.com/2008/10/saliva-soup.html (October, 2008).
5. Saliva Soup, Ibid.
6. Jack, Katherine. "The Nest-gatherers," http://issuu.com/lightmediation/docs/the_nest_gatherers_of_pabellon_Island_4573 (March, 2013).
7. Culibao, Mayet C. "Save this paradise," http://www.seasite.niu.edu/tagalog/Tagalog_Default_files/Philippine_Culture/travel_news_and_features.htm (December 2007).
8. Calcari, Meaghan E. "Indigenous Marine Tenure in a Common-pool Framework: A Philippine Case Study." Project Submitted in Partial Fulfillment of the Requirements for the Master of Environmental Management Degree, Nicholas School of the Environment, Duke University, 2004, p. 28.
9. Coronel, Sheila S., op. cit., p. 27.
10. La Vina, Antonio G. M. "Community-Based Approaches to Marine and Coastal Resources Management in the Philippines: A Policy Perspective," (n.p.), 2002, p. 109.
11. Coronel, Sheila S., op. cit., p. 23.
12. Ibid. p. 24.
13. Ibid.
14. "GPS and 3-D Mapping: Effective Tools to Establish Ancestral Domain Claims," in *Enhancing Access of the Poor to Land and Common Property Resources*, (n.p.: the Asian NGO Coalition for Agrarian Reform and Rural Development (ANGOC) and the international Land Coalition (ILC), 2006), p. 2.
15. Coronel, Sheila S. op. cit., p. 22.
16. Ibid. p. 21.
17. Kali Zingapan and Dave De Vera, op. cit., p. 2.

NOTES TO CHAPTER 4

18. Jack, Katherine, op. cit.
19. Ibid.
20. Ibid.
21. De Guia Merlindo Aguilar, the *busyador* Tagbanua ethnic group at Black Island Busuanga – Palawan. Interview, 6 July 2009.
22. Coronel, Sheila S., op. cit., p. 24.
23. De Guia Merlindo Aguilar. Interview, 6 July 2009.
24. Coronel, Sheila S., op. cit., p. 28.
25. Saragpunta Foundation and PAFID, op. cit., p. 62.
26. De Guia Merlindo Aguilar. Interview, 6 July 2009.
27. Perfecto B. Dabuit Jr., the *busyador* Tagbanua ethnic group at Black Island Busuanga – Palawan. Interview, 6 July 2009.
28. Roy Abella, the *busyadors* of Colon Island the Tagbanua ethnic group at Saragpunta office Colon town Busuanga – Palawan. Interview, 24 May 2008.
29. Perfecto B. Dabuit Jr. Interview, 6 July 2009.
30. Dennis Garcia, the former *busyador* of Cadlao Island the Filipino ethnic at Codognan Resort, El Nido – Palawan. Interview, 9 July 2009.
31. "Species of the Month," *Biota Filipina*, (June–July 2005), p. 7.
32. Fidel E. Mondragon, the vice chairman Saragpunta Federation Brgy. Dobcauon I; Roy Abella and Aldrin G. Caballero, and the *busayadors* of Coron Island the Tagbanua ethnic group at Kayangan lake and Saragpunta office Coron town Busuanga – Palawan. Interview, 23–24 May 2008.
33. Rodolfo Aguilar, the balinsasayaw cave-owner and the chairman of Coron Island the Tagbanua ethnic group at Saragpunta office Coron town Busuanga – Palawan. Interview, 7 July 2009.
34. Jack, Katherine, op. cit.
35. Garcia Dennis. Interview, 9 July 2009.
36. De Guia Merlindo Aguilar. Interview, 6 July 2009.
37. Perfecto B. Dabuit Jr. Interview, 6 July 2009.
38. "Potential for Edible Bird's Nest (EBN) Farming in the Philippines," http://nestfarminginpinas.blogspot.com (May, 2009).
39. Violeta Francisco. The pugad ng balinsasayaw dealer Filipino ethnic group, Coron Town, Busuanga Island, Palawan, Philippines. Interview 6 July 2009.
40. Fidel E. Mondragon, Roy Abella, and Aldrin G. Cabellero. Interview, 23–24 May 2008.
41. Rodolfo Aguilar. Interview, 7 July 2009.
42. Jack, Katherine, op. cit
43. Garcia Dennis. Interview, 9 July 2009.
44. Perfecto B. Dabuit Jr. Interview, 6 July 2009.
45. *Biota Filipina*, op. cit., p. 7.
46. Jack, Katherine, op. cit
47. De Guia Merlindo Aguilar. Interview, 6 July 2009.
48. Garcia Dennis. Interview, 24 May 2008.
49. De Guia Merlindo Aguilar. Interview, 6 July 2009.
50. Rodolfo Aguilar. Interview, 7 July 2009.
51. Garcia Dennis. Interview, 24 May 2008.
52. Violeta Francisco. Interview, 6 July 2009.
53. "Gie of elnodi's Blog," http://gieofelnido.wordpress.com/category/uncategorized/ (March,2013).
54. Perfecto B. Dabuit Jr. Interview, 6 July 2009.
55. Rodolfo Aguilar. Interview, 7 July 2009.
56. De Guia Merlindo Aguilar. Interview, 6 July 2009.
57. Fidel E. Mondragon, op. cit.
58. De Guia Merlindo Aguilar. Interview, 6 July 2009.
59. Fidel E. Mondragon. Interview, 23–24 May 2008.

60. De Guia Malindo Aguilar, Perfecto B. Dabuit Jr., and Rodolfo Aguilar, Palawan. Interview, 6–7 July 2009.
61. Perfecto B. Dabuit Jr.'s wife. Interview, 7 July 2009.
62. Garcia Dennis. Interview, 9 July 2009.
63. Garcia Dennis. Interview, 24 May 2008.
64. Graceffo, Antonio. "By Sea Kayak to the Tagbanua Calamian Tribe Diving on a Japanese Wreck," http://www.escapeartist.com/Travel_Mag/Issues/09/Sea_Kayak_to_the_Tagbanua_Calamian_Tribe.html (November, 2007).
65. De Guia Merlindo Aguilar. Interview, 6 July 2009.
66. Perfecto B. Dabuit Jr. Interview,6 July 2009.
67. Ward, Christain. "Bird's-nest soup," http://we BCache.googleusercontent.com/search?q=cache:bx 8LfkwopWYJ:www.contemporaryliteraryreviewindia.com/2011_07_01_archive.html+busyadors&cd=20&hl=en&ct=clnk&gl=th (March, 2013).
68. "Potential for Edible Bird's Nest (EBN) Farming in the Philippines," http://nestfarminginpinas.blogspot.com/ (May, 2009).
69. Garcia Dennis. Interview, 9 July 2009.
70. Rodolfo Aguilar. Interview, 7 July 2009.
71. "Saliva Soup," http://yapakyakap.blogspot.com/2008/10/saliva-soup.html (October, 2008).
72. Jack, Katherine, op. cit.
73. Srida Sornsri, *The Economic and Political Development of the Philippines*. Bangkok: Kobfai, 2002, pp. 8–9.
74. Zingapan, Kail M. and Dave E. De Vera., op. cit., p. 2.
75. "GPS and 3-D Mapping: Effective Tools to Establish Ancestral Domain Claims," op. cit., p. 2.
76. Saragpunta Foundation and PAFID, op. cit., p. 21.
77. Meaghan E. Calcari, op. cit., p. 28.
78. Saragpunta Foundation and PAFID, op. cit. p. 22.
79. Ibid. p. 23.
80. La Vina, Antonio G. M., op. cit., p. 109.
81. Rodolfo Aguilar. Interview, 7 July 2009.
82. Fidel E. Mondragon, Roy Abella, and Aldrin G. Cabellero. Interview, 23–24 May 2008.
83. Calcari, Meaghan E., op. cit., p. 28.
84. De Guia Merlindo Aguilar. Interview, 6 July 2009.
85. Perfecto B. Dabuit Jr.'s wife. Interview, 7 July 2009.
86. Rey D. Dabuit, Perfecto B. Dabuit Jr.'s son, the *busayador* Tagbanua ethnic group at BGY. Panlaitan Busuanga – Palawan. Interview, 7 July 2009.
87. Jack, Katherine, op. cit.
88. *Biota Filipina*, op. cit., p. 7.
89. Graceffo, Antonio, op. cit. and "Palawan Bird's-nest soup 101," http://eastgatepublishing.com/2011/11/palawan-birds-nest-soup-101 (March, 2013)
90. Dennis Garcia. Interview, 9 July 2009.
91. "Gie of elnido's Blog," http://gieofelnido.wordpress.com/category/uncategorized/ (March, 2013).
92. Rodolfo Aguilar. Interview, 7 July 2009.
93. Violeta Francisco. Interview, 6 July 2009.
94. Culibao, Mayet C., op. cit.
95. "Balinsasayaw / Nido Vegetable Chicken Soup," http://www.the cuisineuer.com/2013/01/balinsasayaw-nido-vegetable-chicken-soup.html (January 31, 2013).
96. "Enchanting Coron," http://www.mysmartschools.ph/web/Enchanting/VisitUs/CoronIsland.htm (July, 2013).
97. Coronel Sheila S., op. cit., p. 21.
98. Coronel Sheila S., op. cit., p. 27.
99. Culibao, Mayet C., op. cit.

100. Calcari, Meaghan E., op. cit., p. 28.
101. "Saliva Soup," http://yapakyakap.blogspot.com/2008/10/salova-soup.html (October, 2008).
102. Jack, Katherine, op. cit.
103. Saragpunta Foundation and PAFID, op. cit., pp. 5–6.
104. Zingapan, Kail M. and Dave E. De Vera., op. cit., p. 2.
105. "GPS and 3-D Mapping: Effective Tools to Establish Ancestral Domain Claims," op. cit., p. 2.
106. Coronel Sheila S., op. cit.
107. Jack, Katherine, op. cit.
108. Bourdieu, Pierre, op. cit., pp. 18, 20.
109. "Balinsasayaw / Nido Vegetable Chicken Soup," http://www.thecuisineuer.com/2013/01/balinsasayaw-nido-vegetable-chicken-soup.html (January, 2013).
110. Srida Sornsri. "Philippines: Politics Economic and Foreign Politics After the Economic Crisis (2540–2550)" in Srida Sornsri, et al. *Southeast Asia: Politics, Economy and Foreign Affairs after the Economic Crisis (B.E. 2540–2550)*. Bangkok: Chulalongkorn University Printing House, 2009, pp. 120, 130, 15.
111. Perfecto B. Dabuit's wife. Interview, 7 July 2009.
112. Hameed Sultan Merican. "The 2007 Malaysian Swiftlet Farming Industry Report," (n.p.: 2007), 4.
113. Chin Mui Yoon. "Swift fortunes await," *The Star Online*, Sunday August 23, 2009.
114. Boyle, Joe. "Welcome to Indonesia's bird nest soup factory town", http://www.b BC.co.uk/news/world-asia-pacific-12274825 (August, 2011).
115. "Scandalous! Fake birds' nests from Malaysia cheated on Chinese people repeatedly," op. cit.
116. "Potential for Edible Birds' Nest (EBN) Farming in the Philippines," http://nestfarminginpinas.blogspot.com/ (October, 2008).
117. Graceffo, Antonio, op. cit.
118. Violeta Francisco. Interview, 6 July 2009.
119. Dennis Garcia. Interview, 9 July 2009.
120. Data from Mayet C. Culibao, op. cit.; Marketman, "Bird's Nests – The Most Expensive Local Ingredient?," http://www.marketmanila.com/archives/birds-nests-the-most-expensive-local-ingredient (April, 2007); "Potential for Edible Birds' Nest (EBN) Farming in the Philippines," http://nestfarminginpinas.blogspot.com/ (October, 2008); Jack, Katherine op. cit.; "Laway Ng Ibon Sa El Nido Ay Ginto," http://gieofelnido.wordpress.com/2010/11/07/laway-ng-ibon-sa-el-nido-ay-ginto/ (November, 2010); "Palawan Bird's-nest soup 101," http://eastgatepublishing.com/2011/11/palawan-birds-nest-soup-101 (November, 2011); Graceffo, Antonio., op. cit., November, 2007; Graceffo, Antonio., op. cit. March, 2013; Violeta Francisco. Interview, 6 July 2009; De Guia Malindo Aguilar. Interview, 6 July 2009; Garcia Dennis. Interview, 9 July 2009; Fidel E. Mondragon, Roy Abella and Aldrin G. Caballero. Interview, 23–24 May 2008; and "Doon po sa Amin: Laway ni Kulas saganang-sagana" http://jevonne020799.wordpress.com/2010/05/17/doon-po-sa-amin-laway-ni-kulas-saganang-sagana (May, 2010).
121. Fidel E. Mondragon, Roy Abella and Aldrin G. Caballero. Interview, 23–24 May 2008.
122. Violeta Francisco. Interview, 6 July 2009.
123. Rodolfo Aguilar. Interview, 7 July 2009.
124. De Guia Merlindo Aguilar. Interview, 6 July 2009.
125. Perfecto B. Dabuit Jr. Interview, 6 July 2009.
126. Wife of Perfecto B. Dabuit Jr., the *busyador*, Tagbanua ethnic group at BGY. Panlaitan Busuanga – Palawan. And the son, Rey D. Dabuit (who fell from the bird's-nest cave). Interview, 7 July 2009.
127. Jack, Katherine, op. cit.
128. Dennis Garcia. Interview, 9 July 2009.
129. Rodolfo Aguilar. Interview, 7 July 2009.
130. Graceffo, Antonio. op. cit.
131. Pattamawadee Phonukul Suzuki and Chon Bunnag, op. cit.
132. De Guia Merlindo Aguilar and Perfecto B. Dabuit Jr. Interview, 6 July 2009.
133. Allen Pang. The quality control of 'Home of Swallows Limited Company' at the sub-meeting room of Hong Kong Polytechnic University, Hong Kong. Interview, 12 October 2009.

134. Srida Sornsri, ibid. p. 1.
135. Akkaraphong Khamkhun. "The History and the Philippines in the History Education Book of the Philippines for the High School Students," *Thammasat Archives Journal*, 12 (June 2008–May 2009), pp. 89, 97.
136. Srida Sornsri, op. cit., pp. 7–9
137. Through the government of the president Emillio Aquinaldo (1899–1901), Manuel Lui Quezon (1935–44), Jose P. Laurel (1943–45), Sergio Osmena (1944–46), Manuel A. Roxas (1946–48), Elpidio Quirino (1948–53), Ramon Magsaysay (1953–57), Carlos P. Garcia (1957–61), Diosdado Macapagal (1961–65), Ferdinand E. Marcos (1965–86), Corazon Aquino (1986–92), Fidel Ramos (1992–98), Joseph Estrada (1998–2001), Gloria Macapagal Arroyo (2001–2010), and Benigno Aquino III (2010–Now 2013).
138. Saragpunta Foundation and PAFID. "Mapping Ancestral Lands and Waters," *Indigenous Perspectives* 2001, 4, No. 2, (December 2001), 21; and Joan C. Bulauitan, "An age-old trade strains a scarce resource," http://mobilemedia.bworldonline.com/projectE/PalawanNorth/PalawanNorth.html (December, 2007).
139. Perfecto B. Dabuit Jr. Interview, 6 July 2009.
140. De Guia Merlindo Aguilar. Interview, 6 July 2009.
141. Sopharat Charusombat. op. cit., p. 83.
142. "*GPS and 3-D Mapping: Effective Tools to Establish Ancestral Domain Claims*," op. cit., p. 2.
143. Saragpunta Foundation and PAFID, op. cit., p.21.
144. Ibid. p. 23.
145. Rodolfo Aguilar. Interview, 7 July 2009.
146. Fidel E. Mondragon, Roy Abella and Aldrin G. Caballero. Interview, 23–24 May 2008.
147. De Guia Merlindo Aguilar. Interview, 6 July 2009.
148. *Biota Filipina*, op. cit., 7.
149. Graceffo, Antonio, op. cit.
150. Dennis Garcia. Interview, 9 July 2009
151. "Gie of elnido's Blog," http://gieofelnido.wordpress.com/category/uncategorized/ (March, 2013).
152. Nitchakarn Qin, op. cit.
153. Scott, James C. Cited by Anan Ganjanapan, op. cit., pp. 164, 167.
154. Mark Anthony S. Blanco the balinsasayaw cave-owner and the chairman of Coron Island the Tagbanua ethnic group at Saragpunta office, Coron town, Busuanga – Palawan, and Rodolfo Aguilar,. Interview, 7 July 2009.
155. Scott, James C. Cited by Pathom Hongsuwan, op. cit., p. 976.
156. ECAN Zones Management and Enforcement Division Enforcement Division (EZMED). *Annual Accomplishment Report 2012*, (Palawan: ECAN Zones Management and Enforcement Division Enforcement Division (EZMED), 2012), pp. 2–17, 20, 24.
157. Jack, Katherine, op. cit.
158. Srida Sornsri, op. cit., p. 4.
159. Nuanchan Kkampang, editor. *Philippines*. Bangkok: Windows on the World Publishing, 2007, pp. 43–45.
160. UNDP Project Document Government of the Philippines United Nations Development Programme PIMS no. 3530 Expanding and Diversifying the National System of Terrestrial Protected Areas in the Philippines (EDNSTPAP), 2009, 7.
161. Sopharat Charusombat. op. cit., pp. 57, 60–2.
162. Ibid. pp. 67–68.
163. Srida Sornsri. op. cit., pp. 76, 130, 150, 173.
164. Sopharat Charusombat, op. cit., p. 55.
165. "Enchanting Coron," http://www.mysmartschools.ph/web/Enchanting/Balinsasayaw_hyperlink.htm (July, 2013).
166. Bulauitan, Joan C. "An age-old trade strains a scarce resource," http://mobilemedia.bworldonline.com/projectE/PalawanNorth/PalawanNorth.html (December, 2007); De Guia Merlindo Aguilar the busyador Tagbanua ethnic group at Black Island Busuanga – Palawan. Interview, 6 July 2009; and Rodolfo Aguilar. Interview, 7 July 2009.
167. http://www.pcsd.ph/resolutions/resolutions/wildlife/res05-246.htm (April, 2013).

168. http://www.pcsd.ph/resolutions/resolutions/miscellaneous/reso4-224.htm (April, 2013).
169. http://www.pcsd.ph/resolutions/resolutions/wildlife/reso4-225.htm (April, 2013).
170. Violeta Francisco, De Guia Merlindo Aguilar. Interview, 6 July 2009; and Rodolfo Aguilar. Interview, 7 July 2009.

Notes to Chapter 5

1. John F. Embree's definition in "Thailand-A Loosely Structure Social System", 1950.
2. Kasem Jandam. *Swiftlet's Nest: Power, Conflict and Wealth*. Bangkok: Mahasarakham University Press, 2007.
3. Suthiwong Phongphaiboon, Dilok Wuttiphanit and Prasit Chinnakan. *Chin Thaksin: Withi lae Phalang*. Bangkok: The Thailand Research Fund, 2001, p. 18.
4. Sa-rup Ritchu, ed. *Art Source Registration in Phatthalung Province*. Phatthalung: Phatthalung Cultural Center, Satri Phatthalung School, 1998, p. 112.
5. Prasit Phanphisut, et al. "Following King Rama V's Visit to Koh Si Koh Ha in Rattanakosin Era 108" in *Commemoration of Enshrining a Royal Monument*, 22 February 1996, Pak Phayun District Phatthalung Province. Phatthalung: n.p., 1996, p. 51.
6. Praeng Phetchamrat. Interview, 7 March 2003.
7. Regional News Team. "Flipping the legend of the dead bird's nest," The benefit of death on the islands Plagued (Warfare)!" *Matichon Daily*, May 22, 1994, p. 9.
8. Prasit Phanphisut, op. cit., p. 51.
9. Natthaphat Chanthawit and Saengchan Traikasem, ed. *A Guide to the Museum National, Nakhon Si Thammarat*. Bangkok: Rungsin Printing 1977, 2000, p. 22.
10. Banchong Wongwichian, et al. *Archeology History of Nakhon Si Thammarat*. Bangkok: Fine Arts Department. p. 96.
11. Narathip Praphanphong, Krom Phra. *La Loubère Annals* (Archives). Bangkok: Khurusapha Printing, 1962, volume 2, pp. 99–100.
12. Sa-ngop Songmeuang. Interview, 19 June 2003.
13. Sa-ngop Songmeuang. "Bird's-nest duty in the south" in the *Southern Thai Culture Encyclopedia*, 1999, Volume 18, p. 8892.
14. Kittisak Nakmeuang. "The National Integration in Five Southern Border Provinces." Individual Study, Master of Arts Program in Political Science, Thammasat University, 1995, pp. 145–46.
15. Ratchadaphon Sriphiban. "The importance of bird's nests to the economy in southern Thailand (B.E. 2310–2482)." Master of Arts Thesis, Thammasat University, 1999, p. 196.
16. Sa-ngop Songmeuang. Research report on Songkhla City Development in the Thonburi and Early Rattanakosin Period B.E. 2310-2444. Songkhla: Srinakharinwirot University, Songkhla, 1980.
17. Ratchadaphon Sriphiban, op. cit., p. 196.
18. Sa-ngop Songmeuang, op. cit., p. 66.
19. Ibid. p. 122.
20. Banchong Wongwichian, et al., op. cit., p. 164.
21. Narong Nunthong. "Administration of Nakhon Si Thammarat Districts in Rattanakosin Period." *A Guide to Nakhon Si Thammarat, 1000 Year Old Historical City*. Bangkok: DLS Printing, 1991, p. 155.
22. Sa-ngop Songmeuang, op. cit., p. 164.
23. Ratchadaphon Sriphiban, op. cit., pp. 196–201.
24. Sa-ngop Songmeuang. "Bird's-nest duty in Chumphon Province" in the *Southern Thai Cultural Encyclopedia*, 1999, volume 18, p. 8901.
25. Ratchadaphon Sriphiban, op. cit., pp. 193–95.
26. Ibid. pp. 155–216.
27. Decho Bunchuchuai. "Bird's-Nest Taxes in Chumphon Province" in the *Southern Thai Cultural Encyclopedia*, 1999, volume 18, p. 8897.

28. Ratchadaphon Sriphiban, op. cit., pp. 216–34.
29. Ratchadaphon Sriphiban, ibid. p. 235.
30. Somphon Nunum. Interview, 8 August 2003.
31. Praeng Phetchamrat. Interview, 7 March 2003.
32. Editorial. "Report: The Unsolved Robbery of Bird Nests in Koh Si Koh Ha Islands". *Leam Thai*, 16–30 April 2003, p. 6.
33. Ibid. p. 6.
34. Somphon Nunum. Interview, 8 August 2003.
35. ASTV *Manager Online*. "Swiftlets Nest Phatthalung Concession Company Contract for Storage concessions." News.thaihomelist.com/2009 / ... (19 August 2009).
36. Khuankhit Muennara. Interview, 3 April 2003.
37. Chaweewan Denphaibun, et al. "Case Study of Swallows at Pak Phanang." *Nakhon Si Thammarat Journal* 34, 3 (March 2004): 36.
38. Kamolsak Lertphaibun. *Nok aen: khwam-lap thi tong chae* (Swiftlets: the secret must reveal). Nakhon Si Thammarat: Kwan Mui Co., Ltd. 2008, p. 8.
39. Cherdphan Phuriphatphan, swallows source owner, Pak Phanang District, Nakhon Si Thammarat Province. Interview, 15 December 2002.
40. Anonymous. Interview, 17 August 2004.
41. Kasem Jandam, op. cit., p. 31.
42. Wit Thiengburanathum. *Dictionary of Birds in Thailand*. Bangkok: Odeon Store, 1989, p. 110.
43. Praeng Phetchamrat. Interview, 7 March 2003.
44. *Teknik kan lieang nok aen* (Swiftlet farm know-how) (n.p / n.d.), p. 1.
45. Liam Chantharamat. Interview, 23 March 2003.
46. Prayoon Chamnina, Panglaema, Koh Thalu, Ao Luek District, Krabi Province. Interview, 2 October 2002.
47. Pratheep Duangkhae. "unveal the secret of swiftlets' white gold." *Advanced Thailand Geographic*, January 2003, p. 153.
48. O-phat Khobkhet. "The Edible-Nest Swiftlet." *The Royal Society Newsletter*, March 2001, p. 3.
49. Liam Chantharamat. Interview, 23 March 2003.
50. Wit Thiengburanathum, op. cit., p. 110.
51. Phakhawat Phonak. "Ecology of the White-Rumped Germain's Swiftlet (*Aerodramus germani Oustalet*) in Koh Chang National Park, Trat Province." Master of Science Thesis (Forest Biology), Kasetsart University, 2004, pp. 4, 9–13, 46, 65
52. Wit Thiengburanathum, op. cit., p. 112.
53. Tuangrat Pho-thiang. *Report on research progress of Ecology and Distribution Species of Aerodramus Fuciphagus*. Bangkok: Department of National Parks, Wildlife and Plant Conservation, 2004, pp. 89, 96.
54. Kamolsak Lertphaiboon, op. cit., Introduction.
55. Saksit Kanwitye. Interview, 4 April 2014.
56. Suwet Ketkaeo, bird's-nest collectors, Koh Sukon, Trang Province. Interview, 29 October 2009.
57. Khieo Chantharamat. Interview, 10 April 2003.
58. Khuankhit Muennara. Interview, 3 April 2003.
59. Prayoon Chamnina, Interview, 2 October 2002.
60. Musa Damchuea. Interview, 21 October 2002. Praeng Phetchamrat. Interview March 7, 2003. and Bae Solae. Interview, 18 April 2003.
61. Uthit Khieokhachi, bird's-nest collector, Koh Rangnoi Thai-Vietnamese ethnicity, Salak Phet House Koh Chang Tai Sub-District, Koh Chang District, Trat Province. Interview, 14 May 2010.
62. Ratchadaphon Sriphiban, op. cit., p. 86.
63. Wiwat Phuntawuttiyanon, "*khon tai pha ha rang nok*" (Cliff-climbers searching for birds' nests), *Sarakadee Magazine*, pp. 69–81.
64. Thin Rueangchuai. Interview, 11 April 2002.
65. Prayoon Chamnina. Interview, 2 October 2002.
66. Donrochet. Interview, 23 October 2002.

67. Musa Damchuea. Interview, 21 October 2002.
68. Prayoon Chamnina. Interview, 2 October 2002.
69. Musa Damchuea. Interview, 21 October 2002.
70. Prayoon Chamnina. Interview, 2 October 2002.
71. Musa Damchuea. Interview, 21 October 2002.
72. Warasri Saengkrachang. "Study of physical characteristics, nutritional value and bioactive substances of white swiftlet nests in Thailand." Master of Science Thesis Department of Agro-Industry, Walailak University, 2011, pp. 96–97.
73. Nisa Phongchu. "The Biology of the Swiftlet Nest (*Collcalia fucifagus*)." Graduate School Thesis (Zoology), Kasetsart University, 1985.
74. "100 percent genuine bird's-nest drink, fact or fool. Research results, Mahidol University. Famous finished bird's-nest beverage includes only 1 percent genuine bird's-nest."
75. Uthit Khieokhachi. Interview, 14 May 2010.
76. Praeng Phetchamrat. Interview, 7 March 2003.
77. Prayoon Chamnina. Interview, 2 October 2002.
78. Bae Solae, Interview, 18 April 2003.
79. Musa Damchuea. Interview, 21 October 2002.
80. Suwet Ketkaeo, Interview, 29 October 2009.
81. ChaweewanDenphaibun, et al., op cit.,, p. 36.
82. Uthit Khieokhachi. Interview, 14 May 2010.
83. Anusit Rueangchuay, swallows island workers, Koh Si Koh Ha Islands, Chumphon villagers, Sathing Phra District, Songkhla Province. Interview, 30 December 2002.
84. Prayoon Chamnina. Interview, 2 October 2002.
85. Nisa Phongchu, op cit., p. 37.
86. Hib Jutharattanakun, swiftlet source owner, Pak Phanang District, Nakhon Si Thammarat Province, Thailand. Interview, 15 December 2002.
87. Sa-rup Ritchu, , op cit., p. 112.
88. Prasit Phanphisut, , op cit., p. 51.
89. Narathip Praphanphong, Krom Phra. op. cit., pp. 99–100.
90. Sa-ngop Songmeuang. Interview, 19 June 2003.
91. Sa-ngop Songmeuang. , op. cit., p. 8901.
92. Kittisak Nakmueang, op cit., pp. 145–46.
93. Ratchadaphon Sriphiban, op cit., pp. 155–216.
94. Sa-ngop Songmeuang. "op cit., p. 8901.
95. Ratchadaphon Sriphiban, op. cit., pp 193–95.
96. Ibid. pp. 216–34.
97. "The Bird's Nest Act, 1939," *Government Gazette*, Volume 56 (30 October 1939), p. 1353
98. Praeng Phetchamrat. Interview, 7 March 2003.
99. Prayoon Chamnina. Interview, 2 October 2002.
100. Bae Solae. Interview, 18 April 2003.
101. Rooney, Sarah, "Thailand's Bird Nest War," *South China Morning Post*, 20 January 2001, p. 1.
102. Anonymous. Interview, 8 August 2003.
103. Somphon Nunum. Interview, 8 August 2003.
104. Karia Chanina. Interview, 5 June 2003.
105. Editorial. "Report: The Unsolved Robbery of Bird Nests in Koh Si Koh Ha Islands". *Leam Thai*, 16–30 April 2003, p. 6.
106. Ibid.
107. Ibid.
108. Thanongsak Supakarn. "(The Chumphon Bird's nests, eyeing on abundant income)". *Khaosod Post*, 23 June 2003, p. 32.
109. Somphon Nunum. Interview, 8 August 2003.

110. "New round of Surat bird's-nest auction earns additional 46 million". *Matichon Daily*, 6 November 2003, p. 22.
111. Chanarong Sawatnaruenat, Pak Phanang Municipal Mayor. Interview, 30 December 2011.
112. Damrong Yotharak. Interview, 9 September 2004.
113. Anan Ganjanapan. *Community dimension: local thinking on rights and resource management*. Bangkok: The Thailand Research Fund, 2001, p. 219.
114. Hary Kusumo Nugroho. Interview, 23 February 2010.
115. Kittisak Nakmueang, op. cit., pp. 145–46.
116. Sa-ngop Songmeuang, op. cit., p. 66.
117. Ibid. p. 122.
118. Prayoon Chamnina. Interview, 2 October 2002.
119. Bourdieu, Pierre. op. cit., pp. 18, 20
120. Seri Siemmai, former bird's-nest collector and concessionaire who collected bird nests on Phetra Islands, Trang Province. Interview, 30 October 2009.
121. Chanya Watthanathawikul, et al. "Bird's Nest Beverage," *Department of Science Service* 46, 144, May 1997, p. 25.
122. Khuankhit Muennara. Interview, 3 April 2003.
123. Suradee Boonyanusat. "Factors affecting the migration and settlement of Germain's swiftlet in Pak Phanang Basin." Master's Degree Thesis in Urban and Regional Planning Program. Department of Regional Planning Faculty of Architecture, Chulalongkorn University, 2006.
124. Hameed Sultan Merican, "The 2007 Malaysian swiftlet Farming Industry Report," (n.p: 2007), p. 4.
125. "New career, clear ideas! The people of Bang Saphan District built the Swallow House," http://www.banRangNok.com/business11.php (9 April 2011).
126. "Scandalous! Fake birds' nests from Malaysia cheated on Chinese people repeatedly," op. cit.
127. Kamolsak Lertphaiboon, President of the Swift's Nest Business Association of Entrepreneurs Thailand. Interview, 8 June 2014.
128. Warasri Saengkrachang, op. cit., p. 1.
129. Ibid. p. 11.
130. "How willingly the 9-provinces committee to revise the swiftlet's nest concession system?" http://www.prachachat.net/news_detail.phpnewsid = 1349941709 & amp; grpid = & amp; catid = 00 & amp; su BCatid = 0000 (October, 2012).
131. Kamolsak Lertphaiboon. Interview, 8 June 2014.
132. Kasikorn Thai Research Center. op. cit., p. 3.
133. Ibid. p. 6.
134. Ibid.
135. Data from the Trang's and Phatthalung's Swiftlets Nests Tax Collecting Board of Directors, 2002–2014; Phakphong Sukontan. Interview, 19 June 2014; Kamolsak Lertphaibun., op. cit., p. 8; Seri Siemmai. Interview, 30 October 2009; Nammon Noima. "Alternative: Analysis on investment of edible-nest swiftlet farms in Banlaem District, Phetchaburi Province". Master of Business Administration Thesis, General Management Program, Phetchaburi Rajabhat University, 2007, p. 2; Chanya Watthanathawikul, et al. "Bird's Nest Beverage," *Department of Science Service* 46, 144, May 1997, p. 25; Regional News Team. "Flipping the legend of the dead bird's nest," The benefit of death on the Islands Plagued (Warfare)! *Matichon Daily*, May 22, 1994, p. 9; Pornthip Angkhapreechaset, "Edible bird's-nest farming," *Science and Technology*, vol. 15-1, (Jan–Apr 2000), p. 49.; Chumphon City Hall, "Chapter 0018/6788, Subject: Determination of selling price on each type of swiftlet bird's nest," 11 April 2001; *Anonymous*. Interview, 6 March 2003; Khuankhit Muennara. Interview, 3 April 2003; Anonymous. Interview, 9 July 2004; Suradee Boonyanusat, op. cit., p. 2; Kasikorn Thai Research Center., op. cit.; "New career, clear ideas! The people of Bang Saphan District built the swallow house.", op. cit.; "How willingly the 9-provinces committee to revise the swiftlet's nest concession system?", op. cit., October, 2012; "Malay–China buy building swallows nest," http://www.komchadluek.net (26 July, 2555) and KittipongSu https://www.facebook.com/profile.php?id=100002370482576 (June 4, 2013). .
136. Kamolsak Lertphaiboon. Interview, 8 June 2014.
137. Kamolsak Lertphaiboon. Interview, 8 June 2014.

138. Praeng Phetchamrat. Interview, 7 March 2003.
139. Prayoon Chamnina. Interview, 2 October 2002.
140. Suwet Ketkaeo. Interview, 29 October 2009.
141. Seri Siemmai. Interview, 30 October 2009.
142. Pattamawadee Phonukul Suzuki and Chon Bunnag, op. cit.
143. Suwet Ketkaeo. Interview, 29 October 2009.
144. Frank Pak. 12 October 2009.
145. Allen Pang. Product Quality Control Department, Home of Swallow Company. Hong Kong. Interview, 12 October 2009.
146. Seksan Prasertkul. "Nation state, ethnicity and modernity." In *The Article Academic Conference Concept Nationalism and Multiculturalism*. Chiang Mai: Regional Center for Social Sciences and Sustainable Development Faculty of Social Sciences, Chiang Mai University, 2008.
147. Suthep Sunthonphesat. *Anthropology and History*. Bangkok: Muang Boran Press, 2005, p. 186.
148. Tanabe, Shigeharu. *Rituals and practices in the Northern Thai Farmer Society*. Chiang Mai: Center for Ethnic Studies and Development, Faculty of Social Sciences, Chiang Mai University, 2012. pp. 33–34.
149. Anan Ganjanapan. op. cit., pp. 237–39.
150. Somchai Phakhaphatwiwat. "Thailand: Politics, Economy and Foreign Affairs after the Economic Crisis (2540–2550)". In Srida Sornsri, et al. *Southeast Asia: Politics, Economy and Foreign Affairs after the Economic Crisis (B.E. 2540–2550)*. Bangkok: Chulalongkorn University Printing House, 2009, p. 339.
151. Department of Curriculum. *Thai history: How to study and teach*. Bangkok: Ministry of Education, 2000. p. 265.
152. Department of Curriculum. *Analytical Thai History*. Bangkok: Ministry of Education, 2003, p. 180.
153. Anan Ganjanapan, op. cit., p. 249.
154. Uthit Khieokhachi. Interview, 14 May 2010.
155. Musa Damchuea. Interview, 21 October 2002. Suwet Ketkaeo and Seri Siemmai. Interview, 29 October 2009.
156. Nichkan Chin. op. cit.
157. Scott, James C. Cited by Anan Ganjanapan. op. cit., pp. 164, 167.
158. *Leam Thai* Editorial. "Report: The Unsolved Robbery of bird nests in Koh Si Koh Ha Islands", 16–30 April 2003, p. 6.
159. Scott, James C. Cited by Pathom Hongsuwan. op. cit., p. 976.

Notes to Chapter 6

1. Wiwat Phuntawuttiyanon. op. cit., p. 77.
2. Sunalinee Nikrothanon, op. cit., p. 153.
3. Valli, Eric and Diane Summers. *Shadow Hunters: The Nest Gatherers of Tiger Cave*. Singapore: Sun Tree Publishing, 1990., p. 4–12.
4. Valli, Eric and Diane Summers, op. cit., pp. 4–12.
5. Earl of Cranbrook. op. cit., p. 33.
6. Passakit Wannawibun. "Bird's nest: Chinese medicine perspective," *Mor Chaoban Magazine*, Vol 389, September, 2011.
7. Valli, Eric and Diane Summers, op. cit., pp. 4–12.
8. Ibid.
9. Chan Shun-Wan. Interview, 13 October 2009.
10. Ng Kar Man. Interview, 13 October 2009.
11. Valli, Eric and Diane Summers, op. cit., pp. 4–12.
12. Chan Shun-Wan. Interview, 13 October 2009.
13. Cheung Hon-yeung, "Comprehensive authenticity verification system for the quality assurance of edible birds' nests," http://qualityalchemist.blogspot.com/2012_10_01_archive.html (August 15, 2013).

14. Frank Pak. Interview, 12 October 2009.
15. Allen Pang. Interview, 12 October 2009.
16. Ismail Mohamed Yusoff, op. cit., p. 6.
17. Stella Blade, Director of Home of Swallows Limited. Interview, 12 October 2009.
18. Allen Pang. Interview, 12 October 2009.
19. Allen Pang. Interview, 12 October 2009.
20. Frank Pak. Interview, 12 October 2009.
21. Allen Pang. Interview, 12 October 2009.
22. Frank Pak. Interview, 12 October 2009. Chan Shun-Wan. Interview, 13 October 2009.
23. Allen Pang. Interview, 12 October 2009.
24. MacKay, Jeanine. "China: Swiftlets and Edible Birds' Nests", www.crystalswiftlets.com/ China_-_Swiftlets_and_Edible_Birds_Nests.doc-, (26 October 2009).
25. Lau, Amy S. M. and David S. Melville, op. cit., p. 10.
26. Lim Chan Koon and Earl of Cranbrook. op. cit., p. 97.
27. Chan Shun-Wan, "Review of Scientific Research on Edible Bird's Nest", http://www.hkfsta.com.hk/articles/special/article7.htm, (11 September 2009).
28. Marshall, Andrew. "Natural Bird Bonanza.", *TIME*, 20 July 2009, p. 42.
29. Allen Pang. Interview, 12 October 2009.
30. Frank Pak. Interview, 12 October 2009.
31. http://www.cgcc.org.hk (18 November 2015).
32. Allen Pang. Interview, 12 October 2009.
33. "Nitrites in Blood-red Bird's Nest," http://www.cfs.gov.hk/english/multimedia/multimedia_pub/multimedia_pub_fsf_62_04.html (December, 2012).
34. Cantor, Joanna G. et al, eds., *Hong Kong*, 21st ed. New York: Fodor's Travel Publication, 2009, p. 365..
35. http://www.in1guide.com, (10 November 2015).
36. Park, Thesese "Bird Nest Soup, Anyone?", http://www.thesesepark.com>bird_nest_soup, (26 September 2009).
37. Cantor, Joanna G. et al, op. cit., p. 368.
38. Frank Pak. Interview, 12 October 2009.
39. Anonymous. Interview, 12 October 2009.
40. Hary Kusumo Nugroho. Interview, 23 February 2010.
41. Ratchadaphorn Sriphiban, op. cit., p. 24.
42. "Scandal! Fake birds' nests from Malaysia repeatedly cheating Chinese people," *ViewNews*.aspx?NewsID=9540000103387&fb_source=message (August, 2011).
43. "Nitrites in Blood-red Bird's Nest," http://www.cfs.gov.hk/english/multimedia/multimedia_pub/multimedia_pub_fsf_62_04.html (December, 2012).
44. "Blood Nest is very safe to be consumed," http://www.naturalnest.com/articles (December, 2012).
45. Ng Alexander, https://www.facebook.com/ng.alexander.589 (9 December 2012).
46. Frank Pak. Interview, 12 October 2009.
47. Frank Pak. Interview, 12 October 2009.
48. Frank Pak. Interview, 12 October 2009.
49. Frank Pak. Interview, 12 October 2009.
50. Allen Pang. Interview, 12 October 2009.
51. Frank Pak. Interview, 12 October 2009.
52. Allen Pang. Interview, 12 October 2009.
53. Bussakorn Lee, op. cit.
54. Meda on returns from swiftlet farming," http://biz.thestar.com.my/news/story.asp?file=/2009/11/13/business/5102837 (1 December 2012).
55. Kasem Jandam, "Bird's Nest Consumption: In the Eastern World Culture," *Documents for the Seminar on Research Culture No. 3*, National Cultural Conference, Bangkok Chada Hotel Bangkok, Department of Cultural Promotion, Ministry of Culture, 11 July, 2013.

REFERENCES

Thai

Akkaraphong Khamkhun. "The History and Philippines in a History Education Book of Philippines for the High School Students." *Thammasat Archives Journal*, 12, June 2008–May 2009.
อัครพงษ์ ค่ำคูณ. "ประวัติศาสตร์และชาติฟิลิปปินส์ในหนังสือเรียนประวัติศาสตร์ ชนชาติฟิลิปปินส์สำหรับชั้นมัธยมศึกษาตอนปลาย." *จุลสารหอจดหมายเหตุธรรมศาสตร์*.

Anan Ganjanapan. "Community Rights in Development." *The Community Dimension: Local Way of Thinking Regarding Rights, Power and Natural Resource Management.* Bangkok: Thailand Research Fund, 2001.
อานันท์ กาญจนพันธุ์. "พหุวัฒนธรรมในบริบทของการเปลี่ยนผ่านทางสังคมและวัฒนธรรม." *บทความแนวคิดประชุมวิชาการชาตินิยมกับพหุวัฒนธรรม*.

———. "Multiculturalism in the Context of Social and Cultural Transition." In *Nation State and Ethnicity*. Edited by Sadtawat Satitphiansiri. Chiang Mai: Regional Center for Social Science and Sustainable Development, Faculty of Social Sciences, Chiang Mai University, 2008, pp. 5–68.
อานันท์ กาญจนพันธุ์. *มิติชุมชน: วิธีคิดท้องถิ่นว่าด้วยสิทธิ อำนาจ และการจัดการทรัพยากร*.

Andaya, Barbara Watson and Leonard Y. Andaya. *A History of Malaysia.* Translated by Pannee Chatpholrak. Bangkok: Foundation for Social Sciences and Humanities Textbook Project, 2006.
พรรณี ฉัตรพลรักษ์, แปล. *ประวัติศาสตร์มาเลเซีย*.

Apinya Fuengfusakul. *Religious Anthropology: Basic Concepts and Theoretical Arguments.* Chiang Mai: Department of Sociology and Anthropology, Faculty of Social Sciences, Chiang Mai University, 2008.
อภิญญา เฟื่องฟูสกุล. *มานุษยวิทยาศาสนา: แนวคิดพื้นฐานและข้อถกเถียงทางทฤษฎี*.

Banchong Wongwichian *et al. Archeology History of Nakhon Si Thammarat.* Bangkok: Fine Arts Department, n.d.
บรรจง วงศ์วิเชียร และคณะ. *ประวัติศาสตร์ โบราณคดี นครศรีธรรมราช*.

"'Brand's golden bird's nest sold out during Mother's Day week, 3.5 million baht." *Thansettakij Daily,* August 6–8, 2009.
"กำลังซื้อเทศกาลวันแม่คึกคัก แบรนด์รังนกเนื้อทองขายเกลี้ยงสัปดาห์เดียว 3.5 ล้าน." *หนังสือพิมพ์ฐานเศรษฐกิจ*.

Chanya Watthanathawikul *et al.* "Bird's-Nest Beverage." *Department of Science Service,* 46(144), May 1997.
จรรยา วัฒนทวีกุล และคณะ. "เครื่องดื่มรังนกสำเร็จรูป" *กรมวิทยาศาสตร์บริการ*.

Chaweewan Denpaiboon *et al.* "Case Study of Swiftlets at Pak Phanang." *Nakhon Si Thammarat Journal,* 34(3), March 2004.
ฉวีวรรณ เด่นไพบูลย์ และคณะ. การศึกษาผลกระทบจากการสร้างเรือนนกที่มีต่อชุมชนเมือง: กรณีศึกษาเทศบาลเมืองปากพนังจังหวัดนครศรีธรรมราช. *สารนครศรีธรรมราช*.

Chayachoke Chulasiriwongs. "The competition between UMNO and PAS to Compete for the People (UMNO-PAS Rivalry and Malay Electorate)." Paper presented at a Seminar on "The Story of Malaysia after the Mahathir Era," Regional Studies Program, School of Liberal Art, Grand Park Hotel, Mueang District, Nakhon Si Thammarat Province, October 18–19, 2003.
ชัยโชค จุลศิริวงศ์. "การแข่งขันกันระหว่างอัมโนกับพาสเพื่อช่วงชิงประชาชน (UMNO-PAS Rivalry and Malay Electorate)." ใน เอกสารประกอบการสัมมนาเรื่อง *มาเลเซียหลังยุคมหาเธร์*.

Chumphon City Hall, "Chapter 0018/6788, Subject: Determination of selling price on each type of swiftlet bird's nest," 11 April 2001.
ศาลากลางจังหวัดชุมพร. หนังสือที่ ชพ 0018/6788 เรื่องการกำหนดอัตราราคาจำหน่ายรังนกอีแอ่นแต่ละชนิด.

Dararat Mattariganond. *Vietnamese History Textbook in Elementary School.* Bangkok: Muang Boran, 2007.
ดารารัตน์ เมตตาริกานนท์. *ประวัติศาสตร์เวียดนามในแบบเรียนชั้นประถม*.

Decho Boonchochuai. "Bird Nest Taxes in Chumphon Province." In *Southern Thai Culture Encyclopedia*, vol. 18, 1999, p. 8897.
เดโช บุญช่วย. "อากรรังนกเมืองมณฑลชุมพร" ใน *สารานุกรมวัฒนธรรมไทย ภาคใต้*.

Department of Curriculum. *Thai History: How to Study and Teach*. Bangkok: Ministry of Education, 2000.
กรมวิชาการ กระทรวงศึกษาธิการ. *คู่มือการจัดกิจกรรมการเรียนการสอนประวัติศาสตร์ "ประวัติศาสตร์ไทย: จะเรียนจะสอนกันอย่างไร"*.

"The legend of the deadly birds' nests: interest v.s. death on war-zone Island.!" *Matichon Daily*, May 22, 1994.
"พลิกตำนาน 'รังนกมรณะ' ผลประโยชน์กับความตายบนหมู่เกาะมีคู่สัญญี!" *มติชนรายวัน*.

Jongjit Attayukti, ed. *Malaysia*. Bangkok: Window on The World Publishing, 2004.
จงจิต อรรถยุกติ, บรรณาธิการ. *มาเลเซีย*.

Kamolsak Lertphaibun. *Nok An: The Open Secret*. Nakhon Si Thammarat: Kwan Mui Co. Ltd., 2008.
กมลศักดิ์ เลิศไพบูลย์. *นกแอ่น: ความลับที่ต้องเปิด*.

Kasem Jandam. "Bird's Nest Consumption in the Eastern World Culture." Paper presented at the National Cultural Conference "Research Culture No. 3," Cha Da Hotel Bangkok, Department of Cultural Promotion, Ministry of Culture, July 11, 2013.
เกษม จันทร์ดำ. "การบริโภครังนกแอ่นในวัฒนธรรมโลกตะวันออก." เอกสารประกอบการสัมมนาวัฒนธรรมวิจัยครั้งที่ 3 การประชุมวิชาการทางวัฒนธรรมระดับชาติ, โรงแรมบางกอกชฎา กรุงเทพฯ กรมส่งเสริมวัฒนธรรม กระทรวงวัฒนธรรม. 11 กรกฎาคม 2013.

―――. *Swiftlet Nest: Power, Conflict and Wealth*. Bangkok: Mahasarakham University Press, 2007.
เกษม จันทร์ดำ. *รังนกนางแอ่น: อำนาจ ความขัดแย้ง และความมั่งคั่ง*.

Kasikorn Thai Research Center. "Swifts Nest: East Carvia … White Gold of the Sea." *Economic Analysis Business Brief*, 13, July 2007.
ศูนย์วิจัยกสิกรไทย. "รังนกแอ่น: คาร์เวียตะวันออก … ทองคำขาวแห่งท้องทะเล".

Kittisak Nakmueang. "The National Integration in Five Southern Border Provinces." Project for the MA Program in Political Science, Thammasat University, 1995.
กิตติศักดิ์ นาคเมือง. "การบูรณาการชาติในห้าจังหวัดชายแดนภาคใต้." สารนิพนธ์รัฐศาสตรมหาบัณฑิต, มหาวิทยาลัยธรรมศาสตร์.

"Livestock push forward the export of house bird's nest along with cave bird's nest." *Thairath*, August 13, 2014.
"ปศุสัตว์ดันรังนกบ้านส่งออกตีคู่รังนกถ้ำ." *ไทยรัฐ*.

Malika Pongparit, ed. *Indonesia*. Bangkok: Window on The World Publishing, 2006.
มัลลิกา พงศ์ปริตร, บรรณาธิการ. *อินโดนีเซีย*.

Najmee Madmarn and Numan Hayimasae. "Discourse on the Nation, the Creation of the Nation and the Heroes of Malaysia: Study through the History of Secondary Education." *TRF Forum*, 2(5), January–March 2011.
นัจมีย์ หมัดหมาน และ นุมาน ทะยีมะแซ. "วาทกรรมเรื่องของชาติ การสร้างชาติ และวีรบุรุษของมาเลเซีย: ศึกษาผ่านแบบเรียนประวัติศาสตร์ระดับมัธยมศึกษา".

Nammon Noima. "Alternative: Analysis on investment of edible-nest swiftlet farms in Banlaem District, Phetchaburi Province". Master of Business Administration Thesis General Management Program, Phetchaburi Rajabhat University, 2007, p. 2.
น้ำมนต์ น้อยมา. "การวิเคราะห์การลงทุนเลี้ยงนกแอ่นของผู้ประกอบการ ในอำเภอบ้านแหลม จังหวัดเพชรบุรี," วิทยานิพนธ์บริหารธุรกิจมหาบัณฑิต สาขาวิชาการจัดการทั่วไป, มหาวิทยาลัยราชภัฏเพชรบุรี.

Nantawan Yotphichit. "Dr. Mahathir and His Role in National Development." Paper presented at a Seminar on "The Story of Malaysia after the Mahathir Era," Regional Studies Program, School of Liberal Art, Grand Park Hotel, Mueang District, Nakhon Si Thammarat Province, October 18–19, 2003.
นันทวรรณ ยอดพิจิตร, "ดร. มหาเธร์กับบทบาทในการพัฒนาประเทศ," ใน เอกสารประกอบการสัมมนาเรื่อง *มาเลเซียหลังยุคมหาเธร์*, โครงการภูมิภาคศึกษาสำนักวิชาศิลปศาสตร์ มหาวิทยาลัยวลัยลักษณ์.

Narathip Praphanphong, Krom Phra. *La Loubère Annals* (Archives). Bangkok: Khurusapha Printing, 1962.
นราธิปประพันธ์พงศ์, กรมพระ. *จดหมายเหตุลาลูแบร์*.

Narisa Chakrabongse. *Land and Forest*. Bangkok: Green World Foundation and Ford Foundation, n.d.
นริศรา จักรพงษ์. *ดินและป่าไม้*.

REFERENCES

Narisa Chakrabongse. *Water*. Bangkok: Green World Foundation and Boonrawd Brewery Co. Ltd., n.d.
นริศรา จักรพงษ์. *น้ำ*.

Narong Nunthong. "Administration of Nakhon Si Thammarat Districts in Rattanakosin Period." In *Take a Tour through Nakhon Si Thammarat, Historical City Over 1000 Years*. Bangkok: DLS Printing, 1991.
ณรงค์ นุ่นทอง. "การจัดการปกครองหัวเมืองนครศรีธรรมราชในสมัยกรุงรัตนโกสินทร์." ใน *นำชมนครศรีธรรมราช เมืองประวัติศาสตร์กว่า 1000 ปี*.

Natthaphat Chantavichit and Saengchan Traikasem, eds. *Take a Tour at the Museum National, Nakhon Si Thammarat*. Bangkok: Rung Sin Printing, 1977, rev. ed. 2000.
ณัฏฐภัทร จันทวิช และ แสงจันทร์ ไตรเกษม, บรรณาธิการ. *นำชมพิพิธภัณฑสถานแห่งชาตินครศรีธรรมราช*.

"New round of Surat bird's nest auction earns an additional 46 million". *Matichon Daily*, November 6, 2003.
"ประมูลรังนกสุราษฎร์ฯ รอบใหม่ได้เงินเพิ่ม 46 ล.", *มติชนรายวัน*.

Nisa Phongchu. "The Biology of the Swiftlet Nest (*Collcalia fucifaga*)." Graduate School thesis (Zoology), Kasetsart University, 1985.
นิสา พงศ์ชู. "ชีววิทยาของนกนางแอ่นกินรัง (*Collcalia fucifaga*)." วิทยานิพนธ์บัณฑิตวิทยาลัย (สัตววิทยา), มหาวิทยาลัยเกษตรศาสตร์.

Nuanchan Kkampang, ed. *Philippines*. Bangkok: Windows on the World Publishing, 2007.
นวลจันทร์ คำปังสุ์, บรรณาธิการ. *ฟิลิปปินส์*.

O-phat Khobkhet. "The Edible-nest Swiftlet." *The Royal Society Newsletter*, March 2001.
โอภาส ขอบเขตต์. "นกแอ่นกินรัง (Edible-nest Swiftlet)." จดหมายข่าวราชบัณฑิตยสถาน.

Pakhawat Photinak. "Ecology of the White-Rumped Germain's Swiftlet (*Aerodramus germani Oustalet*) in Koh Chang National Park, Trat Province." MSc thesis (Forest Biology), Kasetsart University, 2004.
ภควัต โพธินาค. "นิเวศวิทยาบางประการของนกแอ่นกินรังตะโพกขาว (*Collocalia germani Oustalet*) ในอุทยานแห่งชาติหมู่เกาะช้าง จังหวัดตราด." วิทยานิพนธ์ปริญญาวิทยาศาสตรมหาบัณฑิต (ชีววิทยาป่าไม้), มหาวิทยาลัยเกษตรศาสตร์.

Passakit Wannawibun. "Bird's Nest: Chinese Medicine Viewpoint." *Mor Chaoban Journal*, September 2011.
ภาสกิจ วัณนาวิบูล. "รังนก ทรรศนะแพทย์แผนจีน." นิตยสารหมอชาวบ้าน.

Patcharin Suanthitapanya. *Malaysia: Unity and Education*. Bangkok: Thailand Research Fund, 1998.
พัชรินทร์ สวนฐิตะปัญญา. *มาเลเซีย: เอกภาพ กับการศึกษา*.

Pathom Hongsuwan. "Mekong Giant Fish: The Sacred Food and the Competition of Symbolic Meaning in the Community in Thai-Laos Borders." In *Documents of the 9th Annual Humanities Seminar, "Foods and Eating: Political Morals about Foods and Eating No. 3."* Bangkok: Princess Maha Chakri Sirindhorn Anthropology Centre, 2010.
ปฐม หงส์สุวรรณ. "ปลาบึก: อาหารศักดิ์สิทธิ์กับการช่วงชิงความหมายในชุมชนชายแดนไทย-ลาว". ใน *เอกสารประกอบการประชุมประจำปี ทางมานุษยวิทยา ครั้งที่ 9 ปาก-ท้อง และของกิน: จริยธรรมและการเมืองเรื่องอาหารการกิน เล่ม 3*. กรุงเทพฯ: ศูนย์มานุษยวิทยาสิรินธร (องค์การมหาชน).

Phuwadon Songprasert. *Indonesia: The Past and Present*. Bangkok: Chulalongkorn University Press, 2004.
ภูวดล ทรงประเสริฐ. *อินโดนีเซีย: อดีตและปัจจุบัน*.

Pinkaew Laungaramsri. "The Awkwardness of the Ethnic Conception." *Social Sciences*, 19(1), 2007.
ปิ่นแก้ว เหลืองอร่ามศรี. "ความอิหลักอิเหลื่อของมโนทัศน์ ชาติพันธุ์". วารสารสังคมศาสตร์.

Pisit Charoenwongsa. *Analytical Thai History*. Bangkok: Khurusapha Ladphrao Printing, 2003.
พิสิฐ เจริญวงศ์. *ประวัติศาสตร์ไทยเชิงวิเคราะห์*.

Pornthip Angkhapreechaset, "Edible bird's-nest farming," *Science and Technology*, vol. 15-1, (Jan–Apr 2000), p. 49.
พรทิพย์ อังคปรีชาเศรษฐ์. "การทำฟาร์มนกแอ่นกินรัง," วิทยาศาสตร์และเทคโนโลยี.

Praphin Manomaiviboon, trans. and ed. *Chinese Medicine*. Bangkok: Reader's Digest (Thailand) Co. Ltd., 1998.
ประพิณ มโนมัยวิบูลย์ (บรรณาธิการแปล). *อาหารเครื่องยาจีน*.

Prasit Phunphisut *et al.* "Following King Rama V's Visit to Koh Si Koh Ha in Rattanakosin era 108." In *Commemoration of Enshrining a Royal Monument*, February 22, 1996, Pak Phayun District, Phatthalung Province. Phatthalung: n.p., 1996.
ประสิทธิ์ พรรณพิสุทธิ์ และคณะ. "ตามรอยประวัติศาสตร์รัชกาลที่ 5 เสด็จประพาสเกาะสี่ เกาะห้า ร.ศ. 108" ใน *อนุสรณ์การประดิษฐาน พระบรมราชานุสาวรีย์*.

Prateep Duengkae. "Exposing the Secrets of White Gold from Swiftlets." *Advanced Thailand Geographic*, January 2003.
ประทีป ด้วงแค. "ไขความลับของทองคำขาวจากนกแอ่น." *แอดวานซ์ไทยแลนด์จีโอกราฟฟิค*.

Ratchadaphon Sriphiban. "The Importance of Bird's Nests to the Economy in Southern Thailand (b.e. 2310-2482)." MA thesis, Thammasat University, 1999.
รัชดาพร ศรีภิบาล. "ความสำคัญของรังนกต่อเศรษฐกิจในภาคใต้ของประเทศไทย (พ.ศ. 2310-2482)." วิทยานิพนธ์ศิลปศาสตรมหาบัณฑิต มหาวิทยาลัยธรรมศาสตร์.

Sa-ngop Songmeaung. *Research Report on Songkhla City Development in the Thonburi and Early Rattanakosin Period b.e. 2310-2444*. Songkhla: Srinakharinwirot University, 1980.
สงบ ส่งเมือง. รายงานการวิจัยเรื่อง การพัฒนาหัวเมืองสงขลา ในสมัยกรุงธนบุรีและสมัยรัตนโกสินทร์ตอนต้น (พ.ศ. 2310-2444). สงขลา: มหาวิทยาลัยศรีนครินทรวิโรฒ สงขลา.

Sa-rup Ritchu, ed. *Art Source Registration in Phatthalung Province*. Phatthalung: Phatthalung Cultural Center, Satri Phatthalung School, 1998.
สารูป ฤทธิ์ชู, บรรณาธิการ. *ทะเบียนแหล่งศิลปกรรมในจังหวัดพัทลุง*. พัทลุง: ศูนย์วัฒนธรรมจังหวัดพัทลุง โรงเรียนสตรีพัทลุง.

Santisuk Sophonsiri, referred to as "Viriyanan", trans. *Collection of "Nam Cao" Short Story*. Bangkok: Sathienkoset-Nakaprathip Foundation, 1986.
สันติสุข โสภณสิริ, อ้างถึงใน "วิริยนันท์", ผู้แปล. *รวมเรื่องสั้นของ "นามกาว"*.

Seksan Prasertkul. "Nation State, Ethnicity and Modernity." Paper presented at the Conference on "Nationalism and Cultural Pluralism" (in Thai). Chiang Mai: Regional Center for Social Science and Sustainable Development, Faculty of Social Sciences, Chiang Mai University, December 22-23, 2008.
เสกสรรค์ ประเสริฐกุล. "รัฐชาติ ชาติพันธุ์ และความทันสมัย." ในบทความ แนวคิด ประชุมวิชาการ ชาตินิยมกับพหุวัฒนธรรม.

Somchai Phakhaphatwiwat. "Thailand: Politics, Economy and Foreign Affairs after the Economic Crisis (2540-2550)." In Srida Sornsri *et al.*, *Southeast Asia: Politics, Economy and Foreign Affairs after the Economic Crisis (b.e. 2540-2550)*. Bangkok: Chulalongkorn University Printing House, 2009.
สมชาย ภคภาสน์วิวัฒน์. "ประเทศไทย: การเมือง เศรษฐกิจ และการต่างประเทศหลังวิกฤตเศรษฐกิจ (พ.ศ. 2540-2550)." ใน สีดา สอนศรี และคณะ. *เอเชียตะวันออกเฉียงใต้: การเมือง เศรษฐกิจและการต่างประเทศหลังวิกฤตเศรษฐกิจ (พ.ศ. 2540-2550)*.

Sopharat Charusombat. *Enviromental Management in Southeast Asia*. Bangkok: Faculty of Political Science, Thammasat University and Kobfai Publishing, 2003.
โสภารัตน์ จารุสมบัติ. *การจัดการทรัพยากรธรรมชาติและสิ่งแวดล้อมในเอเชียตะวันออกเฉียงใต้*.

Srida Sornsri. "Philippines: Politics Economic and Foreign Politics after the Economic Crisis (2540-2550)." In Srida Sornsri *et al.*, *Southeast Asia: Politics, Economy and Foreign Affairs after the Economic Crisis (b.e. 2540-2550)*. Bangkok: Chulalongkorn University Printing House, 2009.
สีดา สอนศรี. "ฟิลิปปินส์: การเมือง เศรษฐกิจ และการต่างประเทศหลังวิกฤตเศรษฐกิจ (พ.ศ. 2540-2550)" ใน สีดา สอนศรี และคณะ, *เอเชียตะวันออกเฉียงใต้: การเมือง เศรษฐกิจและการต่างประเทศหลังวิกฤตเศรษฐกิจ (พ.ศ. 2540-2550)*.

———. *The Economic and Political Development of the Philippines*. Bangkok: Kobfai Publishing, 2002.
สีดา สอนศรี. *การพัฒนาเศรษฐกิจการเมืองของประเทศฟิลิปปินส์*.

Sriprapha Petchrameesee. *Economic and Political Development in Vietnam*. Bangkok: Kobfai Publishing, 1999.
ศรีประภา เพชรมีศรี. *การพัฒนาเศรษฐกิจและการเมืองเวียดนาม*.

Suradee Boonyanusat. "Factors Affecting the Migration and Settlement of Germain's Swiftlet in Pak Phanang Basin." MA thesis, Urban and Regional Planning Program, Department of Regional Planning, Faculty of Architecture, Chulalongkorn University, 2006.
สุรดี บุญญานุศาสน์. "ปัจจัยที่มีผลต่อการอพยพและการตั้งถิ่นฐานของนกแอ่นกินรัง ในลุ่มน้ำปากพนัง." วิทยานิพนธ์หลักสูตรปริญญาการ วางแผนภาคและเมืองมหาบัณฑิต สาขาวิชาการวางแผนภาค คณะสถาปัตยกรรมศาสตร์, จุฬาลงกรณ์มหาวิทยาลัย.

REFERENCES

Suthep Sunthonphesat. *Anthropology and History*. Bangkok: Muang Boran Press, 2005.
สุเทพ สุนทรเภสัช. มานุษยวิทยากับประวัติศาสตร์.

Suthiwong Phongphaiboon, Dilok Wuttiphanich and Prasit Chinnakan. *Jin Thaksin: Vithi lae Phalang*. Bangkok: Thailand Research Fund, 2001.
สุธิวงศ์ พงศ์ไพบูลย์, ดิลก วุฒิพาณิชย์ และ ประสิทธิ์ ชิณการณ์. จีนทักษิณ: วิถีและพลัง.

"Swiftlet's Nest Duties Act, B.E. 2482." *The Government Gazette*, vol. 56, October 30, 2482: 1353.
"พระราชบัญญัติอากรรังนกอีแอ่น พุทธศักราช 2482." ราชกิจจานุเบกษา เล่ม 56.

Tanabe, Shigeharu. *Rituals and Practices in the Northern Thai Farmer Society*. Chiang Mai: Center for Ethnic Studies and Development, Faculty of Social Sciences, Chiang Mai University, 2012.
ชิเกฮารุ ทานาเบ. พิธีกรรมและปฏิบัติการในสังคมชาวนาภาคเหนือของประเทศไทย.

Techniques for Raising Swifts. n.p., n.d.
เทคนิคการเลี้ยงนกแอ่น. ม.ป.ท., ม.ป.ป.

Thanongsak Supakarn. "The Chumphon Bird's Nest: Keeping an Eye on the Beautiful Income." *Khaosod*, June 23, 2003, p. 32.
ทนงศักดิ์ ศุภการ. "รังนกอีแอ่นชุมพร รายได้งามที่น่าจับตามอง." ข่าวสด.

Thanyathip Sripana, "Vietnam: Politics, Economy and Foreign Affairs after the Economic Crisis (2540–2550)." In Srida Sornsri *et al.*, *Southeast Asia: Politics, Economy and Foreign Affairs after the Economic Crisis (b.e. 2540–2550)*. Bangkok: Chulalongkorn University Printing House, 2009.
ธัญญาทิพย์ ศรีพนา. "เวียดนาม: การเมือง เศรษฐกิจ และการต่างประเทศหลังวิกฤต เศรษฐกิจ (พ.ศ. 2540-2550)." ใน สีดา สอนศรี และคณะ. เอเชียตะวันออกเฉียงใต้: การเมือง เศรษฐกิจและการต่างประเทศหลังวิกฤตเศรษฐกิจ (พ.ศ. 2540-2550).

"The Unsolved Robbery of Bird Nests in Koh Si Koh Ha Islands." *Leam Thai*, April 16–30, 2003.
"รายงาน: ปัญหาโจรลักรังนกที่หมู่เกาะสี่เกาะห้า ฤๅหมดปัญญาหาหนทางแก้ไข." แหลมไทย.

Tuangrat Pho-thiang. *Report on Research Progress of Ecology and Distribution Species of Aerodramus Fuciphaga*. Bangkok: Department of National Parks, Wildlife and Plant Conservation, 2004.
ตวงรัตน์ โพธิ์เที่ยง. รายงานความก้าวหน้างานวิจัยเรื่อง นิเวศวิทยาและการกระจายพันธุ์ของนกแอ่นกินรัง (Collocalia fuciphaga). กรุงเทพฯ: กรมอุทยานแห่งชาติสัตว์ป่าและพันธุ์พืช.

Vitaya Sujaritthanarak, "Indonesia: Political, Economic and Foreign Affairs after Economic Crisis (2540–2550)." In Srida Sornsri *et al.*, *Southeast Asia: Politics, Economy and Foreign Affairs after the Economic Crisis (b.e. 2540–2550)*. Bangkok: Chulalongkorn University Printing House, 2009.
วิทยา สุจริตธนารักษ์. "อินโดนีเซีย: การเมือง เศรษฐกิจ และการต่างประเทศหลังวิกฤตเศรษฐกิจ (พ.ศ. 2540-2550)." ใน สีดา สอนศรี และคณะ. เอเชียตะวันออกเฉียงใต้: การเมือง เศรษฐกิจและการต่างประเทศหลังวิกฤตเศรษฐกิจ (พ.ศ. 2540-2550).

Wanna Alitrakul. "Feasibility Study on a New Tourist Attraction: A Case Study of Homes That Become Bird Nest Houses in Pattani Province." MA term paper (Social Development), National Institute of Development Administration, 2004.
วรรณา อาลีตระกูล. "การศึกษาความเป็นไปได้ในการพัฒนาแหล่งท่องเที่ยวใหม่: ศึกษากรณีโครงการบ้านคนกลายเป็นบ้านนกจังหวัดปัตตานี." ภาคนิพนธ์ ศิลปศาสตรมหาบัณฑิต (พัฒนาสังคม), สถาบันบัณฑิตพัฒนบริหารศาสตร์.

Warasri Saengkrachang. "Study of Physical Characteristics, Nutritional Value and Bioactive Substances of White Swiftlet Nests in Thailand." MSc thesis, Department of Agro-Industry, Walailak University, 2011.
วราศรี แสงกระจ่าง. "การศึกษาลักษณะทางกายภาพ คุณค่าทางโภชนาการ และสารออกฤทธิ์ทางชีวภาพ ของรังนกนางแอ่นชนิดรังสีขาวในประเทศไทย." วิทยานิพนธ์ปริญญาวิทยาศาสตรมหาบัณฑิต สาขาวิชาอุตสาหกรรมเกษตร, มหาวิทยาลัยวลัยลักษณ์.

Wit Thiengburanathum. *Dictionary of Birds in Thailand*. Bangkok: Odeon Store, 1989.
วิทย์ เที่ยงบูรณธรรม. พจนานุกรมนกในเมืองไทย.

Wiwat Phuntawuttiyanon. "Cliff-Climbing searching for Birds' Nests." *Sarakadee*, January 1992, pp. 69–81.
วิวัฒน์ พันธวุฒิยานนท์. "คนไต่ผาหารังนก." สารคดี.

Wutthi Wutthithammawet. *Encyclopedia of Thai Herbs and Medicinal Plants for Therapeutic Use*. Bangkok: Odeon Store, 1997.
วุฒิ วุฒิธรรมเวช. สารานุกรมสมุนไพร รวมหลักเภสัชกรรมไทย.

Engish and other languages

Arief Budiman dan TIM penulis PS. *Budidaya Dan Bisnis Sarang Walet*. Jakarta: Penebar Swadaya, 2008.
Biology Teachers Association–BIOTA Philippines. "Species of the Month," *Biota Filipina*, June–July 2005.
Bourdieu, Pierre. *Raisons pratiques. Sur la theorie de l'action (Economy of Symbolic Property)*. Translated by Chanida Sa-ngiam-phaisan. Bangkok: Kobfai Publishing, 2007.
Calcari, Meaghan E. "Indigenous Marine Tenure in a Common-pool Framework: A Philippine Case Study." Project Submitted in Partial Fulfillment of the Requirements for the Master of Environmental Management Degree, Nicholas School of the Environment, Duke University, 2004.
Cantor, Joanna G., Shannon Kelly and Josh McIlvain, eds. *Hong Kong*, 21st ed. New York: Fodor's Travel Publication, 2009.
Chan, Zora et al. "No Swiftlet Farms in Shophouses Says Naroden." *The Borneo Post*, November 7, 2008.
Chin Mui Yoon. "Swift Fortunes Await." *The Star Online*, August 23, 2009.
Coronel, Sheila S. *Memory of Dances*. Manila: Philippine Center for Investigative Journalism, 2002.
Delaney, Daniel Vincent dan Fakultas Ilmu. *Budidaya Sarang Burung Walet Di Jawa Timur*. Malang: Universitas Muhammadiyah Malang, 2008.
Department of Environment and Natural Resources-Biodiversity Management Bureau and United Nations Development Program. *Expanding and Diversifying the National System of Terrestrial Protected Areas in the Philippines*, no. 3530, 2009.
Earl of Cranbrook. "Swiftlets with Edible Nests: Past and Future." Introduction to *Exposing the Billion-Dollar Bird's-nest Business World*, edited by Patrick Jori and Jirawat Saengthong. Nakhon Si Thammarat: Research Fund and Regional Project Study Bureau, Art Academic Office, Walailak University, 2007.
"EBN palsu turut jadi ancaman." *Mega Utusan Malaysia*, May 7, 2012, p. 10.
Echols, John M. and Hassan Shadily. *Kamus Indonesia Inggris*. Jakarta: Gramedia Pustaka Utama, 2003.
Giles, Francis H. "A Description of the Swifts (*Collocalia Francica* and *Collocalia Innominata*), The Birds Which Build Edible Nests." Translated by Sunalini Nikonthanon for the Commemoration of the Royal Funeral Ceremony of Luang Sawatdisansatphutthi (Sawat Sumit), Wat That Thong, Bangkok, February 25, 1973.
Goloubinoff, Marina. "Swiftlets, Edible Birds' Nests." In *Riches of the Forest: Food, Spices, Crafts and Resins of Asia*. Edited by Citlalli Lopez and Patricia Stanley. Desa Putra: Center for International Forestry Research, 2004.
"GPS and 3-D Mapping: Effective Tools to Establish Ancestral Domain Claims." In *A Resource Book on Enhancing Access of the Poor to Land and Common Property Resources*. Asian NGO Coalition for Agrarian Reform and Rural Development (ANGOC) and the International Land Coalition (ILC), 2006.
Haidar Bin Ali. "Welcome to Niah National Park Delegation of International Heritage Poetry Festival" (Microsoft power point). Niah National Park, Sarawak, Malaysia, November 9, 2008.
Hameed Sultan Merican. *The 2007 Malaysian Swiftlet Farming Industry Report*. Penang: SMI Association of Penang, 2007.
Inscriptions on Noi Island in Nha Trang, Khanh Hoa, Vietnam.
Investment Opportunities Study for Each Province of East, West, Central and South Kalimantan: Executive Summary East Kalimantan. PT Pacific Consulindo International Indonesia, 2005.
Ismail Mohammed Yusoff. "Sustainable Bird Nest Resource Management of Idahan People in the State of Sabah." In *Exposing the Billion-Dollar Bird's-nest Business World*, edited by Patrick Jory and Jirawat Sangthong. Nakhon Si Thammarat: Research Fund and Regional Project Study Bureau, Art Academic Office, Walailak University, 2007.
─────. "Social Control and Bird's Nest Harvesting among the Idahan: A Preliminary Observation." *Southeast Asian Studies*, 37(1), 1999.
Jonker Bird House Malacca. "Thunderstorm introduces Birds' Nest to Zheng He." Heritage Visit display. Melaka: Joon Onn Holdings, 2012.

REFERENCES

La Vina, Antonio G. M. "Community-Based Approaches to Marine and Coastal Resources Management in the Philippines: A Policy Perspective," 2002.

Lau, Amy S. M. and David S. Melville. *International Trade in Swiftlet Nests with Special Reference to Hong Kong Species in Danger*. Cambridge: UK Traffic International, 1994.

Lim Chan Koon. "Bird Nest Business and Bird Nest Farming Development in Malaysia." In *Exposing the Billion-Dollar Bird's-nest Business World*, edited by Patrick Jory and Jirawat Sangthong. Nakhon Si Thammarat: Research Fund and Regional Project Study Bureau, Art Academic Office, Walailak University, 2007.

Lim Chan Koon and Earl of Cranbrook. *Swiftlets of Borneo: Builders of Edible Nests*. Kota Kinabalu: Natural History Publications (Borneo), 2002.

Lim, David Y. C. *Report on the Malaysia Swiftlet Nest Industry Issue*. Federation of Malaysia Bird's Nest Merchants Association, 2002, rev. ed. 2008. http:/worldofswifletfarmimg.blogspot.com

Marshall, Andrew. "Natural Bird Bonanza." *The Times*, July 20, 2009.

Michon, Genevieve et al. *Domesticating Forests: How Farmers Manage Forest Resources*. Jakarta: Center for International Forestry Research and the World Agroforestry Centre, 2005.

Nazrul Azim Sharuddin. "Nilai Hasilan Sarang Burung." *Mega Utusan Malaysia*, May 8, 2012.

Nguyen Quang Phach et al. *The White-Nest Swiftlet and the Black-Nest Swiftlet: A Monograph*. Paris: Boubée, 2002.

Nugroho, E. and I. Whendrato. *The Farming of Edible-Nest Swiftlets Aerodramus fuciphagus in Indonesia*. Semarang: Indonesian Swiftlet Lovers Association, 1994.

Nugroho, E. *The Secrets of a Successful Swiftlet House*. Semarang: Eka Offset, 2001.

Nugroho, E., I. Whendrato and N. Kusomo. *The Farming of Edible-Nest Swiftlets Aerodramus fuciphagus in Indonesia*. Semarang: Eka Offset, 1996.

Oekan Abdoellah et al. "Communities and Forest Management in East Kalimantan: Pathway to Environmental Stability." *Research Network Report 3*. Berkeley: Center for Southeast Asian Studies, University of California, 1993.

Palawan Council for Sustainable Development. *Accomplishment Report 2012*. Palawan, Philippines: ECAN Zones Management and Enforcement Division Enforcement Division (EZMED), 2012.

"Pengelolaan Sarang Walet Tak Jelas." *Serambi*, October 27, 2008.

Persatuan Pengusaha Industri Sarang Burung, Kulai, Johor Baru, Malaysia. *China–Iskandar Malaysia & Bird Nest Business Opportunity*, 2009.

Poole, Colin. "Swiftlet Farming Comes to Cambodia." *Birding ASIA*, 13, 2010.

Rooney, Sarah. "Thailand's Bird Nest War." *South China Morning Post*, January 20, 2001.

Saragpunta Foundation and Philippine Association for Intercultural Development (PAFID). "Mapping Ancestral Lands and Waters." *Indigenous Perspectives*, 4(2), 2001.

Sarawak Forestry. *Sarawak Forestry, Co-management of Edible Bird Nest*. Swiftlets, Metal Signs Exhibition in Niah Cave, Batu Niah, Miri, Sarawak, Malaysia, August 13, 2010.

Scott, James C. *Domination and the Art of Resistance: Hidden Transcripts*. New Haven: Yale University Press, 1990.

———. *Weapons of the Weak: Everyday Forms of Peasant Resistance*. New Haven: Yale University Press, 1985.

Simon, Alina. "Rich Pickings from Swiftlet Rearing." *New Straits Times*, April 24, 2008.

SIRIM Berhad. "The Birds Nest Standards: An Overview of Malaysian Standards Related to Edible Birds Nests." *Standards and Quality News*, 18(2), 2010.

Valli, Eric and Diane Summers. *Shadow Hunters: The Nest Gatherers of Tiger Cave*. Singapore: Sun Tree Publishing, 1990.

Vu Ngoc Phuong. *Khanh Hoa mot tiem nang mot hien thu* (Khanh Hoa: Potential and Propect). Ha Noi: Nha xuat ban chinh tri quoc gia, 2004.

Zingapan, Kail M. and Dave E. De Vera. "Mapping the Ancestral Lands and Waters of the Calamian Tagbanwa of Coron, Northern Palawan." Philippine Association for Intercultural Development (PAFID), March 10, 1999.

Websites

"100 percent-Genuine bird's nest drink, true or false. Research results, Mahidol University. Famous eady-to-eat bird's-nest beverage contained only 1 percent of bird's nest". http://www.mka.co.th/newsdetailgraadmin. Php? Newsid = 404 (21 July 2011)

เครื่องดื่มรังนกแท้ 100% จริงแท้ หรือแค่หลอกลวง. ผลวิจัย ม.มหิดล รังนกสำเร็จรูปชื่อดัง ใส่รังนกแท้แค่ 1% เศษ.

ASTV *Manager Online*. "Phatthalung based swiftlet's-nest concession company signed collection contract.". News.thaihomelist.com/2009/ (19 August 2009)

บริษัทสัมปทานรังนกอีแอ่นพัทลุง ทำสัญญาลงสัมปทานจัดเก็บ

ASTV *Manager Online*, "Scandalous! Fake birds' nests from Malaysia repeatedly cheated on Chinese people." http://www.manager.co.th/China/ViewNews.aspx?NewsID=9540000103387&fb_source=message (August, 2011)

ฉาว! รังนกเลือดปลอมจากมาเลย์ แหกตาคนจีนซ้ำซาก

"Balinsasayaw/Nido Vegetable Chicken Soup." http://www.thecuisineuer.com/2013/01/balinsasayaw-nido-vegetable-chicken-soup.html (January, 2013).

"Banning Thai birds' nests becasue fake 'blood bird's nest' were caught. Who did it?" http://www.prachachat.net/news_detail.php?newsid=1361508066&grpid=&catid=19&suBCatid=1900 (February, 2013)

Bahagian Keselamatan dan Kualiti Makanan, Kementerian Kesihatan Malaysia. "Senarai Premis Pemprosesan Sarang Burung Walit Yang Mematuhi Keselamatan Makanan Bagi Tujuan Pengeksportan Sarang Burung Walit Ke China (Dikemaskini Sehingga 26 Jun 2012)." http://fsq.moh.gov.my/v3/images/filepicker_users/5ec35272cb-78/Aktiviti/Eksport/Sarangpercent20Burungpercent20Walit/Senarai-Premis-Pemprosesan-Mematuhi.pdf (October, 2012)

Bird's-nest soup the Caviar of the East, http://indonesianow.blogspot.com/2006/08/birds-nest-soup.html.

Boyle, Joe. "Welcome to Indonesia's bird nest soup factory town." http://www.bbc.co.uk/news/world-asia-pacific-12274825 (August, 2011)

Bulauitan, Joan C. "An age-old trade strains a scarce resource." http://mobilemedia.bworldonline.com/projectE/PalawanNorth/PalawanNorth.html (December, 2007).

Bussakorn Lee, "The 18th National Congress of the Chinese Communist Party viewpoint: Chinese economy will grow gradually, continuously, and stably in the next 10 years," http://www.thaibizchina.com/thaibizchina/th/china-economic-business/result.php?iblock_id=69&section_id=442&element_id=11655 (November, 2012)

มุมมองจากการประชุมสมัชชาพรรคคอมมิวนิสต์จีน ครั้งที่ 18: เศรษฐกิจจีนจะเติบโตอย่างค่อยเป็นค่อยไปอย่างต่อเนื่องและมีเสถียรภาพใน อีก 10 ปีข้างหน้า

Chan Shun-Wan. "Review of Scientific Research on Edible Bird's Nest." http://www.hkfsta.com.hk/articles/special/article7.htm, (11 September 2009)

Chayaporn Krabi-thong. "Attitude towards Bird's Nest Products (Products from Animals)." *Line* "glum krob ruang nok" and *Facebook* "Swift's nest in Thailand" by The Swift's Nest Business Association of Entrepreneurs Thailand, 14 August 2014.

ชยาพร กระบี่ทอง. "ทัศคติต่อสินค้าประเภทรังนก (สินค้าที่ได้จากสัตว์)." Line กลุ่มครบเรื่องนก และ Facebook รังนกแอ่นไทย โดยสมาคม ผู้ประกอบการธุรกิจรังนกแอ่น ประเทศไทย

Cheung Hon-yeung. "Comprehensive authenticity verification system for the quality assurance of edible birds' nests." http://qualityalchemist.blogspot.com/2012_10_01_archive.html (15 August 2013).

"China may lift import ban on bird's nests." http://www.nst.com.my/nation/general/china-may-lift-import-ban-on-bird-s-nests-1.69626 (April, 2012)

"China will prohibit importing genetically modified fruits, vegetables into the country from November 1," http://www.thaibizchina.com/thaibizchina/th/china-economic-business/result.php?iblock_id=69&section_id=464&element_id=11495 (october, 2012)

WEBSITES

Culibao, Mayet C. "Save this paradise." http://www.seasite.niu.edu/tagalog/Tagalog_Default_files/Philippine_Culture/travel_news_and_features. htm (December, 2007).

"Doon po sa Amin: Laway ni Kulas saganang-sagana" http://jevonne020799.wordpress.com/2010/05/17/doon-po-sa-amin-laway-ni-kulas-saganang-sagana (May, 2010).

Department of Trade Negotiations, Asean office, "The Socialist Republic of Vietnam", www.dtn.moc.go.th/vtl_upload_file//1288605233968/vietnam.pdf., October, 2006.

กรมเจรจาการค้าระหว่างประเทศ สำนักอาเซียน. "ข้อมูลพื้นฐานสาธารณรัฐสังคมนิยม เวียดนาม

Earle, Geoff "Feature: Nest soup taxing Indonesian birds", http://swallow-nest.com/article/2006/03/01/feature-nest-soup-taxing-indonesian-birds/.

"El Nido Town," http://gieofelnido.wordpress.com/category/uncategorized/ (November 4, 2010).

"Enchanting Coron." http://www.mysmartschools.ph/web/Enchanting/VisitUs/CoronIsland.htm (July, 2013). 487

"Gie of elnido's Blog." http://gieofelnido.wordpress.com/category/uncategorized/ (March, 2013).

Graceffo, Antonio. "By Sea Kayak to the Tagbanua Calamian Tribe Diving on a Japanese Wreck." http://www.escapeartist.com/Travel_Mag/Issues/09/Sea_Kayak_to_the_Tagbanua_Calamian_Tribe.html (November, 2007).

Hameed Sultan Merican, "The 2007 Malaysian Swiftlet Farming Industry Report." http://www.smipenang.com/2006SwiftletFarmingReport.html (November, 2007)

History about nyi roro kidul, http://iwansky82.blogspot.com/2010/08/history-about-nyi-roro-kidul.html.

Hoang Ha. "Ấp nở nhan tao va nuoi chim yen hang bằng cong nghệ moi". http://www.ddddn.com.vn.

"How willingly the 9-provinces committee to revise the swiftlet's nest concession system?", http://www.prachachat.net/news_detail.phpnewsid = 1349941709 & amp; grpid = & amp; catid = 00 & amp; su BCatid = 0000 (October, 2012)

วัดใจคณะกรรมการ 9 จังหวัดรื้อระบบสัมปทานรังนกอีแอ่น

http://www.amgadvance.com (June, 2012)

http://www.boi.go.th/thai/asean/Indonesia/sum_n.html/.237

http://www.cgcc.org.hk (18 November 2015)

http://www.ddddn.com.vn.

http://www.ekavietnam.com.

http://www.facebook.com/ccgbirdnest (November, 2012)

http://www.in1guide.com. (10 November 2015)

http://www.joshuaproject.net/countries.php?rog3=ID.

http://www.kebumenkab.go.id/index.php?module=htmlpages&func=display &pid=62.

http://www.pcsd.ph/resolutions/resolutions/miscellaneous/reso4-224.htm (April, 2013).

http://www.pcsd.ph/resolutions/resolutions/wildlife/reso4-225.htm (April, 2013).

http://www.pcsd.ph/resolutions/resolutions/wildlife/reso5-246.htm (April, 2013).

http://www.sieuthihangchatluong.com/?Act=View&DoanhNghiep=yensaokha-nhhoa&Id=EStore.

http://www.tienphong.vn/tianyon/Index.aspx?ArticleID=161548&ChannelID=2.

http://www.www.yen sao.vn, bang gia (thong nhất tren toan quoc).

http://www.yensaonhatrang.com.

http://www.yensaonhatrang.com/Quy.

http://www.yensaokhanhhoa.com.vn.

http://yenvietnhatrang.com.vn/index.php?option=com_content&view=article&id=25:cac-loi-t-yn&catid=3:t-vn-yn-sao&Itemid=4.125

Isa, Faten Saphilla Mohamed. "Burung Walit Import telur burung Indonesia." http://keluarga82.wordpress.com/2011/04/05/burung-walit/ (July, 2012)

WEBSITES

Isahak, Zulhisham. "Pantau kualiti produk sarang burung wallet." http://www.jpvpp.gov.my/index.php?option=com_content&view=article&id=396percent3Apantau-kualiti-produk-sarang-burung-walet&catid=61percent3Aakhbar&Itemid=136&lang=bm (April, 2012)

Jack, Katherine. "The Nest-gatherers." http://issuu.com/lightmediation/docs/the_nest_gatherers_of_pabellon_Island_4573 (March, 2013).

Jegathesan, M. "Bird's Nest Boom Has Malaysian Producers Drooling." http://www.thejakartaglobe.com/bisworld/birds-nest-boom-has-malaysian-producers-drooling/471393 (June, 2012)

"Kenapa Sarang Burung Dari Gua Niah?." http://budidayabirdnest.wordpress.com/2009/11/10/kenapa-sarang-burung-dari-gua-niah/ (July, 2012)

"Laway Ng Ibon Sa El Nido Ay Ginto." http://gieofelnido.wordpress.com/2010/11/07/laway-ng-ibon-sa-el-nido-ay-ginto/(November, 2010).

Lajiun, Jenne. "Swiftlet farms must move out." http://www.theborneopost.com/2012/10/05/swiftlet-farms-must-move-out/#ixzz2EBK5Zunt (October, 2012)

Lim, Jessica and Wilson. "Swiftlet housing boom." http://www.jphpk.gov.my (October, 2007)

MacKay, Jeanine. "China: Swiftlets and Edible Birds Nests." www.crystalswiftlets.com/China_-_Swiftlets_and_Edible_Birds_Nests.doc-, (26 October 2009)

Marketman. "Bird's Nests – The Most Expensive Local Ingredient?." http://www.marketmanila.com/archives/birds-nests-the-most-expensive-local-ingredient (April, 2007).

Marzita Abdullah. "Sarang 'emas' cecah rm 45,000 sekilo," http://www.utusan.com.my/utusan/info.asp?y=2010&dt=1126&pub=utusan_malaysia&sec=Utara&pg=wu_01.htm&arc=hive (May, 2012)

"New career, clear ideas! The people of Bang Saphan District build a swiftlet house". http://www.banrangnok.com/business11.php (9 April 2011)

อาชีพใหม่ไอเดียใส! คน อ.บางสะพาน สร้างบ้านนกนางแอ่น

Ng, Alexander. https://www.facebook.com/ng.alexander.589 (December 9, 2012)

Ngah, Haryani. "Walit Malaysia selamat untuk eksport." http://www.dvs.gov.my (September, 2011)

Ngo, Edmund. "Bird's-nest business between China and Malaysia to resume soon." http://thestar.com.my/news/story.asp?file=/2012/4/26/ metroperak/11175322&sec=metroperak (September, 2012)

Nguyen Tan Tuan. Yen sao Binh Dinh. http://www.baobinhdinh.com.vn/tiemnang-trienvong/2005/2/5394/.

Nichakan Qin, "China is not allowed to bring bird's nest into the country. This may result in a new round of increasing price of bird nest." http://www.thaibizchina.com/thaibizchina/th/china-economic-business/result.php?iblock_id=69&section_id=460&element_id=11519 (november, 2012)

ณิชกานต์ ฉิน. ตั้งแต่วันที่ 1 พ.ย. นี้ จีนเข้มห้ามนำผลไม้ ผัก และสิ่งมีชีวิตดัดแปลงพันธุกรรมเข้าประเทศ

"Palawan Bird's-nest soup 101." http://eastgatepublishing.com/2011/11/palawan-birds-nest-soup-101 (March, 2013).

"Panen Sarang Walet Madina Tak Dinikmati Rakyat." http://groups.yahoo.com/group/sa-roha/message/2465.

Park, Thesese. "Bird nest Soup, Anyone?." http://www.thesesepark.com>bird_nest_soup, (September 26, 2009)

Pattamawadee Phonukul Suzuki and Chon Bunnag, "Power Structure for Natural Resources Allocation and Environment." www.econ.tu.ac.th/doc/seminar/120/sym50_paper3_pat.ppt, (28 March 2011)

ปัทมาวดี พลนุกูล ซูซูกิ และ ชล บุนนาค. โครงสร้างอำนาจในการจัดสรรทรัพยากรธรรมชาติและสิ่งแวดล้อม

"Potential for Edible Birds' Nest (EBN) Farming in the Philippines." http://nestfarminginpinas.blogspot.com (May, 2009).

"Saliva Soup." http://yapakyakap.blogspot.com/2008/10/saliva-soup.html (October, 2008).488

"Supreme Administrative Court allows the Phatthalung bird's-nest auction". http://www.rd1677.com/branch.php?id=53435 (19 August 2009)

ศาลปกครองสูงสุดปลดล็อกเปิดประมูลรังนกอีแอ่นพัทลุงแล้ว

"The great indoor". Timeout. http//72.14.235.104/search?q=cache:zFISSuFa7NcJ:www.vir.com.vn/Client/.

WEBSITES

"Original Bird's Nest International (OBNI) Clean Good Shape and Chemical", http://www.originalnest.com/contact-us.html.

Ramli, Nurhidayah. "1kg bird's nest limit for tourists." http://thestar.com.my/news/story.asp?file=/2012/1/17/nation/10275151&sec=nation (January, 2012)

Reny, Sawitri and R. Garsetiasih, "The Study of Population, Habitat, and Productivity of Thunberg's Swiftlet (*Collocalia fuciphaga*), in South Gombong, Central Java", http://library.forda-mof.org/libforda/data_pdf/620_3_2000.pdf, 43.

Rizka, Agustina, "Swallow Bird's Nest in a Bottle to Maintain Skin Youth", http://webcache.googleusercontent.com/search?q=cache:okigmeioqzoj:fashionesedaily.com/blog/2011/04/22/swallow-birds-nest-in-a-bottle-to-maintain-skin-youth/+birdpercent27s+nest+of+indonesia&cd=13&hl=en&ct=clnk&gl=th&source=www.google.co.th,.

Special Report, Trang Swiftlet Concession, http://77.nationchannel.com/playvideo.php?id=71936. รายงานพิเศษ การประมูลสัมปทานรังนกตรัง

Swiftlet Bird Nests Harvest in East Kalimantan, http://swallow-nest.com/article/2006/10/02/swiftlet-bird-nests-harvest-in-east-kalimantan-2/.

The World Factbook – Central Intelligence Agency. Indonesia. https://www.cia.gov/library/publications/resources/the-world-factbook/geos/print_id.html

The World Factbook – Central Intelligence Agency. Malaysia. https://www.cia.gov/library/publications/the-world-factbook/geos/my.html

The World Factbook – Central Intelligence Agency. Philippines. https://www.cia.gov/library/publications/resources/the-world-factbook/geos/print_rp.html

The World Factbook – Central Intelligence Agency. Vietnam. https://www.cia.gov/library/publications/the-world-factbook/geos/vm.html

Tula ng Paglaya. "Busyador." http://padrepupong.wordpress.com/2012/08/ (March, 2013).

Upacara Ngunduh Sarang Burung Walet di Karangbolong (Kebumen, Jawa Tengah), http://uun-halimah.blogspot.com/2008/12/upacara-ngunduh-sarang-burung-walet-di.html.

Võ Quang Yen. Huyền diệu, Yến sao. http://vietsciences.free.fr/timhieu/khoahoc/biologie/huyendieuyensao.htm.

Ward, Christian. "Bird's-nest soup." http://webcache.googleusercontent.com/search?q=cache:bx8LfkwopWYJ:www.contemporaryliteraryreviewindia.com/2011_07_01_archive.html+busyadors&cd=20&hl=en&ct=clnk&gl=th (March, 2013).

Interviews

2002

April 11
Grandmother of the people who climb up to collect birds' nests, Koh Si and Koh Ha Islands, Pak Phayun District, Phatthalung Province, Thailand
Thin Rueangchuay. Villagers in Chumphon Sub-District, Sathing Phra District, Songkhla Province, Thailand

October 2
Prayoon Chamnina. *Panglaema*, Koh Thalu, Ao Luek District, Krabi Province. Thailand

October 21
Anonymous
Musa Damchuea. People who climb up to collect birds' nests, Koh Lipe Island, Mueang District, Phang-nga Province, Thailand

October 23
Donrochet. Fishermen, Koh Mak Noi Village, Ko Panyi Sub-District, Mueang District, Phang Nga Province, Thailand

December 15
Cherdphan Phuriphatphan, swiftlet source owner, Pak Phanang District, Nakhon Si Thammarat Province, Thailand
Hib Jutharattanakun, swiftlet source owner, Pak Phanang District, Nakhon Si Thammarat Province, Thailand
Sumet Yueannuwong

December 30
Anusit Rueangchuay. Swiftlet island workers, Koh Si and Koh Ha Islands. Chumphon villagers, Sathing Phra District, Songkhla Province, Thailand

2003

March 7
Praeng Phetchamrat

March 23
Liam Chantharamat

April 3
Khuankhit Mhuennara. Bird's nest building owners, Pak Phanang District, Nakhon Si Thammarat Province, Thailand

April 10
Khieo Chantharamat

April 18
Bae Solae

June 5
Karia Chamnina

August 8
Anonymous

2004

August 17
Anonymous

September 9
Damrong Yotharak

2008

May 23–24
Fidel E. Mondragon, Vice chairman of Saragpunta Federation Barangay Dobcauon I, Coron town, Busuanga Municipality, Palawan, Philippines
Roy Abella and Aldrin G. Caballero, the *busyadors* [bird's-nest collectors] of Coron Island, the Tagbanua ethnic group at Kayangan Lake and Saragpunta office, Coron town, Busuanga Municipality, Palawan, Philippines

May 25
Aman Sitanggang. Indonesian oil company workers

October 26–28
Anonymous
Nguyen Duc Vinh, former bird's-nest collector on Cu Lao Cham Island, Hoi An, Quang Nam Province, Vietnam
Nguyen Van Dung, boat driver on Thu Bon River, Hoi An, Quang Nam Province, Vietnam

INTERVIEWS

November 10
Mahli, Sunni, staff member at Niah National Park, Sarawak, Malaysia

November 11
Haidar Bin Ali. Head of the Niah National Park Office, Sarawak, Malaysia
Nuar Bin Haji Jaya. Ethnic Penan group, bird's nest collectors at Niah Great Cave, Niah National Park, Sarawak, Malaysia

2009

June 1
Dieb, Sanest Company bird's-nest collector on Hon Noi Island, Vietnam
Nguyen Nhuu Tri, tour guide at Khanh Hoa-Nha Trang Company

June 2
Female owner of a steamed duck shop in front of the Sanest Bird's Nest beverage factory. Nguyen Sau Ngao, Nha Trang
A taxi driver. Nha Trang
Nguyen Tien Duong, taxi driver in Nha Trang

July 6
Violeta Francisco. The *pugad ng balinsasayaw* dealer Filipino ethnic group, Coron Town, Busuanga Island, Palawan, Philippines
De Guia Merlindo Aguilar. The *busyador* Tagbanua ethnic group, Black Island, Busuanga, Palawan, Philippines
Perfecto B. Dabuit Jr. The *busyador* Tagbanua ethnic group, Black Island, Busuanga, Palawan, Philippines

July 7
Perfecto B. Dabuit's wife. The Tagbanua ethnic group at Panlaitan, Busuanga, Palawan, Philippines
Rodolfo Aguilar, *balinsasayaw* cave owner, Coron Island, the President of Foundation of the Tagbanua Ethnic Group, at Saragpunta office, Coron town Busuanga, Palawan, Philippines
Mark Anthony S. Blanco. At Saragpunta office, Coron town, Busuanga, Palawan, Philippines
Rey D. Dabuit. The *busyador* Tagbanua ethnic group at Panlaitan, Busuanga, Palawan, Philippines

July 9
Dennis Garcia. Former *busyador* of Cadlao Island. The Filipino ethnic group at Codognun Resort, El Nido-Palawan, Philippines

October 12
Anonymous
Allen Pang. Product Quality Control Department, Home of Swallows Ltd, Hong Kong
Stella Blade, director of Home of Swallows Ltd
Frank Pak, owner and manager of the bird's nest business, Home of Swallows Ltd, Hong Kong

October 13
Chan Shun-Wan, researcher/teacher at Hong Kong Polytechnic University
Ng Kar Man, traditional Chinese medicine practitioner at Mahan Chan, New Territories, Hong Kong

October 29
Suwet Ketkaeo. Bird's nest collectors, Koh Sukorn people, Trang Province, Thailand

October 30
Seri Siemmai, former bird's-nest collector and concessionaire on Koh Phetra Island, Trang Province, Thailand

2010

February 21
Mulia and Mahya, Acehnese bird's-nest collectors of Kampung Meunasah, Lampuuk, Lhoknga District, Aceh Province.

February 22
Muzakir, Acehnese bird's-nest collector and leader of Kampung Kampung Meunasah, Lampuuk, Lhoknga District, Aceh Province.
Swiftlet-house farming owner at a motorcycle shop, Samalanga, Aceh Province, Indonesia

February 23
E. Nugroho, researcher on swiftlet and swiftlet house farming in Indonesia and president of the Indonesian Swiftlet Lovers Association, Indonesia
H. Fainal, swiftlet house farm owner at Sigli, Aceh Province, Indonesia

Hary Kusumo Nugroho, businessman and owner of bird's-nest buildings in Semarang and Jakarta, Indonesia

Zafril, bird's-nest trader and swiftlet house farming owner at Bireuen, Aceh Province, Indonesia

February 26
Anonymous

April 7
Tan Boon Siong, researcher and owner of Longevity Wellness Industries Sdn Bhd, manufacturer and exporter of birds' nests, Johor, Malaysia

May 14
Uthit Khieokhachi, bird's-nest collector at Koh Rang Noi, of Thai-Vietnamese ethnicity. Salak Phet Guesthouse, Koh Chang Tai Sub-District, Koh Chang District, Trat Province, Thailand

August 13
Michael Bueng, bird's-nest merchant and former bird's nest harvester, Niah Great Cave, Niah National Park, and the Iban ethnic group of Rumah Changgai, Niah, Sarawak, Malaysia

Johnson Chew, a concessionaire of Niah Great Cave, Niah National Park, and bird's nest merchant, and the ethnic group of Batunah, Sarawak, Malaysia

2011

January 10
Anonymous

Vo Thai Lam, owner of a bird's-nest building business and ready-to-eat bird's-nest industry, Nguyen Viet Company, Ninh Thuan Province, Vietnam

Tran Duc Hung, consultant to Nguyen Viet Company, Ninh Thuan Province, Vietnam

December 30
Chanarong Sawatnaruenat, mayor of Pak Phanang, Nakhon Si Thammarat Province, Thailand

2012

May 10
Siri Neng Buah, Thai ethnicity, resides in Kalantan State, former senior officer of the Ministry of Tourism, Arts and Culture Malaysia

2014

April 4
Saksit Kanwitye

May 1
Thatsawan Srimuangwattana

June 8
Kamolsak Lertphaiboon, president of the Association of Bird's Nest Entrepreneurs in Thailand

June 18
Anan Jongsakchareonkun, Edible-Nest Swiflet Research Center (Thailand) Co. Ltd., Wiang Sa District, Surat Thani Province, Thailand

November 14
Kim Eng. Owners and bird's nest traders in Surat Thani Province, Thailand

INDEX

t=table; *=photograph; **bold** = extended discussion or key reference

Abdul Rozak (nest-collector) **283-288**
Abella, Roy 209
accident 68, 69, 122, 126, 150, **216-217**
Aceh 65, 69, **76-77**, 81, 86, **88-92**, 94, 97, 105*
    civil war (1976-2005) 59, 97, 349
    price of birds' nests (2010) **84t**, 84
    production **58**
    swiftlet-farming 99*
Aceh Besar 88, 94, **96***, 97, 100
Acehnese **58-59**, 62, **64-65**, 67, 71, 72, 93, 94, 97
Administration of Quality Supervision, Inspection and Quarantine (AQSIQ, PRC) 338, 339
advertising and advertisements 23, 25, 35, **53***, 193, **234***, 263, **319***, 318, **344-345***
Aerodramus fuciphagus 62, 115, 183, 184, 246, **247-248**, 301, 352(n138)
    A. germanicus (*vestitus*) 62, 64, 349
    A. maximus 63, **116**, 301
Aguilar, R., 'Kudol' 197, **212-213**, 224, **233***, 365, 389
Aguilar, De Guia Merlindo **213-214**, 360, 365, 388
AIDS 23, 259, 321
Alga Prima Sdn. Bhd. 136, 138, **154-155**, 173*
amino acids 24, **123t**, 260, **261t**, 319, 322, 335
ancestors 9, 22, 26, 119, 121, 130, 131, 148, 151, 177-199 *passim*, 211-214, 223-224, 237, 258, 267, 300
Ancestral Domain Management Plan 198
ancient times
    Indonesia **78-79**
    Malaysia **134-135**
    Philippines **203-206**
    Thailand 246, 271
    Vietnam **32-34**, 346-347
Andaman Sea coast (Thailand) 59, 235, 237, 242, 244, 251, 253, 256, **257-258**, 259-260, 263, 264, 267, 269, 271, 274, 285, 302, 305, 307-308*
animism 7, 26, 72, 118, 119, 125, 143, 146, 188, 193, 258, 264
Aoheng (Penihing) 58, 75-76, 87, 93, 97
Aphichat Kitprasan 268, 274
Apodidae family 1, 182, 246, 248, 250
Apodiformes order 1
Arroyo, G.M. President 206, 228
ASEAN 47
Asian financial crisis (1997) 2, 112, 113, 235, 235, 300
Association of Bird's-Nest Entrepreneurs (Thailand) 301
avian influenza (2008-2009) 86, 306, 331, 336

Awuyuk Dakulo (sacred lake, Palawan) 196
Ayutthaya Kingdom 33, 236, **238**, 265, 268

Ba Chua dao Yen (chief of bird's-nest island) 10, 26
Bach Van (poet) 20
bach yen (white nests) 38
bai tu Yen sao (*yen bai*) (incomplete nest) 34
Bali 61, 86, 99
balinsasayaw (swiftlet) 174, 176, 180, 182*, 182, **183**, 185-186, 190, 193, 209, 230*, 233*
balinsasayaw season 177
bamboo ladders 9, 69-70, 78, 95, 189, 202, 221, 104*, **232***
bamboo scaffolding 32, 40, 47, 52*, 124, 134, 270, 280, 292, 305
Ban thao cuong muc thapdi (1765) 23
Bandung 80, 86
Bangkok 239, 294
Banwang-Daan 177, 196, 223
Bao Nghia Kien Nghiep Hoi 11
Baram (Sarawak) 109, 110, 117, 126
Barangay Panlaitan (Palawan) 180, 198, **214-215**, 233*
Batavia (Jakarta) 56-57, 316
Batu Niah 110, 117, **118-120**, 123, 141
    incentive and welfare system **143-151**
Batu Niah: Rumah Panjang, Kampung Chong 118, 119, 122, 125
Batu Niah National Park **143-145**
beliefs and rituals 4
    Hong Kong **334-341**
    Indonesia **66-71**, **350-351**
    Malaysia **118-126**
    Philippines **185-191**
    Thailand **252-262**, 263, **264**, 267
    Vietnam **19-26**, 347-348
Berau district 76, 94, 97, 352
Best Nest Company Limited 242
Bich Dam village 10-11, 32
Bidayuh 134, 156
Binh Dinh 9, 10, 13, 14, 15, 18, 19, 21, 26, 29, **35**, **37t**, **41-42**
Binh Tay Cuu Quoc Hoi (ethnic group) 33
Bintulu 114, 117, 145
bird's-nest business: prospects **337-339**

bird's-nest business: size
    China 4
    Hong Kong 3, **325-328**
    Indonesia **80-83**
    Malaysia **136-139**
    Philippines **207**
    Southeast Asia (2014) 2, 3
    Thailand **274-276**
    Vietnam **35-37**
bird's-nest cleaners 70, 73*, 78*, 92, 106*, 122, 145, 150, 189, 195, 216, 259, **328***, **344***
bird's-nest cleaning
    Hong Kong 322, 327
    Indonesia 60, 64, 70, 71, 85
    Malaysia 108, 116, 124, 136, 145, 150, 171*, 173*
    Philippines 192, 213, 214, 215
    Thailand 263, 272, 282, **310***
    Vietnam 23, **39t**, 43, **53***
    see also clean nests
bird's-nest collection: belief and fact
    Indonesia **70-71**, 350
    Malaysia **122-124**
    Philippines **190-191**
    Thailand **259-262**
    Vietnam **22-24**, 346
bird's-nest collectors
    employed by government 31
    pay (Vietnam) **43**
    special vocabulary **258**
bird's-nest collectors (by country)
    Indonesia **85-92**, **104***
    Malaysia **170***
    Philippines 186, 190, 196, 200, 208, **209-213**, 220
    Thailand 243, 257, **258**, **278-294**, 300, **307-309***
    Vietnam 31, **43**, **52***
bird's-nest production
    Indonesia 55, **58**, **61-62**
    Malaysia 110, **138-139**
    Philippines **207**
    Thailand 246, **275**, **278**
    Vietnam 8, 13, 14, 36, **37t**, 50
bird's-nest products **323***, **323-324**
    ready-to-consume 220, **345***
    ready-to-drink 25, 36, 43, 44, 46, **53-54***, 136, 137, 138, 155, 157, 211, 260, 275, 294, 296, **310***, 337, 338
    ready-to-eat 4, 14, 31, **53***, 150, 245, 262, 269, 272, 273, 275, 295, **326-327**, **328***, 344
bird's-nest shops **328-329***, 333, 340, **343-345***
    types (Hong Kong) **329**
bird's-nest soup 22, 24, 111, 176, 177, **186***, **190**, 205, **234***, 317, **318**, **318***
Bird's-Nest Taxation Committee 251
bird's-nest traders 332

Bird's-Nest Trading Company 218
birdhouse farming business 102, 113, 132
    see also house-farming
birdhouse store 136
birdhouses 50, 111, 112, 113, 114, 117, 132, 141, 166, 167, 262
birds' nests
    categories **31-34**
    consumed as food, medicine, or beauty products **1-2**
    consumption **272**
    global market (influence of HK) **336-340**
    leading producers **3**
    made using saliva 1, 16
    Malaysia **155-158**
    nesting area and color **38**
    nutrients **71t**, **260t**, **321t**, 322, **323***, **335**
    quality (Thailand) **297**
    quality and color **38**
    rate of collection 2
    raw **324***, **346***
birds' nests: prices
    China 316
    Indonesia **58**, **61**, **83t**, **83-87**, 89, 92
    Malaysia **136**, **140t**, **144**, 159, 160, 162, 165, 297
    Philippines **206-209**, 210, 214, 215, 217, 218
    Thailand 241, 245, **273**, **277-278t**, 279, 283, 291, 292, 297, 303, 305
    Vietnam 12, **34-36**, **38-39**, 46
birds' nests: type and price
    Indonesia **83-85**
    Malaysia **140-142**
    Philippines **208-209**
    Thailand **276-278**
    Vietnam **38-39**
Bireven city **106***, 156
"Bismillah" (poem) **254-255**
Black Island (Palawan) 180, 181, 183, 185, 188, 189, 192, 193, 198, 199, 200, 204, **213-217**, 224, **231***, **232***, **233***
black nests 64, 65, 72, 81, 83t, 86, 89, **105***, 115, 124, 127, 140, **140t**, 141t, **141-142**, **142t**, 145, **146-147**, **169***, **171***, 211, 259, 263, 275, 276, 277t, 289, 291, 303, 305, 335
    Niah National Park **150t**
    price (Aceh) **84t**, 84
    price (Philippines) **208t**
black-nest swiftlet **56-57**, **116**, **169***, **307***
    Aerodramus maximus 16, 115, **116**, 250
    walet sarang hitam **116**
    yen do den 16
Blade, Stella **326-327**
Blanco, M.A.S. 214
blood nests 83t, 83, **160-162**, **335-336**

Bontius **315**
Boon Hui, *Phraya Songkhla* **239**
brands 4, 25, 81, 137, 161, 173*, **263**, 273, 275, 294, 329
Brooke, Rajah James 109, 126, 134
Brunei 155, 156, 295, 337
Bueng, Michael **145-148**
bulo yulo sarang (tool) 124
Bumiputera 168
burung walet (swiftlet) 62, 72, 114, 125
business and management system
    Indonesia **78-95**, **353-354**
    Malaysia **134-158**
    Philippines **203-221**
    Thailand **270-297**
    Vietnam **32-47**, **349-350**
business relationships
    Indonesia **93-95**
    Malaysia **155-158**
    Philippines **219-221**
    Thailand **295-297**
    Vietnam **44-47**
business world (Philippines) **193-202**
Busuanga (people) 185
Busuanga (place) 174, 175, 208
    see also Black Island
busyador (Tagbanua nest-gatherer) 174, 175*, 179, 180, 183-184, 185, **186-191**, 198, 199, 210, 212, 214, **215-218**, 224-225, 226, **230-233***
"Busyador" (poem by Padre Pupong) **186-188**
BYB Business Company Limited 243

Caballero, Aldrin G. 210
Cabugao 177, 197, 224
Cabugao Barangay Council 197
Calamian Tagbanwa 176, 177, 204, 360, 361
Calis Island 203, **204**
cancer 318, **322**
carbohydrates 71t, 260, 321t, 322, 335
caves 51*, 272
Central Thais 266, 269, 295
CEPP Laboratory Services 123
Certificate and Accreditation Administration (PRC) 339
Certificate of Ancestral Domain Claim (CADC) 180, 196, 200, 204
Chailai (goddess) 256, 264
Cham ethnic group 29, 32
Chan Shun-Wan 322, 330
Chao Ju-Kua **175**, 204
Chao Sia Min 317
Chaumont: Alexandre, Chevalier de ~ 265
Cheung Hon-yeung, Dr. **322-323**, 323*
Chavalit Yongchaiyut 242, 268
Chew Hui Chiang, Johnson **148-151**

Chiang Mai 246, 310*
chim yen Hang ('swiftlet') 14
China 3-4, **160-164**, 168, **338-340**
    bird's-nest protocols **338-340**
    nest-consumption **315-318**
    relations with Thailand 241
China market **315-318**, 324, 328, 330, **333-334**, **340-342**
    for Indonesia 57, 62, 81, 86, 92, 93, 94, 95
    for Malaysia 95, **136-137**
    for Philippines **220-221**
    for Sarawak **109-110**
    for Thailand 95, 245, 268, 274, **276t**, 294-295, **296-297**, 301, 303
    for Vietnam 8, 32, 44, 46, 95
Chinese people 1, 2, 23, 46
    Hong Kong 3, **318-346**
    Indonesia 57, **61**, 76, 79, 80, 87, 93, 94, 95, 97, 100, 337
    Malaysia 118, 128, 129, 137, 156, **157-158**, 168
    Philippines 176, 177, 179, 180, 181, 194, 196, 197, **199**, 204, 205, **207**, 210, 211, **212-213**, 214, 215, 217, **220-221**, 224, **221**, 226, 337-338
    Sarawak 144, **145**, 147, **148-151**
    Thailand 236, 237, **238-240**, 259, 265, 267, **269-270**, 274, 281, 282-283, 295, 297, 299, 302, 303, 335
    Vietnam 7, 11, 27, 29, 32, 33, 46
Chinese language 62, 80, 137, 207, 269, 274
Chinese monopolies (Thailand) **241**
chinteng (sub-manager) **282-283**
Christianity 125, 188, 193
Christians 7, 119, 120, 146
Chulalongkorn University 260
Chumphon Province **240-241**, 242, 243, 250, 256, 264, 266, 267, 274, 303, 305
chung thuy 19
CITES 50, 305
clan 131, 145, **151-152**, 156, 178-179, 195, 220, 202, 224
clean nests 39t, 81, 83, 86, 136, 140t, **141**, 142, 154, 196, 197, **234***, 273, 282
    see also bird's-nest cleaners
Codognun Island (Palawan) 182*, 217, 218, 230*
collecting season
    Indonesia **65**
    Malaysia **117**
    Philippines **184-185**
    Thailand **251-252**, 257, 283
    Vietnam **17-19**
Collocalia genus 62, 100, 115, 330
    Collocalia fuciphaga 60, 62, 72, 182, 186
    Collocalia fuciphaga germaini oustalet (swiftlet) 15
Collocaliini tribe 1

colonial era   11, **27–29**, 33, 74, 79, 126–127, 130, 131, 151, 158, 172*, 195, 206, **222–223**, 298, 327
color   **320**
'communal property'   45, 75, 76, 93, 129, 131, 132, 133, 155, 200, 201, 202, 219, 270, 295
Communist Party of Vietnam   **47**
community cooperatives   58, 65, 75, 76, 77, 87, 88, 89, 94, 97
Community Forest Stewardship Agreement (CFSA, 1990–)   **197**, 224
'complexity of rights'   75, 76, 78, 129, 132, 133, 201, 202
Concepcion, Fray J. de la   176
cong nhan (nest-collectors)   21
conservation   5, 8, 14, 18–19, 31, 264, 299
'Conservative Society' era   **315–318**
Coron Island (Palawan)   **176–181, 183–184**, 185, 188–204 *passim*, **209–213**, 214, 223, 224, 226, 229, 233*
Coron Town   180, 186, 193, 194, 196, 200, 203*, **208t**, 210, 224, 227, 231*, 233*
corruption   97–98, 99, 149–150, 165, **296**
cosmetics   **346***
CP Charoen Pokphand   263
Cranbrook, Earl of   330
Cu Lao Cham   8, 9, 18, 21, **25–26**, 28, 29, 35, **40–41**, **52***
culture, traditions, wisdom   4, **340–342**
    Indonesia   72–73
    Malaysia   **125–126**
    Philippines   **192–193**
    Thailand   **264**
    Vietnam   **25–26**, 349
Cuyonon (ethnic group)   179, 185, 189, 191, 195, 196, 199, 200, 203, 217, 220, 224, 230*, 232*
CV Bintang Sejahtera company   94, 97

Da Nang   12, 13, 35, 36, **37t**
Dabuit Jr., P.B.   **215–216**
Dabuit, R.D.   **216–217**, 233*
dai duong (diabetes)   23
Dai Nam Nhat Thong Chi   9, 33
Dai Viet   9, 29
Dao Tan Hiep   9, **25–26**
dao yen (swiftlet islands)   14
dau tien (nest collectors)   9
Davao del Sur   192, 234*
Dayak   57, 62, 93, 94, 99, 100
death   122, 150, 156
deforestation   99, **165**, 228
Democratic Centralism   30, 47
Dennis, Garcia   189, **217–218**, 361, 362, 364, 386
Department of Environment and Natural Resources (DENR, Philippines)   180, 200
Desa Langap   57

Desa Naga Umbang   97
Development Diplomacy (Philippines)   206, 228
dia tu Yen sao (yellow or black nest)   34
diabetes   23, 33
doa Teungku ceremony   69, 73
doa peusijue(k) ritual   69, 73
doa selamat   125
Doi Moi (Renovation) policy (1986–)   25, 30
Dubai   155, 156, 334
Duties on Birds' Nests Act:
    (Thailand, 1939)   241, **266–267**
    (Thailand, 1997)   242, 268
'dynamism of rights'   129, 133, 201

East Kalimantan   65, **75–76**, 81, 87, **94**
Ecolite Biotech Manufacturing Sdn. Bhd.   154–155
ecology
    Indonesia   **98–102**, 352
    Malaysia   **164–168**
    Philippines   **227–229**
    Thailand   **304–306**
    Vietnam   **49–50**, 347
edible-nest swiftlets *see* swiftlets
eggs   248, 250
El Nido (Palawan)   **176**, 183, 185, 186, 193, 199–200, 201, 204, 208, **208t**, **217–219**, 225, 226, 227*, 229, 234*
El Nido: Cadlao island   181, 190, 192, **218**
elders   **131**, 152, 200, 213, 257
elements [minerals]   **123t**
emas putih (white gold bird's nest)   78
environment
    Indonesia   **98–102**, 352
    Malaysia   **164–168**
    Philippines   **227–229**
    Thailand   **304–306**
    Vietnam   **49–50**, 347
Environmental Impact Assessment (EIA)   164
epidermal growth factor (EGF)   322
equipment and tools
    Indonesia   **71–72**, 105*, 350
    Malaysia   **124**
    Philippines   **192**, 218, 221
    Thailand   **262–263, 280**, 282, 285, 288, 291, **307–308***, 310*
    Vietnam   **24–25**, 346
ethnic groups   4
    China   **315–318**
    Indonesia   **93–95**, 96, 98
    Malaysia   107, **125–126, 155–158**, 163
    Thailand   **264**, 301
    Vietnam   7, **25–26, 28–31**, 32, 33

INDEX

ethnic relations
　Indonesia **93-95**
　Malaysia **155-158**
　Philippines **219-221**
　Thailand **295-297**
　Vietnam **44-47**
'ethnic rights' 75, 76, 98, 132, 133, 201, 202, 301
Eu Yan Sang **324-325**
'exclusive rights' 30, 76, 77, 129, 132, 133, 177, 178, 196, 197, 198, 200, 202, 224
export markets
　for Indonesia **80-81, 82t**, 93
　for Malaysia **155**, 156-157
　for Philippines **219**
　for Thailand 274, **275-276t**, 294-295
　for Vietnam 44, 46-47

factories 39, **43**, 46, 48, 53*, 94, 106*, 278, 388
Fainal, H. 90
fakes 3, 136, **153-154**, 157, **160-162**, 207, 225, 273, 297, 301, 329, 332, **335-336**, 337-338, **340***
feudalism 28, 29, 56, 74, 127, 135, 195, 200, 205, **237-240**, 265, 267, 268, 269, 298
Filipinos (Tagalog) 191, 195, 199, 203, 211, 217, 219-220, 225
food 22-24, 32, 33, 134, **219**, 237, **315-317**, 320, 324
food sovereignty
　Indonesia **80-95, 353-354**
　Malaysia **135-158**
　Philippines **206-221**
　Thailand **272-297**
　Vietnam **34-47**, 350
Foundation of Tagbanua for Coron Island 211
France 11, 33, 238, 295, 298
Francisco, Violeta 186, **210**, 368, 391

GAM (*Gerakan Aceh Merdeka*) 59, 97
Germain's swiftlet 15*, 56, **249-250**, 370, 372, 380, 382
Gia Long, Emperor (r. 1802-1820) 9, 10, 26, 29, 33
ginseng 316, **323***, 324, 326, 333, **346***
global market **336-338**
globalization 2, 227, **241-244**, 299, 318, 342
Golden Company Nathet Company Limited 243
golden nests 134, 166, 276, 325, 326t
Golden Sat Company 244
Gomantong Cave (Sabah) 135, 156
Gombong Selatan (Middle Java) 56
grass-nest swiftlet (*Collocalia esculenta*) 16, 39, 60, 182*, 183, 217, 230*
　'glossy swiftlet' (*Collocalia esculenta*) 114, 115
　see also *seriti*
Gua Niah *see* Niah Cave
Gua Sarai 100
Gua Tugung 100

Guangxi Province 160
guard huts **51***, 234*
guards 21, 39, 40, 42, 43, 45, 93, 118, 129, 130, 132, 144, 147, 149, 156, 169*, 196, 218, 220, 224, 227*, 242, 290, 293, 308*
Guerera, Eduardo 179
Guha Rayeak **58-59**, 64, **69**, 72, 73, 77, 94, 97, **103-105***
Gulf of Thailand coast 7, 235, 237, 242, 243, 251, 258, 259, 264, 266, 267, 269, 274, 302, 305
Gumbang Cave 109, 126

Haidar Bin Ali **143-144**
hang (caves) 14, 15
Hang Trong Hon Ngoai 20
Hanoi 36
Hao Yieng, *Phra Songkhla* **238-239**, 271, 316
Haryoto Kusnoputratanto 102
Ho Chi Minh City 12, 13, 36
Ho Thao and Ho Kae (spirits) 237, 256, **308***
Ho Van Hoa 9, 10, 26, 29, 33
Hoh Yen shrine (for Ho Van Hoa) 10, 26
Hoi An 8, 9, 16, 18, 21, 25, 26, 28, 35, 40
　categories of bird's-nest 34
Home of Swallows Limited 46, 95, 157, **220-221**, 296, **324-327**, 331
Hon Lao Island 26
Hong Kong (HK) **314-347**, 375-376
　bird's-nest prices **324-326**
　bird's-nest products **326-327**
　classification of bird's-nest business **324-326**
　discourse (bird's-nest business) **331-336**
　ethnic Chinese community 3, **318-346**
　ethnic Chinese community (size of bird's-nest business) **328-331**
　imports of birds' nests (estimated value, 1975-2008) **331t**
　modern capitalism **321-324**
　nest-consumption (modern capitalism) **321-324**
　nest-consumption culture **318-320**
　principal consumers of birds' nests 3
Hong Kong: Centre for Food Safety 332, **335***, 338
Hong Kong: Sheung Wan 333, **333***, 343*
Hong Kong: Wing Lok Street **328-329***, **333***, 333, 334, **343-344***
Hong Kong market 317, **340-342**
　for Indonesia 62, 80, 81, 82t, **85-87, 92, 95**
　for Malaysia 110, 136-137, **157**, 159, 165
　for Philippines 207, **220-221**, 229, 329
　for Thailand 269, 273, 274, **276t**, 294-295, 296-297, 303
　for Vietnam 31, 34-35, 44, 46, 337
Hong Kong Polytechnic University 331
Hong Kong Trade Development Council 332

Hong Kong Traditional Chinese Medicine-Dealers'
    Association (1928–) **332***, 332, 343*
Hop tac xa Yen sao Vinh Nguyen 33
house-farming (of swiftlets)
    Indonesia **59–62**, 63*, 80, **90–92**, 98, 101–102,
        103*, **105–106***, 351–352
    Malaysia **111–114**, 153, 160
    Philippines **181**, 206, 229
    Southeast Asia **2**
    Thailand **244–246**, 269, 270, **278**, **300**
    Vietnam **12–14**, 31
    see also birdhouses
house-farming: buildings 50, 111, 133–134, 137, 158,
    159, 160, 163, **166–167**, 171–173, 192, 229, 270,
    272, 274, **309***
hunter-gatherers 47, 221, **270–272**
huyet yen (red nest) 38
Hydrochous gigas (giant swiftlet or waterfall swift)
    115

Iban 110–111, 118–120, 122, 123–124, 125, 141, 144,
    145–148, 149, 151, 156, 170*, **171***
Idahan 109, 114, 117, 119, **120–122**, **125–126**, **129–132**,
    134–135, **151–152**, 156
incentive and welfare system
    Indonesia **85–92**
    Malaysia **142–155**
    Philippines **209–221**
    Thailand **278–294**
    Vietnam **39–44**
'inclusive rights' 78, 129, 133, 201, 202
India 1, 155, 157, 276t, 295, 334
indigenous people 225
    Indonesia **55–62**, 351–352
    Malaysia **108–114**
    Philippines **175–181**
    Thailand **236–246**
    Vietnam **8–14**
Indigenous People's Rights Act (IPRA, Philippines,
    1997) **196**, 198, 205, 214
Indonesia **55–106**, **351–355**
    bird's-nest business (size) **80–83**
    export and import companies **80–81**
    exports of birds' nests 81, **82t**, **93**
    house-farming (of swiftlets) **59–62**, 351–352
    house-farms (number, 2011) 62
    role model 262
    world's largest producer of nests 55, 337
Indonesian Swiftlet-Lovers' Association 61
informal market **302–303**
inheritance 3, 31, 45, 75–78, 94, 98, 118, 119, 128–133,
    148, 156, 174, 178, 179, 180, 185, 195–202
    passim, 214, 215, 216, 223–224, 225, 228, 270,
    300, 301

Internet 36, **41–42**, 87, 217, 218
interviews 85, **233***, 301, **384–387**
Islam **90–91**, 94, 118–119, 121, 125

Jakarta 80, 81, 86, 92, 157
Jakuibantara (Iban spirit) 119–120, 146
jang got jin (black birds' nests) 72
Japan 57, 82t, 93, 95, 194, 206, 207, 219, 220, 276t,
    295, 337
Java 61, 65, 68, **79**, 99, 104*, **105–106***
    house-farming 99*, 111, 112
    nest-collectors 56*, 56
Javanese 62, 93
Jesus, Fray Luis de 176
JETA Corporation Limited 268, 290, 293
Johor 172*, 173*
jorhor (someone who knows where to find nests)
    281–282, 302

kae **308***
Kalamian municipality (Palawan) 178, **196**, 204,
    223–224
Kalat Island **284–286**
Kalimantan 61, 65, 146
    East Kalimantan **57–58**
kalipatpat (swiftlet) **183**
Kamolsak Lertphaiboon 301
Kantang Cave 281
kara-ut ('a dirty bird') **183**
Karang Bolong Cave (Java) 66–67, **68–70**, 74–75,
    79, 100
Karanganyar 74, 79
Kartasusa, Raja 70, 74, 79
Kayan 109, 126, 134, 156
Kebumen (Java) 67, 68, 70, **74–75**, 79, 100
Kedah 116, 136, 138, 155, 173*
Keko Manufacturing (M) Sdn. Bhd. **154–155**
Kelantan 113, 117, 137, 138, 172*, 239
Kenyah 57, 75, 87, 93, 134, 156
khae (bamboo trunk) **285**
Khanh Hoa 10, 13, 14, 15, 18, 20, 29, 33, 35, **37t**,
    51–52*, 53*
    birds' nests 'legendary' **11**
Kiai Surti **68–69**
kidneys 314, 316
killings/murder 144, 211, 213, 214, 225, 226, 242, 268,
    282, 283, 284, 302, 303
Kirimu Shaman or Miring (Iban ritual) **120**
Kitti Kittipinyo 301
Ko Bun (Aphichat Kitprasan) 268, 284, 290, 291, 293
Ko Tong (Patchuban Angchotpan) 293
KOC Import [company] 243, 244
Koh Laetong 256
Koh Lao Liang **292**

INDEX

Koh Mu (Pig Island) 290–291
Koh Na Tay Wada 308*
Koh Pha-ngan 266
Koh Phetra (Phetra Island) 256, **288–294**, 291, 292, 300, 302, 372
Koh Rang (Trat) 299, 307*, 309*
   incentives and welfare **278–280**
Koh Rang Noi (Trat) 256
Koh Si Koh Ha (Phatthalung Province) 236, 237, 238, 239, 241, 242, 243, 253, 256, 263, 264, 267, 271, 300, **302–303**, 307–308*
   incentives and welfare **280–283**
Koh Thalu (Phang-nga) 256, 264, 271, **283–288**, 300, 308*
kola-kola (grass-nest swiftlet) 182*, **183**, 217, 230*; same as *Collocalia esculenta* 217
Kong Yun-Cheng, Professor 315, 318
Koperasi Sarang Burung Walet 76, 87, 94
Kosa Pan 238
Krabi Province 251, 256, 264, 266, 267, 268, 274, 303, 305
Kuching 145, 147, 150
KUD setempat (community cooperatives) 75

Laem Thong Bird's-Nest (Siam) Company Limited 242, **267**, 281, 300
Lagsonic, M.T. 213
Lahad Datu 109, 117, 119, **120–122**, 125, **129–132**, 134–135, 156
   incentive and welfare system **151–152**
lam thaeng 288
lampong (iron tool) 124, **170***
Lampuuk (Aceh) 58, 64, 65, 69, 72, 77, 89, 97, 100
Langham, N. 112
Langpute, J.A. 267
Lanh Nam tap ky [book title] 22
lap (secret) 302
Lau, Amy S.M. 327
law
   China 331, 336
   Hong Kong 3, 325
   Indonesia 74, **76–78**, 85–102 *passim*
   Malaysia **126–127**, 129, 130, 133, 144, 153–154, 155, 159, 164, **167**
   Philippines 174, 185, **195–196**, 197, 198–199, 201–202, 211, 219, 223, **226**
   Southeast Asia 3
   Thailand 242, 266–267, 269, 270, 279–280, 289, 301, 305, 306
   Vietnam 28, 30, 31, 40, 45, 46, 48, **49**
Le hoi yen sao (harvest ritual) 10, 26
Le Loi, Emperor 26–27
Le Thi Huyen Tram (Dao Chu Thanh Mau) 10, 11, 32–33

Le Van Dat (nobleman) 10, 26, 32
Le Van Quang 10, 11, 32–33
lebon (palm-leaf basket) 192
legal pluralism 77, 78, 133, 202
legal systems **26–31**, 346
Leti Vien Trom 21
Lhoknga district (Aceh) 58, 64, 65, 69, 72, 77
   'Lhoknga' 97, 100
Li Shizhen (1518–1593) *see* Ly Thoi Tran
licenses 91, 113, 114, 128–129, 211, **231***
Lich Su Nghe Yen Sao 10
Lim Chan Koon 327
'linear concept of rights' 30, 75, 76, 129, 132–133, 200, 201
'linear system of management' 30, 75, 76, 77, 129, 132, 200, 269
Loarca, Miguel de 177, 204
Loire, L. de la 33, 237
Long Apari **57–58**, 75–76, 87, 94
Long Peso 75–76, 87, 94
Low, Hugh 109, 126
lubang (small cave) 148, 151, 170*
Lubang Perintah (Niah) 143
luk chuek **281–282**
luk tho (supporter to a *Jorhor*) **281–282**
lullabies **253**
luray (nest) **176**, 182, 210
Ly Thoi Tran 8, 23, 33
lysine 335

MacKay, J. 327
Madai (Sabah) 109, 117, 129–130
Madina district 97
Mahathir bin Mohamad 164, 168
Mahya **88**
Mahidol University 260, 261
Makassar 80, 86
Malays 118, 122, 126, 128, 146, 147, 149, 156
   see also Muslims
Malaysia 3, 82t, **107–173**, **337**, **356–362**
   basic facts **107**
   companies **137–138**
   Indonesian refugees 111–112
   role model 262
   swiftlet vocabulary **114–115**
Mandailing Natal 97
Mandelslo, J.A. de 108, 134
Manila 174, 180, 211, 215, 217, 234*
Manlavi, D. 176
mao yen (bird's nest recently completed) 34
Marcos, F.E. 204, 223
Marshall, A. 330
Mataram 68–69
Maytegued Island 179

390

Medan 73*, 78*, 80, 81, 86, 89, 92, 95, 106*, 157
medicines 1, 4, 21, **23**, 32, 33, 34, 49, 68, 69, 70, 79, 93, **109**, 110–111, 119, 122, 134, 155, 186, 190, 203, 237, **259**, 260, 262, 263, 271, **317–320**
Melaka/Malacca 108, 169*, 172–173*
Melville, D. S. 327
mestizo/mestiza 196, 221, 224, 338
Meunasah, Kampung 58, 64, 65, 67, 69, 72, 77, 88, 103*
Middle East 155, 157, 337
mieu tho (shrine) 9
Ming Dynasty 32, 108, 109, 134, 236, 237, 264, 316–317
Minh Mang, Emperor (r. 1839–1841) 11, 19, 22, 29, 33
Miri 114, 117, 142, 146, 147, 150, 171*
mo vang trang (platinum ingot) 12
Mohamed Yusoff Ismail **151–152**, 321, 360, 372 (n16), 385
Mondragon Jr., Fidel E. 209
monopolies 31, 45, 47, 48, 75, 76, 77, 78, 93, 95, 97, 129, 131, 132, 133, 151, 156, 158, 159, 200, 202, 220, 221, 223, 240, **241**, 265, 266, 267, 295, 297
Moosang (Penan spirit) 119
mossy-nest swiftlet (*A. salanganus*) 115
Mt. Rabang 109
mu pa (wild pigs) 290
mua khai thac (nest-collecting season) **17–19**
Muara Wahau district 76, 94, 97, 350
Mulia **88**
'multiple systems of management' 75, 77, 129, 133, 201, 202
Muslims 118, 120, 143, 151
  Thai-Malay 253, 256, 257, 262, 263, 264, 267, 269, 271, 288–289, **290–294**, 295, 296, 300, 302
mutu bulu (bird's nest with feathers) 83
mutu sarang hancuran (bird's-nest biscuit) 84
mutu sarang pecah (broken bird's nest) 84
mutu sarang rampasan (bird's nest before egg-laying) 83
mutu sarang tetasan (bird's nest after hatching eggs) 84
Muzakir **89**
MV Civil Company Limited 243
mythology **33**, 66, 191, **334–336**

Na Nakhon family 266
Na Songkhla family 266, 271
Naga Umbang Cave 100
Najib Razak, Prime Minister 160
Nakhon Si Thammarat **238**, 240–241, 244–245, 250, 261n, **265–266**, 271, 294
Nanyang (Southeast Asia) 57, 110
Narai, King 237, 238, 265
Narathiwat Province 261t, 301

National Economic and Social Development Plan (Thailand, 1961) 272
nen van hoa yen sao (bird's-nest cultural events) 9
nest-rebuilding **248**
Netherlands 55–57, 74–75, 79, 96, 93, 95, 126, 295, 315, 337
New Economic Policy (Malaysia, 1971–1990) 135
Ng Kar Man 318, 320
ngoi nha yen (artificial bird-farms) 13
NGOs **213**
Ngui Island 21
Nguoi Cham 9
nguoi gat yen (nest-collector) 21
nguoi lam nghe khai thac yen (professional collectors) 26
nguoi tho khai thac Yen sao (nest-collector) 18
Nguyen Anh, King 11, *see* Gia Long Emperor
Nguyen Duc Vinh **40**
Nguyen Dynasty 9
Nguyen Sau Ngao (Nha Trang) **43–44**
Nguyen Tien Duong (taxi driver) **42–43**
Nguyen Trai (1380–1442) 26–27
Nguyen Van Dung **40–41**
Nha Trang 10, 11, 12, 13, 18, 21, 25, 26, 30, 31, 35, **37t**, **42–44**, 50, **51–53***
Niah (Sarawak) **108–109**, 148
Niah Cave (Gua Niah) 117, **118**, **122**, 124, 125, 128, 134, 143, 156, **169–171***
  decline in number of swiftlets 165–166
Niah National Park 118, 119
  black nests (1935–2002) **150t**
nido (nest) 176, 177, 186
Noi Island 10, 45, **51–52***
Northeastern Thailand 245, 269, 295
Nuar Bin Haji Jaya **143–145**
Nugroho, E. 61, **85–87**, 90
Nugroho, H.K. **85–87**
Nyi Roro Kidul (goddess) **66–70**, 72

oil palm/palm oil **99**, 107, 112, 145, 148, 155, **165**
ong to nghe yen (nest-collectors) 9
ong to nghe yen ceremony 26
open-access regimes 45, 93, 155, 219, 295
over-harvesting 110, 158–159, 165–166, 226, 229

pa-ong (bamboo scaffolds) 158
Pabellon Island (Palawan) 176, **179–180**, 183, 184, 185, 189, **199**, 200, 204, 205, **217**, 224, 226, 230*, 232*
Pabillion Island: same as 'Pabellon Island' 176
Pahang 113, 117, 138, 153, 155, 172*, 356
pahtar (exclusive buyers) 76, 97
Pak, Frank 328

INDEX

Pak Phanang District (Nakhon Si Thammarat) 250, 252, 270, 273, 294, 306, 307*, 310*
Pak Phanang House **244-245**, 300
Pak Phanang Municipality 262, 306, 309*
Pak Phayun District, Phattalung 237, 238, 264, 281, 302-303
Palawan **174-234**, 329
Palawan Council for Sustainable Development (PCSD) 195, 223, 229
Palawan Wildlife Report Rescue and Conservation Center (PWRCC) 226
Palembang 56
Pang, Allen 328
pang-lae-ma or *pang-li-mo* ('elder', 'head of collectors') 257, **259-260**, 271, 284, 285, 286
panyaan (sacred place, Palawan) 196
Passengers' Belongings Act (Thailand, wef 2012) 301
Pattani 239, 244, 262, 266, 300, 303, 306, 309*, 381
Pe, M. 210, 213
Pen Chao Kang Mu Su Yee (Chao Sia Min) 317
Penan 110, **118, 119**, 123-124, 125, 128, 134, **143-147**, 149, 156
Penang 112
Peninsular Malaysia **111-113, 132-133**
    incentive and welfare system **152-155**
    law 167
Perak 113, 116, 137, 138, 153, 156, 169*, 171*
Persatuan Pedagang Sarang Burung Malaysia (Bird's-Nest Merchants' Association of Malaysia) **152-153, 160**
Phang-nga Province 240, 242, 244, 251, 266, 267, 268, 274, 305, 370, 387
    see also Koh Thalu
Phatthalung Province 236, **237-238, 241-244**, 251, 256, 264, 266, 267, 274, 302-303, 305
Phetchamrat, Kra Praeng **280-283**
Phibunsongkhram, FM Plaek 266
    'FM Pibulsongkram' 241
Philippines **174-234, 337-338, 363-368**
    domestic market 336-337
    'sacred heresies' **188-190**
Poland 82t, 93, 95, 334
poles 24, 180, 285, 291, 292
politics
    Indonesia **95-98**, 354-355
    Malaysia **158-164**
    Philippines **221-227**
    Thailand **298-299**
    Vietnam **47-48**, 352
pollution 165, 306
    noise pollution 50, 102, 167
Pony Testing International Group 321t
power relations 28, **29**, 45, **48**, 74, 75, 76, 126-127, 133, 164, **194-195**, 202, 220, 221, 270, 296

Prachuap Khiri Khan Province 241, 242, 243, 245, 251, 264, 266, 267, 274, 305
Prajadhipok, King 266
Prapai Srisirikan **261-262**
predators **183-184, 250**, 279-280
private property 45, 76, 77, 93, 132, 133, 155, 201, 219, 295
private sector 30, 166, 229, 306, 331
protein 24, 260t, 260, 321t, 321-322, 335
PT Cipta Karisma company 98
Puerto Princesa (Palawan) 226, 234*
pugad ng balinsasayaw (swiftlet's nest) 182, 203
Pupong, Padre (poet) **186-188**
purih (bamboo ladders) 69, 70, 72
puya koh ('island ceremony') 256, 257, 263, 284, 285, 287, **308***

Qin Shi, Emperor 22
quan yen sao (white nest) 34
Quang Nam Province 21, 25, 28, 29
Quang Ngai 12
Quang Trung, Emperor (r. 1788-92) 10
Quy Nhon 14, 21

rada (three-pronged iron tool) **285**, 288, 291, **307***
radak kenueku 72
Rama III (Nangklao), King 266
Rama V (Chulalongkorn), King 298
Ramos, F. 196, 206, 228
Rang Noi Island (Trat) 256, 263, 264, 278
Rang Nok Tai Company Limited 241
raw nests 3, 4, 44, 85, 86, 135, 144, 154, 272, 273, 275, 310*, 320, 324, 324*, 329, 335, 345*
Ray, John **315-316**
red nests 3, 24, 38, 140, 141t, 248, 273, **319***, 320, 325, 326t, 344*
res nullius regimes 45, 93, 155, 219, 295
Reserve and Wildlife Protection Act (1992) 269
Rian River 57
rights and legal systems
    Indonesia **73-78**, 353
    Malaysia **126-134**
    Philippines **193-202**
    Thailand **264-270**
    Vietnam **26-31**, 349
'rights of access' 129, 132, 133, 201
'rights of management and control' 129, 133, 201
Rongkop (Java) 66
ropes 120, 124, 180, 189, 203, 218, 221, 233*, 258, **281-282**, 285
rowhouses 111, 112, 113
Ruen Cave (Koh Si Koh Ha) 307*, 309*

Sa-ngop Songmeuang (historian) 265
Sabah 109, 117, **120–122**, 125, **129–132**, 134, 137, 150, 153, 166, 317
    incentive and welfare system **151–152**
    swiftlet-house farming 114
    see also Lahad Datu
Sadrana village 70, 74
sahing (torch) 189, 192, 203, **232***
Saiburi family 266
saleng (torch) 198
Sandakan 119, 167
Sanest (beverage) 25, 36, 42, 43, 46, **52–54***, 350
sao chia (nest-collector) 21
sapalung 192
sarang burung:
    ~ *berwarna hitam* (black nests) 140
    ~ *berwarna kuning* (yellow nests) 140
    ~ *berwarna merah* (red nests) 140
    ~ *berwarna putih* (white nests) 140
sarang burung walet (swiftlet's nest) 62, 78, 115, 134
sarang darah 83
sarang emas 134, 166
sarang hitam (black nest) 65, 115
sarang merah (red nest) 115
sarang puteh (white nest) 65
sarang putih (white nest) 115
Sarawak **108–109**, **118–120**, 122, 124, 126, **127–129**, 134, 137, 138, 153, **165–166**, 167
    incentive and welfare system **143–151**
    production of nests 110
    swiftlet-house farming 114
Satun Province 239, 240, 242, 244, 251, 256, 261n, 264, 266, 267, 268, 274, 284, 305
scales (for weighing birds' nests) **231***
secret information 209
security huts 103*
Sedaya (Gresik, Java) 2, **59–60**
Selangor 116, 137, 138, 154, 160, 173*
semah ritual (Penan) **118**, 125
Semarang 61, 63*, 80, **85–87**, 91, 103*, 106*
Seri Siemmai **290–294**
seriti (*C. esculenta*) **64**, 72, 83t, 101, 103*
sexual performance 2, 109, 110, 124, 190, 191, 253, 259, 305, 316
    erectile dysfunction 22, 71
Shah Alam (Selangor) 137, **154–155**, 173*
shipwrecks 215, 271, 287, 364
shophouses 111, 124, 127, 137, 152, 153, 167, 274, 357
Sia Lek 290, 293
Siam Nest Company Limited 244
Siam Rang Nok Thalay Tai Company Limited 243
Sigli (Aceh) 84, **90**
Singapore 12, 35, 44, 46, 57, 81, 82t, 89,93, 94, 99, 155, 156, 245, 276t, 295, 317, 328, 337

Siri Bin Neng Bua **149–151**
Sirih Cave 109, 126
skin cream **323***, 324, **346***
smuggling 154, 179, 226, 227, 303, **333–334**
social class 44, 70, 74, 133, 135, 154, 202, 211, 218, **234***, 294, 321
Socialist Market Economic system (SRV) 47
society
    Indonesia **80–98**
    Malaysia **135–164**
    Philippines **206–227**
    Thailand **272–303**
    Vietnam **34–48**
Songkhla **238–242**, 243, 245, **265–266**, 280, 283, 303, 369
Songkhla Lake 241, 242, 256, 271
sopa de nido (bird's-nest soup) 186*, 190
Sooksant Wongsearint (photographer) 311–313*
Southeast Asia 1–5, 50, 57, 71, 157, 162, 177, 192, 207, 225, 229, 273, 297, 298, 300, 301, 316, 328, 329, 330, 333, 336, **336–339**, 342, 343*
Southern Andaman Company 243
Southern Thais 253, 256, 262–271 *passim*, 295, 296, 300, **302–303**
spirits 21, 26, 52*, 67, 68, 72–73, **118–122**, 125, 152, **188–189**, 193, 253, 256, **257–258**, 264, 288, 358
St. John, Spenser 109, 126, 134
state property 45, 76, 77, 93, 133, 155, 178, 196, 201, 219, 224, 295
status 2, 44, 154, 194, 204, 262, 294, 295
Strong Republic Vision (Philippines) 206
Su U Yi Ji (medicine textbook) 317
Sue (Penan spirit) 119
sugpit (bamboo prong) 192
Suharto, President 96, 97, 98
suk-pit (tool) **231***
Sukarno, President **95–96**
Sumatra 61, 91, 97, 111
Summers, Diane 330
Sung Dynasty 174, 176, 194, 204, 236
Sungai Peta 57, 76
Sunni Mahli 143
Surat Thani, Province 241, 242, 244, 251, 264, 266, 267, 274, 301, 303, 305
Suryawati 68, 69
sustainable development 195, 223, 228, 229, 305
Suwet Ketkaeo (nest-collector) **288–290**
swiftlets
    Chinese terminology 312
    collecting season **17–19**
    'condo' 245, 252, 253
    'do not like smoke' 148–149, 165
    eggs 51*, 230*
    geographical range 1

swiftlets (*continued*)
   species 1
   time taken to build nests 250
   time taken to learn to fly 249
   Vietnamese names 14–15
swiftlets: characteristics
   Indonesia 62–65
   Malaysia 114–117
   Philippines 182–185
   Thailand 246–252
   Vietnam 14–19
swiftlets: habitat
   Indonesia 65, 99
   Malaysia 116–117
   Philippines 184
   Thailand 251, 256
   Vietnam 16–17
swiftlets in nature
   Indonesia 55–59, 351
   Malaysia 108–111
   Philippines 175–181
   Thailand 236–244
   Vietnam 8–12

ta chop (hook) **308***
taboos 121, **257–258**, 288
Tagbanwa (or Tagbanua) 174, 175, **176–200**, 203, 204, **210–216**, 220, 224, 226, 232*, 337
Tagbanwa Foundation of Coron Island (TFCI) **197**
Taiwan 3, 35, 44, 46, 82t, 93, 94, 155, 156, 245, 276t, 294, 297, 336, 337
Takbai Island **291–292**
Taksin, King **238–239**, 265, 271
tali punsung payan (equipment) 124
Tan Thuy Hoang, King 22, 33
tang cuong tinh duc (erectile dysfunction) 22
Tang Wap ritual 257
taxation 2, 3, 325, 331
   Indonesia 77, 79, 86, 88, 90, 91
   Malaysia 130, 145, 151, 153
   Philippines 178, 179, 196, 197, 198, 199–200, 205, 210, 214, 217, 218, 224, 225
   Thailand **238–240**, 265, **266**, **267–268**, 283
   Vietnam 9, 10, 11, 29, 31, 33, 41–42
Tay Wada Cave (Koh Si Koh Ha) **309***
Taytay Bay 205
technology 32
Telang Teba 57, 76
Terengganu 113, 117, 172*
tet (New Year) 18
Thai-Vietnamese 256, 262, 263, 264, 267, **278–280**, 295, 296, 299, **309***

Thailand 82t, **235–310**, 333–334, **335**, **366–371**
   agricultural exports **275t**
   communal collection **237**
   companies (listed) **273**
   coup d'état (Siam, 1932) 240, 266, 272, 299
   duties 274
   economic system **299**
   export markets (2004–2007) **276t**
   feudal property system (Siam) **237–241**
   globalized capitalism **241–244**
   imports (2003–2007) **276t**
Thailand: Constitution (1997) 268, 272
Thailand Research Fund (TRF) viii
Thailand Science Research and Innovation (TSRI) vi
Thairath (newspaper) 301
Thais 237, 253, 255, 257, 259, 262, 263, 264, 272, 274, 288, 304
Thanh Binh-Ninh Thuan (cinema) 12
Thanh Chau (village) 9, 29
That Thada (poet) **254–255**
Thawee Chulasap, Chief Marshal 241, 281
theft 31, 40, 41, 98, 100, 144, 149, 150, 151, 156, 163, 165, 197, 211–227 *passim*, 237, **242**, 267, 268, 282, **283**, **289**, 290, 291, **296**, **302–303**
Thian Seng, *Phraya Sunthonnurak* 239
Thien kim phuong (medicine) 33
Thien Limthanakul 260
thien tu Yen sao (blue nest) 34
Tien Ching, *Phra Songkhla* **239**
Time 327
to chim do (red birds' nests) 23
To Ye Trong Nha (House Nest) 38
to yen mau hong (pink nest) 39
to yen vun (smaller nest) 39
Tohir Sukarama (Java) 59
Toon Wongsupasawat 275
torches 24, 178, 189, 192, 198, 203, 218, 221, 232*, 289, 291
tourism 25, 40, 42, 46, 73, 88, 120, 154, 162, 193, 234*, 288, 306, 327, 358, 381
Tra pho tap van [book title] 22
traditional Chinese medicine 317, **318–320**, **322**, **332***
Traditional Chinese Medicine Association 332
Trang Province 251, 264, 266, 267, 268, 274, 296, 305
   see also Koh Phetra
Trat Province 243, 245, 251, 256, 261n, 263, 264, 267, 274, **278–280**, 299, 305, 307*, 312*
tre (bamboo) 21
Trung Quoc [book title] 33
Trung Viet [book title] 23
trust 46, 92, 95, 149, 157, 220, 284, 286, **329**, 334

Truyen thi lao trai hoan 23
tsunami (2004) 58, 65, 70, 77, 88, 89
tu ha xa (a traditional medicine) 23
tuberculosis 316
Tuyen Nam tap chi [book title] 22, 32

ubangon (bamboo ladders) 69, 70, 72, 104*
ulama 67, 69, 70, 90–91
UN Earth Summits 228, 305
United East India Company (VOC) **56–57**
United States 335, 337
upacara keselamatan (safety ritual) 68
Uthit Kieokhachi **278–280**

Valli, E. 327
vang trang (white gold) 20
Veterinary Health Mark (VHM) 154
Viet luc (*Six Vietnamese*) 22
Vietnam **7–54**, 294, **347–350**
 basic facts 7
 development of house-farming **12–14**
 domestic market **336–337**
 export market **44**, 46–47
 foreign policy 47
 incentive and welfare system for nest-collectors **39–44**
 indigenous people and birds' nests **8–14**
 nests (type and price) **38–39**
 number of swiftlets 15
 pioneer of nest business 8
 production 8, 13, 14, 36, **37t**, 50
 rights and legal systems **26–31**, 349
 size of bird's-nest business **35–37**
 swiftlets in nature **8–12**
Vietnamese Constitution (1992) **30–31**, 34
Vietnamese ethnic group 3, 30
Viking Cave xii–xvi*, 287
Vinai Dithajohn (photographer) xii–xvi*
Vinh Nguyen 11, 29, 30, 33
Vision 2000 policy (Philippines) 206, 228
vitamins 24, 181, 186, 190

Wai Yuen Tong (Cantonese company) 329, **345***
walet sarang goa (*A. germanicus* or *vestitus*) 64
walet sarang hitam (*A. maximus* or *lowi*) 64, **116**
walet sarang putih (*A. fuciphagus*) **63–64**
Wangsit (supernatural mandate) 69
war of bird's-nest resources 164, 303
Ward, Christian (poet) **190–191**
Wawasan 2020 (Malaysia) 135, 164
wayang kulit **68**, 73
weapons of weak 48, 98, **163–164**, 226, 302
websites 41, 44, 154, **335***, **386–389**
'white gold' 1, 20, 78, 203, 229, 314

white nests 62, 63, 65, 83t, 83, 86–87, 89, 105*, 112, 114, 115, 124, 126, 136, 140, **140t**, 141t, 142, 146, 169*, 248, 263, 275, 276, **277t**, 291, 292, 307*, **320**, 324, **325**, 326t, 344*
 amino acids **261t**
 price 84t, 84, 208t
white-nest swiftlet 169*, 183
 Aerodramus fuciphagus **115–116**
 C. fuciphaga germani 16
 chim yen hang 16
 walet sarang putih **115–116**
white-rumped swiftlet (*A. germani oustalet* or Germain's swiftlet) 246, 248, 307*
 general characteristics **249–250**
wildfires (1997–98) 99
women 10, 22, 26, 43, **122**, 144, 145, 146, 150, 177, **189–190**, **195**, 214, **216**, 256–257, **258–259**, 282, 288, 294, **309***, 327, **328***, 344*
Wong Chi Men (naturalist) 312
World Trade Organization 47
World War Two 57
WTA Company Limited 243

Xi Nghiep Quoc Doanh Yen sao Nha Trang **11–12**, 30

yellow nests 62, 140, 141t, 248, 276, 277t, 325, 326t
yen dia 39
yen hang (cave swiftlet) 38
yen huyet sao (red nest, blood nest) 23, **33–34**
Yen sao Khanh Hoa Company 11, **13–14**, 30, 35, **36**, 42, 43, 46, 50, **52–53***
yen sao to nho (pure swiftlet nest) 39
Yen va nguoi (film, *Swiftlets and Man*) 20
Yongle, Emperor 108, 134

Zafril (Chinese-Acehnese man) **92**
Zhejiang 136, 153, 161, 207, 273, 334
Zheng He, Admiral 108, **134**, 316
Zhong Yau Da Ci Dian 1978 (Chinese Dictionary 1978) 109

About the Author

Kasem Jandam while relaxing during the field trip in Northeastern Thailand, January 2021.
Photograph by Kitti Pagkam.

KASEM JANDAM is from a farmer's family in Koh Phasuk Village, Khon Hat Sub-District, Cha-uat District, Nakhon Si Thammarat Province. He is an independent researcher of the Thai Research Fund (TRF) and the National Research Council of Thailand (NRCT). His works included "Conditions of the Farmers' Existence in Khon Hat Sub-District, Cha-uat District, Nakhon Si Thammarat Province (1985)" and Birds' Nests: Power, Conflict, and Wealth." The latter was part of the research project, "Mapping the landscape of the South: Economic Base and Cultural Capital (2002–2005)," funded by TRF, led by Prof. Suthiwong Phongpaiboon. From 2009-2010, Kasem received the TRF fund to study the Transnational Research Project: "Ethnicity and Birds' Nests Resources in Southeast Asia." The research work, "Birds' Nests: Business and Ethnicity in Southeast Asia," was published first in Thai in 2017, translated and published in English in 2021.

In 2019 the Guangdong Bird's Nest Industry Association awarded Kasem, an expert's official recognition. From 2020–2021, Kasem received a grant from the NRCT for the research project, "Bird's Nest Cleaning Process Industry in Thailand." His latest book in Thai is *The Global Bird's Nest Industry* (2020).

www.ingramcontent.com/pod-product-compliance
Lightning Source LLC
Chambersburg PA
CBHW080353030426
42334CB00024B/2862